Adapted Aquatics Programming

A Professional Guide

Monica Lepore, EdD
West Chester University

G. William Gayle, PhD
Wright State University

Shawn F. Stevens, EdD
Edgemoor Community Center

Human Kinetics

Library of Congress Cataloging-in-Publication Data

Lepore, Monica, 1956–
    Adapted aquatics programming : a professional guide / Monica Lepore, G. William Gayle,
Shawn F. Stevens.
        p.   cm.
    Includes bibliographical references (p.   ) and index.
    ISBN 0-88011-695-1
    1. Swimming for handicapped persons. 2. Aquatic exercises--Therapeutic use.
    3. Physically handicapped--Rehabilitation. I. Gayle, G. William. II. Stevens, Shawn F., 1956-   .
III. Title.
    GV837.4.L47 1998
    797.2'1'087--dc21   98-22953
                                                                                            CIP

ISBN: 0-88011-695-1

Developmental Editor: Jim Kestner; Managing Editor: Rebecca Crist; Editorial Assistant: Laura
Majersky; Copyeditor: Bonnie Pettifor; Proofreader: Sue Fetters; Indexer: Marie Rizzo; Graphic
Designer: Robert Reuther; Graphic Artist: Doug Burnett; Photo Editor: Boyd LaFoon; Cover
Designer: Jack Davis; Photographer (cover): Monica Lepore; Illustrator: Tim Offenstein; Printer:
Edwards Brothers.

Human Kinetics books are available at special discounts for bulk purchase. Special editions or
book excerpts can also be created to specification. For details, contact the Special Sales Manager
at Human Kinetics.

Printed in the United States of America
10 9 8 7 6 5 4 3 2 1

Human Kinetics
Web site: http://www.humankinetics.com/

United States: Human Kinetics
P.O. Box 5076
Champaign, IL 61825-5076
1-800-747-4457
e-mail: humank@hkusa.com

Canada: Human Kinetics
475 Devonshire Road Unit 100
Windsor, ON N8Y 2L5
1-800-465-7301 (in Canada only)
e-mail: humank@hkcanada.com

Europe: Human Kinetics, P.O. Box IW14
Leeds LS16 6TR, United Kingdom
(44) 1132 781708
e-mail: humank@hkeurope.com

Australia: Human Kinetics
57A Price Avenue
Lower Mitcham, South Australia 5062
(088) 277 1555
e-mail: humank@hkaustralia.com

New Zealand: Human Kinetics
P.O. Box 105-231, Auckland 1
(09) 523 3462
e-mail: humank@hknewz.com

This book is dedicated to our families and to the thousands of individuals with disabilities from whom we learned the skills included in this book.

≋ Contents ≋

Preface ix

    Organization of This Book ix

    Trends and Controversies in Adapted Aquatics x

Acknowledgments xi

Credits xiii

Part I Foundations of Adapted Aquatics **1**

Chapter 1 Introduction to Adapted Aquatics 3

    The Evolution of Adapted Aquatics 3

    Legislation for Individuals With Disabilities 7

    Benefits of Aquatic Participation 12

    Applications of Aquatic Participation 14

    Summary 16

Chapter 2 Models for Adapted Aquatics Programming 17

    Medical-Therapeutic Model 18

    Educational Model 21

    Therapeutic Recreation Model 26

    Collaborative Model 29

    Summary 33

Chapter 3 Inclusion and the Least Restrictive Environment .. 35

    Concepts of Placement 36

    Continuum of Placements 37

    Prerequisites to Inclusion 42

    Developing and Maintaining Successful Inclusion Groups .. 46

    Framework for Task Presentation 53

    Activities to Facilitate Inclusion 55

    Summary 59

Chapter 4 Individualized Instructional Planning 61

    Planning for Assessment 61

    Developing the Individualized Aquatics Program Plan (IAPP) .. 71

    Implementing the IAPP 75

    Summary 76

Chapter 5   Program and Organizational Development   77

Organizational Foundations   77

Communications and Promotion   82

Financial Development   83

Facilities Acquisition and Safety   84

Program Development and Evaluation   86

Human Resource Management   90

Summary   95

Chapter 6   Facilities, Equipment, and Supplies   97

Facilities   98

Equipment and Supplies   105

Summary   111

Part II Facilitating Instruction   **113**

Chapter 7   Prerequisites to Safe, Successful, and Rewarding Programs   115

Essential Communication Skills   116

Transferring Techniques   118

Hydrodynamics: Properties of Water and Implications for Movement   132

Positioning and Supporting Participants   134

Participant Care and Safety   138

Addressing Problem Behaviors   144

Summary   147

Chapter 8   Instructional Strategies   149

The Process of Learning   149

The Process of Teaching, Facilitating, and Guiding Participants to Goals   154

Summary   161

Chapter 9   Specific Needs of Adapted Aquatics Participants   169

Atlantoaxial Instability   171

Attention Deficit   171

Auditory Perception Disorders   172

Autonomic Dysreflexia or Hyperreflexia   173

Balance Disorders   174

Brittle Bones   174

Cardiovascular Disorders   175

Circulatory Disorders   176

Contractures and Limitations to Range of Motion   177

Deafness and Hard of Hearing   179

Head Control Difficulties   180

High Muscle Tone   182

Hyperactivity   183

Interaction Difficulties   184

Joint Dysfunction   185

Kinesthetic System Disorders   186

Memory and Understanding Problems   186

Multisensory Deprivation   189

Oral Motor Dysfunction   191

Paralysis, Paresis, and Atrophy   192

Posture Disorders   194

Primitive Reflex Retention   195

Proprioceptive Disorders   196

Range of Motion Dysfunction   196

Receptive-Expressive Language Disorders   196

Respiratory Disorders   196

Seizures   197

Tactile System Disorders   198

Temperature Regulation Disorders   199

Vestibular System Disorders   199

Visual Impairment and Blindness   200

Visual Perception Deficits   202

Summary   203

Part III Program Enhancement   **205**

Chapter 10 Adapted Aquatics Program Selection   207

Program Environments   207

Program Purposes   212

Types of Participation   213

Nationally Sponsored Aquatics Programs   213

Summary   216

Chapter 11 Competitive and Recreational Activities   217

Competitive Swimming for Individuals With Disabilities   217

Equitable Competition and Classification   223

Coaching Swimmers With Disabilities   225

Recreational Aquatic Activities   228

Summary   231

Chapter 12 Aquatic Fitness and Rehabilitation   233

    Health-Related Physical Fitness Concepts and Aquatic Exercise   233

    Physical Conditions and Tips for Aquatic Rehabilitation   241

    Summary   243

Glossary of Common Disabilities   245

Glossary of Terms   248

Appendix A: AAHPERD-AAALF-Aquatic Council—
Adapted Aquatics Position Paper   253

Appendix B: Assessment Forms   256

Appendix C: Games and Activities for Various Age Groups   278

Appendix D: Information Gathering Forms   285

Appendix E: Adapted Aquatics Program Resources   291

References   298

Index   307

About the Authors   314

≋ Preface ≋

Adapted aquatics is the offspring of adapted physical education and general aquatics, both of which have undergone many changes during the last 25 years. Besides the changes in the parent disciplines, federal legislation has helped water-related activities for individuals with disabilities evolve from therapy-based programs to include cross-disciplinary programs that embrace the talents of professionals in many disciplines to create recreational, therapeutic, and educational aquatic programs.

We have written this book for aquatic instructors who are looking for more information and guidance in meeting the needs of individuals with disabilities in general or adapted aquatics programs. It will also serve as a resource for swim coaches, special educators, physical and occupational therapists, therapeutic recreation specialists, and aquatic therapists, who may use aquatics for habilitation and rehabilitation programs. This book will provide you—no matter what your approach to aquatics—with information, activities, resources, and references for planning, implementing, and evaluating aquatic programs along a continuum of services for individuals with disabilities. You'll find up-to-date information about individuals with disabilities and their needs in the aquatic environment as well as tips for successfully applying the methods, materials, and resources we'll describe in this book.

ORGANIZATION OF THIS BOOK

We have divided this book into three parts. Part I, "Foundations of Adapted Aquatics," will introduce you to the various philosophies and issues having to do with initiating adapted aquatics programs. Chapter 1 will give you an historical prospective, discuss related legislation, and describe the benefits of aquatic activity. In chapter 2, you'll compare the therapeutic, educational, recreational, and collaborative models for structuring a program. Chapter 3 describes the principles and practices for implementing inclusion policies and creating the least restrictive environment in the aquatic setting. Chapter 4 explores assessment, planning, and development of the Individualized Aquatics Program Plan. Chapter 5 examines components of organization and program development, which lay a foundation for implementing quality adapted aquatics programs. Chapter 6 discusses facilities, equipment, and supplies, identifying relevant functional and safety considerations.

Information on competencies and resources for adapted aquatics personnel is the focus of part II, "Facilitating Instruction." Chapter 7 discusses essential communication skills, transferring and positioning techniques, participant care and safety, and behavior management. Chapter 8 outlines the process of teaching, learning, facilitating, and guiding participants to a goal. Chapter 9 provides insights into common challenges to aquatic participation, implications for the aquatic environment, and modifications of swimming skills and equipment.

In part III, the focus switches to "Program Enhancement." Chapter 10 reviews considerations for choosing a program that best meets the needs and desires of the participant and provides you with examples of model programs to help you enhance your own program. Chapter 11 examines the status of aquatics within sports organizations in the United States, issues regarding disabled sport participation, and nonswimming recreational and enrichment aquatic activities. Chapter 12 introduces aquatic fitness concepts, shows you how to modify fitness activities for participants with disabilities, and offers tips for common physical conditions requiring aquatic rehabilitation.

TRENDS AND CONTROVERSIES IN ADAPTED AQUATICS

In this book, we'll address several current trends and controversies in adapted aquatics today. We'll look at integration of educational, therapeutic, and recreational concepts, the resulting cross-disciplinary professional roles, competitive opportunities, and water fitness for special populations. In addition, because of the inclusion of individuals with disabilities into regular aquatic programs and the changing role of the adapted aquatic specialist, we'll discuss in detail inclusive settings, and support and adaptations within inclusive settings, as well as how to decide when segregated classes and programs meet participants' needs better. We'll show you how to make decisions regarding safe, effective, and relevant aquatic programs for individuals with disabilities on an individual basis, in compliance with federal legislation, including the Individuals With Disabilities Education Act and the Americans With Disabilities Act.

The issue of including individuals with disabilities into regular aquatic programs versus placing them in specialized, self-contained programs remains controversial. Instructor programs in adapted aquatics have waned since the 1970s, due to legal and ethical drives to include individuals with disabilities in mainstream aquatic programs and classes. Unfortunately, general aquatic instructors who conduct the inclusion classes have limited training in teaching individuals with disabilities, yet are expected to provide adequate aquatic instruction to this varied population within the regular aquatic program. While appropriate inclusion of individuals with disabilities into regular aquatic programs is a viable option, it requires individual assessment by aquatic instructors who know the common attributes of individuals with disabilities and discussion of placements with participants (if able) and caregivers before swim instruction begins. Appropriate inclusion also involves education of and support for the general aquatic instructor through co-instruction with adapted aquatic instructors, available paraprofessionals, adapted equipment, and Individualized Instructional Plans. In some cases, an appropriate option is "reverse mainstreaming" in which the focus of the program is on the needs of individuals with disabilities and individuals without disabilities are brought into the program to practice their swim skills and facilitate age-appropriate friendships. Yet, when appropriate, individually based segregated aquatic placement of individuals with disabilities still has its place.

We embrace the belief that each person is a unique individual and has a right to a full productive life, whatever his or her potential might be. Appropriate use of aquatics facilitates the educational, recreational, and therapeutic fulfillment of that potential. How? Individualization is the key to safe, effective, and relevant programming. Thus, never assume that all characteristics associated with any of the disabilities identified in this book are endemic to each person with that diagnosis. Generalizations serve merely to present a wide scope of information that may pertain to swimmers with any particular disability. How, then, do you meet the needs of each participant? Teach each swimmer sufficient safety and swim skills to become as safe and comfortable as possible during aquatic activities. Tailor the choice and presentation of skills to meet the specific needs of each individual.

Aquatics for individuals with disabilities is a diverse and expanding profession with a multitude of professionals claiming turf rights. Throughout this book, we'll list and discuss comprehensive and contemporary resources to help you learn about all the pertinent issues. You'll find the information you need—whether you're an aquatic instructor, swim coach, physical or occupational therapist, therapeutic recreation specialist, kinesiotherapist, special educator, physical educator, adapted physical education specialist, aquatic director, an aquatic participant with a disability, a parent, or another caregiver of individuals with disabilities.

In conclusion, we have written *Adapted Aquatics Programming: A Professional Guide* to encourage you to ensure that your adapted aquatics program makes individuals with disabilities safe, comfortable, and independent in the water by encouraging participants to make the transition from passive observation to active participation in the enjoyable world of aquatics. Make it your goal to help more individuals with disabilities become comfortable in the water, realizing the educational, recreational, and therapeutic benefits of aquatics.

≋ Acknowledgments ≋

The authors would like to acknowledge the following people for their assistance:

Volunteers, parents, teachers, and participants of the West Chester University and Wright State University adapted aquatics programs for their assistance with photographs and permission forms

Clients from Brian's House, West Chester, PA

Clients of CK Center from Rome House and Mary Hall of Springfield, PA

Clients of Elwyn of Pennsylvania

Clients and staff of the Mary Campbell Center in Wilmington, DE

Aquatic staff of the A.I. duPont Hospital for Children, Wilmington, DE

Campers and staff of Camp ABILITIES, SUNY-Brockport, NY

Paul Dietrich and Maria Lepore-Stevens for their assistance with photographs

Kelly Butterworth for Camp Ability Photos

All of our anonymous reviewers for their comments and recommendations

Jim Kestner and Rebecca Crist of Human Kinetics for their help and guidance

≋ Credits ≋

Figure 1.1 Courtesy of Roosevelt Warm Springs Institute.

Figure 1.3 Courtesy of Diane LaTourette at Mapleton Center, Boulder, CO.

Figures 1.4 and 1.8 Photo by Lauren Lieberman, Ph.D. SUNY-Brockport.

Figure 1.6 NCA 1996.

Figure 3.2 Adapted, by permission, from C.B. Eichstaedt and B.W. Lavay, 1992, *Physical activity for individuals with mental retardation: Infancy through adulthood.* (Champaign, IL: Human Kinetics), 177.

Figure 3.3 Adapted, by permission, from M.E. Block and P.L. Krebs, 1992, "An alternative to least restrictive environments: A continuum of support to regular physical education," *Adapted Physical Activity Quarterly* 9(2), 104.

Figure 3.4 Reprinted from Carter, Dolan, and LeConey, 1994.

Table 6.1 Reprinted from the Department of Justice, Office of the Attorney General, 1991.

Figure 6.7 Photo by Aquatic Access, Louisville, KY.

Figure 6.10 Photo by Triad Technology.

Figure 6.12 Courtesy of *Aquatic Therapy*, 123 Haymac, Kalamazoo, MI 49004

Figure 6.13 Courtesy of Excel Sports Sciences, Inc., Eugene, OR.

Figure 7.11 Photo by Phil Conatser, Charlottesville, Va.

Table 8.1 Reprinted, by permission, from P.D. Miller, 1995, *Fitness programming and physical disability* (Champaign, IL: Human Kinetics), 193-199.

Figure 8.3 Courtesy of Chester County Family Academy of West Chester, PA.

Figure 9.10 Adapted, by permission, from S. Grosse, 1985, "Instruction of a deaf-blind swimmer," *National Aquatic Journal* 1(3):16.

Figure 10.4 Courtesy of Osborn Aquatic Center, Corvallis, OR.

Figure 11.1 Courtesy of Gail M. Dummer, Michigan State University Department of Physical Education and Exercise Science.

Figure 11.2 Photo by Curt Beamer. Copyright Sports 'N Spokes/Paralyzed Veterans of America, 1996.

Figure 11.3 Reprinted, by permission, from J.P. Winnick, 1987, "An integration continuum for sport participation," *Adapted Physical Education Quarterly* 4:157-191.

Figure 11.4 Copyright Sports 'N Spokes/Paralyzed Veterans of America, 1994.

Figure 12.7 Courtesy of Sprint-Rothhammer International, Santa Maria, CA.

Pages 256-263, 283 Reprinted with permission from Special Olympics International, the sports organization that provides year-round sports training and athletic competition in a variety of Olympic-type sports for people eight years of age and older with mental retardation.

Special Olympics

Special Olympics International, 1325 G Street, NW, Suite 500, Washington, DC, USA 20005; phone 202-628-3630; fax 202-824-0200

Part I

FOUNDATIONS OF ADAPTED AQUATICS

INTRODUCTION TO ADAPTED AQUATICS

Because of the support afforded by water, many people whose disability impairs mobility on land can function independently in an aquatic environment without the assistance of braces, crutches, walkers, or wheelchairs. Indeed, water is a medium in which individuals with disabilities may participate in fulfilling physical activity, safely and successfully. You can help such individuals discover this freedom. Specifically, your continuing professional development will help you better understand the benefits of aquatics for individuals with disabilities, federal legislation mandates, and the need for positive community attitudes. In this chapter, you'll learn how the field of adapted aquatics has evolved, how others have advocated equal opportunity in community programs, and about aquatic programs others have created for individuals with disabilities.

THE EVOLUTION OF ADAPTED AQUATICS

Although aquatic participation for therapeutic purposes has a long history, individuals with disabilities have not had full access to swimming and water safety instruction for educational and leisure purposes. Until recently, both society and professionals who work with individuals with disabilities have not generally encouraged such individuals to participate in the general program of community aquatics due to numerous barriers, including conflicting philosophies about service delivery and professional responsibility. Water provides such a unique opportunity for development of physical and motor fitness, however, that opportunities have expanded from passive, therapeutic programming (figure 1.1) to include instructional swimming (figure 1.2), recreational aquatics and even international competition.

Using water as a therapeutic tool predates all other modalities of physical medicine (Campion 1985), extending back to the time of Hippocrates (Harris 1978). For example, the Greeks and Romans used water in naturally occurring hot springs for healing purposes (Moran 1979). Many other forms of treatment have come and gone but the use of water endures. Nowadays, fitness centers and posh hotels offer spa treatments.

Figure 1.1 Historic theraputic swimming.

Figure 1.2 Integrated or "inclusive" aquatics programs provide expanded opportunities.

The Twentieth Century

Therapeutic aquatic activities began in the United States immediately before World War I as a program for individuals with rheumatic disorders. In this century, we can consider Charles Lowman as the father of water exercise for therapeutic purposes. His work in the 1930s systematized **hydrotherapy**, the treatment of disease, disability, and ill health using water as the therapeutic medium. The post-World War II polio epidemic increased the clientele using water exercise for rehabilitation. But public fear of people with polio using swimming pools restricted water rehabilitation programs to hospitals and spas. Researchers carefully studied several programs and concluded that water exercise had many benefits for rehabilitation (Bryant 1951).

Injuries to soldiers and civilians during World War II increased awareness of and demand for rehabilitation programs, creating greater need for therapeutic aquatic activities. The armed forces initiated training programs for instructors and the American Red Cross

(ARC) developed its own programs. These initial efforts led to many other efforts for meeting the needs of individuals with disabilities, including programs created by the YMCA, Special Olympics International, the National Multiple Sclerosis Society, the American Alliance for Health, Physical Education, Recreation and Dance (AAHPERD), and the National Safety Council.

The American Red Cross

The American Red Cross responded to World War II by developing its "Convalescent Swimming Program" in the early 1940s, which offered swimming and water activities to accommodate disabled veterans; in 1949, they added a training course for instructors to ensure program quality (American Red Cross 1977a). The program focused on adapting swim strokes for persons with physical disabilities such as amputations and paraplegia. The American Red Cross revised the program in 1955, renaming it "Swimming for the Handicapped."

In the 1970s, the American Red Cross broadened the scope of swimming for persons with disabilities and changed the program content to include individuals with all types of physical, mental, and emotional disabilities, calling it the "Adapted Aquatics Program." ARC national headquarters supported instructor and instructor aide certification provided by local chapters. The philosophy was that through swimming and water safety instruction, individuals with disabilities could experience the thrill and fun of aquatic activity, participating in programs available in their communities.

The American Red Cross Adapted Aquatics Program and instructor certification was popular until the beginning of the 1990s when the Red Cross decided to include information about individuals with disabilities in their regular Water Safety Instructor (WSI) Program. Much of the resource information for WSIs regarding adapted aquatics is contained in the American Red Cross text, Swimming and Diving (1992a; 1996). Ultimately, its embracing of the philosophy of inclusion of individuals with disabilities in regular programs resulted in the elimination of segregated adapted aquatics programs and instructor certifications on the national level.

Young Men's Christian Association (YMCA)

Beginning in the late 1960s and continuing throughout the 1980s, other organizations became involved in adapted aquatics. In 1960, the Longview, Washington YMCA published an aquatics manual for special populations. Edited by Grace Reynolds and Esther Dedrick, it was presented at a YMCA conference in the Pacific Northwest. In April 1970, the YMCA conducted a research project under the leadership of Grace Reynolds to study the YMCA swimming programs for special populations. She presented the results of that study at the 1970 YMCA National Aquatic Conference. As a result, the YMCA adopted seven proposals to develop training materials, budgeting guidelines, safety standards, personnel recruitment standards, record maintenance guidelines, and skill progressions (Reynolds 1973). In 1972, the YMCA introduced two levels of certification: "Aquatic Leader: Swimming for the Handicapped," for assistant instructors, and "Instructor: Swimming for the Handicapped," for those who planned and implemented adapted aquatics programs. The YMCA now calls these certifications "YMCA Aquatic Assistant" and "YMCA Specialist Instructor/Leader in Aquatics for Special Populations." Subsequently, the YMCA

has introduced a third level, "Aquatic Director/ Administrator for Special Populations."

Throughout the years, the YMCA has directed several projects of interest, such as Project Aquatic Mainstreaming and Project Mainstreaming Activities for Youth. These two projects helped to disseminate information to aquatic instructors and recreational personnel about the needs of people with disabilities and the importance of integrating them into recreational and educational programs conducted by the YMCA.

In 1974, Kit Wilson of the Whittier YMCA in California, developed a community-based arthritis aquatic program called "Twinges in the Hinges" (YMCA and Arthritis Foundation 1985). It gained considerable notoriety on the West Coast and was taken to the National Arthritis Foundation Medical and Scientific Committee for review, which subsequently approved it for widespread distribution. In April 1983, the national YMCA and Arthritis Aquatic Program Task Force met and approved a nationwide program called "Arthritis Foundation YMCA Aquatic Program" (AFYAP), which included set procedures for certifying leaders and instructors. They held the first instructor training workshop in October 1983, using videotapes of approved exercises and an instructor manual. Since that time, the program (figure 1.3) has expanded to include an aerobic endurance component and strength and **flexibility** exercises (Arthritis Foundation and the National Council of YMCAs of the USA 1990).

Special Olympics International

In 1968, Special Olympics was founded to provide competitive sports events—including swimming—for individuals with mental retardation (see also chapters 10 and 11). This organization has made tremendous strides in making swimming programs accessible to the hundreds of thousands of individuals with mental retardation in the United States and the world. In fact, the first international games, held in 1968, featured swimming as an official event (Shriver 1972). Now officially called Special Olympics International, this organization provides sport skill training and vital physical activity for individuals with mental retardation aged five and older and competition for individuals aged eight and older at the international, national, and local levels. State chapters offer training programs for coaches while local chapters offer training programs for athletes.

Figure 1.3 Arthritis aquatic program in session.

Participation in Special Olympics aquatic programs has traditionally been segregated with both individual and group instruction. Activities are structured and based on long-term goals and short-term **objectives** for each participant. The Special Olympics Swimming and Diving Sports Skills Instructional Program (Special Olympics n.d.) provides program personnel with information about skill assessment, **task analysis,** teaching suggestions, and coaching tips. Special Olympics Aquatics: Sport Management Team Guide provides program personnel with key technical information needed to conduct high-quality sport programs (Special Olympics International 1994).

The National Multiple Sclerosis Society

In 1991, in response to clients with multiple sclerosis (MS), the National Multiple Sclerosis Society—Georgia Chapter developed a comprehensive aquatic program for community facilities, such as YMCAs, YWCAs, and private health clubs, to use (National Multiple Sclerosis Society Client and Community Service Division 1993). The primary mission of the program is to provide people with MS an opportunity to engage in structured exercise after they are discharged from a formal physical therapy program. In addition, the aquatic setting allows participants to become reinvolved in social activities within the community following diagnosis or exacerbation (flare-up).

In order to conduct an MS aquatic program, you must attend a one-day MS aquatic training workshop for aquatic instructors. Prerequisites include CPR certification and American Red Cross certifications in Community Water Safety, Water Safety Instructor, or Lifeguard Training. Following successful completion of this course, you receive a certificate of attendance. The organization recommends that you take a refresher course every three years.

American Alliance for Health, Physical Education, Recreation and Dance (AAHPERD)

AAHPERD (originally AAHPER) has been an advocate of swimming for individuals with disabilities since 1969 when it published A Practical Guide for Teaching the Mentally Retarded to Swim. In 1981 under the guidance of Joan Moran and the Aquatic Council, AAHPERD published Handicapped Swimming: A Syllabus for the Aquatic Council's Courses Teacher and Master Teacher of Handicapped Swimming. With the phasing out of the national American Red Cross Adapted Aquatics Instructor course and the reintroduction of the AAHPERD instructor course in 1993 and position paper on adapted aquatics in 1996 (see appendix A), AAHPERD has moved to the forefront in adapted aquatics.

National Safety Council and Ellis and Associates

Another recent entry on the national swimming instruction scene is the National Safety Council Learn-to-Swim Program. Developed in conjunction with Ellis and Associates and endorsed by the National Recreation and Park Association, this program teaches basic swimming skills. Although this Learn-to-Swim program is not specifically designed as an adapted aquatics program, it features developmentally appropriate, progressive skills that facilitate the inclusion of children and adults with disabilities in a standard aquatic program. It is intended as a community-based program in which instructors decide what, when, and how to teach. The program is administered by licensed coordinators who must meet training and auditing criteria to retain their licenses.

In 1996, Ellis and Associates released a manual, Adapted Aquatics (Priest 1996), intended as a supplement to the instructor's resource manual for Learn-to-Swim, providing additional information regarding the teaching of swimming to children with mild to moderate disabilities. Sections in the manual include general principles, performance factors, descriptions of specific disabilities, and aquatic games.

LEGISLATION FOR INDIVIDUALS WITH DISABILITIES

The forces of federal legislation have mandated the demise of architectural barriers and served as catalysts for encouraging school and agency programming to accommodate all members of the community. In addition, legislation has created funding opportunities to subsidize local and state fiscal concerns for renovation of existing structures and construction of new facilities. Thus, individuals with disabilities are not only

more visible but also more vocal, as the laws empower them to make their own decisions, thereby resulting in greater independence. As this is a rapidly developing and ever-changing area of the law, programs should seek professional advice as to current regulations and allowable exceptions.

PL 93-112: The Rehabilitation Act of 1973

In 1973, section 504 of the **Vocational Rehabilitation Act** was enacted. It mandates that all programs and facilities receiving federal support must be made accessible to individuals with disabilities. Consequently, federally funded organizations removed architectural barriers and the U.S. Architectural and Transportation Barriers Compliance Board developed accessibility codes. Many services became available to people with disabilities for the first time. For example, federally funded organizations made parking spaces, pools, bathrooms, university classrooms, and government offices accessible (figure 1.4). Specific to aquatics, all federally funded facilities had to make their pools accessible through such means as Hoyer lifts, removable stairs, or transfer tiers.

PL 94-142: The Education for All Handicapped Children Act

The **Education for All Handicapped Children Act** continued integrating individuals with disabilities into society. It mandates free, appropriate public education in the **least restrictive environment**, including special education. As stated in the Federal Register, a government publication that contains regulations pertaining to laws, special education is defined as specially designed instruction to meet the unique needs of children with disabilities, including physical education. Physical education is defined as "(I) . . . The development of: (A) physical and motor fitness; (B) fundamental motor skills and patterns; and (C) instruction in aquatics, dance, individual and group games, and sports (including intramural and lifetime sports)" (Federal Register 1977a). Including aquatics in the definition of physical education provides schools with the option of including swimming in the curriculum for students with disabilities.

Figure 1.4 Ramping enhances integration.

Another important aspect of this law is the **Individualized Educational Program** (IEP). This document, assembled by educators, related service professionals, and parents, plots the goals a student is expected to accomplish within the educational environment as well as the steps necessary to achieve the goals. If aquatics is not specifically mentioned on the IEP, it is not a required school service. But if a child or young adult attends a community aquatic program, you should ensure that any related IEP goals are incorporated into the aquatic program (see chapter 4).

It would be remiss to mention the Education for All Handicapped Children Act without two of its important amendments, PL 99-457, the **Education for All Handicapped Children Act (reauthorization of 1980)**, and PL 101-476, Individuals With Disabilities Education Act (reauthorization of 1990). PL 99-457 expanded the age range of services covered by the law from 3 to 21 to include infants and toddlers from birth to 3 years old. Accordingly, parents of young children with disabilities and personnel of early intervention programs may seek out community aquatic programs as appropriate motor activities for young children. If you are familiar with these laws, you can better meet the special needs of infants and toddlers with disabilities.

You should also be familiar with the **Individualized Family Service Plan (IFSP)**, which was a result of PL 99-457. The IFSP contains individ-ual goals, objectives, and methods for the family, child, and service providers for infants and toddlers with disabilities. Appendix C, in which we describe games for inclusion, also has some tips for aquatic participants ages 6 to 36 months.

PL 101-476: Individuals With Disabilities Education Act

Public Law 101-476, the **Individuals With Disabilities Education Act**, was enacted in 1990 as an amendment to the Education of All Handicapped Children Act. PL101-476 (amended in 1997 as PL105-17) changed the term "handicapped" to "individuals with disabilities," added autism and tramatic brain injury as disability categories, and stressed the importance of transitional services within the IEP. Thus, the IEP must now include goals and objectives as well as a plan for the transition to the community. This plan, called the **Individualized Transition Plan**, projects what skills participants should have when they leave the school. "Transition" means the plans to bridge the gaps between (1) infant, toddler, and preschool programs and school programs and (2) high school programs and lifetime pursuits (figure 1.5). As an aquatic instructor in a school and community facility, you might be called on to contribute to such a plan, especially for the young adult. Seize these opportunities whenever possible. After all, what better lifetime recreational pursuit is there than aquatics?

So far, the three main laws we have mentioned focus on educational institutions, whereas the Rehabilitation Act of 1973 and the Americans With Disabilities Act have implications for school and community public and private facilities that are open to the public.

PL 101-336: Americans With Disabilities Act

The **Americans With Disabilities Act (ADA)**, passed in 1990, mandates the elimination of discrimination against 43 million Americans with disabilities with standards enforced by the federal government (Bedini and McCann 1992). The ADA has widespread implications for almost every area of life in the United States, including recreation and aquatics. The law makes illegal all discrimination based on disability and provides for ". . . full and equal enjoyment of the goods, services, facilities, privileges, advantages, or accommodations of any place of public accom-

modation by any person who owns, leases (or leases to), or operates a place of public accommodation" (Division of Vocational Rehabilitation, Dept. of Labor 1991, p. 6). The law covers employment, public services, transportation, public accommodations, services operated by private entities, telecommunications, and activities of state and local government (Winter 1992).

The specific terminology and intent of the law clearly apply to the aquatic realm. In the following sections, we'll look closely at the specific terminology of this all-encompassing law and then summarize its minimum requirements.

Qualified Individual

Congress adopted the same definition of disability first used in the Rehabilitation Act of 1973 (Federal Register 1991). The law defines a "qualified individual" as a person with physical or mental impairment that substantially limits one or more of life's major activities (Recreation Resources 1993). We can describe major life activities as self-care, manual tasks, walking, seeing, hearing, speaking, breathing, learning,

Figure 1.5 Learning personal safety skills enhances transition.

and working. Individuals with mobility or sensory impairments, mental retardation, and other mental and physical impairments as well as those with hidden disabilities, such as diabetes, cancer, epilepsy, heart disease, mental illness, and people with HIV, are all covered by this law. In addition, the law includes people who have a previous record as having an impairment (e.g., cancer in remission) and also those perceived by others as disabled, such as those who are HIV-positive but asymptomatic (Scott 1990).

Undue Hardship

An "undue hardship" is something that would lead to profound costs or difficulty for an organization with respect to the size and financial resources of the organization in its efforts to accommodate an individual or to provide general access. A small, not-for-profit organization, for example, might have a pool deck so narrow that it cannot fit a transfer lift into the area to make it accessible. To make the necessary accommodations, such an organization would need to build a new addition, knocking down the wall to extend the deck. They may, in this case, plead undue hardship, though the Internal Revenue Code provides a tax credit to remove barriers and a small business tax credit may be available to qualified businesses (Osinski 1993). Organizations who believe that their financial situation would be overwhelmed by the cost of compliance with the law can apply for an exception to the law and show how the modifications pose an undue financial burden. The IRS (as cited in Osinski 1993) considers applications for this exemption on a case-by-case basis. In many cases, however, an organization will be able to make reasonable accommodations.

Reasonable Accommodation

Although "reasonable accommodation" is not firmly defined in the ADA, experts consider it to be some action that provides access to individuals with disabilities by making modifications to policies, procedures, and practices. The law specifically addresses issues of discrimination in public accommodation and services operated by private entities. An organization cannot exclude a person from participating in services, programs, or activities based solely on her disability: "If the individual meets the requisite skill requirement for the activity, he or she should be allowed to participate" (Bedini and McCann 1992, p. 41). Courts consider it discrim-

ination to place a person in a segregated adapted aquatics program based only on her disability, rather than on her ability. This means that a facility cannot offer a person with a disability *only* the segregated, adapted program or class. The segregated program may be the one that is chosen by the participant, caregivers, and the aquatic instructor in concert, but stereotyping an individual and forcing her to accept an adapted program is not permissible. Thus, one of the purposes of the ADA is to integrate individuals with disabilities into the mainstream of society. Therefore, staff of each facility need to assess program admission policies, looking for possible barriers to participation. Some examples of reasonable accommodations in aquatic programs include the following:

- Providing flotation devices for individuals who cannot stand on the bottom of the pool while they wait for instructions during swim lessons (e.g., those with paraplegia or dwarfism)

- Allowing a person who has a urine bag to wear long, baggy shorts over the swimsuit to avoid embarrassment

- Allowing an aide to participate, at no additional cost, with an individual who needs support

- Providing a water chair and incorporating arm movements into water aerobic classes for those with lower body impairments

- Designating an area on deck for guide dogs, crutches, wheelchairs, and other mobility equipment

- Installing a nonslip carpet strip from the shower area to the pool ladder or a lift for individuals who need such help for balance, crutch traction, orientation, or mobility

- Providing auxiliary aids and services, such as alternate formats (e.g., Braille, computer disk), for registration, handouts, and certificates

- Providing family/caregiver restrooms and changing areas for caregivers of the opposite sex to enable them to provide assistance

- Removing requirements that discriminate, such as height requirements of "being able to stand on the bottom of the pool," which individuals who use wheelchairs or have dwarfism may not be able to meet

Exceptions to the law are also made for program modifications that would significantly alter the primary purpose of the set aquatic program. For example, a person with **atlantoaxial instability** syndrome, for which diving is contraindicated, may not be reasonably accommodated in a competitive diving meet.

Readily Accessible

The law uses the phrase **"readily accessible"** to describe a facility that is easily and immediately usable and accessible, in other words, a facility in which a person with a disability can move around and use to a high degree (Scott 1990). A readily accessible aquatic facility is one that already has ample parking for those with disabilities with an easily identifiable access route, pools with handrails and ramps, Braille signs, family restrooms, usable lifts, or movable pool floors.

Readily Achievable

"Readily achievable" focuses on the ease of which a facility can remove a barrier. If it can be removed easily, it is considered readily achievable. Some examples of readily achievable in an aquatic facility include having locker rooms in which bolted-down benches can be removed and locker room hooks can be lowered, purchasing a transfer tier for getting into the pool, printing aquatic manuals in Braille, removing concrete door risers between shower and locker area, and removing footbath or water collection troughs on decks or in showers.

Minimum Requirements

To meet all pertinent legislation, where should your program start? When modifying existing facilities, at least one accessible means of getting in and out of the pool should be available, either by ramp, stairs or transfer tiers, or lifts. Stair treads must be made of such material and depth, width, and riser height so that a person who uses a wheelchair can use it for transferring by easing down the steps one at a time. Although the ADA guidelines for accessibility specify that wheelchair and platform lifts permit *unassisted* operation, the Recreation Access Advisory Committee of the U.S. Architectural and Transportation Barriers Compliance Board (1994) and the National Center on Accessibility (1996) recommends that pool lifts do not have to comply with this and lifts that require attendant assistance are acceptable (1994). See figure 1.6. For more information, see chapter 6, "Facilities, Equipment, and Supplies," and consult the article by Osinski (1993), the chapter on the ADA in Leisure Opportunities for Individuals With Disabilities: Legal Issues by Stein (1993), and "Recommendations for Accessibility Guidelines: Recreational Facilities and Outdoor Developed Areas" by the Recreation Access Advisory Committee of the U.S. Architectural and Transportation Barriers Compliance Board (1994).

It is not acceptable to claim inconvenience or inaccessibility of a facility as prohibitors. Moreover, you cannot claim that a program is unavailable because the staff is untrained. Furthermore,

---

General Recommendations for Swimming Pool Accessibility

- One accessible water entry and exit for each swimming pool located on an accessible route; and two accessible water entries and exits for pool with more than 300 linear feet of pool wall.

- Pools with only one accessible means of water entry and exit shall provide a pool lift, wet ramp, or zero depth entry.

- Pools with a second means of water entry and exit shall provide a transfer wall, transfer steps, movable floor, stairs, swimming pool lift, wet ramp, or zero depth entry. Lifts, wet ramp, or zero depth entry may not be used as the second accessible means if used as the first accessible means.

- If a second accessible entry and exit exists, it should be located to complement the first accessible entry and exit to serve both ends and sides of the pool.

Figure 1.6 Recommendations for accessability (NCA 1996).

your program must avoid "barriers of omission," overlooking the special needs of certain individuals. An example of omission is a flyer or announcement circulated about a program that does not include accessibility information and therefore will not attract individuals with disabilities. The ADA demands that a program have an attitude of accessibility, including seeking to improve awareness and knowledge of how to provide service to individuals with disabilities.

BENEFITS OF AQUATIC PARTICIPATION

The benefits of aquatic participation can foster physical, psychosocial, cognitive, and leisure skill development. Yes, participants will learn valuable motor skills, but so much more can come from appropriate planning.

The Appeal of Water

As we've discussed, water's recreational, educational, and therapeutic value has long been recognized. More than 100 million Americans participate in such endeavors yearly (American Red Cross 1992a). Facilities for swimming and other water-related activities are widely available and usually inexpensive. Aquatic activities provide a form of exercise that is perceived as relaxing and socially acceptable. Although water activities do not provide a magical solution to life's problems, they may add quality to one's life through physical and mental health benefits (American Red Cross 1977b). For individuals with disabilities, an empty wheelchair and crutches laid on the pool deck means freedom of movement and a feeling of success, enhancing self-image. In short, swimming is a fun, enjoyable activity that has many physical, psychosocial, cognitive, and recreational benefits—appealing to participants, therapists, and instructors alike.

Physical Benefits

Although adapted aquatics does not focus on therapeutic water exercise, warm water itself facilitates therapeutic goals. Some therapeutic psychomotor effects of exercise in warm water are muscle relaxation, relief of pain and muscle spasms, maintaining or increasing **range of motion** in joints, reeducation of paralyzed muscles, and

improving muscle strength and endurance (Skinner and Thompson 1983). The aquatic environment helps establish early patterns of movement that may constitute the first time a person is able to explore movement possibilities. Specifically, swimming strengthens muscles that enhance posture, thereby helping to develop the stability needed to learn locomotor and object control skills (Horvat, Forbus, and Van Kirk 1987).

Lack of physical movement and aerobic exercise often causes individuals with disabilities to have decreased vital capacity of the lungs. Vital capacity is the amount of air a person can exhale after the deepest possible inhalation. Adapted aquatics activities can help improve breath control and cardiorespiratory fitness. Blowing bubbles, holding the breath, and breathing out through the mouth and nose all improve respiratory function as well as oral motor control, which can aid speech and decrease drooling and feeding problems (Martin 1983). In addition, swimmers tend to breathe deeper than usual due to the pressure the water exerts on the chest and the greater need for getting a sufficient amount of air during rhythmic breathing (Canadian Red Cross 1969).

It is easier for instructors to develop aquatic-based, rather than land-based, fitness programs for individuals who have difficulty moving against gravity (Reid 1980). The water supports the body and lessens the effects of gravity so that a person who may not be able to walk on land may be able to walk in water, thereby strengthening the muscles needed for walking on land.

Water also acts to stimulate the sites where we "take in" information (perceptual stimulant), such as the skin, vestibular system (the system that facilitates balance), and visual and auditory systems (Campion 1985). Skin must react to different temperatures and sensations (e.g., through water, towels, and pool floor and walls), the vestibular system to the turbulence of the water, the eyes to the ever-changing water surface, and the ears to compensate for increased pressure when submerged. Thus, for individuals with disabilities who require sensory stimulation, water can be an important part of therapy and rehabilitation. By sharing goals, physical and occupational therapists can help the aquatic instructor provide activities that are therapeutic as well as instructional, possibly leading to increased benefits for the participant. In fact, the more the participant can practice the same skills in a variety of environments, the more they can generalize the skills to other situations.

Finally, a person with a disability may build on aquatic fitness and swim skills gained in your class to enable him to participate in enrichment aquatic activities, such as boating, water skiing, and scuba diving (see chapter 11).

As you can see, aquatic activity can be a fun way to improve vital lung capacity, flexibility, muscle tone, and overall fitness without putting undue pressure on joints (Exceptional Parent 1993).

Psychosocial Benefits

Participation in an aquatic program can facilitate psychosocial as well as physical wellness (American Red Cross 1977a). As an individual with a physical disability learns to move about in the water without assistance and enjoy the water, self-esteem and self-awareness improve (Martin 1983). "For young people, whose sense of self may be a direct result of body image and athletic proficiency, residual motor impairment can be a particularly negative variable" (Telzrow 1987, p. 538). Moreover, the freedom of movement made possible by water not only boosts morale but also gives individuals with disabilities the incentive to maximize their potentials in other aspects of rehabilitation (Skinner and Thompson 1983). Indeed, one aquatic program's objective was to "prepare the handicapped through aquatics to be contributing members of society" (Muhl 1976, p. 43).

Appreciation and knowledge of aquatic activities is an added benefit of aquatic programs for individuals with disabilities (Canadian Red Cross Society 1980). The opportunity to participate in fun, leisure activities can lead to increased awareness of age-appropriate, community experiences. Potential benefits include improving mood, reducing anxiety and depression, and increasing self-esteem (Exceptional Parent 1993). A sense of well-being and freedom temporarily releases an individual from tension and stress, which in many cases may compound the effects of physical disabilities.

Cognitive Benefits

The motivational and therapeutic properties of water provide a stimulating learning environment for even individuals with more severe disabilities (Dulcy 1983a). Movement exploration helps participants understand their own bodies and how they move. It can be of particular benefit to persons with traumatic injuries who may

tend to lack knowledge about how their bodies now move. Some instructors have even integrated academic learning with adapted aquatics, successfully reinforcing cognitive concepts (American Red Cross 1977a). For example, these creative instructors have centered games and activities around math, spelling, reading, and other concepts. Participants may count laps, dive for submerged plastic letters, or read their workouts. These activities also help participants improve their judgment and orientation to surroundings.

In general, about 4.5 million school-aged children require special education services. In addition, a relatively new population of individuals with disabilities is availing themselves of the cognitive benefits: Approximately 40 percent of people with traumatic brain injury are under 18 (Bigler 1990). This means as many as 18,000 youngsters in the United States with traumatic brain injury may need special academic programs (Savage and Carter 1984). A trained instructor can properly plan and present activities that focus on problem-solving experiences, counting, speaking in full sentences, performing memory exercises, and working from left to right to reinforce reading—all in the aquatic environment.

Recreational Benefits

Recreational activities take place at leisure yet are perceived to be constructive, not merely diversional (Kraus 1971). Aquatic recreation can make worthy, yet enjoyable, use of leisure time as well as help meet participants' cognitive, physical, and psychosocial goals. Statistics show that many individuals with disabilities have a higher than average amount of leisure time (West 1991). Using leisure time wisely can often make the difference between a person who is socially isolated and has poor self-esteem and one who is stimulated through socialization with others to achieve self-actualization (Austin and Crawford 1991).

Promoting independent functioning and enhancing health may be part of a comprehensive therapeutic recreation program. "Therapeutic recreation may be viewed as a process of systematic use of recreation activities and experiences to achieve specific objectives" (Carter, Van Andel, and Robb 1985, p. 16). Participation in an aquatic program that has individualized goals and objectives and uses swimming, water safety, and fun aquatic activities surely is a recreational activity with therapeutic benefits, but you cannot call such a program "therapeutic recreation" unless it is overseen by a certified therapeutic recreation specialist (CTRS; see also chapter 2).

APPLICATIONS OF AQUATIC PARTICIPATION

"Adapted aquatics" is a term that can mean many different things. Aquatic instructors use the term when referring to aquatic programs involving individuals with disabilities and necessary modifications for instructional strategies, facilities, and equipment, mobility from one area to another, and communication and movements to perform swim strokes, water safety, and other aquatic activities. In this arena, the application of adapted aquatics is to improve fitness, water safety, and quality of leisure time through instructional tasks, corrective feedback, and structured practice. As we've discussed, other applications of adapted aquatics are less educa-

tional and more therapeutic (see also "Medical-Therapeutic Model" section in chapter 2).

Adapted water exercise programs use active (not passive) exercises usually done on land, within the medium of water. Aquatic professionals adapt land exercises to the needs of individuals with acute or chronic disabilities. The goals are similar to hydrotherapy, but adapted water exercise programs do not use whirlpools, contrast baths, or passive exercise. Aquatic instructors trained specifically for the arthritis aquatic programs and the National Multiple Sclerosis Society's aquatic programs as well as kinesiotherapists, physical educators, athletic trainers, and physical therapists all use this form of exercise with success. **Therapeutic water exercises** are aquatic movements specially prescribed for a particular individual. Therapeutic water exercise protocols should be authorized by a physician and conducted by a physical therapist, athletic trainer, or kinesiotherapist who has aquatic training (figure 1.7). Aquatics programs using the medical model, such as hydrotherapy and adapted and thera-

Figure 1.7 Therapeutic water exercise should be monitored by medical personnel.

peutic water exercise, are often categorized under the broad category of **aquatic therapy** (see also chapter 2).

An **adapted swimming program** modifies swim strokes for individuals who do not have the strength, flexibility, or endurance to perform the "standard" version. Adapted swimming is part of adapted aquatics. **Adapted aquatics** is the more comprehensive label for programs that use swimming, water safety, and aquatic recreational activities to promote health and rehabilitation. While such a program encompasses more than swim strokes, it does not include therapeutic water exercise, hydrotherapy, or aquatic therapy. Some professionals in the field would prefer to call this approach "adapted swimming" when referring to the nonmedical aspects of this field rather than "adapted aquatics." Their concern is that potential participants and medical personnel might misunderstand the implications of adapted aquatics, thinking that a program labeled "adapted aquatics" includes therapeutic water exercise. These professionals believe that adapted aquatics reflects the entire scope of adapted water activities including swimming, exercise, rehabilitation, safety, and recreation.

In this book, however, the term "adapted aquatics" reflects the philosophy of adapting swimming, safety, and aquatic recreational activities to the needs of individuals with unique needs. Adapted aquatics is a method, program, and process that parallels **adapted physical education**, its equal on land.

As a method, adapted aquatics strives to change, adapt, or modify any existing swim stroke, game, or activity to meet the needs of individuals with special needs (Sherrill 1993). As the instructor, you can do this within an integrated or segregated swim program. Acceptance of all people and an open, creative mind are beneficial instructor attitudes (figure 1.8). Sherrill states that all ". . . good teaching implies adapting the curriculum to individual needs so as to minimize failure and preserve ego strength" (1993, p. 3). Whether you intend to specialize in adapted aquatics or not, you should familiarize yourself with methods for adapting aquatics activities so you can integrate individuals who may benefit from regular aquatic activities. Specialized study, reading, and practical experience with instructors who practice adapted aquatics can help you, as a general swim instructor, become more profi-

Figure 1.8 Aquatics improves the human condition.

cient in this field. Indeed, adapted aquatics methods may apply to individuals with disabilities or any person who may need adaptations in order to learn swimming and water safety.

As a program, adapted aquatics can be a segregated placement for those individuals with unique needs that you cannot accommodate within any other program. Individuals or their caregivers may opt for a separate program of aquatics games, activities, swim strokes, and recreation to meet their own comfort and needs. But remember, federal law mandates that segregated programs not be the sole program that individuals with disabilities are offered.

As a process, adapted aquatics focuses on the delivery of a full range of aquatic programs to individuals with disabilities. This process includes identification, **assessment**, recommendation of placement, teaching, and evaluation of that placement as appropriate. We have adapted our view of adapted aquatics as a service delivery system (process) in aquatics from Claudine Sherrill's position on adapted physical education (1993). More on this in chapter 3.

SUMMARY

Although aquatics programs have long provided therapeutic benefits, adapted aquatics is a philosophy that encompasses swim strokes, water safety, and recreational aquatic activities that may or may not be considered therapy. Therefore, though the use of aquatics with individuals with disabilities grew out of therapy programs in the 1920s and 30s (and even those more ancient), you should not confuse aquatic therapy, therapeutic water exercises, and hydrotherapy with adapted aquatics.

Why adapted aquatics? As an aquatics professional, you should advocate for the hard-fought changes in accessibility to facilities and programs, particularly in light of the proven benefits of aquatics for people with disabilities. Indeed, the appeal of water leads to many psychosocial, cognitive, and physical benefits. Thus, throughout this book, we'll focus on swimming, water safety, and recreational uses of aquatics for individuals with disabilities who cannot successfully or safely participate in regular aquatic programs or who have special needs in the inclusive setting. Whether you're learning about teaching adapted aquatics for the first time or a seasoned instructor, in this book we will provide you with not only theory but also practical, field-tested suggestions for providing safe, successful, and relevant aquatic programs as you strive to accommodate individuals with disabilities—with the dignity all participants deserve.

CHAPTER 1 REVIEW

1. Trace the historical theme in aquatics programming for individuals with disabilities.

2. Approximately how many individuals participate in aquatics programs annually?

3. Describe the purposes of the Rehabilitation Act of 1973, Education for All Handicapped Children Act (1975), Individuals With Disabilities Education Act (1990), and the Americans With Disabilities Act (1990).

4. Explain the psychomotor benefits of aquatics participation and how water enhances individuals with disabilities' opportunities to achieve these benefits.

5. Explain the differences between adapted water exercise, therapeutic water exercises, adapted swimming, and adapted aquatics.

6. Discuss the terms "reasonable accommodations," "readily accessible," and "readily achievable."

MODELS FOR ADAPTED AQUATICS PROGRAMMING

The number of individuals using aquatics for physical improvement has increased tremendously for many reasons. One reason is the development of organizations such as the Aquatic Exercise Association, the American Physical Therapy Aquatic Therapy Section, and the aquatic network of the American Occupational Therapy Association, all of which provide training seminars for professionals who conduct a variety of different programs for individuals with temporary or permanent disabilities. Because of the influence and involvement of these organizations, allied health care professionals have joined aquatic instructors in using aquatic facilities, focusing on delivering programs centered around activities or exercise other than swimming and water safety. Naturally, federal legislation requiring that facilities and programs be made accessible to individuals with disabilities has also increased participation. In addition, senior citizens with and without disabilities have become aware of the benefits of aquatic activity. Finally, individuals with temporary physical disabilities have come to the water for rehabilitation. Indeed, an entire water exercise industry has emerged through the participation of individuals with back pain, sport injuries, and work-related disabilities (The Back Letter 1991).

In this chapter, we'll profile four models used in developing programs to serve the basic needs of individuals with disabilities: the medical-therapeutic model, the educational model, the therapeutic recreation model, and the collaborative model. We'll examine distinct components, goals, and **objectives**, and the roles played by various professionals involved in the delivery of services for each model, including how to apply each model in the aquatic realm.

MEDICAL-THERAPEUTIC MODEL

Over the centuries, English, Greek, and Roman physicians have prescribed healing baths—a practice which evolved into the therapeutic use of aquatics, called hydrotherapy. Its meaning is derived from two Greek words, hydro (water) and therapia (healing). To apply this model, the medical profession has typically used various tests to diagnose a problem, assigning it a medical term or disability category and then prescribing a specific course of treatment to remediate, cure, or control the symptoms.

Aquatics as a medical prescription follows this model, known as the medical-therapeutic model. In the United States, the treatment of disease, disability, and ill health through aquatics is called hydrotherapy, aquatic therapy, or aquatherapy. Physicians prescribe it for the short- or long-term treatment of burns, peripheral vascular disorders, and all types of orthopedic and neurological impairments and athletic injuries.

Distinct Components

The distinct components of the medical-therapeutic model of aquatic service include physician prescription or referral, problem-oriented reporting, disability-specific treatment, and specific active and passive exercises conducted by therapy specialists.

Physician Prescription or Referral

Typically, physicians who specialize in physical medicine, orthopedics, rehabilitation, **neurology**, or **rheumatology** are the most knowledgeable about the benefits of aquatic activity and, in general, refer the most patients to aquatic therapy. When physicians refer or prescribe aquatic therapy, they will often prescribe the number of sessions per week, the total sessions they believe will be beneficial, the types of exercises suggested, and, most importantly, the specific objectives the therapy should achieve. Prescribed objectives may be as vague as "to increase range of motion" or as specific as "to increase range of motion in the knee to 130 degrees."

Problem-Oriented Reporting

Working to solve specific problems is a distinct component of the medical-therapeutic model. Once the physician has prescribed the therapy, the patient seeks out a therapist who will communicate with the physician to draw up a problem-oriented report (POR). The POR focuses on the problems the patient is having, how to solve those problems, treatments the medical team will apply, and which health professional is responsible for solving each problem. Meticulous record keeping is typical in the medical-therapeutic model with the therapist writing weekly reports and monthly summaries of progress and setbacks toward goals and objectives. Third-party insurance reimbursements that occur with programs following the medical-therapeutic model generally demand such attention to detail.

Disability-Specific Treatment

Another distinct component is the focus on the disability. Often a specific treatment plan is set into motion in response to a diagnosis. This is known as a categorical approach in which the medical team builds exercises, activities, and **contraindications** around typical characteristics of a disability and uses these generically with all or most patients who have that disability. Disability-specific treatment takes into account a large amount of information regarding physical and mental conditions, ensuring important safety information is available if the person is subject to **seizures**, ataxic movements, impulsive acts, or abnormal movements due to neurological dysfunction.

Specific Exercises

Professionals, such as physical and occupational therapists, kinesiotherapists, and athletic trainers (sports medicine specialists), usually develop distinctive exercise protocols for specific disabilities and modify these protocols for each individual's specific physical characteristics. Methods of treatment include positioning, using anatomical movements underwater, and progressions of developmental sequences. "Hydrodynamic properties of the water, which influence the individual's position and movement in the water, are the basis of exercise progression" (Dulcy 1983a, pp. 15-16).

Goals and Objectives Within the Medical-Therapeutic Model

Goals are broad outcome statements aimed at guiding a program or an individual within a program. Objectives are specific statements of intent that reflect a future observable and measurable outcome for an individual within a program. In this section, we will describe typical goals of programs that operate within the medical-therapeutic model and give examples of goals and objectives for participants in those programs (see also chapter 10).

The main goals of any medical-therapeutic aquatics program are to facilitate restoration, maintenance, and development of functional capacities through positions, exercises, and activities that reduce pain and prevent deformity and further disability and to develop or improve motor skills and muscular strength and endurance so that patients may function at their maximum potentials (Sherrill 1993). Specifically, medical-therapeutic aquatic programs emphasize using hydrodynamics and underwater exercise to improve the condition of an individual (Dulcy 1983a). Goals and objectives for aquatic therapy programs that operate under the medical-therapeutic model generally follow the therapeutic land protocol but aquatic activities are generally easier and more enjoyable than therapeutic exercise on land and are therefore quite popular in achieving specific therapeutic goals.

Goals that might guide a program under the medical-therapeutic model include but are not limited to the following example.

The goals of the program are to provide exercises and activities that

1. improve range of motion,
2. improve independent **ambulation**,
3. decrease abnormal muscle tone,
4. facilitate weight-bearing tolerance in transferring activities, and
5. facilitate improvement of vital lung capacity.

Goals, assimilated from the model, delineate what participants will do within a specific program. The treatment team then translates these general program goals into goals and objectives for individual participants based on individual needs. The following lists outline typical goals and objectives for participants in programs guided by the medical-therapeutic model.

PARTICIPANT GOALS

1. To improve range of motion in extremities
2. To maintain vital lung capacity
3. To increase weight-bearing tolerance

PARTICIPANT OBJECTIVES

1.1 Participant will increase range of motion in elbow by 20 degrees by March as a result of elbow flexion and extension exercises during aquatic therapy sessions.

2.1 Participant will maintain vital lung capacity of 23 liters of oxygen per minute by swimming the front crawl for 200 meters, four times per week.

3.1 Participant will show increased weight-bearing tolerance by standing on flat feet in four feet of water for 5-minute intervals, three times per 60-minute aquatic therapy session, three times per week.

Settings

The settings for aquatic services within the medical-therapeutic model include community settings as well as hospital-based facilities. Private and public pools may be rented by hospitals, rehabilitation centers, or private practice therapists for one or several hours per week to facilitate community outreach. Additional settings in which the medical-therapeutic model in aquatics is evident are in rehabilitation centers, nursing homes, intermediate- and long-term care facilities, health and wellness facilities, and sports medicine centers (see also chapter 10).

Providers

The field of aquatic therapy, operating within a medical-therapeutic model, is reaching the masses in these settings through professionals called aquatic therapists. Who are aquatic therapists? They are specialists in the area of aquatics, movement, and chronic and acute disabilities and diseases. They have degrees in sports medicine, **kinesiotherapy**, adapted physical education, physical or **occupational therapy**, or **therapeutic recreation**. In a few years this question will be further defined as the American Physical Therapy Association and the American Occupational Therapy groups expand their aquatic networks and as the aquatic council of the American Alliance for Health, Physical Education, Recreation and Dance (AAHPERD) makes recommendations about aquatic therapy certification.

Aquatic therapy provided by physical therapists has always functioned under the medical-therapeutic model. Aquatic activities are delivered under a physician's direction or prescription and are supervised by a licensed physical therapist. Some states do not require a prescription from a physician and individuals therefore have direct access to physical therapy. Physical therapy assistants may provide one-to-one contact in the pool and conduct some of the active therapy. In the last decade, other allied health professionals have used water as a therapeutic medium to meet treatment goals. Sports medicine specialists, also known as athletic trainers, are also providers of aquatic therapy, in particular using it for the rehabilitation of athletic injuries. Athletic training/sports medicine functions under the medical-therapeutic model much like physical therapy.

Occupational therapists (OT) provide a setting where individuals with disabilities can acquire, practice, and refine activities that are necessary to function in daily life. Occupational therapy is the ". . . therapeutic use of self care, work and play activities to increase independent function, enhance development, and prevent disability" (Hopkins and Smith 1988, p. 4). Occupational therapists work in hospitals, rehabilitation centers, nursing homes and schools to introduce skills involving dressing, transferring, self-maintenance, **sensory integration**, vocational training, and leisure. In the aquatic setting, occupational therapists work with their clients to develop sequencing of normalized movements, provide proper positioning, and encourage self-care. The water also provides the perfect setting to develop sensory integration as it requires constant adjustment to changing depth, surface movement, and pressure (see figure 2.1).

Kinesiotherapists treat the effects of disabilities, injuries, and diseases with education and exercise in aquatic and nonaquatic settings. In the past they were known as corrective therapists and worked mainly within the veterans' administration hospitals, but they have recently entered private practice to offer their services to clients in a variety of community health care facilities. Kinesiotherapists work with physicians to ". . . act as a bridge between traditional physical therapy in hospitals or clinics, work tolerance programs and return to work" (Meyer 1994, p. ii).

The certified therapeutic recreation specialist (CTRS), who has received additional training in aquatics, works with individuals with disabilities to help them reach their full physical, emotional, cognitive, and social potential through recreational aquatic activities. They are employed in both clinical and community settings.

Important Issues

Applying the medical-therapeutic model to the aquatic setting has several shortcomings. For example, programs that operate with the medical-therapeutic model as their guide often are guilty

Figure 2.1 Sequencing of manipulative skills are enhanced through therapeutic aquatics.

of losing sight of aquatics as a medium for enjoyment and learning. Often this narrow view can lessen benefits simply by becoming monotonous.

Therapists who do not have training in aquatic safety may be unaware of the potential contraindications of a disability in the aquatic setting or the specific precautions required for safety. Without the skills to assess, plan, implement, and evaluate aquatic skills, inadequately trained therapists may overlook safety hazards, compromising their abilities to foresee, prevent, and respond to aquatic emergencies. In addition, therapists may be comfortable walking in the shallow end of a pool but may pose a risk to themselves and others if they lack swimming and water safety abilities in deeper water.

Finally, experts often view the medical-therapeutic model as categorical in that it groups individuals according to common pathology. It is common for hospitals to have separate programs for different disabilities. To make matters worse, such programs often use negative terminology and sometimes focus care based on the individual's disorder, diagnosis, or disability, rather than on abilities. Thus, the medical-therapeutic model may not allow an adequate view of the whole person.

EDUCATIONAL MODEL

The educational model of adapted aquatic instruction has developed as a result of several factors including the American Red Cross (ARC) and YMCA progressive swim models; the adapted physical education service delivery model, resulting from the Education for All Handicapped Children Act (now Individuals With Disabilities Education Act [IDEA]); and the social minority model of viewing individuals with disabilities. The educational model is quite different from the medical-therapeutic model in that it focuses on education rather than treatment, strengths rather than problems, water safety and swim skills rather than facilitation of movement.

The progressive swim models of the ARC and YMCA guide instructional programs by listing water safety and swim skills in a hierarchy. Individuals build on the skills learned earlier and progress up the hierarchy much like graded classrooms in schools. When an organization defines skill progressions, as in appendix

B, participants see the big picture of water safety and skill instruction, and this minicurriculum can serve as a guidepost for progress.

Because of the mandates of the Education for All Handicapped Children Act (now IDEA; see chapter 1), as an aquatic professional providing service in the educational model, you must be more accountable. Educational aquatic programs in schools and community agencies often contribute to a child's individualized educational program and operate within the educational model. Expect and ask to be part of creating an individualized plan if you are to be the aquatic instructor.

The service delivery model of adapted physical education, developed by Claudine Sherrill (1993), incorporates all of the required concepts. This model stresses identifying participants with needs in the psychomotor area; providing appropriate assessment; planning, implementing, and evaluating participants; and providing instruction in the least restrictive environment (see also later in this chapter as well as chapters 3 and 4).

The social minority model has also greatly influenced the education model. This model espouses the philosophy that individuals with disabilities are different, not defective, inferior, or less than others—simply different. Looking at any issue surrounding individuals with disabilities from this standpoint tends to be a more positive approach; assessment tends to rely on individualized data, and education to empower becomes the goal.

Distinct Components

The distinct components of the educational model of aquatic service include the focus on learning theory and its application to teaching aquatic skills, the notion that an individual has unique strengths and weaknesses (as opposed to a general categorization of problems assigned to a person when a specific diagnosis is made in the medical-therapeutic model), the concept of least restrictive environment for the acquisition of skills, the development of an individualized plan focusing on the improvement of skills versus solving problems, and the content of each session, which focuses on swimming and water safety skills rather than therapy.

Learning Theory

Not surprisingly, learning theory is the foundation of the educational model. Lesson plans control instruction by listing individual or group goals, objectives, instructional strategies, activities to achieve objectives, and evaluation activities. Instructors plan each aquatic session to provide experiences that encourage learning through sequential progressions of skills. They introduce skills by explaining the reasons for the skills, demonstrating the skills, and guiding participants' practice of the skills with appropriate feedback. Instructional strategies, such as academic reinforcement games, provide participants with challenges that motivate as well as help them test their new skills.

Another aspect connected to learning theory and therefore important to mention in the educational model is developmental aquatic readiness (Langendorfer, Harrod, and Bruya 1991). This concept recognizes that individuals come to the pool with a variety of different aquatic backgrounds as well as developmental levels. As an aquatic instructor (or therapist), you need to recognize that aquatic readiness plays a critical role in an individual's willingness to participate in aquatic activities. You can assess aquatic readiness by observing initial behaviors and by interviewing a swimmer and caregivers. If you find that an individual is afraid of the water or lacks readiness in any other way, you may need to include a sequential progression of water orientation activities. No matter the model, all practitioners should address readiness.

Assessment of Needs

The second distinct component of this model is the focus on assessment of individual needs, giving caregivers, significant others, and the participant a say in what strengths and weaknesses they want to develop. To apply this model, you must examine functional ability and functional limitations, rather than accept the medical diagnosis or assign a disability category. Progressing from a medical-therapeutic model to an educational model, in which you teach rather than treat the participant, is an important step in empowering individuals to assume active roles in self-actualization, a concept that comes from the social minority model.

Least Restrictive Environment

Another aspect of the educational model, which resulted from legislation, is the concept of **least restrictive environment (LRE)**. You should seek to place children with disabilities in an environment that best meets their needs, provides appropriate socialization and instructional opportunities, and encourages full potential while they receive education alongside typically developing individuals to the maximum extent possible. Some professionals believe that individuals with disabilities should be totally included in all regular aquatic programs with the necessary support. We, however, believe that individuals should have the opportunity to participate in integrated aquatic programs if they can acquire skills in a group setting with necessary support. If this is not possible due to health, physical, emotional, cognitive, or other reasons, then you should explore other placements (see also chapter 3).

Individualized Plans

The Individualized Educational Program (IEP) for individuals 5 to 21 years, the Individualized Family Service Plan (IFSP) for infants, toddlers, and pre-schoolers, the Individualized Transition Plan (ITP) for individuals over 14, or the Individualized Aquatics Program Plan (IAPP) for adult participants is another distinct characteristic of the educational model. These plans define the educational goals and provide an individualized curriculum based on students' needs and desires, caregivers' goals, availability of equipment, personnel, and facilities, and the focus of the aquatic program (see also chapter 4).

Lesson Content

The content of each session is another major distinguishing factor in programs that use the educational model. As the instructor, you must analyze swim strokes to determine which tasks the participant must master and to develop a learning progression based on learning style, physical, mental, and emotional abilities, and the difficulty of each task. Moreover, you must integrate water safety information into each lesson and link skills to their usefulness in fitness, recreation, and survival pursuits. You can teach aquatic games, stunts, and swim strokes using the educational model of adapted aquatics.

Goals and Objectives Within the Educational Model

The main goal of any aquatic program following the educational model is to teach an individual with a disability how to safely enjoy the aquatic environment (figure 2.2). Instruction in aquatic skills facilitates safe enjoyment. But the range of aquatic skills you can teach will vary among individuals. In a regular aquatic program, instruction proceeds so that all participants complete the same skills, such as being able to bob in deep water 20 times or perform a standing front dive off the pool deck. Individuals with disabilities who need prerequisite or adapted skills may each finish the program with different outcomes, however. As a general aquatic instructor, you can help participants accomplish objectives within a swim class of same-age peers, using an adapted aquatics instructor as a co-instructor, or you can work one-on-one or with a small group of individuals with and without disabilities.

Goals that might guide an educational adapted aquatic program come from the educational model's philosophy of swim and water safety instruction and may include, but are not limited to, the following.

The goals of the program are to provide instruction and activities that improve

1. knowledge and appreciation of pool rules and safe behavior,
2. correct use of steps, ramps, ladders, lifts, or transfer equipment,
3. mouth closure when a wave or splashing occurs,
4. breath control,
5. swim strokes,
6. competitive starts and turns,
7. synchronized swimming movements,
8. mask, fins, and snorkel competence,
9. swimming in a tube or life jacket,
10. rolling from front to back and vice versa,
11. ability to inflate clothing for survival swimming,
12. direction changes while swimming,
13. recovering from horizontal position,
14. treading water, and
15. making a reaching rescue.

Your program could expand this list to include community water safety, lifeguard training and instructor skills, boating, scuba, competitive and synchronized swim skills, diving, and water polo.

Since IDEA identifies aquatics as a specific activity under the definition of physical education, the implications are twofold: (1) physical educators may use aquatics as part of the physical education program and (2) if parents or caregivers believe that aquatic experiences are beneficial to the total education of the child with a disability, they can argue that the school must provide a swimming program in addition to

Figure 2.2 Flotation assistance diminishes anxiety while enhancing safety.

physical education on land (Dunn 1978). Thus, goals and objectives may include nonswim skills, such as balancing on one foot, hopping, jumping, and underwater stunts and running. These skills may be typical physical education land goals, but performing them in the water generates resistance, which can help individuals be more aware of what their body parts are doing (see figure 2.3). In Canada, a program called Aqua-Percept does just this. It is a prototype program that strives ". . . to build and maintain confidence; to bridge gaps in motor development; and to teach each child to swim" (Fitzner 1986, p. 8). (Refer to appendix E for the address of this program.)

Examples of typical goals and objectives for participants in programs guided by the educational model of adapted aquatics follow.

PARTICIPANT GOALS

1. To improve breath control.
2. To increase cardiorespiratory endurance.
3. To improve swim stroke mechanics.
4. To improve fundamental locomotor skills.

Figure 2.3 Physical education activities can be adapted for the pool.

PARTICIPANT OBJECTIVES

1.1 Participant will improve breath control by performing 20 consecutive bobs in deep water each session.

2.1 Participant will increase cardiorespiratory endurance by swimming the front crawl for 300 yards more per session.

3.1 Participant will improve swim stroke mechanics as shown by proper hand placement during the catch phase of the front and back crawl, 75 percent of the time.

4.1 Participant will run with coordinated cross-**lateral movement** for 50 yards, 75 percent of the time.

As mentioned earlier, you can use the educational aquatic program to incorporate objectives typically taught in an academic classroom. In addition to the strategies we've already discussed, you can use the water to reinforce and teach the words and concepts of under, on top of, over, and so on; this can be important for individuals needing concrete, hands-on, learning experiences. But you don't need to design total lessons around the concepts—simply incorporate them into the already existing lesson through emphasizing the concept whenever possible. For example, during the front crawl, cue phrases such as "elbow up" with a tap on the elbow can emphasize the word and concept "up." Often you will find yourself reinforcing what the special educator has taught in the classroom, but sometimes you can initiate a concept in the pool through special planning, coordinated with the classroom teacher. We encourage you to look for ways to plan instructional units using goals and objectives to teach swimming, academics, and movement all at once.

Settings

The settings in which programs following the educational model take place include schools, community centers, and camps. Summer camp is a setting in which many children first learn to swim. Schools provide educational adapted aquatic programs as part of the physical education curriculum to replace, supplement, or complement the regular or adapted physical education class.

Sometimes when schools don't have a facility but an IEP calls for an educational aquatic program, they subcontract with a pool in the community to provide adapted aquatics programs. When this happens, the school will dictate that the program be geared toward the educational model of service. The school provides transportation to a community-based facility to fulfill this requirement (see also chapter 10).

Providers

Providers of adapted aquatic service within the educational model include regular and adapted aquatic instructors, regular and adapted physical educators, and, occasionally, special educators and therapeutic recreation specialists. Regular aquatic instructors gain formalized training in the educational model by attending classes and passing tests that are given by the American Red Cross, YMCA, American Alliance for Health, Physical Education, Recreation and Dance (AAHPERD), or the National Safety Council. Aquatic instructors will get cursory lectures about or brief experiences with individuals with disabilities in an effort to make them comfortable with inclusion. Aquatic instructors who have no other training in teaching swimming and water safety skills to individuals with disabilities may gain job training by working with an experienced co-instructor. We recommend, however, that formal training from an agency such as AAHPERD or the YMCA accompany informal training, because formal training helps you provide safe, effective, and relevant educationally based aquatic programs, creating an environment in which a higher rate of learning and socialization will take place. Furthermore, formal training will make it easier for you to make appropriate decisions regarding each individual.

As the aquatic instructor, you should receive input from the school-based physical educator about the individual's motor skills on land and her behavior in groups. The regular and adapted physical educator might make recommendations as to whether a child could benefit from a totally inclusive aquatic program or learn better in a small group, one-on-one, or segregated placement and about how you can teach or reinforce land-based skills in the water. Consulting, sharing information, and advocating for aquatics in the IEP are functions the adapted physical education specialist could serve. Thus, if you're an aquatics instructor who teaches in the school

setting or collaborates to provide aquatic services for the school in community-based settings, you need to understand the process of assessment and the IEP, IFSP, ITP, and the IAPP (see chapter 4).

The special education teacher, although not usually versed in aquatics, may try to use pool time to incorporate goals and objectives from the academic classroom. Activities of daily living, spatial concepts and following directions can be easily merged into the aquatic lesson. The special education teacher may be a great advocate for aquatic programming in the educational setting. The special education teacher may work with the individual in a self-contained class, in a learning or physical support setting, or as a consultant to an individual's inclusion program. No matter how much or little the contact is, the special education teacher can provide you with valuable information about academic level, learning style, and overall behavior of the student. Academic level may not seem to be a concern to you as the aquatic instructor, but knowledge about mental age, reading and comprehension levels, and what concepts are being presented in class should have a large impact on what and how you may choose to present information in the pool.

As a member of a team within the educational setting, a certified therapeutic reaction specialist may use the concepts from the educational model during the skill acquisition phase. The learning of aquatic skills in the transition from rehabilitation center to community setting requires the instruction of new skills and changing of behaviors. Crossing over the boundaries from instructional to recreational makes therapeutic recreation (and sometimes kinesiotherapy) unique in its role.

Important Issues

With each individual with disabilities, ask yourself "What is the most appropriate place for this individual to learn water safety and aquatic skills and who should be conducting the instruction?"

The most pressing and controversial issue is total inclusion versus least restrictive environment. Yet, the educational approach to aquatic programming can take place in any kind of setting; thus, the issue of settings should not dictate what will be learned and how (see also chapter 3).

The role of the regular aquatic instructor in providing instruction for individuals with disabilities continues to be an issue that is unresolved. It is clear that regular aquatic instructors with no formal training find it difficult to integrate the individual with special needs into aquatic programs. Thus, all participants with disabilities should have access to an instructor with formal training in adapted aquatics. An adapted aquatics specialist does not need to be the principal instructor, but assessment, planning, placement, monitoring of appropriate instruction and opportunities, and evaluation of the progress toward individualized goals and objectives should be done by him or an adapted physical educator or certified therapeutic recreation specialist with aquatic instructor certification. The adapted aquatics instructor may be the instructor, support person, consultant, assistant, or simply the monitor of the plan, but in some fashion, a trained adapted aquatics specialist must be involved.

THERAPEUTIC RECREATION MODEL

Although many of the components of the therapeutic recreation (TR) model seem to be governed by the medical-therapeutic model and some by the educational model, the crossover between models makes this model unique enough to look at separately. Therapeutic recreation is a health-related profession that seeks to bring about a change in behavior through recreational experience (O'Morrow 1980). The contemporary therapeutic recreation model developed from the rehabilitation movement starting in the early 1900s when key figures such as Dorothea Dix brought attention to inadequate care of individuals in institutions for the mentally retarded and mentally ill. Her fight for residential clients' rights enhanced recreation opportunities in institutions throughout the United States. Other key figures such as Richard Nixon, who began mandated deinstitutionalization, and Howard Rusk, who helped establish recreation as an adjunct therapy, helped recreation become a viable tool for rehabilitation. Legislation such as the Vocational Rehabilitation Act of 1963 and the Developmental Disabilities Services and Facilities Construction Act of 1971 also affected the growth of recreation for therapy, helping create therapeutic recreation as a profession. In 1978, the

National Therapeutic Recreation Society developed the first standards of practice for the delivery of therapeutic recreation in community-based programs and, in 1979, for clinical and residential service settings. These historical events began to shape the profession as well as define "therapeutic" (Crawford 1991).

Historically, practitioners have approached therapeutic recreation in two ways: therapeutic recreation and special recreation. Therapeutic recreation focuses on recreational activities for rehabilitation and treatment while special recreation centers on adaptations to activities for leisure. For example, carving out handles into a kickboard for someone to participate easier in recreational swimming is special recreation; a therapeutic recreation specialist carrying on a conversation with a participant learning to use a kickboard and the etiquette for swimming laps using a kickboard is therapeutic recreation.

Special recreation has no model for the provision of services; practitioners only seek to make accommodations necessary for the person to participate. Here we will focus on the therapeutic recreation model, because it is so closely aligned with adapted aquatics. Apply this model to aquatics when an individual with a disability who needs intervention in lifetime leisure skills shows an interest in aquatics or the physician, caregiver, and therapist decide to introduce the participant to the water. Proponents of the TR model use it to develop aquatic programs that focus on socialization, enjoyment, aquatic skill acquisition for lifelong use, and appropriate leisure behaviors.

Distinct Components

The distinct components of the therapeutic recreation model of aquatic service include links with the medical-therapeutic model, links with the educational model, and a focus on independent participation in lifetime leisure skills.

Links to Medical-Therapeutic Model

In a clinical setting, referral to therapeutic recreation is made by a physician, who prescribes goals. Solving the patient's problems during recreational activities (increasing range of motion) and solving problems about participation in recreational activities (learning skills needed to participate) are the main focuses. As in the medical-therapeutic model, therapeutic recreation specialists may write weekly and monthly patient summaries noting progress, do complex charting, and may even deal with insurance reimbursements. But unlike in the medical-therapeutic model, the therapeutic recreation specialists often teach individuals with disabilities the skills they need to know to participate in recreation and leisure activities that they have expressed interest in. Generally, certified therapeutic recreation specialists (CTRSs) work with teens, adults, and senior citizens (figure 2.4).

Links to Educational Model

The second component, leisure counseling and education, stems from the educational model. Once the therapeutic recreation specialist determines what the client wants to try, she usually has to teach the physical, cognitive, and affective skills necessary so the individual with disabilities may participate during leisure time. The educational model may guide this aspect of the aquatic program under the TR model as the TR specialist follows a session plan and instructional strategies for teaching swim and water safety skills.

Independent Pursuit of Leisure

The third component of the TR model encourages participants to be as independent during leisure pursuits as possible, to enjoy themselves, and to learn and practice appropriate social behaviors in order to have a desirable, fulfilling experience through a recreational activity. Following therapeutic intervention, leisure counseling, and education, the participant acts alone. No longer directed by a certified therapeutic recreation specialist (CTRS), the participant is encouraged to choose his own recreational aquatic activities. Whether segregated, adapted, or totally inclusive, the TR specialist helps individuals with disabilities use aquatics during free time, by facilitating communication, providing equipment, or modifying facilities, thus giving them valuable opportunities to further develop confidence and competence.

Goals and Objectives Within the Therapeutic Recreation Model

The general goal of aquatic programs that follow a therapeutic recreation model is to provide experiences in the aquatic environment that nurture an individual to be the best she can be physically, cognitively, spiritually, and emotionally. Some specific sample goals follow.

The goals of the program are to provide activities and opportunities that

Figure 2.4 Therapeutic recreation teaches skills necessary for participation in community leisure activities.

1. facilitate independent leisure time functioning,
2. improve self-confidence so that participants will try other new recreational activities,
3. encourage participants to engage in lifelong fitness routines,
4. increase appropriate socialization with others,
5. allow exploration of strengths and weaknesses,
6. improve swimming and water safety skills, and
7. increase self-actualization.

A TR specialist helps participants achieve these goals through planned activities, which include getting from the car to the locker room, dressing, transferring, and participating in exercise, water sports, swim and water safety instruction, socialization, or competitive swimming. Goals and objectives developed for individual participants may include the following.

PARTICIPANT GOALS

1. To improve range of motion.
2. To develop cooperative relationships with others.
3. To increase independence while using an aquatic facility.

PARTICIPANT OBJECTIVES

1.1 Participant will improve upper body range of motion by performing back crawl with proper hand and arm entry 75 percent of the time.

2.1 Participant will observe swim etiquette when getting in pool and sharing a lane provided with only one verbal reminder per session.

2.2 Participant will initiate an appropriate conversation during cool-down of water-walking with others, once per session.

3.1 Participant will put a magnet on her locker, without being reminded, to indicate which is her locker.

3.2 Participant will exit pool within five minutes of target time, without a reminder.

Goals and objectives for participants in aquatic programs that operate under the TR model become part of the Individualized Treatment or Individualized Aquatics Program Plan (ITP or IAPP). The treatment team should prioritize goals and then provide specific strategies to guide the aquatic TR specialist, who will implement the plan. If an individual does not have a treatment team, the participant and significant others should serve as reviewers. An evaluation plan, specifying methods of achieving goals and dates of initiation and completion of services, should be agreed upon by the team, including caregivers and, if appropriate, the participant. Implementation begins when the treatment team, caregivers, and if feasible, the participant, agree to the program.

Aquatics as recreation provides very successful carryover therapy. Instead of being a time filler or a passive activity, aquatic endeavors in the TR model, carefully selected by the guidance of an aquatic TR specialist, have meaning for participants, offer pleasure and satisfaction, and provide opportunity for skill mastery (Austin and Crawford 1991).

Settings

Aquatic programs that follow the TR model are found in a multitude of settings, including summer camps, community centers, intermediate- and long-term care facilities, and rehabilitation hospitals.

Providers

The certified therapeutic recreation specialist (CTRS) is the primary provider of aquatic service within this model. These professionals have a bachelor's or master's degree in therapeutic recreation, have passed a national certification exam and, in addition, possess an aquatic instructor or water safety instructor certificate. Occasionally, kinesiotherapists and adapted physical educators use this model, but you should not call a program a therapeutic recreation program unless it is guided by a CTRS.

In a rehabilitation hospital or center, the aquatic TR specialist may work with the physical and occupational therapist during aquatic therapy and provide programs at other times, possibly during evenings and on weekends. Using the pool at this time facilitates participation by families and friends and also outpatients who may be involved in support group programs. In a hospital, the aquatic TR program may be very medically oriented and prescribed by a physician or fully diversional with few structured goals and objectives and little record keeping.

Important Issues

The most pressing issue surrounding the TR model comes from within the profession itself: What constitutes therapeutic intervention and separates therapeutic aquatic activities from adapted aquatic activities? The answer relates to the end product of "Why aquatics?" To learn swimming and water safety skills? (Educational model.) To improve physical functioning through reduced gravity exercise and hydrodynamic principles? (Medical-therapeutic model.) To achieve self-actualization and independent leisure skills through the use of aquatics as a pleasurable, fun, and motivational recreational activity? (Therapeutic recreation model.) Often, since TR embraces the medical-therapeutic and educational models, it is difficult to draw the fine line that separates them. Functioning in two different models sometimes causes a bit of "turf wars," leaving the TR specialist feeling like he is stepping over his boundaries onto other professional "toes."

Another issue is the manner in which clinical TRs view community-based TR programs. In a community setting, a CTRS who conducts an aquatic program within the TR model usually gets no third-party reimbursement and little respect from colleagues who are in hospital-based therapeutic recreation. Many CTRSs subsequently avoid community-based programming and community recreation programs suffer.

A final issue that causes controversy is that non-CTRSs often advertise their aquatic programs as recreation "therapy" but do not possess the knowledge to function within the therapeutic recreation model and therefore don't make aquatic experiences actually therapeutic. When this happens, the program is not conducted within the therapeutic recreation model and does not result in the benefits of a bona fide TR program. Outsiders may not recognize it is not conducted by a CTRS and therefore develop an erroneously poor perception of TR aquatic service. Unfortunately, this causes wariness among consumers, physicians, insurance companies, and allied health professionals about what exactly happens during a TR session conducted in the pool within the TR model.

COLLABORATIVE MODEL

Because of legislation providing access to various services in the United States, such as recreation activities, educational programs, and vocational opportunities, human services personnel have emerged to help facilitate each of these services, leading to the development of the collaborative model during the 1970s, 80s, and 90s (see figure 2.5). Because of the large number of professionals all striving to help the individual with a disability become the best he or she could be, conflicts arose as to what were priorities in that person's life. In the 1970s the multidisciplinary model of service was common. Used in IDEA (1990) the term multidisciplinary commonly refers to many different professionals who have come to an understanding that they all have important contributions to make in the education and treatment of individuals with disabilities (United Cerebral Palsy 1976). Professionals in a multidisciplinary team (M-team) share and review their assessment results, goals and objectives, and progress reports. Members of the M-team know what the others are trying to accomplish and are aware of the methods the others are using. Often, professionals employing this model discuss additional services that the individual may need and make recommendations for services.

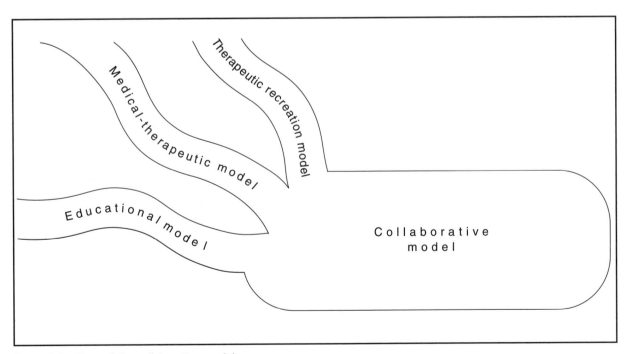

Figure 2.5 Flow of the collaborative model.

In the 1980s the concept of interdisciplinary service began to be developed. The interdisciplinary model builds on the multidisciplinary model to promote collaboration among professionals in planning and implementing programs. These professionals may present assessment information at a team meeting and reach agreement together about goals, objectives, and strategies in order to act more as a unit in their service provision. If you are an aquatic instructor cooperating within this model, you are responsible for incorporating the other disciplines' goals. For example, if the team has specified that the individual needs to develop left-

right discrimination, you must be sure to provide appropriate feedback and skill development during instruction. In this way, individuals with disabilities receive more comprehensive services in aquatics.

Recognizing that the unidisciplinary model has failed and that the multidisciplinary and interdisciplinary models were still not doing enough, Dulcy conceptualized a collaborative model for aquatics. As seen in figure 2.6, Dulcy (1983a) demonstrates that the unidisciplinary model for providing aquatics for individuals with disabilities has limited benefits. The division of aquatic programming into therapeutic, recreational, and

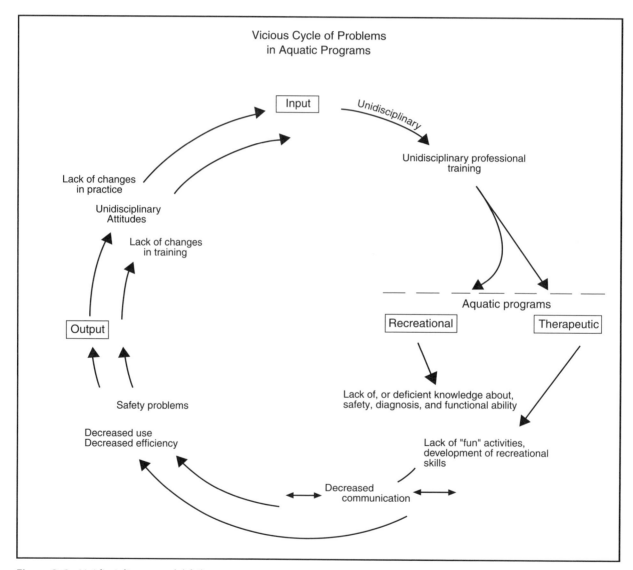

Figure 2.6 Unidisciplinary model failure.

Reprinted, by permission, from F. Dulcy, 1983, "Aquatic programs for disabled children," *Physical and Occupational Therapy in Pediatrics* 3(1): 18.

educational approaches does not sufficiently meet the needs of participants and may cause a cycle of problems. In the medical-therapeutic model, therapists often sacrifice fun for exercise related to specific goals, but patients with cognitive difficulties may lose interest and may need motivation through fun activities. In the recreational model, professionals using the special recreation approach lack medical input in regard to diagnosis, functional abilities, and developmental needs. In the educational approach, instructors may be unaware of therapeutic positioning. The therapeutic recreation approach seems to be most closely aligned with a collaborative approach, although it still has a more narrow focus on leisure behavior and may put more value on non-swimming type goals, such as etiquette, socialization, and appropriate use of free time.

Distinct Components

The distinct components of the collaborative model are the release of roles by each member of the collaborative team, the integration of each service within an existing program, and an overview of the person as a whole rather than as a list of separate needs.

Role Release

Role release is a way of introducing a specific discipline to others on a collaborative team. Initially, it consists of *role extension*, in which members of a team describe their role; *role enrichment*, in which members of a team share important information about basic practices in their discipline with regard to a participant; and *role expansion*, in which members of a team explain how others can use their practices in their own setting. As the team works together, role exchange and role support take place. When professionals practice *role exchange*, they implement techniques from other disciplines into their setting. In *role support*, team members provide each other with support to take on each other's roles with a specific individual (Woodruff and McGonigel 1988). The following demonstrates some ways you as an aquatic specialist might participate in this process.

1. The aquatic specialist teaches the other members of the team about the specific methods and benefits of swim strokes, water safety skills, and aquatic games for the program participants.

2. The aquatic specialist learns the function of each of the other disciplines and has enough knowledge to integrate other curricular areas and therapeutic methods into the aquatic program.

3. The aquatic specialist occasionally includes other members of the team in pool sessions for group assessment or teaching and therapy sessions.

4. The aquatic specialist becomes familiar with medical and academic classroom terminology to communicate more effectively.

5. The aquatic specialist functions as a bridge between recreational, educational, and therapeutic aspects of swim and water safety skills.

6. The aquatic specialist provides opportunities for individuals with disabilities to practice and generalize academic concepts, activities of daily living, leisure choices, and motor skills.

7. The aquatic specialist is aware of the interaction of the individual with the environment and uses many sources of professional input for modifying that environment.

Thus, the collaborative model differs from the multidisciplinary approach in that team members truly understand each other's roles, having learned to function in each other's capacities.

The integration of each professional, the service, and the benefits of that service within an existing program can be part of the collaborative process. Instead of a therapist seeing an individual separately, the therapist comes into the pool with the aquatic instructor and facilitates therapeutic goals as well. In this way, the aquatic instructor and therapist (or the special education teacher) can provide maximum benefits, share ideas, and see these goals in progress. The participant benefits by having medical, therapeutic, educational, and recreational goals incorporated into one session. It's not as if the therapist works five minutes on one aspect, and the teacher another five minutes on another aspect. If the participant was walking as a warm-up, the therapist or aquatic instructor gives a prompt to encourage good posture while engaging in appropriate social interaction. These three separate behaviors—warm-up, posture, and social interaction—receive intervention from the treatment team, so that the participant practices skills from other disciplines in a single setting: the pool.

In the past, those professionals who provide therapy, education, and recreation to individuals with disabilities worked in isolation. Focusing on the important aspects of their own work and their own goals, they lost the view of the whole child or adult. The collaborative model champions the idea that an individual with a disability cannot be adequately served when dissected into parts, such as the brain and legs. Instead, following this model, the person working with the participant will understand the need and will be able to incorporate cognitive, social, physical, and affective (emotional) goals within each activity.

Goals and Objectives Within the Collaborative Model

The goals and objectives of the collaborative model include the goals of the three models previously described, focusing on **transdisciplinary** sharing and cooperation. The team of professionals, with the caregivers and participant, prioritize goals and provide input in a collaborative manner. Goals for a program that have adopted a collaborative model might include some of the following examples.

The program's goals are to provide activities and opportunities that

1. develop functional walking patterns during aerobic aquatic class,
2. maintain vital lung capacity during breathing exercises and swim strokes,
3. increase range of motion while swimming laps,
4. improve transfer skills while getting into the pool,
5. develop socialization skills during water jogging,
6. increase cooperative behaviors while waiting in line to pay or present membership card at the pool,
7. improve arm and shoulder strength while treading water,
8. decrease abnormal muscle tone during swim instruction, and
9. increase awareness of the opportunities in aquatics for leisure pursuits.

The following lists include examples of goals and objectives for participants within programs conducted under the collaborative model.

PARTICIPANT GOALS

1. To improve posture through aquatic activities.
2. To improve communication and cooperation during swim class.
3. To develop lifetime leisure skills of swimming and water aerobics.
4. To increase self-confidence through learning to dive.
5. To understand the relationship between swimming and fitness.
6. To maintain vital lung capacity through performing rhythmic breathing during front crawl.

PARTICIPANT OBJECTIVES

1.1 Participant will keep head and neck in alignment during treading water for one minute.

2.1 Participant will wait for a turn and respond "me" when it is his or her turn, 75 percent of the time.

3.1 Participant will learn two swim strokes and two water aerobics steps and perform them independently, 100 percent of the time during warm-up.

4.1 Participant will show increased self-confidence by performing a standing front dive from the diving board.

5.1 Participant will demonstrate an understanding of the relationship between swimming and fitness by correctly answering several questions pertaining to that issue.

6.1 Participant will demonstrate maintenance of vital lung capacity by performing rhythmic breathing during 100 meters of the front crawl without stopping.

As you can see, it is important to go beyond a single-minded (unidisciplinary) medical-therapeutic, educational, or therapeutic recreation focus. Coordinating efforts among various professionals allows both adult and juvenile participants to practice recreational, educational, and therapeutic skills in a natural setting. In this scenario, the team can achieve its primary objective: to improve or maintain functioning of the individual. Trying to meet all objectives that a person is working on in his or her life during one session is not the intent; rather, you should incorporate a variety of objectives to meet specific long-term goals prioritized by the team of professionals and the participant. Thus, in this model, all professionals involved have a better understanding of the overall goals and objectives for each individual they serve.

Settings

The cooperative nature of the collaborative model opens many natatorium doors. Collaborative programs may take place anywhere you find a pool: community centers, hospitals, schools, residential living facilities, or treatment centers.

Providers

Specialists who may be involved in a collaborative model of aquatic service include regular and adapted aquatic instructors, regular and adapted physical education specialists, physical therapists, physical therapist aides, occupational therapists, occupational therapist aides, speech and language pathologists, certified therapeutic recreation specialists, rehabilitation or physical medicine physicians, kinesiotherapists, special education or regular education teachers or aides, play therapists, parents or caregivers, nurses, or coaches.

Important Issues

Significant issues involved in making the collaborative model work are communication among members of the team, changing typically unidisciplinary training, and exploration of legal issues involved with role release.

Communication

Not surprisingly, extensive communication is integral to this model. The involvement of role extension, expansion, and release, as we mentioned earlier, becomes critical to success. Communication goes beyond reporting what has been done with an individual during a session. Sharing problems and concerns with one another and including participants and significant others in discussions of successful approaches, skill sequences, and environmental influences is crucial to the success of the collaborative model.

Typical Unidisciplinary Training

Institutions of higher education and community organizations that train special educators, therapists, and aquatic personnel must make an effort to include information about collaborative methods in their curricula to foster this philosophy, rather than the unidisciplinary approach. Believing that the approach used in one discipline is the only and best approach and engaging in turf wars inhibits sharing and cooperation. Some professionals even go so far as trying to deter others from infringing on areas that they believe to be their exclusive domain. As professionals, however, we must reinforce mutual goals and relinquish control over some skills that can be safely and successfully carried out by others under supervision.

Legal and Safety Issues

Although we recommend the collaborative approach, you should observe some legal and safety constraints. Legally, as an aquatic specialist, you are not a therapist and therefore should not provide manipulations, such as massage, joint compression, and passive range of motion exercises with medically diagnosed individuals. Moving healthy limbs for the purpose of **tactile** or kinesthetic teaching is acceptable, however. Likewise, therapists and educators who are not trained in water safety instruction should not be teaching swimming, working with frightened swimmers, or moving into deep water without consulting an aquatic instructor. As you know, using progressions for teaching various water safety skills is imperative for safe aquatic programming.

SUMMARY

Whatever model your aquatics program follows, your primary focus must be on providing the best possible service to each participant. To accomplish this, you must assess each participant's needs; tailor a program to meet those needs, bringing in other service providers when necessary or, if appropriate, referring the participant to another program; and evaluate your program periodically. Therefore, you must be adequately trained and appropriately certified to perform the services your program offers.

The best way to maintain a flexible service to meet the needs of each individual is to follow the collaborative model, which provides for your team of professionals to collectively use your expertise—sometimes all at the same time—to pool resources, knowledge, and expertise in order to serve individuals with disabilities in a more efficient and proficient manner. Yet extensive communication, sharing of roles, and attention to legal issues of role release are important issues that your program must address in order to achieve a comprehensive and effective approach to aquatic service delivery.

CHAPTER 2 REVIEW

1. How do aquatic programs' objectives differ when conducted by allied health care professionals applying the medical-therapeutic model, and by aquatic instructors using the educational model?

2. What is meant by a "categorical approach" to aquatic therapy?

3. What are some of the ways that an aquatic instructor can incorporate other professional roles into instruction?

4. What constitutes therapeutic intervention, separating therapeutic aquatic activities from adapted aquatic activities?

5. Discuss the importance of communication and how this facilitates collaboration among aquatic professionals.

INCLUSION AND THE LEAST RESTRICTIVE ENVIRONMENT

Inclusion of individuals with disabilities into regular educational, vocational, recreational, and social settings is by far the most emotional issue among people with disabilities. As we have discussed, the Americans With Disabilities Act (ADA) and the Individuals With Disabilities Education Act (IDEA) guarantee access to services and facilities to people with disabilities and mandate support services in regular educational programs. In this chapter, we'll identify several concerns and issues regarding inclusion, including the following:

- Appropriate placement of individuals with disabilities
- The continuum of appropriate placements
- Prerequisites to successful inclusion
- Developing and maintaining successful inclusion groups

In addition to the availability of placements, answers to the following questions should help instructors, participants, parents, significant others, and therapists make the decisions about placement in aquatic programs. Keep them in mind as you study this chapter.

1. How many of the participant's targeted goals and objectives match what will take place in the general aquatic program?
2. Can the participant follow rules and guidelines within the regular aquatic program so as not to compromise the safety of all?
3. Is there an age-appropriate class available?
4. Does the placement provide an emotionally and physically safe environment?
5. Is the ultimate goal of the placement to be able to participate in aquatic activities in an integrated setting?
6. Does the placement meet other goals in addition to instructional goals, for example, recreational or therapeutic goals?

CONCEPTS OF PLACEMENT

The concept of placement comes from educational services for individuals with disabilities from birth to 21, but extends into adult services. When an individual with a disability seeks entrance into an aquatic program, you should assume that the correct placement will be within the regular curricula without support. However, the participant, caregiver, or you as the aquatic instructor may suggest that an assessment is warranted prior to admission to determine if the participant needs support services to enhance learning (see figure 3.1). Remember, individual assessment is an integral concept within the guidelines of the ADA and IDEA. Thus, you must help individuals with disabilities discover the most appropriate aquatic program that is as integrated with nondisabled persons as possible. Ensure that you do this on a case-by-case basis without stereotyping the person according to his or her disability label.

Use the results of your assessment as one factor helping you determine if the regular class is the optimal learning setting or if additional or alternative services are warranted within an "array of services," a new concept that supports the inclusion of individuals with disabilities in high-quality educational, recreational, social, and work settings with an assortment of services (National Council on Disability 1994). In contrast is the concept of a "continuum of services," a term historically used to denote the possibilities of placements and services that exist leading up to fully included experiences within regular educational or recreational settings. The National Council on Disability believes that inclusion into regular programs is a civil right and strongly supports the array of services approach (National Council on Disability 1994). This is a progressive, humanistic view, in drastic contrast to the extreme segregation of the first 75 years of the 20th century. But totally inclusive settings should not be the only available environments. Thus, we support both concepts as does the Council for Exceptional Children (Council for Exceptional Children 1993). If parents and caregivers really have a say in the education of their disabled child and service delivery professionals are striving to empower individuals with disabilities to make choices, then no justification exists for only one placement option.

We believe in providing an aquatic setting in which an individual learns best—regardless of

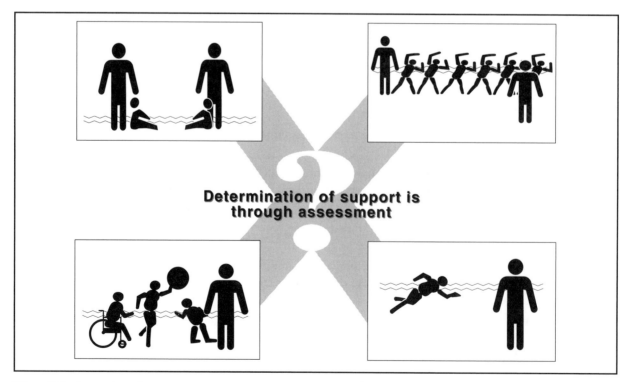

Figure 3.1 Support services.

politics. Thus, you should always carefully examine assessment results, drawing conclusions that will best serve the individual, not someone else's ideals. While we believe socialization and integration are important, these should not be the overriding factors driving a placement decision in a program that stresses physical skill acquisition. So the vital questions to ask yourself when looking for an individual's proper placement within a range of aquatic class opportunities are "Where will that person safely and successfully learn swimming and water safety skills best? Parallel to or within the regular aquatic class and its curriculum?" This approach takes into account opportunities to acquire aquatic skills that typically developing individuals are learning, in a setting as close as possible to the setting in which participants will use these skills in leisure pursuits. Finally, you must consider the health and safety of the individual with disabilities as well as the others in the potential group.

The practice of placing an individual in an environment that matches individual abilities with appropriate services while preserving as much freedom as possible is called seeking the least restrictive environment (LRE) (Sherrill 1994). Sherrill offers the following definition of LRE: "LRE philosophy is an integration/inclusion-with-support-services conceptual framework based on the belief that assessment, placement, instruction, and evaluation should be individualized and personalized in each school subject, as well as in nonacademic and extracurricular areas, through adherence to collaborative home-school IEP protocol and use of a continuum of placement options and services" (p. 27). This placement strategy differs from total inclusion because it may include a variety of settings whereas total inclusion always takes place in the regular setting with support services complementing that setting.

The least restrictive environment should be synonymous with the placement in which the individual should learn best. Specifically, if you carefully match the ability of the participant with an appropriate aquatic learning environment, the participant will be successful in attaining swimming and water safety skills. Naturally, this environment should have an instructional level commensurate with the learning ability of the participant, and it should also emphasize individualized instruction, ensure safety of all participants, provide age-appropriate social interaction, and enable active participation instead of passive spectatorship (Auxter, Pyfer, and Huettig 1993).

In the 1990-1991 school year, approximately 70 percent of all individuals with disabilities aged 6 to 21 were served in a regular class setting for all or a good part (21 to 60 percent) of the school day (United States Department of Education 1993). Proceed with caution, however, before generalizing this statistic to the aquatic setting since data is unavailable as to aquatic inclusion. Only a small number of individuals with more challenging disabilities can best be served in a noninclusive environment. Such individuals might have an intensified need for smaller groups, more sterile environments, additional space and equipment, increased numbers of instructors (e.g., two instructors to one participant), different delivery of reinforcement, medical supervision, or an environment with heightened safety components. They may be more successful in a setting that falls along the "continuum of services" available, such as a partially segregated group (small group apart from larger group, sharing same space), a reverse mainstream group (individuals with disabilities are the focus and individuals without disabilities integrated in), or a separate class in a segregated facility in which the air and water temperature, pool depth, and overall physical comfort level may be more appropriate than a community-based integrated facility.

Don't let yourself get lost in the concepts of appropriate placement, continuum of services, inclusion, and least restrictive environment, however. Concentrate on seeking an aquatic setting in which learning is best facilitated for each individual. Avoid buying into one particular philosophy, thereby causing a disservice to individuals with disabilities. The development of swimming and water safety skills depends upon a program that has a flexible curriculum, informed professionals who provide the best environment for each individual regardless of educational fads, and accommodates all participants safely and successfully. This is where the continuum of placements concept can truly help you provide the best for each participant.

CONTINUUM OF PLACEMENTS

You should conduct aquatic activities with age-appropriate goals in the setting that is most conducive to learning and is as close as possible to the regular environment. If you determine through formal assessment of aquatic readiness, your professional judgment, parental and participant input, and trying the regular setting first that the regular aquatic class is not the appropriate setting, consider some of the options in figures 3.2 and 3.3.

The existing models of continuum of placements grew out of the concept of the least restrictive environment, beginning with Deno's work, published in 1970, and continuing with interpretations of the Education for All Handicapped Children Act. The continuum concept is based on a series of placements that are sequenced in regard to the amount of integration with individuals without disabilities as well as available services (Grineski 1994). The underlying notion in this continuum is that individuals must be ready for the next environment before they can move along the continuum, allowing individuals to move as they change, as appropriate and necessary (Stein 1994). The continuum concept is being

challenged as a violation of civil rights, as a method of keeping a dual system of education in place (special education versus regular education), and as a way to continue denying individuals with disabilities their rightful place in society. We mention it to give you an historical perspective of what is a current practice so that you can provide important information for consumers, parents or caregivers, and other aquatic instructors to use in their quest for the best way for individuals with disabilities to acquire aquatic skills.

Models of Continuums of Placements in the School Setting

In the following sections, we'll examine several continuums of placements that work best in the school environment. We have adapted figure 3.2

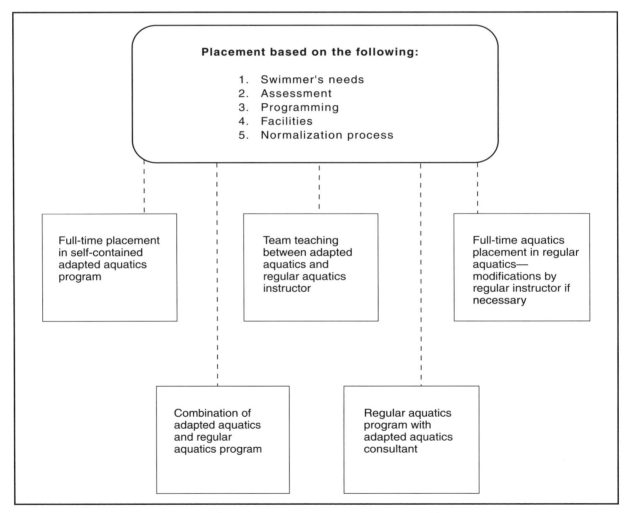

Figure 3.2 Adaptation of Eichstaedt and Lavay's least restrictive environment model.

Adapted from Eichstaedt and Lavay 1992.

from Eichstaedt and Lavay's (1992) least restrictive environment flowchart. Your program may not offer a variety of placements within a particular aquatic program, but if you have individuals who will benefit from alternative placement, you should encourage and pursue such placement.

Block and Krebs (1992) see this subject not as a continuum of placements, but as a continuum of support to the regular physical activity placement. We have adapted their model by replacing physical education with aquatics as the activity (figure 3.3).

This continuum of support revolves around the belief that integral to all learning is for individuals with disabilities to be with individuals without disabilities. The most support in this model comes from the concept of reverse mainstreaming (reverse inclusion). Reverse mainstreaming allows participants with disabilities to work one-on-one or in small groups in semi-integrated settings. Allowing nondisabled swimmers to share pool time provides role models for people with disabilities and informal education for nondisabled swimmers regarding disability issues.

Models of Continuums of Placements Outside the School Setting

The models we have discussed so far have been devised for the individual with a disability receiving services within the schools. The following three models for aquatic services have been developed with community, recreational, and transition from school to leisure pursuits goals in mind. The underlying philosophy is that unless individuals can use community facilities, it is unlikely that skills will carry over from school, hospital, and residential settings. The models presented here, from the Canadian Red Cross (1989) and Carter, Dolan and LeConey (1994),

---

Continuum of Supports for Regular Aquatics

Level 1: No support needed
- Swimmer makes necessary modifications on his or her own.
- Regular aquatics instructor makes necessary modification for student.

Level 2: Adapted aquatics instructor consultation with recommendations such as
- Peer tutor watches out for swimmer.
- Peer tutor assists swimmer.
- Paraprofessional assists swimmer.

Level 3: Adapted aquatics instructor provides direct service in regular aquatics class
- Adapted aquatics instructor as co-teacher.
- Adapted aquatics instructor one-on-one within regular class.
- Adapted aquatics instructor intervenes only as necessary.

Level 4: Part-time adapted aquatics and part-time regular aquatics
- Flexible schedule with reverse mainstreaming.
- Fixed schedule with reverse mainstreaming.
- Participant in segregated aquatic program attends regular aquatic program once a month.

Level 5: Reverse mainstreaming in special program
- Nondisabled students come to segregated adapted aquatics program 2 to 3 times per month for reverse mainstreaming.
- Students with and without disabilities meet at community-based aquatic facility and work out together.

Figure 3.3 Adaptation of continuum of supports.

Adapted from Block and Krebs 1992.

attempt to go beyond meeting the needs of the school-aged population to address lifelong aquatic participation issues.

Carter, Dolan, and LeConey (1994) have diagrammed a continuum of services (figure 3.4). This model of service recognizes that individuals with disabilities possess a variety of levels of aquatic skills and that a participant skill continuum (with inclusion as the ultimate goal) is the model that best addresses an individual's assessed needs. "This approach recognized that specific participation outcomes are influenced by participant functioning capacity, and that the degree of staff intervention is dependent upon participant functioning level" (p. 4). Level I is where individuals who need prerequisite skills, such as increased range of motion, balance, and tolerance of frustration, and those with fragile health needs receive services. Level II is where individuals learn adapted aquatic skills and other skills they need to participate in aquatic activities, such as self-care. Participants in level III receive additional experience to function in an integrated setting. Level IV (not depicted) is called LINK (leisure integration network) and involves inclusion with resource support. The

support comes from advocates for individuals with disabilities and staff who act as resources and facilitators in the community or facility.

The Canadian Red Cross adapted the continuum of aquatic integration by Lister-Piercy (Canadian Red Cross 1989; Lister-Piercy 1985). In this model, participants acquire skills in a segregated environment during phase 1. At this level, the student-to-instructor ratio is low and may be even one-to-one. Once a participant has acquired several skills, he moves up to phase 2. In this phase, the instructor helps the participant generalize the skills he learned in phase 1 to two different pool settings with two different instructors. If this criterion is not feasible, vary some aspects of the instructional setting such as the point of entry into the water. Phase 3 involves reverse mainstreaming with select nondisabled participants. Phase 4 expands the instructional environment to include friends and family in integrated recreational activities. Phase 5 is an included setting with maximum assistance. The instructor who has been with the participant from the beginning provides physical and learning support within the regular aquatic setting. In phase 6, the instructor begins

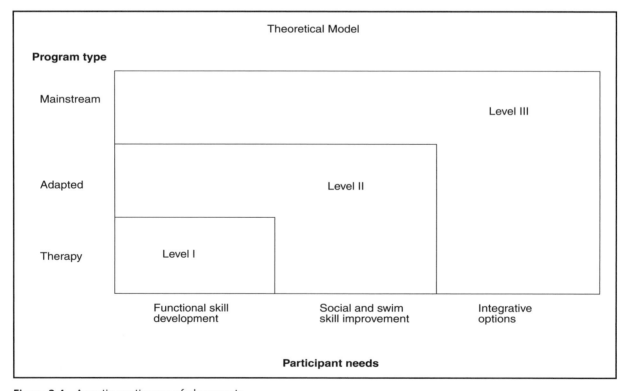

Figure 3.4 Aquatic continuum of placements.

Reprinted from Carter, Dolan, and LeConey 1994.

Figure 3.5 Inclusion Assistance Steps. (a) Prone gliding with a kickboard is a functional skill (b); independent swimming in a lane is an important social and swim skill (c); generalization of skills enhances integrative options.

to eliminate some of the support within the included setting by maintaining verbal and visual support but removing himself from the water. The final phase (7) eliminates the adapted aquatic instructor from the pool area, and the person is now self-sufficient in the regular aquatic class. Some individuals may be able to progress through the entire continuum, some will start and finish at various stages along the way. Some participants will stay where they started or not much higher. Whatever happens, it is important that the participant, caregivers, and aquatic personnel are willing to be flexible, moving up or down the continuum as needed.

Recommendations and Concerns

The Canadian Red Cross-Lister-Piercy continuum serves as a role model for aquatic programs in the quest for quality inclusion of individuals with disabilities in community aquatic programs. Another helpful resource for integration is presented in Johannsen (1987). Also, a model that has been adapted from Sherrill's adapted physical education continuum is shown in figure 3.6.

According to the interpretations of the ADA and IDEA, a continuum of placement opportunities offers reasonable accommodations. Yet many people have concerns about continuum of placements; many facilities do not offer a wide enough selection of options to their members, and individuals with severe disabilities may never acquire the necessary skills to join integrated programs. With this second concern the ques-

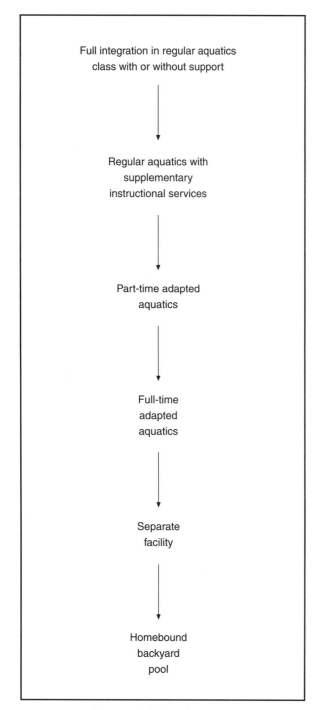

Figure 3.6 Adaptation of Sherrill's cascade of services.

Adapted, by permission of McGraw-Hill, from Sherrill, 1993, Adapted Physical Activity, Recreation and Sport. (Dubuque, IA: Wm. C. Brown), 184.

tion is "Should we never encourage individuals whose disabilities severely limit their participation to enter integrated programs because they lack the skills?" Only with informed parents, caregivers, consumers, and educated adapted aquatic and regular aquatic instructors may we as a profession even begin to discuss this question.

PREREQUISITES TO INCLUSION

Continuums of placements stem from the belief held by many professionals that a participant with a disability must meet certain prerequisites before she can safely and successfully participate with nondisabled peers in an aquatic setting. The categories of prerequisites include participant prerequisites, environmental prerequisites, and programmatic prerequisites.

Participant Prerequisites

Participants should have a minimal level of basic skill competencies and health criteria as prerequisite to inclusive aquatic classes. Participant prerequisites include medical and health considerations as well as fundamental social, cognitive, and aquatic readiness that are vital to inclusive group integrity and individualized learning.

Consideration of medical and health conditions may serve as the foundation for safe accommodations into a class or program or serve as a catalyst for discrimination. Thus, you should avoid making general judgments and statements about one type of disability or medical condition regardless of your experience with individuals of similar disability; such generalizations are by their very nature stereotypical and therefore against the intent of all civil rights legislation. Moreover, generalizations often lead to false assumptions regarding an individual's abilities, resulting in loss of credibility, strained relationships, and wasted instructional time. You must assess each individual's situation on a case-by-case basis to determine whether health conditions require an alternative to the regular setting, support from an adapted aquatic specialist, a smaller group size, peer or volunteer assistance, health care provider assistance, or no assistance.

To help you handle the issue of prerequisites and make the best placement for each individual with disabilities you serve, examine the examples of health or safety concerns that may hinder performance in a regular setting or interrupt the regular group on a continual basis so that learning is hindered for others. Each situation is a scenario that would force the professionals and family involved to discuss a more restricted placement for aquatic instruction and participation.

Health and medical reasons are but one set of concerns that may preclude inclusion into regular aquatic classes. Issues of safety and comfort for the individual and group, and behavior and cognitive skills also require support outside the regular setting. However, as with medical conditions, never assume that participants with behavior or cognitive deficits automatically need emotional or learning support, nor that either the regular or alternative class setting is appropriate. Instead, discuss the behaviors that the participant exhibits with members of the team, including parents, seeking the best match of participant with setting. You may uncover valuable information. Some individuals, for example, have fewer behavioral outbursts with an instructor of a particular gender, voice modulation, height, weight, race, ethnicity, or the like. Although the goal is to have participants respond appropriately to anyone, you may need to adjust your thoughts and actions to initially accommodate the individual, gradually bringing in others to help the participant get used to a variety of people within the aquatic environment.

Although age-appropriate groups are desirable, participants with severe cognitive disabilities may not reach their full potential in an included setting with same-age peers due to problems with **receptive** or **expressive language** and the complexity of directions and tasks. Some professionals believe that if the individual with a severe cognitive disability has the appropriate learning support, the individual can work on tasks similar but not identical to the tasks the group is doing. Such an approach would only be acceptable if the support person is an adapted aquatic specialist. Think about it: Why should the individual with the most intense needs be taught by a volunteer or paraprofessionals with little experience while the others have a trained aquatic instructor providing feedback and instruction?

Individuals who will be included in regular aquatic classes need to have behavioral characteristics that respond to applied behavioral analysis principles without compromising the entire group's integrity. Students who bite others, pinch, kick, scream, throw objects, or call out inappropriate statements at every opportunity

INCLUSIVE SETTINGS: HEALTH AND SAFETY CONCERNS

1. Individuals with any type of open sores such as those with decubitus ulcers are prohibited from swimming in a public pool but may use an individual Hubbard tank in which staff changes the water after each user.

2. Individuals who have a large number of seizures leading to emergency removal from the pool and causing clearing of the pool for each seizure due to medical emergency.

3. Individuals with tracheostomy tubes or who are **ventilator**-dependent may require shallow water, qualified health care professionals, heavily grounded electrical cords, and calm water with no splashing.

4. Individuals with certain neuromuscular conditions who require a certain water temperature, which may not be available in the general aquatic facility.

5. Individuals with certain neurological conditions who require gradual change from water to air temperature due to inadequate thermoregulation systems.

6. Individuals with high susceptibility to infection may need more sterile environments, such as closer locker rooms to prevent chilling, higher temperatures in water and air, or few or no other people around.

7. Individuals with allergies to chlorine, requiring pools with alternative cleaning mechanisms or chemicals.

8. Individuals with behavior disorders, whether noncompliant behaviors or uncontrolled aggression, who would compromise the safety of others.

9. Individuals with hemophilia possibly requiring calm water, limited bumping into other participants and equipment, and modified pool temperatures due to arthritic conditions.

10. Individuals with detached retinas who need to avoid projectiles such as balls and any other bumping of the head and face.

may have a better chance of being successfully included if those behaviors are addressed in a smaller group or one-on-one setting, rather than if you immediately place them in a large aquatic class. When an individual with a disability poses a health and safety threat to the instructor, other aquatic patrons, or themselves, even when reasonable accommodations have been provided, you can legally deny participation.

Remember, though, that a program cannot establish rules and regulations related to entrance into a course which exclude individuals with disabilities; "however, rules can be established which are necessary for the safety or health of participants, which happen to screen out some individuals with disabilities" (Osinski 1993). For example, a policy that prohibits individuals with behavior disorders from participating in a specific aquatic program is illegal, but a policy that prohibits individuals who bite others may be warranted. Legal advice for your particular situation should be sought.

Aquatic skill prerequisites may be necessary for success in some aquatic classes, especially if there is no additional personnel support. Even if the task is simple, such as holding the pool gutter, closing the mouth when someone splashes, or not drinking pool water, these skills might be necessary for success in the regular class (figure 3.7). This is not to say that a person who cannot do these things shouldn't be included, only that certain prerequisite skills might be necessary for *successful* inclusion, if there is no additional help or equipment provided. With proper support, you can be flexible and, whenever possible, include individuals who will never achieve the prerequisites but who are good candidates for successful skill acquisition within a regular group. In short, while you should carefully consider aquatic skill prerequisites when providing appropriate matches between participant and setting, you should not use them to exclude.

Environmental Prerequisites

Each aquatic setting brings with it a group of environmental conditions that either support or negate the inclusion of individuals with disabilities. Although we cannot stress enough that you should view each participant as an individual, some general environmental conditions support inclusive, successful settings. We can further divide environmental issues into physical and learning environments or climates.

The physical environment prerequisites will be unique to each person, but you can make an appropriate match between participant and environment when you consider the right questions, such as the following:

Figure 3.7 Some individuals need to perform simple prerequisite skills such as holding a pool gutter

1. Does the target setting match the individual's needs? For example, does the participant work better with a pool temperature greater than 85°F? Less than 85°F? Is the participant comfortable in a large open space or does she require a smaller, more contained setting?

2. For health reasons, does the participant have to be cautious about moving from one temperature extreme to another? For example, does the target setting have greater than a four- or five-degree difference in air and water temperature?

3. Does the deck space have adequate storage space for wheelchairs, crutches, walkers, canes? Does this affect safe accessibility?

4. Is the individual allergic to chlorine or **bromine**?

5. Does the participant have difficulty maintaining attention? For example, are there too many people in the area, possibly distracting the participant?

6. Are there materials in the area that may be an attractive nuisance to an impulsive or noncompliant participant?

7. Do the acoustics of the pool encourage yelling or screaming to hear echoes? Is this a major problem with the participant?

8. Does the participant have intense medical or health needs? Specifically, is the environment physically safe for the individual?

Consideration of physical environment generally comes last in the minds of parents, participants, and caregivers. But issues including facility location, architectural accessibility, and air and water temperature are important considerations in selecting an adapted aquatics program.

The learning environment is an even more crucial aspect of the overall environment. A caring instructor with the prerequisite knowledge about aquatic activity modifications, contraindications, cross-disciplinary techniques and communication, ethical treatment of individuals with disabilities, and the skills to individualize aquatic programs is a more important prerequisite than space and equipment. Use the following questions to help you monitor learning environment:

1. Do instructors treat individuals with disabilities with dignity and respect?

2. Do individuals with disabilities receive opportunity to respond to tasks and assignments?

3. Do instructors accept differences in performance?

4. Is cooperation the main thrust of the class?

5. Do individuals with disabilities feel emotionally safe to try the skills presented?

6. Have other participants in the class been educated about inclusion and aspects of ability, diversity, and acceptance of differences?

As important as the learning environment prerequisites are, they may be greatly influenced by the third category, programmatic prerequisites.

Programmatic Prerequisites

Programmatic prerequisites for successful inclusion include, but are not limited to, the following suggestions for what should be in place in a particular program.

PROGRAMMATIC PREREQUISITES

1. Program and instructional goals and objectives are clearly stated. You cannot adapt a program unless you can start with the basic directives.

2. Task progressions should have enough flexibility to allow for achievement by those who have disabilities that preclude success in one part of the progression. For example, the task progression for the breaststroke should be flexible enough to allow a person who has had both legs amputated to bypass using the leg kick and progress to the arm stroke.

3. Program educates staff, including locker room workers, desk clerks, instructors, and lifeguards, before initiating an inclusion program to identify and improve their attitudes, skills, and knowledge.

4. Program educates other participants and patrons of the program and facility before the program begins regarding acceptance of diversity and facts about various disabilities. This can be done through a "town meeting" format at the facility or by a flyer describing inclusion.

5. Primarily, formal assessment should drive placement, but you should take secondary factors into consideration.

6. Assessment results should dictate how you individualize programs.

7. Prerequisites to entering a class must be flexible. For example, the prerequisite for getting into a "learn to swim" program may be to be able to stand on the bottom of the pool with face above water. A program must be flexible enough to reasonably accommodate an individual with dwarfism even though he or she may not meet the height requirement.

8. The administration must be flexible about allowing individuals to move from one class placement to another in order to meet their needs.

9. Facilitators of the program communicate with the participant in his or her desired mode or make adaptations to accommodate an interpreter.

10. Program offers proper support and assistance in and around the pool or allows parents, caregivers, or aides to be in and around the pool at no additional cost.

11. Administrators highly respect and encourage collaboration among instructors, therapists, parents, caregivers, and participants.

12. Instructors place participants with disabilities into the regular aquatic program in naturally occurring proportions, which suggests a maximum of 10 to 15 percent of individuals with disabilities in a class.

13. Participants who need help outside the regular aquatic program receive that help to achieve more.

14. Instructors present activities in an age-appropriate manner.

15. Instructors use a variety of teaching methods.

You should base successful inclusion of participants with disabilities in aquatic programs on the tenet that the participants have the prerequisite skills for safe and successful participation, that the physical and learning environment is matched with the needs of the participants, and that the program has the flexibility to accommodate a variety of abilities and learning styles (see figure 3.8).

DEVELOPING AND MAINTAINING SUCCESSFUL INCLUSION GROUPS

Although this chapter stresses the readiness of participant, instructor, environment, and program for inclusion and that various places exist for learning, in the remainder of this chapter, we'll focus on the practices that develop and maintain high-quality integrated aquatic groups. The major purpose of inclusion in aquatic classes is to provide opportunities for all to learn and recreate together—the way they will in the rest of society. Some benefits of inclusion include the opportunity to learn in natural environments, with age-appropriate role models, greater potential for friendships and social contacts, and an opportunity to change attitudes of the nondisabled to being more accepting of differences. And lastly another benefit is that it meets the spirit of the ADA.

In general, the types of considerations for developing and maintaining successful inclusion groups center around instructor preparation, learning and physical support, age consid-

Figure 3.8 Integrated aquatic classes may need additional adult help.

erations, group size and makeup, and task or skill progression and presentation. In the following sections, we'll look more closely at specific examples of how you might meet the concept of "reasonable accommodations," according to the ADA.

Instructor Preparation

Not surprisingly, experts support the notion that a key factor to successful inclusion is the instructor (Reid 1979; Weiss and Karper 1980). Insufficient training of staff and inadequate education and experience of instructors conducting integrated aquatic programs are major reasons why these types of programs fail (Priest 1979). Naturally, poor instructor preparation has a negative impact on the success of the program. What, then, are the remedies? Training opportunities exist on three levels: formal certification programs (preservice), conferences and seminars, and in-house training (inservice).

Formal Certification

Formal certification of adapted aquatic instructors in the United States consists of attending a course given by one of two organizations providing specialty certificates for instructional aquatic programs. Attending either the American Alliance for Health, Physical Education, Recreation and Dance (AAHPERD) or Young Men's Christian Association (YMCA) adapted aquatic instructor courses and earning certification prepares an instructor for working with individuals with disabilities. Other individuals who possess the skill, knowledge, and attitude necessary to conduct integrated or segregated aquatic programs might be water safety or aquatic instructors with advanced degrees in adapted physical education, special education, and therapeutic recreation. Physical and occupational therapists who have aquatic instructor certification should also be able to provide quality adapted aquatic experiences. Organizations other than the YMCA and AAHPERD conduct certification programs but they are not truly instructional (see also chapter 1).

Conferences and Seminars

Conferences and seminars can provide up-to-date, accurate information about practical techniques and theoretical concepts as well as a forum for new or controversial issues. Experts can present their research on specific issues related to aquatics, exercise, swimming, and individuals with disabilities in a short amount of time and are easily accessible for questioning.

Unfortunately, however, aquatic instructors with an interest but no formal background in disability issues often feel overwhelmed due to a lack of background knowledge or high-tech professional jargon. Small seminars at which the facilitator asks everyone's background may demonstrate more sensitivity to the novice than a conference or convention speaker. Another concern in regard to regional conferences is they tend to be far away, ignoring the fact that travel funds are usually limited for community, recreational, or educational professionals. Some professionals, however, participate in conferences as a means of earning continuing education units (CEUs), which they apply to certification requirements in their respective health care professions. In addition, such travel expenses and conference fees are probably tax deductible for you as an individual; check current tax code.

Inservice Programs

The most informal method of education in adapted aquatics is a site-based inservice program (figure 3.9). In this setting an expert who is on staff or from an outside agency comes to a facility to train the staff. Such training is low-cost; only the presenter travels; the expert can tailor presentations to the specific staff, facility, and population served; and it takes little effort to organize the training.

The information the expert presents should include concepts of safety related to balance problems, lack of motor control, sensory input problems, aspects of wheelchair-to-pool transfers, and positioning and handling various emergency situations, such as seizures, asthma episodes, and diabetic incidents. In addition, the trainer should cover issues related to identifying and changing attitudes and task and activity analyses as well as offer tips for inclusion and for adapting stroke propulsion and water safety skills. Inservice education also facilitates informal brainstorming and professional case study discussions of clientele.

A disadvantage of the in-house inservice is that the attending instructors tend to focus on their specific problems and may ignore the broader issues. Another disadvantage is that inservice training is usually mandated, which tends to restrict the enthusiasm of the group, resulting in a lot of **coping behavior**.

Figure 3.9 Materials and information specific to an aquatic staffs' needs can be addressed in an on-site inservice workshop.

Learning and Physical Support

Another critical factor in developing inclusion programs is to provide learning and physical support (see figure 3.10). The Canadian Red Cross has outlined categories of support that some individuals with disabilities might require:

1. Special services might be assistance in transportation to the facility or help in changing.
2. Equipment could involve swimming pool modifications or flotation devices.
3. Instruction could include one-on-one ratio or the addition of a teacher aide or peer tutor (Canadian Red Cross 1989, p. 23).

However, although one-on-one assistance in instruction, equipment adaptations, and special services can take place within the fully inclusive instructional setting, keep in mind that some participants cannot be included no matter how much support you offer.

Physical Support

Physical support is any person or device that helps participants who have issues regarding physical safety or comfort to be included. Examples of physical support include an extra adult to physically help individuals who cannot hold the wall, maintain head control, stand in the pool, or close their mouths to prevent swallowing water. You should evaluate what physical support participants need before the classes begin rather than automatically assuming it is needed. Moreover, participants with support needs may still be fully included instead of using this need as an excuse to exclude.

Learning Support

Likewise, learning support, which is any device, technique, or individualized instruction that is in addition to the general program that aids learning, is a positive aspect of support within the inclusive setting. The expertise of all personnel, including volunteers, special education teachers, interpreters, adapted aquatic instructors and aides, parents, and related service personnel, may serve as vital learning support. Participants who spend part of the time with the aquatic class and the remaining time working one-on-one with their aquatic learning support person is one method of using support.

Another method is to provide the aquatic learning support during the entire inclusive aquatic experience. While this support could be provided by a variety of individuals trained to meet the needs of the participant, an adapted aquatic instructor is the most competent and highly qualified choice to provide learning support for individuals with intense needs. She can

Figure 3.10 Physical support should be provided within the aquatic class to facilitate successful inclusion.

individualize and interpret instructions, adapt the task or skill so it is within reach of the participant, or carry out instructions related to Individualized Aquatic Program Plan goals. Other learning supporters such as special educators or parents may be the more appropriate choice for participants who require continuous structure and consistency of behavior management programs.

Peer Tutors

In addition, adapted physical education and adapted aquatics literature has mentioned the appropriate use of **peer tutors** to help provide learning support (Block 1994; Canadian Red Cross 1989; Houston-Wilson 1993). Peer tutors are assistants to the participant with a disability who are approximately the same age as the participant. They may help support learning by repeating directions or providing cue words when working together; however, a participant may not require such assistance for every activity or task. Some other learning support tasks that a peer tutor might perform are using sign language or other gestures to clarify instructions, repeating a demonstration of the skill or task, helping count laps, time, or repetitions, reminding the peer what to do next, showing how to use a piece of equipment, or reading task cards at individual aquatic stations.

In general, peer tutors can increase support in the aquatic class by providing physical or learning assistance as well as by acting as safety lookouts. In physical education classes in the gym, peer tutors have had a positive effect on learning in an integrated setting (DePaepe 1985; Webster 1987).

How do you determine how much peer support a participant needs in an inclusive setting? Block asserts that no magical formula exists for answering this question. He says: "There is no clear cut way to determine how much support a particular student will need. Teams should work together to make an informed decision based on as much information as they can collect regarding the student, teacher, peers, and environment" (Block 1994, p. 111).

Peer tutors should be responsible, caring, and specifically trained as to what they should and should not say and do. According to a study by Houston-Wilson (1993), trained tutors were able to increase the **academic learning time** and improve motor performance on five discrete motor skills in individuals with developmental disabilities included in a regular physical education class more proficiently than untrained peer tutors. Finally, providing peer tutor with tasks that are compatible with their abilities is important (see figure 3.11).

Physical education practitioners have developed a variety of peer tutor models, based on inclusion in regular classrooms and physical education classes. Some of the most applicable models to physical activity settings are Project PEOPEL (Long et al. 1980), Project CREOLE (Wright 1986) and the Partners Club (Special Olympics International n.d.).

Project PEOPEL (Physical Education Opportunity Program for Exceptional Learners), one of the best known peer tutor models in physical education, originated in Arizona and was developed to provide one-on-one assistance to students with disabilities from trained high school students. Classes are comprised of 12 students with disabilities and 12 peer tutors with one instructor. You can use the concept of Project PEOPEL in an aquatic class to increase individual attention for participants with disabilities who do not need the expertise of a one-on-one session with you but do need one-on-one attention to stay focused. (See also Long et al. 1980.)

Project CREOLE uses a peer tutoring approach to teaching high schoolers with severe disabilities functional skills for use at home, school, and community (Wright 1986). This curriculum includes task analysis of activities used in physical education and leisure pursuits. Tutors teach social skills, wheelchair mobility and transfers, and physical and emotional

health skills. Although the program doesn't include aquatic skills, the curriculum guide will help you develop a peer tutoring program involving severely disabled individuals.

A type of peer tutor program that is geared toward participants with mental retardation in Special Olympics sports skills training programs is the Partners Club (figure 3.12). This club was created by the Joseph P. Kennedy, Jr. Foundation for the purpose of bringing high school students and Special Olympics athletes together to practice sports skills (Special Olympics International n.d.). Since swimming is an official summer sport of the Special Olympics, you can contact local high schools and initiate the formation of an official club. The Partners Club handbook has a step-by-step checklist for the formation of a Partners Club chapter and can be obtained by writing to your local Special Olympics office or Special Olympics International, Sports Department (see appendix E). You may also obtain information about the Sports Partnership program, in which a school's swimming team (or any other team) forms a partnership with a Special Olympics swim team. The Unified Sports program goes one step further and combines athletes with and without mental retardation together on one team (see also chapter 11).

Figure 3.11   Peer tutors can help in an integrated aquatic class.

Figure 3.12 Partners Club programs pair individuals with and without disabilities.

Table 3.1

Suggested Age Ranges for Groups of Age-appropriate Peers	
Infants	6-18 months
Toddlers	18-35 months
Young children	3-5 years
Young elementary	6-8 years
Older children	9-11 years
Adolescents	12-14 years
Teens	15-17 years
Young adult	18-21 years
Adult	21+

Age Considerations

To fully embrace the general philosophy of inclusion, individuals with disabilities should have the opportunity to participate in age-appropriate activities whether in small or large groups. This concept includes gearing tasks, activities, peer interaction, and materials to a participant's chronological rather than functional age. Appropriate music, names of games, age ranges, and equipment all help create an age-appropriate aquatic experience.

Age-Appropriateness of Activities

The philosophy of providing age-appropriate groupings and functional skills is that in order to function in the community and participate in lifetime leisure skills in pools, fitness centers, parks, and playgrounds, an individual must participate in ways similar to same-age peers (see table 3.1). Likewise, functionality of an activity is defined by the participant's age and the environment in which the individual must function. For example, 18-year-old men and women swimming in the community pool usually do not glide like Superman, bob like rocket ships, or dive for Big Bird tokens, but they might have a cannonball jumping contest, perform glides as far as they can underwater, and play water tube basketball.

The easiest way to determine what is age-appropriate is to integrate individuals with disabilities into same-age peer groups. Ask the participants to do what they wish for 10 minutes and observe. Typically, adults will water walk or jog, use a kickboard, do some stretching exercises, swim laps, dive, or tread water. Teenagers might get into tubes, throw a ball around, swim underwater, try to sit and surf on kickboards, dive, jump, or swim laps. Elementary students will have breath-holding contests, toss and pick up rings and coins from the pool bottom, lie on kickboards, paddle in tubes or rafts, splash and spit water at each other, and jump into the pool a thousand times. Young children who can stand in the pool will practice the doggie paddle, do underwater twists and turns, attempt to sit on and touch the bottom, try to open their eyes underwater, throw balls, float in tubes shaped like animals, kick their feet, jump up and down, and attempt to jump into the pool a hundred times. Typically, infants and toddlers, when held or sitting in shallow water will splash themselves, play and reach for toys, suck and bite equipment, and drink the pool water. While not all individuals will exhibit these behaviors, they are fairly typical behaviors of the age groupings.

Although many individuals with disabilities may not have the prerequisites to engage in common age-appropriate activities, you must make some informed decisions—introducing certain skills the participant may never have the prerequisites for. For example, even when the participant is working on grasping a ball in order to fully play inner tube water polo, if possible, go ahead and let the participant play anyway (maybe with full physical assistance). The participant may work on ball grasping during the actual water polo game by holding the ball for the entire time the team is on offense or by throwing the ball in. Keep in mind that feeling fully included is a tremendous motivator.

Presentation and Teaching Techniques

Age-appropriateness refers to selection of activities that are socially appropriate for chronological age groupings. Although activity selection should be based on age-appropriateness, you should base your presentation on functional or developmental age, including the teaching methods, cue words, expressiveness and detail of instruction, and learning modes (visual, auditory, tactile learner) you choose. The younger the participant, the narrower the age span the group should include due to the tremendous differences in growth and development during this time.

Unlike land-based physical activities, often an individual with a disability cannot participate in aquatics with same-aged peers due to lack of ability. For example, if the entire instructional unit is taking place in the diving well and the individual is overly fearful, the parents or caregiver and individual must communicate with the instructor about what is needed, desired, and feasible. Alternatives might include having the participant work on fitness swims with an instructor aide, opting temporarily for a segregated program, or working with an adapted aquatic instructor in the shallow end during the same time frame. Even so, look for one or two activities the person can participate in with same-age peers.

Group Makeup and Size

Whether they have disabilities or not, individuals who participate in aquatic classes are often quite diverse in ability, interests, and motivation levels. Many aquatic programs group individuals according to ability, giving some consideration to age and instructor-pupil matching. Instructor-pupil matching are dynamics in the makeup of groups that can cause a class to succeed or fail.

Makeup

If you carefully consider, then modify the mix of participants in a group, you can often positively affect how effectively a group works together. Of course, inclusion groups, with their diversity of physical, mental, and social abilities, are a challenge in interpersonal dynamics. Social development and function of each member of the group may play an important role in the success of the group. Social interaction may be a secondary outcome of the group, but individuals who cannot get along with the teacher or others in the group cause conflict within the group. Yet diversity does not have to preclude positive interactions. In fact, diversity can enhance this aspect of the learning environment. As the instructor, you must take the lead in developing awareness of group dynamics, teaching the rules that govern group behavior, and demanding some semblance of group cooperation.

No recipe, however, can be written for balanced group makeup. Individuals with special needs do not have similar behaviors, so the ingredients you must deal with will change from class to class. Forming smaller groups that are homogeneous in ability is one helpful hint and preparing the group for possible interruptions or for diversity issues is another. It is practical to include individuals with disabilities into groups that have been prepared. Instructors should explain diverse behaviors and learning styles to the group and show a positive attitude about inclusion of individuals with disabilities. Typical comments to the group may include: "All individuals do not have the same abilities and we need to be patient with everyone in the group." "Sam, who has Down's syndrome, sometimes needs me to help him while you are practicing." "Loretta, who has spina bifida, will need to wear shorts over her suit because of a special device that helps her stay healthy."

Size

Use the questions and class size recommendations that follow to help you determine the number of individuals in any particular aquatic class. While these numbers were set by the American Red Cross for participants without disabilities, you can modify and adapt them to individual situations as you strive to meet best practice standards.

- How large is the available pool space?
- How many lifeguards are on deck?
- What is the instructor-participant ratio set by the program?
- What support staff and equipment are available?
- What are the ages of the participants?
- What are the aquatic skill abilities in the group?
- Can the participants stand with their faces above the water?
- Can the participants hold the edge of pool independently?
- How many individuals in the group need intense individualized instruction?
- Are there any participants who require a very small group environment?

AMERICAN RED CROSS RECOMMENDATIONS FOR CLASS SIZE (1992A)

≋

Infants and Toddlers (6 months to 3 years)

6 to 8 parent (or caregiver) and child pairs to 1 instructor

Although infants under six months of age do participate in water play, the American Red Cross, Council for National Cooperation in Aquatics, and the American Academy of Pediatrics do not recommend their participation in organized water orientation and play classes. The American Red Cross advocates using a parent or caregiver one-on-one with each child in the pool until the age of three.

≋

Preschoolers (3 to 5) Without Caregiver

4 to 5 per instructor if water is more than chest deep

6 to 8 per instructor with an aide if the water is more than chest deep

4 to 6 per instructor if water is chest deep

8 to 10 per instructor with an aide if the water is chest deep

5 Years Old and Above

10 participants per instructor

Each state's department of education has maximum class size mandates for classes in which individuals with disabilities are enrolled. When applying these to aquatics, consider such maximums cautiously, however, because some exceed recognized standards such as the American Red Cross maximum of 10 students per one instructor.

Remember, no more than 10 to 15 percent (the natural proportion of people with disabilities) of the aquatic class should consist of individuals with disabilities if it is to be a successful inclusion experience (Block 1994). When you're placing a participant who poses a challenge to aquatic group structure, communication, or safety, limit the number of participants without disabilities to five for a total of six.

But even six may be too large or too small depending on the situation. Each situation is unique. Careful assessment of the individual, proper planning, and the ability to communicate with family, caregivers, and professionals who work with the participant are the key considerations in developing successful inclusion groups.

FRAMEWORK FOR TASK PRESENTATION

It is imperative when planning lessons for any aquatic class, but especially when the class includes participants with physical or mental disabilities, that you analyze the activities, tasks, and progression that you wish to present. Think about the physical, cognitive, and social demands each activity will demand of participants. Write out the physical aspects of each activity: the motor movements and patterns and physical fitness demands. Establish what cognitive abilities for successful participation each activity will require, such as the ability to follow directions, remember rules, know right from left, understand simple directions in space, plan strategies, read, sequence numbers, and interpret verbal and nonverbal communication. List the possible social requirements, such as skills in cooperation, rule following, displaying acceptable winning and losing behaviors, getting along with others, and waiting for a turn.

The process of task analysis is necessary for part-whole and progressive-part teaching styles. In each of these areas, break down the skills into simpler parts so that participants can successfully reach the terminal (target) objective. The target objective may be an aquatic physical or knowledge skill, an auxiliary skill, such as dressing, washing, toileting, or a social behavior. Beyond this, you must present the tasks in an acceptable progression to the entire class as well as to the individual who may have a disability that precludes them from functioning at the same level. Often aquatic instructors fail to distinguish between the activity analysis, task analysis, and progression to teach. See the example for the activity called "Raft Ball" to help you get started.

ACTIVITY ANALYSIS, TASK ANALYSIS, AND PROGRESSION FOR RAFT BALL

Description: Participants lie on blow-up rafts and paddle with their arms. They try to scoop up the small beach ball and pass it to their teammates. Someone tries to swim the ball over the goal line while on the raft.

≋

Activity Analysis

Physical skills necessary include the following:

Butterfly or front crawl arm stroke

Backward push stroke (like a backward butterfly)

Balanced reach for the ball

Ball toss to partner

Ball scoop

Ball catch

Swimming with the ball while on the raft

Righting self after falling off the raft

Cognitive skills necessary include the following:

Awareness of group and concept of team

Ability to remember which is their goal

Ability to switch roles from defense to offense quickly

Social skills necessary include the following:

Sharing ball with other teammates

Using the right amount of assertiveness versus aggressiveness for defense and offense

Self-confidence, so as not to be intimidated by the others

Cooperation with instructor and peers

Following the rules

Maturity to handle own strengths and weaknesses as compared to others

≋

Task Analysis

For this example, we'll analyze only one of the physical skills.

Task analysis of butterfly arm stroke on raft:

1. Balance self on stomach on raft, head raised, arms in water, 10 seconds.
2. Same as #1 but with people splashing water around participant.
3. Lift arms out of the water at the same time, while balancing on raft lying on stomach.
4. Place hands in water in front of shoulders, arms extended.
5. Pull arms back and slightly under raft to propel self forward.
6. Pull stronger with one arm to make turns.

≋

Progression for Teaching

1. Instructor supports raft while participant gets on, lying on stomach.
2. Instructor pulls raft around pool, participant maintains balance.
3. Instructor encourages participant to look ahead and put arms in water while pulling participant around.
4. Instructor encourages participant to place feet in water in various positions to feel balance changes while being pulled around.
5. Instructor encourages participant to keep balance while being pulled around and instructor makes turbulence.
6. In a stationary position, instructor demonstrates proper arm position while participant sits on steps, side of pool, or water chair.

7. While floating on the raft, participant tries arm position.

8. Participant tries arm stroke on raft across pool.

9. Participant paddles on raft length of pool with others swimming around him.

10. Participant paddles on raft length of pool with others in his way.

How do you go about determining which activities and tasks you must analyze? Look at the assessment and the Individualized Aquatic Program Plan phase (see chapter 4). See what skills and activities the participant and caregivers would like developed, what skills are necessary to be included with peers, what therapeutic and healthful activities are desirable, and what can or does your program offer in these regards. Once you know how your program matches the participant's needs, you should target and analyze the related activities and skills. Then ask yourself "How many steps should I break each task into?" The answer depends on how physically, cognitively, and socially challenged the individual is. You must use your professional judgment, based on information you have gleaned from assessment, to help you make decisions about how and when to analyze a task.

ACTIVITIES TO FACILITATE INCLUSION

Participants find success and satisfaction in aquatic activities that are challenging, yet attainable. Although the factors of instructor competency, learning and physical supports, and progression and presentation of tasks provide an essential base to a successful inclusion program, safe and enjoyable activities that are inclusive make the entire package work. Activities and teaching styles using the inclusive philosophy use many performance standards—not just one standard for all—so that all can participate on whatever level they are capable of. So don't emphasize mastering the activity in one exact way; instead, stress performing aquatic activities to the best of one's ability and, most of all, stress enjoyment. Mosston was famous for developing this concept, illustrated by the slanted rope activity, in which the instructor asks participants to jump over a rope held in the air by two peo-

ple (Mosston and Ashworth 1986). The rope can be high at one end to challenge the more-advanced jumpers and lower at the other end to accommodate the less-skilled jumpers. When you find ways to accommodate abilities this way, you can use the same activity with little modification, thereby including and challenging all participants without singling out any individual. Moreover, allowing everyone to choose her level of difficulty puts everyone at ease—whether or not they face special challenges. In the following sections, we'll identify common principles that should guide you as you develop and adapt activities to be inclusive (see specific activities in appendix C).

Best Practices

Good teaching practices and heightened interpersonal skills are two important tenets to the success of inclusive aquatic activities. Here we'll look at best practices for physical activity in general and show you how to apply them to aquatics.

First, however, we cannot stress enough that your attitude and education are two key factors in successful inclusion programs, but, most critical is how you apply what you know and feel in the learning environment. One sensitive way to approach inclusion is to focus on cooperative rather than competitive learning activities. For example, downplay "fastest" and concentrate on "best as you can" and avoid elimination activities in which the individuals with poorest skills are "out" first.

Games

The opportunity for learning during games is great if you carefully consider the needs of all participants during planning. A playful atmosphere—even with adults—decreases pressure on those who don't perform as well as others (American Red Cross 1977a). Moreover, putting skills to use in activities and games is a natural motivator and reinforcer. To this end, you must remember to continue to teach during the game or activity, avoiding turning it into mere free time. "Aquatic games are not rote drills, highly structured competitive sports or relay races. They are activities that all can enjoy, are active and serve a purpose" (Langendorfer, German, and Kral 1988).

You can modify any activity that you have previously used in instruction by using Morris and Stiehl's "games analysis model" (1989), which facilitates participating in activities in more than one way or changing an activity's competitive nature to a cooperative one. Morris and Stiehl listed six components you can adapt, including (1) number of participants who are playing, (2) equipment used in the game, (3) movements used for participation, (4) patterns of organizing the participants in the activity, (5) limitations of the activity as seen in rule changes, and (6) purpose, in terms of the goals and objectives of the activity. If you have an individual who cannot participate in the game of water volleyball or Marco Polo, for example, brainstorm (and even ask participants) as to how to best adapt any of the six components to make the game more inclusive and developmentally appropriate for each participant. Use the example that follows to help you modify other games and activities.

Remember, when using games analysis or cooperative games, planning for successful experiences is a must. Realistic expectations, consistent instruction, clarity of class rules and procedures, and setting up the area for maximal safety and participation can increase the time involved in instruction and practice. If you are conducting a regular class that includes individuals with special needs, you must structure swim instruction so that all individuals are actively pursuing the objective of the lesson and the individualized program for two-thirds of the class time (Wessel and Kelly 1986). Thus you must ensure that proper placement, appropriate physical and learning support, and effective teaching behaviors mesh to produce a setting in which learning time for all is

Example of the Games Analysis Model

Game: Marco Polo

How to Play: "It" is blindfolded or closes eyes. It continues to say "Marco" and the players say "Polo" until It can locate players by sound and tag someone, who then becomes It. To avoid being tagged, all others try to swim around and under the water in a designated area after they say "Polo."

Adaptations

Players: Many people mean more chances of success. The mix or makeup of the group can lend itself to success by ability grouping or size and strength grouping.

Movements: Consider having more-proficient individuals swim a certain way, such as sculling on the back, in order to equalize the game for individuals who are slower.

Equipment: A life vest or tire tube can help individuals with severe physical disabilities enjoy this game. A soft foam reaching pole will assist an individual with limited range of motion when It.

Organizational pattern: If the space for players is limited and the area is cordoned off, players with limited mobility and sight are in a better position to have an equal chance to succeed.

Purpose: You can change any of the game's purposes (to develop judgment, to improve auditory focusing, and to improve changing direction in the pool) to accommodate individuals' specific goals—for example, to improve underwater swimming, have everyone swim underwater.

Limitations (rules): When an individual with mobility impairment is It, you could (1) limit all players by saying they may only move one step in any direction after saying "Polo," (2) when an individual who is deaf or hard of hearing is It, require players to splash gently toward It, (3) when an individual who uses a flotation device is It, ban players from going underwater, or (4) limit players to being It two times per game to avoid the slower individuals being caught all the time.

maximized. We have taken the following suggestions from Achievement-Based Curriculum Development in Physical Education (Wessel and Kelly 1986). Use them to maximize time on-task for the participants in the included aquatic setting.

1. Have equipment ready before participants arrive.
2. Have enough equipment for each participant.
3. Use location cues for where you want the students to go when moving from one place to another.
4. Use signals that all understand to stop and start activity.
5. Use physical assistance if necessary.
6. Use parents or caregivers to bring students to restroom, move equipment, and count laps.
7. Adapt distance, time, equipment, and movements for those with fitness and motor skill limitations.

Suggestions for Various Age Groups

Infant, toddler, and preschool children with disabilities may have developmental delays that hinder their participation in aquatic programs. Lack of head control can cause the face to flop close to the water. Low muscle tone in the trunk can lead to inadequate sitting and upright posture control. Poor oral motor control, causing them to swallow water, and underdeveloped respiratory systems, causing them to have trouble coughing out inhaled and swallowed water, can lead to their taking water into the lungs or stomach. Excess ingestion of water can lead to hyponatremia, a sodium imbalance.

Children 6 to 36 Months Old

Orient children ages 6 to 36 months with and without disabilities to the water in a gentle manner and allow them to be accompanied by a significant other, such as parent, guardian, or caregiver. The group size should be no more than six to eight pairs per instructor. The holding techniques in the American Red Cross "Infant/Preschool Aquatic" video are an excellent parent and instructor training tool as are the infant and preschool sections in the American Red Cross's Water Safety Instructor's Manual (1992b).

Children 3 to 5 Years Old

Most children with disabilities 3 to 5 years old will be able to function without a one-on-one caregiv-

er-child ratio, but learn best in very small groups of three to five children, depending on severity of needs and water depth. Often, children with disabilities of this age need extra assistance and would benefit from the assistance of an additional certified swimming instructor or an adapted aquatic instructor and a water table if pool depth is above their chins. At this age, keep verbal directions to a minimum: use visual demonstrations as the primary means to teach. Giving short verbal cues directly to the individual rather than the whole group, however, can be very successful.

Children 6 to 8 Years Old

Children ages 6 to 8 generally enjoy the water and just about any activities that you might present. At this age, children are beginning to develop skills to keep themselves afloat in deep water, jump into deep water independently, and swim for long periods of time (maybe up to 25 yards). You must ensure that the individuals with disabilities who are included into the regular aquatic class will at this point have the prerequisite skills to benefit from the instruction and have a safe and successful experience or that the participant without prerequisite skills has the proper physical and learning support to maintain a safe, successful, and satisfying experience for all.

Children 9 to 11 Years Old

In general, children with disabilities ages 9 to 11 who have been exposed to swimming for a few years have usually mastered some type of technique to keep themselves afloat. This age group may be more mobile because they can usually touch the bottom of the pool or perform a unique version of the dog paddle, double-arm backstroke, or treading water. They begin to find themselves physically at a disadvantage at this time, when compared with their nondisabled peers, due to the physical or cognitive complexity of the skills presented. Thus at this stage, they will need help refining skills that they have. In addition, because girls and boys begin to become aware of some physical differences in strength between genders, you will need to adapt the activities you choose for many individuals within the aquatic class, challenged or not.

Children 12 to 14 Years Old

Participants who are 12 to 14 years old are looking for acceptance and adventure. They do not want to fail around their friends and often prefer to show off and get into trouble. They are beyond baby games and think they are much too sophisticated to even be in swim class, let alone play a game. At this point, you should refer to games as "activities" to promote cooperation.

Teens and Young Adults

In general, people ages 15 years and older without disabilities usually do not participate in swim lessons, making it difficult to create age-appropriate inclusion group swim lessons. Usually, the types of activities teens and adults may participate in include aqua-aerobic exercise classes and single-focus activities, such as water polo, diving lessons, synchronized swim groups, recreational swimming including fitness swims, aquatic stunts and fooling around, and competitive swim teams.

About the age of 15, many individuals with disabilities find themselves at a proverbial fork in the road. Activities that their same-age peers are involved in tend to be team sports and competitive games. Activities that are instructional and noncompetitive are usually offered in segregated programs catering to the needs of individuals with disabilities. Moreover, a greater difference in skill level into the teen and adult years exists, and many individuals with disabilities find themselves lacking skills needed to safely participate. Aquatic instruction at the late teen and early adulthood level may take place only in high school aquatic physical education classes, college physical education required courses, summer camps, and segregated instructional programs for individuals with disabilities.

Remember that individuals with disabilities who are in their teens through age 21 will have formal Individualized Transition Plans (ITPs) to prepare them for other activities in the community. So whenever possible advocate adding swimming and water safety to the transition plan. Write goals and objectives as to what the participant needs to accomplish to function as fully as possible at the local pool in the aquatic programs he or she chooses. Like all people their age, choice is vital to self-esteem and self-actualization. So ensure that young adults (and adults) receive sufficient orientation to aquatic opportunities so they can make informed decisions for themselves. Thus, instructional programs in schools that lead up to adulthood and transition should expose participants to a variety of experiences as well as work to improve specific skills.

Adults

Naturally, by adulthood, needs vary from one individual with disabilities to another even more than in the general population. Moreover, as with adults without disabilities, they differ from teenagers and children in their goals, attitudes, and desires. Adults may be motivated by many different factors to attend an aquatic program. Usually fitness is a primary concern or a focused skill such as scuba diving. In the following section, we'll discuss issues that commonly arise when attempting to include adults and teenagers with disabilities into water exercise, competitive, instructional, and recreational programs (see also chapters 11 and 12).

In aqua-aerobic courses, as with any included setting, individuals with disabilities and their advocates must determine how much support is needed (if any at all) in the locker area, on the pool deck, and in the program itself. Next, you should compose a list of typical movements the exercise class performs. Then, you should demonstrate the movements to the individual and perform a skills assessment. Perhaps the participant should spend a few sessions working on those skills with the adapted aquatic instructor, then move into the class with the adapted aquatic instructor as support, and finally, if able, participate independently with adapted equipment or other support (see also chapter 12).

Although, in general, we discourage using competition for teaching skills in instructional programs, an entire aquatic option exists in the competitive arena. Segregated competitive programs exist to serve almost every type of disability group, and integrated competitive opportunities exist, fostered by U.S. Swimming, Inc. (See also chapter 11.)

Adults may find an occasional beginner swim class offered in a continuing education program but these are few and far between. How, then, can you help the adult with disabilities learn to swim? Tips for including adults and teens in instructional programs in high schools and continuing education programs follow along the same principles we've been advocating in this chapter. In colleges and universities, a different scenario exists as individuals with disabilities will tend to have more physical or sensory disabilities and fewer mental disabilities. In the college setting, you'll generally find a greater amount of support for your teaching endeavors due in part to the presence of disabled student services on campus. This means that you're more likely to be able to offer integrated instructional programs in swimming, canoeing, and SCUBA (see also chapter 11).

Although many games are unsuitable for teen and adult participation, you should still create activities to reinforce skills. You can use the following ideas throughout any aquatic program to make it more fun and age-appropriate for teens and adults.

Using music that is popular with the group is a common means of making activities age-appropriate. Put a fast-paced song on when participants are treading water and ask them to tread for the whole song. Incorporate dance steps into water exercises that can transfer into community dancing.

Use adult-type equipment. Hoops, sinkable flowers, and floaties are children's toys, while inner tubes, wet vests, coins, and water-ski belts are more adult in nature. And don't forget to use age-appropriate names for activities.

Age-appropriate aquatic programs that serve young adults and older adults, whether included or segregated, should strive to treat individuals with the respect and dignity they deserve as adults. Preserve dignity by being especially sensitive to encouraging choices, providing socially appropriate experiences, and speaking in respectful tones.

SUMMARY

You and your programs cannot make excuses that you do not have the knowledge, equipment, or services to facilitate access to individuals with disabilities. Use the guidelines we've presented in this chapter to assimilate individuals into aquatic programs, establishing the least restrictive environment possible for participation. Work to ensure that your inclusive groups are successful by assessing the individuals you're striving to accommodate, preparing fully, providing adequate support within the aquatic environment, adjusting group size, and presenting lessons appropriately.

Avoid the all-too-common trap of using aquatic games and activities as time fillers, rather than as carefully planned steps to enhance aquatic or movement skills. With forethought, games and activities can replace drills and the repetitive practice sessions that may lead to boredom and discouragement. Use the suggestions we've made in this chapter to adapt and modify to existing aquatic activities. Be creative and enjoy!

CHAPTER 3 REVIEW

1. Discuss the concepts of appropriate placement, continuum of services, inclusion, and least restrictive environment.

2. What steps would you take to promote the inclusion of individuals with disabilities into a fully included setting?

3. List and explain prerequisites that should be in place before a participant with a disability can safely and successfully be included in an aquatics setting with his or her nondisabled peers.

4. Which health or medical concerns may hinder performance in a regular aquatics setting?

5. What are the benefits of the inclusion philosophy in an aquatics setting?

6. Discuss the concept of chronological age-appropriateness.

4

INDIVIDUALIZED INSTRUCTIONAL PLANNING

Critical to implementing programs that are safe, effective, and relevant is the underlying notion that those in charge have planned for success, ensuring that the aquatic learning environment is at its best. Specifically, after your director has designed the overall adapted aquatics program, including designating the curriculum and model and creating or adopting tools to assess participants, the director must plan in more detail for the day-to-day functioning of the instructional program, including individual and group programming. In this chapter, we'll introduce concepts of individualized instructional planning, including planning for assessment, developing the Individualized Aquatics Program Plan (IAPP), and strategies for implementing the plan. Keep in mind that individual assessment and individualizing lessons meet the spirit of the Americans With Disabilities Act's mandate to offer reasonable accommodations.

Individualized instructional planning begins with defining what skills a participant needs to learn and assessing his present level of performance in those skills. Whether it is a therapeutic exercise, swim stroke, or learning how to circle swim in a lane, as the aquatics specialist, you must plan out the goals, objectives, strategies, activities, equipment, and evaluation needed for the long-term (annual) goals as well as for each session. The IAPP usually forms the basis of a daily or weekly lesson plan. Any lesson plan format is acceptable as long as the plan helps you move from one activity to another in a safe and time-efficient manner.

PLANNING FOR ASSESSMENT

You should perform an aquatic assessment to determine present level of performance, helping you place a participant in the right program with the proper level of support services. And when we say we are testing a participant, we are describing the collecting of data, using formal and informal observations. Along with interviewing and reading background records, gathering information through testing forms the basis for making placement and planning decisions.

Naturally, however, before performing the actual aquatic assessment, you should determine the skills you will assess. To prioritize, ask questions such as "What is the participant interested in learning? What does the caregiver believe to be important skills for the participant to acquire? Where will the participant use the skills outside of class? What are same-age peers doing in aquatics? What equipment does the family have available to them? What are the medical, therapeutic, educational, and recreational needs of the participant?" After writing down the answers to these questions, look over the list and determine what activities and concepts are common to a few of the areas—these are the priorities. Develop assessment items that will determine the present level of performance in these skills.

Once you have collected the data, view it in the context of the big picture. The following questions will help you use assessment data appropriately: Do I need to compare the assessment data to previous data? Do I need to compare the data with other participants' data? How should I use the data to determine where the person will experience the most success in learning aquatics skills? How should I use the data to determine meaningful gain or mastery? How should I use the data to determine what skill components the person should practice next? How should I use the data to determine feedback for individual stroke propulsion mechanics? Use some or all of the answers to these questions to evaluate test results accurately.

Most often, you should use testing in adapted aquatics to determine specific goals and objectives and the ". . . appropriateness of placing students into regular classes, since it is this extrinsic standard against which all other students in regular classes are compared" (Seaman and DePauw 1989, p. 130).

As an aquatics specialist, you could, depending on the situation, use testing information to compare individuals to themselves, others, and preestablished criteria. Then you can decide the most appropriate learning environment, the plan for teaching, and the desired expected outcomes. Finally, given that instruction and ongoing assessment are synonymous, you need to

continue gathering information about an individual's performance, to evaluate that information, and continuously make decisions as to placement, support services, and projected goals and objectives.

What you assess and how you assess will be dictated by the model under which you are working and therefore the goals of the program, the facilities and equipment available, your expertise, and the individual's age, needs, wants, and capabilities. In the following sections, we'll look at the particulars of assessment in regard to each of the four treatment models we introduced in chapter 2.

Medical-Therapeutic Model of Aquatic Assessment

Remember that in the medical-therapeutic model, the focus is on treating specific, diagnosed problems. In general, medical-therapeutic aquatic assessment deals with specific movements, prescriptive exercises, anatomical positions, and ambulation to indicate present level of functioning. The assessment battery may also include basic swimming, water safety, and socialization skills, but these aspects are not of primary importance. Each specialist approaches assessment in a slightly different way, however.

Occupational Therapy

As an occupational therapist (OT) with aquatics expertise, you may develop an instrument for collecting data that includes assessing self-help skills, use of equipment, reflex involvement, swim ability, movements that increase or decrease pain, abnormal muscle tone, muscle spasms, posture and positioning, sensory integration, hand functioning, strength and endurance, oral facial control, balance, edema, joint stability, relaxation, mobility, play skills, bilateral motor, coordination, or gravitational security.

On land, an OT may choose from many standardized tests to use with children and young adults. For example, functional skills tests are based on current and future environmental tasks of daily living. The OT will most often evaluate adults with functional skills checklists, vocational tests, tests of manual dexterity, activity and task analysis, and range of motion, balance, strength, and endurance tests. An OT will either use a standardized assessment (e.g., the

Sensory Integration and Praxis Tests [Ayres 1989], Milani-Comparetti Motor Development Screening Test [Milani-Comparetti 1967], Bruininks-Oseretsky Motor Development Scale [Bruininks 1978], or the Motor-Free Visual Perception Test [Calarusso and Hammill 1972]) or conduct functional life skills tests that are ecologically based (i.e., nonstandardized tests designed specifically for the participant's current environment). The OT uses standardized testing in the area of motor development to determine the underlying causes of problems (balance, sensory deficits) an individual may be experiencing (Pratt and Allen 1989).

In the water, the OT may evaluate the differences in land versus water performance in all of the areas we've mentioned, taking notes about vestibular, visual, auditory, **proprioceptive**, and tactile reactions to the pool environment. Observations could also include manipulation of pool toys and equipment such as kickboards, hand grasp of pool gutters and railings, and head and body control during locomotion and propulsion in a gravity-reduced environment. The information in figure 4.1 is a sample occupational therapy assessment of aquatics behaviors and skills.

Besides actual aquatic therapy, the OT conducts land exercises in the pool to increase motivation (see figure 4.2). Patients who may be working on sitting balance while manipulating equipment or toys can be brought to the pool as a way to avoid burnout from traditional land therapy. Adults who attend the Maryvale Samaritan Medical Center Pool in Phoenix, Arizona, have job tasks simulated in the pool. They engage in physical exercises to increase activities of daily living, decrease pain, and increase confidence (Thiers 1994). OTs have discovered the success of therapy in the water even with the most difficult and frustrated patients, due to the relaxing atmosphere and the elements of fun (Smith 1992). In fact, in 1994 there were more than 600 OTs in the aquatics therapy network of the American Occupational Therapy Association. Occupational therapists use aquatics therapy to facilitate the same goals as on land (Mastrangelo 1992) and therefore, aquatic assessment by OTs is primarily based on land assessment with anecdotal notes about the way the person handles themselves in the water. OTs focus on gathering information about skills necessary for children and adults to enjoy an independent and satisfying life.

Physical Therapy

Physical therapists' approaches to assessment vary, based on the diagnosis, current land programs, age, and cognitive and physical abilities. Since PTs commonly use aquatic therapy for postorthopedic surgery patients, range of motion and strength assessments are critical (Framroze 1991). PTs usually take these measurements on land because it is hard to measure accurately in the water. In addition, patients who have had extensive bed rest may be deconditioned so the PT will typically assess for endurance.

A PT assesses ambulation in an aquatic physical therapy program. A therapist might look at forward, backward, and sideways walking as well as running and stair climbing. The PT will note positions of comfort and discomfort, posture, body mechanics, and confidence while moving in various depths of water. The assessment may also include weight-bearing status, transfer ability, and amount of assistance needed for activities and exercises. Figure 4.3 shows a sample PT aquatic assessment from the duPont Hospital for Children.

Kinesiotherapy

Since kinesiotherapy is a bridge between traditional therapy and the full return to daily functioning, some items on a kinesiotherapy aquatic assessment resemble physical and occupational therapy as well as adapted aquatics and therapeutic recreation. For example, the kinesiotherapist assesses patients on dry land, taking an oral or written history to assess swimming and floating abilities, exercise capacity, and tolerance for various positions required in the pool (Meyer 1994). Next the kinesiotherapist asks patients which activities they prefer to do in the pool. The aquatic assessment is then based on the patients' needs in fitness, leisure, and vocational settings.

Sports Medicine

In the field of sports medicine, aquatic specialists ask patients to perform various anatomical movements to assess whether exercise should be buoyancy-assisted, buoyancy-supported, or buoyancy-resisted. For athletes with **stress fractures**, **shin splints**, and overuse syndrome of the lower body, the aquatic specialist will assess ambulation, taking anecdotal notes to record movements that cause or relieve pain and the overall comfort level of the patient in the pool.

4 = Performs independently
3 = Performs with equipment or technique adaptations
2 = Completes but not in a practical time frame
1 = Attempts but requires assistance of the therapist to complete
0 = Does not attempt activity

Child assessment	Initial assessment	Post-assessment
1. Stair or ramp entrance (circle one)		
2. Holds pool gutter		
3. "Spidering" (hand-walking) on pool gutter		
4. Sits for 1 minute on water table		
5. Holds sitting balance while water is turbulent (1 minute)		
6. Grabs and holds toys just out of reach from sitting		
7. Stands on water table		
8. Holds standing balance while water is turbulent		
9. Walks on water table		
10. Grasps flotation device		
11. Holds and uses flotation device		
12. Grasps weighted ring (from standing) on pool bottom without submerging		
13. Tolerates water splashing nearby		
14. Tolerates water on face and head		
15. Closes lips when putting face in water		
Adult assessment	Initial assessment	Post-assessment
1. Stair, ramp, side entrance (circle one)		
2. Holds sitting balance for 3 minutes		
3. Ambulates in chest-deep water		
4. Runs in chest-deep water		
5. Walks backward in chest-deep water		
6. Grapevine step in chest-deep water		
7. Ball catch with partner while standing in chest-deep water		
8. Recovers from fall or swim underwater		
9. Closes lips when water is splashed toward face		
10. Closes lips when submerging		
11. Recovers from supine position (back float)		
12. Holds and uses flotation kickboard or barbells		
13. Relaxes on flotation device for 2 minutes		

Figure 4.1 Occupational therapy aquatic assessment.

Figure 4.2 Reaching and crossing midline are occupational therapy activities that can be adapted to a pool setting.

Educational Model of Aquatic Assessment

As we stated in chapter 2, the goals of an educational adapted aquatic program focus on teaching individuals with disabilities how to safely enjoy the aquatic environment. Since swim strokes, water safety, and other aquatic skills are paramount, assessment revolves around determining present level of performance in those areas, focusing either on curriculum-based needs or individual skills that the person can use to function better in her current or future environment (ecological assessment) or both.

As in the medical-therapeutic model, assessment takes place before meeting the participant with a review of medical, educational, and aquatic records continuing during initial contact and subsequent sessions. You should create information forms or select one from appendix D to ascertain present status about home, school, and medical considerations. After reviewing this material, you will know the potential swimmer well enough to begin to plan the aquatic assessment.

Curriculum-Based Assessment

Curriculum-based assessment is based on the notion that in order for the individual with disabilities to succeed in a regular swim program or with peers in recreational swimming, he needs to be able to learn the skills that peers are doing in that setting. Thus, as the instructor, you should base the assessment on the actual skills that you will be teaching to the class, such as the Red Cross Progressive Swim Levels I-VII or SCUBA skills (see table 4.1). You can task-analyze these skills or take them from a task-analyzed skills package, such as the Data-Based Gymnasium Program (see later in this section). Appendix B contains many valuable assessment tools as well.

Ecologically-Based Assessment

Ecologically-based assessment may include components of the curriculum-based assessment, but may also include individual skills not addressed in the regular curriculum. Skills such as exiting and entering the pool area, dressing, appropriate use of language in a swim group, performing stretching exercises before swimming, knowing how to swim in a circle, using an inner tube for flotation, and clearing the mouth of water are skills that an individual needs to learn but will not learn within a regular swim curriculum. Use a specially designed ecologically-based assessment tool to assess these skills (see appendix B).

In his book, *A Teacher's Guide to Including Students With Disabilities in Regular Physical Education*, Block (1994) includes four questions you should ask when conducting evaluations:

duPont Hospital for Children
Gross Coordination Evaluation in Water

Name: _____ Diagnosis: _____
History: _____
Experience in water: _____
Date: _____ Instructor: _____

Activity	Completes without difficulty independently	Completes with difficulty with minimum assistance	Moderate assistance	Maximum assistance	Unable to complete (abnormal)	Depth of water	Time	Comments
Amb. forward								
Amb. backward								
Amb. sideways, right								
Amb. sideways, left								
Amb. crossover step								
Running forward								
Running backward								
Skipping								
Jumping jacks								
Hopping right								
Hopping left								
Jumping								
Throw and catch ball with bilat. UEs								
Throw and catch ball with dominant hand								
Throw and catch ball with nondominant hand								
Run and catch ball								
Tread water with support								
Tread water without support								
Pendulum swing								
Swim strokes, right side								
Swim strokes, left side								
Butterfly								
Front crawl								
Back crawl								
Walk up and down steps								
Walk up and down ramps								
Additional:								

Figure 4.3 Physical therapy aquatic assessment.

Table 4.1

Sample Participant Educational Swim Program Checklist										
Course **Skills**	**1**	**2**	**3**	**4**	**5**	**6**	**7**	**8**	**9**	**10**
1. Water adjustment										
2. Blowing bubbles and bobbing										
3. Breath holding										
4. Prone glide and float										
5. Prone glide and kick										
6. Entries and exits										
7. Back glide and kick										
8. Stroke in prone position										
9. Stroke in supine position										

1. What do we teach?
2. Where do we teach it?
3. What is the present level of performance in the targeted skills?
4. How well does the participant follow routine?

The answer to the first question should hinge on the educational, vocational, home, health, and/or social values the activities have. If the activities are relevant to the participant's life, you should assess how well the participant can perform them.

You must answer the second question, "Where do we teach it?" on a continuous basis. A swimmer who has mastered the crawl stroke in a small group or one-on-one adapted aquatic setting may now be ready to use it on the community swim team or at recreational swim, but may need work in other areas. Identify individuals who need more or less assistance in learning aquatic skills as quickly as possible and modify the environment accordingly. A good way to evaluate is to look at the progress of a participant and of her peers in a group. Poor progress might signify a problem in placement, makeup of the group, or teaching methods.

Answering the question "What is the present level of performance in the targeted skills?" will help you decide if you must modify the placement, individualized program plan, group format, staff, or activities.

The question "How well does the participant follow routine?" demands that, as the aquatic instructor, you and support staff identify the tasks that the participant must be able to perform in the aquatic setting and during class, recreation, or team practice. Then you must consistently provide a routine to follow. Follow up by continually verifying whether or not a participant is following a routine with identifying verbal, visual, and physical cues and the level of assistance the participant needs in order to follow the routine.

Performing Assessments and the Data-Based Gymnasium Program

You can perform aquatic assessment in a variety of ways, including informal observation during free swim or formal observation while working with another instructor or one-on-one. Be aware, however, that if the participant is not familiar with you, he may hesitate to perform. This is especially true for the frightened swimmer, newly injured, or those who are dependent on physical assistance (e.g., quadriplegics). Individuals who are unsure of their abilities in the water may experience loss of balance, depth perception difficulties, and lack of coordination in this new environment, which may cause fear and uncertainty. Young children may feel more comfortable showing their skills in a wading pool on the deck or standing on steps or a water table (see figure 4.4). Thus, the initial contact in the pool may not yield accurate results of a participant's present level of performance. Patience and ongoing assessment, however, will provide you with a better indicator of accurate abilities.

Because of the tendency of many individuals to hesitate to perform initially, you should conduct a general assessment during the initial meeting and collect more detailed data in subsequent sessions. An example of such an assessment is the **Data-Based Gymnasium Program (DBG)** (Dunn, Morehouse, and Fredericks

Figure 4.4 Steps or ramps can provide a secure spot for fearful participants to demonstrate their skills.

1986), a task analysis and data recording model. In addition to the unique application of behavior management techniques to the movement setting, this system provides assessment and a teaching approach that makes it easier for you to individualize instruction and conduct ongoing assessment data. Twenty aquatic skills are provided in the DBG, including task analyses and a **terminal behavior** for each. During planning, you review the current information from the participant interview, caregiver feedback, aquatic history, and physical, and cognitive, and social behavior; then you pick ten skills or so to test. In order to identify the skills to teach, you must also assess what the person can currently perform and what he may be able to do in the future as a result of appropriate instruction. Where, exactly, should you head? Target activities that the participant can use in the future, making the participant more functional and therefore the program more relevant. Deciding what the participant will master is paramount so that you can eliminate less helpful items and target functional skills critical to success (Block 1994).

To apply the DBG model, begin testing by demonstrating the terminal (target) behavior for a skill (e.g., front crawl) and then requesting that the participant do it three times. If the participant can perform the target behavior two out of three times (trials), you should consider that individual to possess the skill components and should not pinpoint that skill for learning. Note successes, however, so you can have the participant practice it in times of frustration or use it to improve endurance.

For those skills that the participant does not show mastery of during the assessment, analyze skill performance again, determining what parts of the skill are present and what parts are missing. To do this, compare the participant's performance with the task analysis. You can compose your own task analysis by writing down the simplest components of a skill in the order in which the participant needs to perform them. You can develop behavioral objectives for the individual plan directly from this task analysis model of service delivery. The skill component that the participant achieved is the present level of performance, and the next component in the task analysis is the logical short-term objective and starting point at which you should begin teaching. For example, if swimming underwater for five body lengths is the terminal objective and the task analysis for swimming underwater consists of seven basic components, the participant who achieves levels 1 and 2 would have level 3 as a short-term objective and may have level 7 (terminal behavior) as the annual goal. See the example that follows for more information.

DATA-BASED GYMNASIUM TASK ANALYSIS

≋

Underwater Swim

Terminal behavior: Swimming underwater five body lengths and surfacing without choking.

Prerequisites: Being able to hold breath underwater for 10 seconds and the judgment to come up when air is needed.

Short-term objectives

1. Submerge full body underwater while holding instructors' hands, twice per session by February 2.
2. Submerge full body underwater and move to a horizontal position, with instructor's assistance in positioning him or her, by March 9.
3. Submerge full body underwater five times per session by April 4.
4. Submerge full body underwater and move to a horizontal position ready to swim by April 9.
5. Submerge full body underwater and swim using arms, touch bottom of four-foot-deep pool, for 10 feet, by May 9.
6. Submerge full body underwater and swim 15 feet using arms and legs by June 9.
7. Swim fully underwater for five body lengths by July 9.

Several examples of the Data-Based Gymnasium task analyses for aquatic skills are located in appendix B, which also contains examples taken from other resources, including Designing Instructional Programs for Individuals With Disabilities (Carter, Dolan, and LeConey 1994) and the I CAN: Aquatic Skills (part of the I Can Instructional Skill Curriculum) (Wessel 1976).

Recreational Model of Aquatic Assessment

Observing and interviewing are the most commonly employed therapeutic recreation techniques for assessment (Austin and Crawford 1991). As long as the observer gives the participant rules and limits to start with, natural observation of an unstructured recreation swim can provide valuable information. As a therapeutic recreation specialist, you might use a video camera, take notes, or use a checklist to help you spot specific behaviors. As a certified therapeutic recreation specialist (CTRS), you might set up a specific recreation situation in the pool and observe how the participant works within the situation.

In an interview, the participant may complete a written questionnaire or an oral interview. You should ask about the participant's aquatic history, leisure desires and needs, and perceived strengths and weaknesses.

As a therapeutic recreation specialist conducting an adapted aquatic program, you should also use interviews and observations to find out more about the participant's social and psychological well-being. Your interviews should discover how well she accepts herself and others, and if she appreciates her accomplishments and feels a sense of belonging to a group and family. You should also discern if she has the ability to take on challenges as well as has self-confidence, leisure and recreation habits, self-control, self-determination, self-actualization, an appropriate body image, and a well-developed value system.

Many organizations that provide therapeutic recreation services have their own checklists or inventories, but you may wish to adapt your own checklist from the following instruments: Mirenda Leisure Interest Finder (Mirenda 1973), Self Leisure Interest Profile (McDowell 1974), or the Leisure Diagnostic Battery (Witt and Ellis 1985). An example of a therapeutic recreation aquatic assessment as shown on page 70. In addition to these items, you may also wish to use information from task analysis and swim checklists (see appendix B).

Collaborative Model of Aquatic Assessment

As we discussed in chapter 2, one main ingredient in the collaborative approach to assessment is to ensure that all involved recognize the merit of the others' disciplines. In other words, you

Therapeutic Recreation Aquatic Assessment
Using Community-Based Aquatic Facilities

Participant's name: Date of birth:

Date of assessment: Recommended sessions:

Aquatic experience:

Diagnosis and applicable history:

Collaborative team goals:

Client goals:

Take notes on the following areas while observing participant in community-based recreation swim and swim or exercise class.

Building entry:

Front desk and sign-in procedures:

Toileting:

Pool deck routine:

Pool entry:

In-pool etiquette:

In-class protocol-following:

Independent swim behavior:

Social skills:

Pool exit:

Locker and shower area behavior:

Facility exit:

must look beyond what you have determined are the goals of assessment and see the "big picture" through collaboration with the other team members involved.

Ideally, the most effective and relevant way to assess would be to have all the professionals concerned with increasing function through aquatics present at land and water assessments. Observations might come from different perspectives, but the perspectives will come from the same picture. The specialist who will work most in the water with the participant should lead the assessment, with others involved, if the participant can handle it. A functional assessment approach, as in the collaborative model, involves structured observation during a typical adapted aquatics session. The observation should include locker room and toileting behaviors, transfers and deck movement, interaction with other participants and staff, entering and exiting the pool, use of equipment, water adjustment, swimming and recovery, ambulation, balance, and propulsion of self. Observers may combine assessment tools or use their own, as long as all professionals know what the others are looking for. If all professionals cannot attend, they should submit specific items that they would like to see answered by the assessment.

DEVELOPING THE INDIVIDUALIZED AQUATICS PROGRAM PLAN (IAPP)

Developing the Individualized Aquatics Program Plan should also involve a collaborative effort, with professionals and swimmers coming together to reach toward common goals through ongoing dialogue and feedback. If the participant is a child or young adult (less than 21 years old), and aquatics is part of the educational services, then the IAPP is only part of the IEP. The law (IDEA) mandates that the IEP be developed by a team, including the participant, when appropriate, and parents, teachers, therapists, and a local educational agency representative. Remember, a collaborative team approach maximizes the participant's overall development, gives the team greater problem-solving abilities, and enables all professionals to use best teaching practices (Block 1994). In addition, you can use collaborative teamwork (Rainforth, York, and Macdonald 1992) with adults in reha-

bilitation. Adults who are not connected with rehabilitation centers could have a team composed of themselves, the aquatic instructor, a significant other, the physician, and any professional who may add significantly to the team.

As we discussed in chapter 2, each team member maintains responsibility for a certain focus of skill development, but the team cross-trains each other so they may help carry out each other's goals. In the following section, we will focus on how you can translate assessment information into an IAPP, using the collaborative model.

Stating the Present Level of Performance

You must use the information you gather during initial assessment to name strengths and determine goals. Statements of probability and inference are not usually a strong basis for the development of goals and objectives. Thus, you should base the statements you make regarding the present level of performance of an individual with disabilities in aquatics on what you and the team have actually observed. The following is an example of an accurate statement of a present level of aquatic performance, based on observations:

"Kate is a 24-year-old woman with mild **hemiplegia** cerebral palsy and average intelligence. Her left side involvement includes slight flexion of elbow, wrist, and fingers and internal rotation of the left leg with ankle plantar flexion. She can enter the pool independently but needs spotting and an occasional boost on exit. Kate has difficulty with mouth closure when her face is submerged and therefore has trouble blowing all air out during rhythmic breathing. She can perform front crawl with an underwater recovery on the left side, and overwater recovery on the right. She can perform the following skills: back glide with kick, treading water one minute, jumping into deep and surfacing, survival floating for one minute, swimming underwater for 15 feet, and turning to the left while swimming front crawl."

The present level of performance should also include social and emotional behavior exhibited in the setting in which the participant may eventually function independently.

"Kate needs assistance maneuvering through the locker room as well as pulling up her swim suit. She is friendly toward others, but tends to speak too loudly and not stay in her lane while swimming. Kate is unaware of swim etiquette during recreational swim and gets overly embarrassed when confronted with a new rule. Kate enjoys swimming, but her endurance is low and she stops often to wipe her face and catch her breath."

Determining Annual Goals and Short-Term Objectives

Moving from the present level of performance to **annual goals** and short-term objectives is the most difficult part of planning. When moving from what the participant can do to what the participant should be doing takes a great deal of thought, discussion with others, and, finally, decision making. Many factors go into the selecting and prioritizing of goals for an individual. Since specific activities are targeted in the planning phase and assessed in the next phase, the third phase is to develop a list of skills needed by the participant and logically sequence a program for the acquisition of those skills. Then you must prioritize the needs list.

Setting Priorities

To help you set priorities, we have adapted the checklist on page 73 from "A Systematic Procedure for Prioritizing IEP Goals" (Dardig and Heward 1981) for you to use as an example. Feel free to make copies of this checklist. Write each task or activity on the top of a page and evaluate each against the 17 statements. Add the numbers up, and the activities with the highest totals are the ones you should target.

Determining Logical Sequence

Once you set the priorities, you can then sequence those skills that are prerequisites to one another, determining in what order the participant might be able to accomplish the skills. Determining how many skills you can teach depends on factors such as (a) group size, (b) teacher-to-student ratio, (c) support staff needed, (d) equipment available, (e) time of day, (f) instructional time per week, (g) instructor experience, (h) participant ability, and (i) pool and air temperature. In addition, factors including participant fitness level, medications, developmental readiness, and other considerations will also play a role. Don't fall into the common trap of trying to teach too

many skills, resulting in exposing the participant to so many skills that he cannot master any. Indeed, it is reasonable to choose only five skills to master in a year for a participant who attends instructional adapted aquatics class for 45 minutes once a week in a group of five other participants. Table 4.2 provides an example of how to calculate instructional time.

Writing Goals and Objectives

Once you and the team prioritize and sequence the goals, write them as broad statements, grouping compatible objectives into categories that have common instructional relevance (see figure 4.5).

The goals for the areas listed in figure 4.5 might include the following: (a) to demonstrate increased water confidence, (b) to perform entries more safely, and (c) to swim with improved propulsion. For each goal statement you should be able to justify and explain the intent behind the goal, the purpose of reaching for that goal, and the significance or motivation for the participant to achieve the goal (Davis 1989).

Write long-term goals as broad statements under which the skill objectives and criteria the participant needs will fall. Then you can develop the relevant short-term performance objectives. Consider the example of a one-year goal "To improve water confidence by June of next year." Use the assessment results of one of the priority tasks or activities in that category and write a measurable, observable statement, assigning a short-term date. For example, "Jamal will improve water confidence as shown by increasing the amount of time treading in deep water to two minutes by the end of March."

Water confidence	Entries	Propulsion
Treading	Diving	Back glide with kick
Deep bobbing	Jumping in	Sidestroke arms
Turning over		
Using kickboard		

Figure 4.5 Grouping of objectives into goal areas.

Checklist for Prioritizing Goals

0 = Strongly disagree 1 = Somewhat disagree 2 = Somewhat agree 3 = Strongly agree

_____ a. Participant can use task in current environments.

_____ b. Participant can use task in future environments.

_____ c. The activity provides opportunity for socialization.

_____ d. Task prepares participant for a greater goal.

_____ e. Task is age-appropriate.

_____ f. Task fosters independence.

_____ g. Task fosters another discipline's goals.

_____ h. Task meets a medical need.

_____ i. Participant rates task as a high priority.

_____ j. Significant other or caregiver rates task as a high priority.

_____ k. Task promotes a positive view of the individual.

_____ l. Individual has access to this activity after the program ends.

_____ m. Task improves fitness and wellness.

_____ n. Participant can engage in activity with family, friends, or independently.

_____ o. Related service professionals support task or activity.

_____ p. Equipment is available for task.

_____ q. Facilities are available and accessible for activity.

Table 4.2

Estimated Calculation of Instructional Time	
1. Number of weeks in aquatic session	10 weeks
2. Days per week of aquatic class	2 days/wk
3. Total number of days per session (multiply item 1 x item 2)	20 days
4. Number of minutes of instruction per class	50 minutes
5. Total number of minutes of class instruction for the session (multiply item 3 x item 4)	1000 minutes
6. Estimate lost instructional time (sickness, weather, etc.) 10% (.10 x 1000)	100 minutes
7. Total time available for instruction	900 minutes
$900 \div 60 = 15$ hours available for instruction, about enough time for a student to master one objective.	

Adapted from Wessel and Kelly, 1986.

Working backward from the target (terminal) behavior, use experience and what you know about the participant in order to determine the projected time, equipment, and support needed to teach the skill. If you write the objectives well and analyze the task correctly, it may take from 10 to 12 hours of instruction (three to four months) to achieve an objective. But it may take twice as long for a participant with multiple disabilities or severe cognitive disabilities. You may need to further task-analyze a goal that takes too long to achieve. Consider breaking tasks that will take longer than 10 to 12 hours of instruction into smaller intermediate time frames, perhaps setting goals that will take as little as 4 or 5 hours of instruction to achieve. It takes practice to judge the time it may take a participant to progress, so be flexible and learn from your mistakes.

In addition to stating a time interval, objectives should include the performance (action) the participant will be doing, the conditions under which the performance will take place, and the criteria by which you will deem the skill acceptable (quantity and quality of performance). Use an action verb to make the statement observable, such as "swim," "perform," "demonstrate," or "participate." The criterion is a statement of accuracy that might answer how well, how fast, how deep, or how many times the participant must perform the action with acceptable quality. The condition refers to the environmental surroundings during the action, such as, "in the diving well," "using a kickboard," "with a verbal prompt," or "during a regular swim class." The following are some examples of well-written performance objectives:

1. Maria will demonstrate bobbing in the diving well 20 consecutive times by August 8.
2. Carlos will perform standing front dive from a one-meter board within one minute of a request, 100 percent of the time, by June 13.
3. Lauren will properly don a life jacket, with verbal cues only, three out of four sessions, by February 20.
4. Shawn will hold kickboard while being pulled across pool in horizontal position for 30 seconds by April 28.
5. Susan will tolerate being held in a vertical position in the water, as demonstrated by her not kicking, screaming, or biting for 10 consecutive minutes each session by, May 1.

Additional Components of the IAPP

Included in the IAPP, in addition to present level of performance, annual goals, short-term objectives, and starting and ending dates for the program, should be statements about the specific aquatic services the participant will receive, including special instructional materials and learning, physical, or emotional support the participant needs to participate in aquatics. Moreover, a plan is not complete without reference to the extent to which the individual will participate in regular aquatic programs and a justification for the aquatic placement (see chapter 3). A final section should describe how these skills projected for mastery will help the individual succeed in leisure pursuits, work, play, school, or home, and how mastery will improve the quality of life. As a contract, the IAPP should be signed by all involved as an agreement of what will be provided, how, and for how long.

IMPLEMENTING THE IAPP

You'll have the most success implementing an individual plan when (1) the class has a low participant-to-instructor ratio, (2) the individual's goals match to some degree with the goals of the class, and (or) (3) each participant with an individual plan has another instructor or instructor aide with him or her in the pool. Examples of successful hints for working on individual goals and objectives within a group follow.

SUCCESSFUL HINTS FOR ACHIEVING INDIVIDUAL GOALS WITHIN A GROUP SETTING

- Target the behavior you want to see and communicate it to the participant.
- Determine the components the group is working on so that all can work on different phases of the same task.
- Provide activities in which individuals with different goals can perform an activity together while doing different aquatic skills.
- Know each participant's goals and objectives well.

- List objectives for the group as well as individuals in the lesson plan.
- Pair students with similar goals.
- Provide specific feedback for the area within each skill for which the individual needs correction.
- Use station teaching, having participants only go to the stations they need to work at.
- Change distances, movements, speed, and equipment to individualize the goal for each participant.
- Modify rules, expectations, and requirements to meet individual capacities.
- Adapt communication mode, teaching methods and strategies, and amount of feedback to meet individual needs.
- Analyze tasks and activities to ensure that each participant has prerequisite cognitive, social, and physical skills to participate in various activities; if not, provide support.
- Use laminated task cards with instructions or pictures for tasks that can be practiced alone or with minimal intervention.

Refer often to chapter 3 for more information about successful inclusion of individuals with disabilities in aquatic programs.

Lesson planning involves looking at where the individual (or group) is presently, where you want them to go, how to get them there, how to do it within the setting they are involved in, and how to know if you've been successful (Canadian Red Cross Society 1989). The manner in which you organize your lessons is pivotal to their success. Lesson planning includes the preparation of materials and the strategy conceived to facilitate learning. A complete lesson plan includes statements of goals and objectives compatible with individual program plans, specific activities you have determined will help meet the goals and objectives, and a time line for moving from activity to activity. Incorporate individual goals into group goals if they match and plan adaptations when the IAPP and the group lesson do not match. When goals do not match, use an adapted aquatic specialist, a peer tutor, or an aide as a co-teacher. When preparing lesson plans or evaluating colleagues' plans, use the following as a handy checklist.

LESSON PLAN EVALUATION

1. Goals are compatible with individual program plans.
2. Performance objectives describe learner behavior, not teacher behavior.
3. Performance objectives contain condition, observable behavior, and criterion level.
4. Performance objectives reflect functional behaviors.
5. Performance objectives reflect individual program plan.
6. Activities to meet objectives are age-appropriate.
7. Activities are developmentally appropriate.
8. Plan includes how each member of the group will participate in each activity if different from primary goal of activity.
9. Plan includes mechanism for teacher to know if students achieved objectives.
10. Plan includes progressions or task analysis.
11. Plan includes specific intervention for affective and cognitive learning.
12. Plan includes how students and teacher will use equipment.
13. Plan includes methods for practice.
14. Plan includes strategies for intervention and feedback.

SUMMARY

Follow the guidelines in this chapter on your journey from planning and assessing participants to developing and implementing individual program plans. Along the way, remember to keep overall age-appropriate goals as well as individual needs in mind when planning for and assessing individuals with disabilities in aquatics. Ensure that the needs of the individual drive the assessment process, objectives, and activities. Specifically, base the placement on health and wellness needs, desires, and functional skills the individual needs to participate in in present and future settings. Remember, although time-consuming, the IAPP is the key to a personalized curriculum, thereby meeting federal law. These plans signify the collaboration and agreement of instructor, participant, parents or caregivers, significant others, and other professionals as to the appropriate course of action. The tasks and activities you choose, introduce, and have the participant practice should flow directly from the IAPP. Lesson plans help to make the transition from objectives to skill acquisition.

The IAPP and the lesson plans that flow from it create the vision that will help individuals with disabilities move from point A to point B. Indeed, a well-written IAPP serves to facilitate that vision, convey it to others, and implement effective and relevant programs.

CHAPTER 4 REVIEW

1. What should you do before performing an aquatic assessment of individuals with disabilities?
2. Why must aquatic assessment take place before aquatic participation?
3. How do you determine an individual's present level of aquatic performance?
4. Explain why instruction and ongoing assessment are synonymous.
5. What is one main ingredient of using a collaborative approach to assessment?
6. What are the determining factors that influence the number of skills that a participant can learn during the year?
7. What are the components of a behaviorally stated performance objective?
8. What are some questions you might ask to determine placement in aquatics programs?

PROGRAM AND ORGANIZATIONAL DEVELOPMENT

Implementing adapted aquatics programs requires more than merely good intentions and quality instruction. As a program continues to expand and starts taking on the characteristics of an organization or as successful programs become more integrated with an organization, program planning becomes more complex and comprehensive. Effective organizational development cultivates community support, helps secure appropriate resources, improves and expands program development, and leads to a leadership structure for sustaining the organization.

Well-managed administration is the key to developing a successful adapted aquatics program. It includes several elements. Effective staff development ensures that sufficient, qualified staff are available to maintain and improve programs. Indeed, effective management of human resources can positively impact the quality and continuity of program delivery. Appropriate funding and facilities are basic to program survival. Developing community support through networking and collaboration enhances program success. Adherence to **risk management** guidelines and procedures creates a safe service delivery environment and limits exposure to expensive legal actions. Appropriate communication with the public, advocacy agencies, community leaders, the media, other aquatic professionals, and program constituents contributes to the development and support of the adapted aquatics program. In this chapter, we'll give you a brief overview of each of these components of organizational and program development.

ORGANIZATIONAL FOUNDATIONS

Several organizational building blocks can facilitate an organization's long-term survival. A realistic and visionary strategic plan can guide the organization to continued success. Appropriate funding, facilities, and resources provide the means for sustaining programs. Effective governance, leadership, community support, program development, and risk management carry the organization through growth and conflict.

WHERE DO WE GROW FROM HERE?

A professor at a local university started a community adapted aquatics program to meet a community need and to provide practicum experiences for students in her adapted physical education course. Meeting 6:00 to 7:00 P.M. one evening a week, this program served 10 children with various disabilities during each semester of the first year. By the end of the next year, 25 children participated each semester. In the third year, the professor added an additional evening session and 50 children were being served. In order to have enough instructional staff to maintain the program, the professor found it necessary to supplement her student staff by recruiting volunteers from other courses.

The professor became increasingly aware of the additional resources needed to maintain the program. However, the community need was great, parental support was high, and everyone was committed to maintaining the program. More time was spent recruiting, training, and organizing volunteers. Instructional equipment was needed, so grants were solicited from local companies and foundations. Parents started to organize and discuss other issues regarding programs and services for their children. Scheduling facilities became increasingly difficult as other courses and community groups competed for pool time. Plans were also being made to develop a two-week summer camp program and further expand the current program in the coming year.

What started out to be a simple adapted aquatics class was evolving into a complex series of processes and activities aimed at achieving a broader mission. The program was taking on all the characteristics of an organization with human resources development, marketing, strategic planning, budgeting, funding, and the acquisition of equipment and facilities. Such is the case when programs are successful and community need is great. However, continued success requires the ability to effectively and efficiently develop the organization.

Strategic Planning

A strategic plan can successfully guide an organization as its adapted aquatics programs evolve by providing sufficient structure to keep the organization on track over a three- to five-year period. An effective strategic plan is also flexible, allowing the organization to adapt to new conditions and dynamics that might result from serving a diverse population, meeting legislative mandates and staff and facility needs, and seeking new funding resources. Although many management models for developing a strategic plan exist, we may consider the following components, as depicted in figure 5.1, to be a basic template.

External and Internal Issues

A strategic assessment includes an environmental analysis of those external and internal issues and trends that directly influence the organization and its programs. External issues include, for example, legislation (e.g., Americans With Disabilities Act) that impacts services and funding for individuals with disabilities, availability of and access to aquatic facilities in the community, advocacy from the professional community for inclusion programs, and community support for programs for individuals with disabilities. Internal issues include, for example, leadership support for adapted aquatics programs, intraorganizational competition among different departments for program resources, and levels of awareness among organizational staff regarding the needs of individuals with disabilities.

An initial step in strategic planning is to list the internal and external issues and trends specific to your organization as a way of determining what realistic plans your organization might develop. Staff may proceed with a SWOT analysis, which assesses organizational strengths (S) and weaknesses (W) in confronting trends and issues identified as opportunities (O) or threats (T) to organizational success (Wilbur, Finn, and Freeland 1994).

The Mission

The mission of your organization should be summarized in a clear and concise statement describing the organization's purpose, philosophy, uniqueness, and reason for existence. Such a statement reflects the credibility and recognition of your organization and how it positions itself compared to other organizations. The mission of Special Olympics International is as follows:

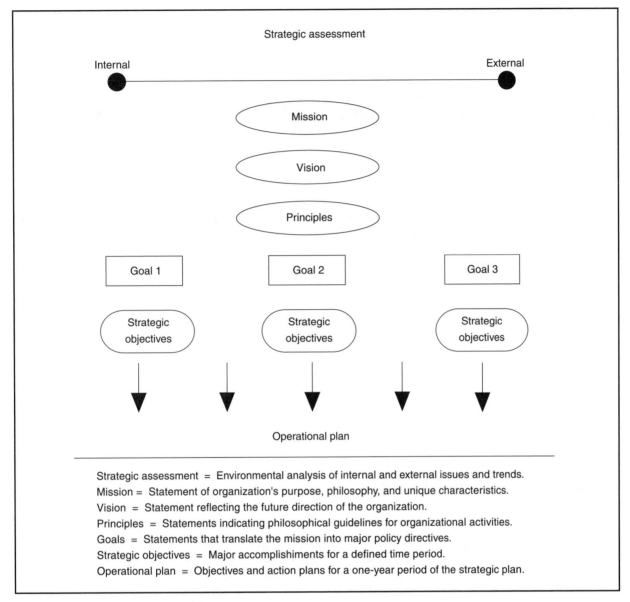

Strategic assessment = Environmental analysis of internal and external issues and trends.

Mission = Statement of organization's purpose, philosophy, and unique characteristics.

Vision = Statement reflecting the future direction of the organization.

Principles = Statements indicating philosophical guidelines for organizational activities.

Goals = Statements that translate the mission into major policy directives.

Strategic objectives = Major accomplishments for a defined time period.

Operational plan = Objectives and action plans for a one-year period of the strategic plan.

Figure 5.1 Strategic planning model.

To provide year-round sports training and athletic competition in a variety of Olympic-type sports for children and adults with mental retardation, giving them continuing opportunities to develop physical fitness, demonstrate courage, experience joy and participate in a sharing of gifts and friendship with their families, other Special Olympics athletes, and the community (Special Olympics International 1994).

Similar to the comprehensive mission statements of the American Red Cross, the YMCA, and the National Safety Council, this mission statement encompasses but does not specifically identify aquatic programs. The mission statement for our fictional model organization, Aqu-Achievements (see figure 5.2), is a sample statement specific to an aquatic organization.

The Vision

An organization's vision establishes where it plans to be at some future point, as it strives to grow. It reflects how the organization wants to be viewed by its customers, membership, and the community. Accordingly, Aqu-Achievements' vision requires the commitment of its resources to strive continually for this vision.

<table>
<tr><td colspan="3" align="center">**Aqu-Achievements**</td></tr>
</table>

Strategic assessment	Strength or Weakness	Opportunity or Threat
Internal environmental issues and trends		
Modern aquatic facility with complete accessibility		
Segregated programs emphasizing physical and skill development		
Resources for staff recruitment and training		
Budget to support program development		
External environmental issues and trends		
Specific legislation supporting programs for individuals with disabilities		
Climate supporting advocacy and inclusion programs		
Competition for corporate and foundation funding		

Mission

Aqu-Achievements provides individuals with disabilities opportunities for personal challenge, self-confidence, fitness, socialization, lifestyle enrichment, and development of physical, motor, and safety skills through educational, recreational, competitive, and therapeutic aquatic programs.

Vision

Aqu-Achievements will provide the most accessible, available, and comprehensive aquatic programs for any individuals with disabilities desiring to participate in aquatic activities.

Principles

- Programs that provide increased opportunities for physical, personal, and social development should be made available and accessible to individuals with disabilities.
- Aqu-Achievements supports community efforts to increase public awareness about disabilities and to increase opportunities for individuals with disabilities to participate equitably as members of the community.
- Aqu-Achievements promotes the inclusion of individuals with disabilities in its organizational governance, staffing, and program development.

Goals and strategic objectives

Program development—Increase the types of aquatic programs available to individuals with disabilities.

- Initiate three competitive swimming programs targeted to specific individuals with disabilities.
- Implement an inclusive aquatic program that provides educational and recreational aquatic activities for children with disabilities and their typically developing siblings.
- Develop and implement a year-round therapeutic aquatic program.

Facility development—Implement facility modifications to improve accessibility and attract a more diverse population of individuals with disabilities.

- Build new male and female locker room facilities at ground level and adjacent to the pool to provide improved accessibility.
- Build a ramp extending into the shallow end of the pool so as not to depend on the hydraulic lift for entry and exit.

Human resource development—Provide opportunities for individuals with disabilities to serve the organization in paid staff and leadership positions.

- Ensure a significant representation (at least 25%) of individuals with disabilities serving on the board of directors and other leadership committees.
- Promote paid staff positions to ensure that individuals with disabilities are recruited as applicants prior to interviews and selection.

Figure 5.2 Sample strategic plan.

Principles

An organization is comprised of people whose collective principles or values provide a foundation for directing policy decisions, initiatives, and programming. Clearly identifying these principles permits organization leadership, paid staff, volunteers, and supporters to better understand and embrace the governance and direction of the organization. A commitment to principles, such as those of Aqu-Achievements, can make it easier for leaders to decide how to implement programs, recruit staff, allocate funds, and advocate for clients.

Goals

Organizational goals refine the organization's mission by stating policy directives. Such goals guide all subsequent management decisions regarding the resources and activities an organization needs to achieve its mission. Goals promote continuity and stability by keeping the organizational leadership focused. In contrast, an organization not guided by its goals might simply react to environmental conditions and the whims of organizational constituents, thereby derailing its own efforts to serve. Ultimately, goals articulate opportunities for proactively achieving the organizational mission and establishing an image that promotes credibility, support, and confidence.

Developing goals involves translating your organization's mission into a limited number of broad statements that focus on ways to achieve the mission. Goal statements are useful if they meet the following criteria:

- They clarify the mission.
- They specify major organizational purposes.
- They provide a basis for developing program activities and operational plans.
- They provide a basis for determining organizational priorities. (Wilbur, Finn, and Freeland 1994).

The sample goals for Aqu-Achievements (see figure 5.2), provide examples of how your organization might write goals.

Following the development of goals, organizational leaders must then define the strategic objectives that will become the major accomplishments for a defined period of time. These strategic objectives help you measure in a concrete way whether or not your organization is succeeding in its mission. Such strategies might focus on diversifying services, developing collaborative pro-

grams with other organizations, developing new and improved resources to enhance programs, or attracting more customers. The sample strategic objectives for Aqu-Achievements (see figure 5.2) demonstrate how strategic objectives evolve from goals and how they quantify or qualify the broader goal statement. Use the Aqu-Achievements model to help your organization define and write strategies that further clarify how it should allocate organizational resources, assess accomplishments, and plan activities for the fiscal year.

Once complete, the strategic plan can then guide the activities of your organization, including resource allocation, budgeting, financial development, marketing, and service delivery. Staff may further refine the plan by developing a short-term, operational plan, identifying the objectives and action plans your organization will accomplish over the next operating or fiscal year. Generally, such a time period conforms to a budget cycle, making it much easier for you to focus on the plan.

After your strategic plan is in place, ensure that each objective, activity, and action that your organization includes in the operational plan is a concrete and measurable aspect intended to achieve the strategic objectives and goals of the strategic plan. Finally, your organization should establish its annual budget based on its operational plan. Although leadership may compile information from many sources to develop strategic and operational plans, ultimately, they should agree that the plan is sufficiently complete, comprehensive, and achievable and that appropriate organizational resources are available.

Governance and Leadership

Some adapted aquatics programs may operate on a "for-profit" basis. More typical are those programs that are provided through not-for-profit organizations. Many of these organizations carry the Internal Revenue status of 501(c)(3) and are subject to Federal rules of governance and financial management and are guided by set laws, policies, and procedures.

A common practice of a nonprofit, community-based organization is to create a board of directors to govern the organization. Its officers and directors establish policies and supervise the fiscal management of the organization. Directors tend to represent specific interests that can support the success of the organization through their influence, affluence, high public profile, or expertise.

A board of directors of an organization that provides adapted aquatic programs benefits from including individuals with disabilities among its representatives. Such a practice demonstrates support of the organization's mission, lends credibility to its programs, provides expertise useful to policy and program development, and ensures appropriate sensitivity to customers served by the organization. The board might improve their effectiveness by supplementing their membership with committee structures, advisory boards, paid and volunteer staff, and other leadership volunteers.

COMMUNICATIONS AND PROMOTION

Effectively communicating and promoting the purpose, contents, and outcomes of adapted aquatics programs will help sustain and develop your programs. In chapters 2, 6, and 7, we describe the reasons for communicating with other aquatics professionals, the importance of cross-disciplinary communication, and appropriate methods for sharing information. Here, however, we'll examine the importance of communication and promotions about your organization, which provide additional opportunities to increase program participation, funding, community support, staff recruitment, and customer satisfaction. In general, it is best to direct these communication and promotions efforts through external communications with the public, media, and other organizations, and through internal communications with program customers and constituents.

External Communications

Any opportunity that can present a positive image of your organization and its programs enhances public awareness and establishes a foundation for future support. You can be certain that modesty does not build identity or recognition! So encourage participants, volunteers, organizational leadership, and paid staff to tell the organization's story. Actively solicit opportunities to relate the mission and vision of the organization and its value to the community. Seek opportunities to gain organizational and program recognition through speaking engagements with schools, civic organizations, funding organizations, professional groups, support and advocacy groups, and employee groups. Apply for community and professional awards. Participate in community events such as fairs and conferences. Regularly communicate with business and industry leaders, state and government officials, and other community leaders. Encourage such leaders to speak on the organization's behalf. Develop and distribute publications, such as brochures, newsletters, and annual reports. The amount of effort expended to raise public awareness can significantly pay off by obtaining financial, human, and materials resources for program development.

One method by which organizations increase public awareness is through interaction with the media. Accordingly, your organization might find effective ways to engage the media and develop its media relations. Consider asking local media to serve on advisory committees or the board of directors. Developing personal contact with the media could increase the possibilities of placing news releases or securing feature articles and radio spots.

Interagency Communications and Advocacy

Coalitions and councils have become common, formal ways for developing interagency communication. Your organization, however, may build informal networks by communicating with peers and colleagues in other organizations. You can compile information in news releases, newsletters, reports, and brochures and routinely distribute them via mail, fax, E-mail, and Internet bulletin boards and chat groups.

Communication among organizations with related missions, programs, operations, and customers can achieve several objectives:

- Organizations can promote each other's programs, providing more ways to recruit and service customers.
- Organizations can share staff with specific managerial, functional, or technical skills.
- Organizations can build advocacy for programs and services impacting a target population.
- Several organizations can collaborate to solve common problems and service delivery issues.

Communicating With Customers and Constituents

The survival of any program certainly requires the support of its customers and constituents. Customers include those individuals who directly participate in the adapted aquatics program and those indirectly affected by the program such as the parents, relatives, friends, and caregivers of the participants. Constituents include all individuals and groups who support or associate with the adapted aquatics program such as parent support groups, funding sources, volunteers, and referral sources. Since these individuals are most involved with the adapted aquatics program, they are in the best position to promote it. An organization can influence the way its customers and constituents promote the program by providing targeted, quality communications. Newsletters, brochures, and other internal communications should educate customers and constituents about the purpose, contents, features, and benefits of the adapted aquatics program so they can then provide appropriate word-of-mouth promotion. Informal and formal program orientations and recognition provide another opportunity to excite individuals about the program and encourage them to tell the program's good news.

Community Support

The backing of key community leaders and groups who have influence, affluence, or expertise can sustain your organization, help it grow, and raise its recognition and credibility throughout the community, giving it the competitive edge in gaining community support. To elicit such support, your organization must tailor its statements of objectives to show others how they may impact your programs positively. Consider, for example, the impact of achieving the following organizational objectives if an organization such as Aqu-Achievements has sufficient and appropriate support from the community.

—Aqu-Achievements wants to submit a state grant-in-aid application for $20,000 to expand its adapted aquatics program in the next fiscal year. The competition for these funds mandates that Aqu-Achievement gain the support of several key legislators. Aqu-Achievements must also rally the support of influential customers, corporate leaders, agency heads, advocacy groups, and parent groups to lobby on its behalf.

—During the next year, Aqu-Achievements wants to provide four satellite, adapted aquatic programs in the two-county region. The program will be delivered year-round so pools must be secured accordingly. Volunteers are needed to solicit other organizations for pool-time, preferably as an in-kind donation.

—Aqu-Achievements is planning a capital campaign for funding a state-of-the-art, outdoor aquatic facility. The two million dollar campaign will require solicitation of corporate and foundation grants and major gifts. The steering committee and solicitors leading the campaign must cultivate major givers in the regional area.

—Over the next two years, Aqu-Achievements wants to position itself as a leader in providing therapeutic aquatics programs, supplemental to medical care and physical therapy. Aqu-Achievements expects to partially recover program costs through the clients' insurance carriers. The advice, expertise, and influence of clients, the medical community, and allied health professionals will be instrumental in developing and implementing this program.

Note how specific each objective is, allowing potential supporters the chance to see clearly how they may help the organization as well as how their sponsorship may pay off for them, whether through increased publicity or using their more established programs.

Achieving each objective requires more than the efforts of paid and volunteer staff committed to an adapted aquatics program. For example, competition for resources can occur internally, among departments and programs within an organization, and externally, among community organizations trying to maintain and expand their own programs. Your organization can confront such competition by developing community support through increased recognition of the existence and the value of its program, thereby increasing participation in those programs.

FINANCIAL DEVELOPMENT

Equipment, facilities, materials, personnel, and administrative expenses are only a few of the many costs associated with providing aquatic programs. Funding sources and ways to secure funding are only limited by the initiative, creativity, and drive of those seeking the funding. In any geographic area, hundreds, even thousands, of nonprofit and charitable organizations compete for funds to support their programs. It may not be a matter of who has the most worthwhile programs, but who is the most organized in soliciting funds.

Revenue Generation

Perhaps the most tangible way to obtain program funds is through a revenue generation program that charges fees, based on membership and program fees. Many organizations such as YMCAs, Boys and Girls Clubs, and Jewish Community Centers take in significant operating funds through fees. Some individuals or groups participating in adapted aquatics programs, however, may not have the discretionary income to pay such fees. Moreover, some costs associated with providing adapted aquatics programs may be proportionally more than other programs, resulting in higher fees. Thus, your organization may have to look elsewhere for funds to support or supplement program expenses.

Direct Solicitation

Your organization may choose from many different methods for directly soliciting individuals and groups for financial support, including annual giving or direct mail campaigns, corporate sponsorship, grant solicitation, and major gifts programs. Each of these funding methods requires organization, expertise, and a support structure to ensure success. Annual giving campaigns involve personal and mail solicitation, maintenance of a database to track contributors and their giving histories, correspondence with and recognition of contributors, and the financial management of incoming contributions. Soliciting corporate sponsorships and foundation, corporate, or government grants requires researching the most appropriate contributors for adapted aquatics programs, cultivating relationships with the contributors, securing key individuals such as community representatives and volunteers to assist with the funding request, developing and presenting a case for giving, processing grant applications, and communicating effectively. Major gifts programs require making potential contributors sensitive to the mission of the organization and the need for support.

In-Kind Support

In-kind support, non-cash contributions of goods or services, is another method of financial development that can defray the costs of operating adapted aquatics programs. For example, you can solicit much of the instructional equipment and materials from local vendors and manufacturers, including life jackets, kickboards, inflatables, other flotation aids, pool toys, tot docks, transfer tiers, wet vests, goggles, stop watches, and lifts. Pool time is another type of in-kind donation appropriate for adapted aquatic programs, whether your organization is conducting a single program or trying to expand the program to various locations in the community. Finally, you may be able to secure services through in-kind donations, including legal services, nursing services, and PT or OT services.

Special Events

Special events have been the mechanism by which many groups have raised funds to support programs. But don't underestimate how labor-intensive and time-consuming such events can be. Still, special events are often worth the effort as they also provide an excellent opportunity for program promotion and recognition. An active, diverse, and committed committee should plan carefully for success.

FACILITIES ACQUISITION AND SAFETY

Perhaps your group or organization offers adapted aquatics programs but is not fortunate enough to own a pool; instead, you have found an affordable, accessible alternative by using another organization's facilities. Or maybe you have the aquatic facilities but have not considered the feasibility of expanding your programs to include adapted aquatics programs until now.

Where should you look for aquatic facilities to use if you don't have one or need ideas for adapting the facilities you do have? Many types of for-profit and nonprofit organizations may be able to help you, including

- private, community-based facilities known to provide year-round aquatic programs such as YMCA, YWCA, Boys and Girls Clubs, and Jewish Community Centers,

- public and private schools,
- organizations providing direct services to individuals with disabilities such as United Cerebral Palsy, Easter Seals, and Special Olympics,
- summer camps sponsored by any organizations,
- hospitals and rehabilitation centers,
- residential facilities,
- colleges and universities,
- publicly funded organizations such as parks and recreation facilities and community centers,
- community-based and corporate, private, fitness facilities,
- hotel and motels, and
- residential facilities such as developments and condominiums. (See also chapter 2 for the four treatment models settings.)

These organizations may provide opportunities for developing adapted aquatic programs by (a) incorporating your programs into their existing lines of service, (b) renting their facility to your group, whether your group is internal or external to the organization, (c) providing the facility to your group as an in-kind donation, (d) initiating a collaborative program that is mutually beneficial to their organization and yours, or (e) adding an adapted aquatics program to enhance the programs they currently offer. Finally, in the "Where Do We Grow From Here?" feature at the beginning of this chapter, the adapted aquatics program provided a practicum experience, thereby enhancing the adapted physical education course.

One approach for soliciting pool space is to market the benefits your organization will derive from sponsoring an adapted aquatics program. Consider an example whereby a Special Olympics chapter secures pool space from a local YMCA. Special Olympics has the opportunity to offer an aquatic program at an organization recognized for its aquatic programs, which is also structured to deliver services to the community. The YMCA has opportunities for program outreach, expanding its customer base, developing a partnership with another community organization, and achieving its mission by providing a needed service.

Risk Management

The ceiling over the pool collapses. A fire destroys the locker room facilities. A participant trips over some instructional equipment, falls on the pool deck, and breaks his arm. A parent threatens to file a lawsuit because she feels your organization has not provided an appropriate accommodation. An instructor provides some inaccurate and sensitive information to the media about medical issues pertaining to one of the program participants. These situations demonstrate a few of the risks that might confront your organization and its staff and customers. Responsible organizations implement risk management programs to anticipate and avoid such situations. Specifically, risk management programs strive to develop basic measures that identify, evaluate, eliminate, reduce, and transfer risks (Rakich, Longest, and Darr 1985).

Many ways exist to manage risks, including the following (Horine 1995; Rakich, Longest, and Darr 1985).

- **Insurance Protection:** Consider sufficient coverage to protect against financial losses from liability, fire, theft, and vehicle accidents and to provide for workers' compensation. Circumstances might also warrant unique or additional insurance coverage for volunteers, athletic events, and so on.

- **Policies and Procedures:** Emergency action plans, communication protocols, operations manuals, and personnel policies manuals are types of documents your organization might develop to guide the actions of staff in preventing or dealing with hazardous situations. Such documents should clearly define roles and responsibilities and provide guidance for appropriate actions. Most importantly, the administration must disseminate, explain, and review the information in these documents regularly.

- **Records and Reports:** Opportunities to identify risks, then follow up and prevent future risks result from comprehensive records and reports. Many aquatic facilities use accident, injury, and incident report forms to document follow-up and preventative measures. Registration records, participant information forms, and medical release forms can also help you identify potential risks related to specific individuals or groups.

- **Safety Audits:** Through comprehensive and regular investigations of facilities and equipment, an audit could identify potential hazards that your organization may be able to eliminate or control. Items such as loose bolts on a diving block, a jagged edge on the stairs entering the pool, or a missing skimmer cover might easily go unnoticed and possibly cause injury if an organization fails to conduct regular safety audits.

• **Staff Training:** Since situations of risk involve people, it becomes critical that those responsible for managing risks are trained accordingly. It seems obvious that first aid, CPR, and lifeguarding skills enable aquatic staff to manage risks, however, each organization must determine what other training related to risk management is appropriate for which staff. Staff training should answer these types of questions: Do staff have appropriate pool operator training to handle pool chemicals? Who can communicate with program participants who are deaf in an emergency? How will participants who require a lift to enter the pool be removed if that lift breaks?

• **Customer and Participant Education:** Since there are usually more program participants than staff in an aquatic program, it makes sense to engage the participants in preventing accidents and avoiding risks. For this reason, aquatic facilities should post rules, orient program participants to the program and the facilities, have everyone involved practice emergency drills, and provide literature about the program. Creative efforts to educate pool patrons provide a more proactive approach to risk management than attempts to discipline patrons after they have engaged in an activity that increases the risk of an accident.

• **Equipment:** Quality safety, rescue, and instructional equipment can help staff prevent accidents and effectively intervene if an accident does occur. Adequate backboards, rescue tubes, ring buoys, and first aid kits are basic equipment for effective lifeguarding. Be aware, too, that accidents and injury can easily result from broken kickboards, damaged life jackets, leaky face masks, and sharp-edged toys.

• **Facility Modifications:** Nonslip surfaces, temperature-controlled showers, appropriately designed handrails, and easily accessible entrances and exits are a few of the many facility features that can reduce and prevent injury. Identify necessary modifications through past injury reports and consultation with pool design companies.

• **"Hold Harmless" and Parental Consent Forms:** In an effort to transfer risk, many organizations have required participants to sign forms indicating the participant agrees not to sue if some

future accident should occur. In many instances, parents sign for minors. Since these types of "hold harmless" or exculpatory agreements cannot excuse ordinary negligence nor gross, wanton, or intentional acts, there are many circumstances for which they would not hold up in court (Horine 1995). Perhaps a better approach to more clearly informing parents and participants about a program is through a parental consent form, which should include permission to participate, an overview of program content and risks, medical insurance information, emergency notification information, participant medical information (relevant to risk prevention and emergency care), and permission to provide emergency medical treatment (Horine 1995). Because laws and court decisions affecting these issues vary and change from jurisdiction to jurisdiction, however, your program should seek advice from an expert in the field of liability insurance.

Your organization's process of risk management must ensure that it identifies, controls, and resolves risks. Organizational policies, procedures, and detailed job descriptions should clearly define responsibility for risk management. Many organizations have legal counsel and designated management staff who implement various components of the risk management program. It is best to structure staff meetings, customer surveys, and accident and incident reports so that leadership can collect, review, and analyze crucial feedback about managing risks.

PROGRAM DEVELOPMENT AND EVALUATION

Critical to the implementation of programs that are safe, effective, and relevant is the underlying notion that adequate planning has been done to ensure the optimal aquatic learning environment. Designing the overall adapted aquatic program, including assessment tools, individual and group plans, and an evaluation system, takes time, creativity, dedication, and a broad knowledge base, regarding adapted aquatics, individuals with disabilities, special education, general aquatics, and multidisciplinary functioning. In the following sections, we'll introduce concepts, elements, and evaluations of programs that provide quality aquatic programs for individuals with disabilities.

Elements of Program Design

Planning for the program begins with the selection of the service model and corresponding goals; this is known as defining the program. As described in chapter 2, the selection of the model will depend on factors, such as setting and facilities (e.g., school, community center, rehabilitation center), service provider (e.g., aquatic instructor, therapist, recreation specialist), as well as the target population (e.g., people with physical disabilities, cognitive disabilities, senior citizens). The target population may be one that has traditionally been underserved, one that is already served in your particular facility, or one that has expressed interest through a community needs survey.

Although we recommend the collaborative model, usually, a specific, unidisciplinary thrust will be necessary. In addition, another philosophy that might guide a program might be a competitive sports approach. This approach shares components of the educational and recreational models, offering instruction and providing individuals with leisure time skills for pleasurable recreational experiences. Competitive programs may function in any of the settings we've addressed under the direction of aquatic instructors, parents, therapists, or recreational specialists who are interested and trained in coaching swimming.

Beyond defining the thrust of the program, the amount of collaboration desired, and the general goals of the program, your organization must develop a specific curriculum. Whether the thrust of your program is educational or not, the philosophy, goals, and scope and sequence of skills involved in your program should comprise the major parts of your curriculum. The major purpose of writing curriculum, whether it is for one individual or a group, is to provide direction and continuity. Specifically, center your curriculum around aquatic skills and their application in the lives of individuals with a particular disability. Ask yourself, "Are the goals relevant to the current needs of the target group of the program?" Use the guidelines for age-appropriate activities in chapter 3 to help you tailor your program's goals further.

Curriculum goals serve the mission statement, guide the program, and reflect program philosophy. They give the program purpose, determine the content, and are outcome oriented. In compliance with the mission statement, the program director first delineates the program goals, which can then be translated into desired outcomes. These statements should reflect what the program and participant should accomplish. Figure 5.3 shows the relationship between program and participant goals. Next, the program staff identifies the skills to be taught each class session, appropriate learning progressions, and specific behavioral objectives for each participant (see chapter 8).

The program staff continues program planning by examining time, facilities, equipment, personnel, and the effects of these on content. Ultimately, this program information serves as the basis for assessments and goals of the individuals who attend the program.

Components of Program Evaluation

Administration and staff must evaluate the many parts of the adapted aquatic program to determine if participants are making meaningful gains and if the program itself is safe, effective, relevant, and age-appropriate. Indeed, ongoing evaluation can quickly uncover problem areas that your

Program goals	Participant goals
To provide social experiences during aquatic participation	To increase number and quality of social contacts
To provide instruction in swim strokes	To perform 5 basic swim strokes
To increase independent movement	To perform independent transfers for entering and exiting the pool
To provide instruction in skills which promote safety and survival in the water	To perform floating and self-rescue skills in the deep water

Figure 5.3 Relationship between program and participant goals.

organization needs to address in terms of facility planning, program plans, staff development, and customer satisfaction. While some programs opt for monthly, quarterly, semiannual, or yearly evaluation, ongoing evaluation will help your program respond in a more timely fashion to issues regarding quality and appropriateness of instruction, environment, and planning.

While programs vary too much for us to suggest a single method of evaluation, the following considerations will give you examples and suggestions for ongoing and postprogram evaluation, pertaining to facilities, program development, staffing, and customer satisfaction. Adapt these ideas to fit your program's needs.

Assuming that the staff has done a full accessibility survey (see chapter 6), facility evaluation may consist of maintenance concerns and upgrades that increase the level of accommodation and expand program options. Well-maintained, clean decks and locker rooms, chemically balanced water, and accessible areas are basic to any program. Use the questions that follow to help identify facility characteristics and features that may affect program quality in addition to these basics.

Does the lighting provide maximum visibility throughout the entire facility?

Are there areas in which accidents have occurred?

Are water and air temperatures satisfactory?

Are there any drafty areas?

Do the swimmers feel the facilities and programs are accessible, usable, and desirable?

Are there family changing areas that are accessible?

Are there waiting areas for parents, caregivers, and significant others?

Is the pool/instructional space too large or too small?

Are extraneous noises and sounds of concern?

Are obstacles and objects in close proximity to working areas?

Are changing tables available in dressing rooms?

Are shower chairs or benches available in the shower area?

Does the pool have a variety of depths to facilitate a variety of activities?

Are there adequate options for entry and exit?

While evaluation of individual program plans, group lessons and activities, and personnel should be continual, evaluation of program goals may not be so frequent. Although administrators and staff of adapted aquatic programs should constantly ask themselves questions about the mission, philosophy, and goals of a program, it may be years before they changes their program goals substantially. Possible goal changes for a program may emerge from changes in community, society, and personnel. For example, as discussed in chapter 1, aquatic programs for individuals with disabilities went through great changes in the 1970s when federal legislation mandated education programs and federally funded programs and again in the 1990s with the renewed trend toward inclusion into all aspects of life. When personnel change, a program might subsequently change due to differences in philosophy, training, and knowledge. Still other changes may be brought about by reexamination of the types of individuals in the program as in the example that follows:

An adapted aquatic instructor for a community agency was planning to give a presentation about her program and prepared some statistics regarding the variety of individuals with disabilities. This process revealed that half the participants were individuals with traumatic brain injury, forcing this instructor to reexamine the program goals and add more goals directly related to interaction, communication, following rules, and physical fitness. Subsequently, she determined that these goals better met the specific needs of this group.

When you are conducting an aquatic program evaluation, you may also wish to examine the quality of interactions between instructor and participants and among the participants themselves as well as how participants react to task difficulty and the entire process of how they are served in your aquatic programs. Modified from "A Needs Assessment Instrument for Local School District Use in Adapted Physical Education Needs" (Sherrill and Megginson 1984), the information in the Program Evaluation Form examines the process and practices of an organization and its staff when providing appropriate aquatic services for individuals with disabilities. Use this checklist as a general guide for observing an overall program.

Program Evaluation Form

Respond "yes" or "no" to each of the statements. "No" answers could indicate areas for improvement.

Assessment, Placement, and Individualized Program Plans

Y N   1. The aquatic staff has an established procedure for accommodating individuals with disabilities.

Y N   2. The aquatic program provides a continuum of placements, including segregated, partially included, and totally included settings for aquatic participation and instruction.

Y N   3. Aquatic assessment is conducted by an adapted aquatic specialist in conjunction with other professionals if warranted (regular aquatic instructor, therapists, or the like).

Y N   4. The adapted aquatic specialist uses an observation instrument for assessment.

Y N   5. The aquatic personnel attend team meetings to present information when appropriate.

Y N   6. All members of a transdisciplinary team of professionals, parents, caregivers, significant others, and participant have voices in placement, goals, and objectives.

Y N   7. Individual programs are evaluated at least four times per year.

Y N   8. The individual plan includes present level of performance, annual goals, rationale for goals, short-term objectives, including projected dates to start and finish, and criteria for evaluation.

Instruction and Programming

Y N   1. The adapted aquatic program is periodically reviewed by outside expert evaluators.

Y N   2. A curriculum manual is available describing overall program goals, philosophy, rationale, benefits, assumptions, and aquatic instructional services for individuals with disabilities.

Y N   3. Aquatic instruction for individuals with disabilities takes place under the guidance of certified adapted aquatic instructors.

Y N   4. Adapted aquatic instruction for individuals with severe disabilities takes place with one support person per participant.

Y N   5. The content of the adapted aquatic program contains a variety of swimming, water safety, and leisure time aquatic activities.

Y N   6. Instructors base aquatics instruction on individual goals as outlined in the Individualized Program Plan.

Y N   7. Individuals with disabilities included in regular aquatic classes have the proper learning, emotional, and physical support as defined by the IAPP.

Y N   8. The program focuses on what an individual with disabilities needs to participate now and in the future in lifetime and leisure pursuits.

Y N   9. Aquatic programs for individuals with disabilities include goals for strengthening self-esteem.

Y N 10. The organization gives individuals with disabilities who can succeed in regular competitive athletics opportunities to do so.

Personnel

Y N   1. The organization leader ensures that staff and participants in the program are prepared to embrace the diversity of abilities of individuals with disabilities.

Y N   2. Sufficient number of qualified personnel are available to meet the needs of individuals with disabilities.

Y N   3. Certified adapted aquatic instructors deliver adapted aquatic services and instruction to individuals with disabilities.

Y N   4. Administrators understand the scope of adapted aquatic services.

Y N   5. Administrators ensure that regular aquatic instructors have at least one inservice training session each year on adapted aquatics concepts by specialists in this area.

Y N   6. Administrators ensure that instructor aides have appropriate inservice training each year by an adapted aquatic specialist.

Y N   7. Administrators encourage aquatic instructors who want to improve knowledge in the area of adapted aquatics.

Y N   8. Administrators grant release time for adapted aquatic instructors to attend team meetings.

Y N   9. Administrators understand the difference between adapted aquatics and aquatic therapy.

Y N 10. Staff maintains communication with parents, caregivers, and significant others.

Y N 11. Staff maintains communication with other professionals.

Y N 12. Instructors provide education to encourage family and caregiver involvement.

Next, we'll look specifically at how to evaluate aquatic instructors. As a function of successful program implementation, as a program manager, you must examine the teaching behaviors of the program's aquatic instructors. First, however, the organization must clearly identify the functions of an aquatic instructor working with individuals with disabilities. Then to determine effectiveness, you must find a way to measure how well the instructors demonstrate these functions. You can develop an observation checklist for evaluating effective teaching behaviors with the statements listed below, adapted from Randall's functions of physical educators, as criteria for assessing instructor effectiveness (1992). By rating the instructor on each point on a scale from one to five, as the observer, you determine the degree of instructor effectiveness, with five indicating very effective and one, very ineffective.

FUNCTIONS OF AN ADAPTED AQUATIC INSTRUCTOR DURING CLASS

- Reviews previous skills
- Reviews prerequisite physical, cognitive, and affective skills for new skill
- States lesson goals and objectives
- Uses task-analyzed teaching progressions
- Provides proper explanations and demonstrations
- Uses concrete examples
- Uses key terms and cues
- Checks for participant understanding
- Includes all participants in instruction
- Modifies tasks when too easy or hard
- Displays enthusiasm for task presented
- Uses a variety of communication modes
- Brings participants back on-task if off-task
- Allows ample time for practice
- Responds to all participants at a high rate
- Gives tasks to participants that meet their individual goals
- Structures practice so that participants spend a high percentage of time engaged in motor activity
- Aims for high success rate

- Provides general corrective feedback
- Gives specific corrective feedback
- Uses positive reinforcement
- Uses applied behavioral analysis principles when necessary
- Uses routines for participants who need them
- Directs paraprofessionals or aides to perform specific tasks
- Offers safety tips
- Motivates participants to learn new activities
- Makes smooth transitions from one activity or space to the next
- Applies rules consistently
- Promotes positive self-images of all participants

A final vital area of evaluation—too often neglected—is determining how participants, caregivers, or significant others view the entire program and overall aquatic experience. Interviews, observations of compliance, and surveys are ways to obtain input from the consumers your program serves. Participants should be directly involved in this process, but if they are unable to respond it may be necessary to question significant others. The Consumer Satisfaction Survey models effective evaluation statements for assessing consumer satisfaction. You can survey consumers semiannually or more frequently. Use the results to examine your current practices and to plan for the future.

HUMAN RESOURCE MANAGEMENT

As we have discussed, a sound organizational structure with appropriate and adequate facilities and a solid funding base are essential to help your organization function well. Delivery of services, however, depends on sufficient, qualified, trained staff who understand their jobs and the purpose of the organization. Competent staff, including the program director, instructors, lifeguards, aides, and other personnel, ensure that your program achieves its objectives, maintains quality and customer service, and delivers its services safely, efficiently, and effectively.

Consumer Satisfaction Survey

Help us measure the success of this aquatic program. Check one box for each of the numbered categories. Please explain "disagree" and "strongly disagree" ratings. If you have ideas as to how we might improve the program, please share them with us.

	Strongly Agree	Agree	Disagree	Strongly Disagree	Unable to Judge
1. Facilities met my accessibility needs.	❏	❏	❏	❏	❏
2. Facilities were well kept.	❏	❏	❏	❏	❏
3. Facilities were conducive to learning.	❏	❏	❏	❏	❏
4. It was easy to join this program.	❏	❏	❏	❏	❏
5. I felt comfortable with the process of being assessed and discussing goals.	❏	❏	❏	❏	❏
6. Ongoing assessment was shared with participants.	❏	❏	❏	❏	❏
7. Program staff collaborated with others effectively.	❏	❏	❏	❏	❏
8. Communication lines were always open.	❏	❏	❏	❏	❏
9. Individualized Aquatics Program Plans were developed with participant and, if appropriate, significant others.	❏	❏	❏	❏	❏
10. The atmosphere of the classes was positive and conducive to learning.	❏	❏	❏	❏	❏
11. The instructor provided specific goals to be achieved at each session.	❏	❏	❏	❏	❏
12. The instructor provided ample opportunity to practice.	❏	❏	❏	❏	❏
13. There was positive interaction among individuals with varying abilities.	❏	❏	❏	❏	❏
14. Instructor adapted activities and tasks to individuals' levels of performance.	❏	❏	❏	❏	❏
15. Instructor communicated in preferred mode.	❏	❏	❏	❏	❏
16. Instructor included you in the entire session.	❏	❏	❏	❏	❏
17. Instructor chose activities that helped you meet your goals.	❏	❏	❏	❏	❏
18. Enough equipment was available during sessions.	❏	❏	❏	❏	❏
19. Equipment was of good quality.	❏	❏	❏	❏	❏

Reasons for disagreeing with any statement: _____

Suggestions for improvement: _____

Following a simple model of human resource development, your organization should first determine and define which jobs will help you achieve organization and program goals (see figure 5.4). This information should then drive decisions regarding job prerequisites, appropriate credentials for applicants, classifications and number of positions, performance management, and training and development programs for maintaining qualified staff.

Job Analysis

A job analysis is the process of studying a job to determine its contents, a process appropriate for both paid and volunteer staff positions associated with adapted aquatics programs. The resulting information indicates the types of skills, experience, and training required for positions and guides decisions for the effective recruitment, selection, and orientation of new staff (Rakich, Longest, and Darr 1985). Organization and program leadership may conduct a job analysis through observation, questionnaires, and interviews.

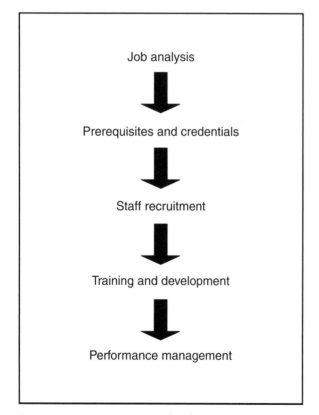

Figure 5.4 Human resource development model.

Information obtained through a job analysis becomes the basis for a job description, which summarizes job relationships, responsibilities, qualifications, and conditions. The analysis also assists in documenting job specifications related to appropriate education, experience, physical skills, communication skills, initiative, judgment, training, and so on (Rakich, Longest, and Darr 1985). These specifications provide much guidance when recruiting for new positions and when interviewing job applicants.

Prerequisites and Credentials

A table of organization, such as figure 5.5, identifies a hierarchy of staff positions. Each position requires prerequisites and credentials for successful job performance. An organization providing adapted aquatics programs might expect its staff to possess the following general characteristics: positive attitudes; willingness to do many tasks; flexibility, realism, and adaptability in meeting the needs of customers; and acceptance of diversity among its customers. These characteristics apply to both paid staff and volunteer job positions, including program directors, lifeguards, greeters, instructors, and locker room and pool aides.

Each position within your organization should also require specific prerequisites and credentials to ensure a standard of performance and safety upon entering a job. The job analysis should determine such information, which should, in turn, be documented in the job description and job specifications. As an example, consider the positions listed under the manager of instructional and personal development programs in figure 5.5. For such a position, you might expect an applicant to have received related training from organizations such as the American Red Cross, YMCA, AAHPERD, Aquatic Exercise Association, U.S. Swimming, and the National Safety Council so that she may adequately supervise aquatic instructors and therapists. In addition, your organization might require academic credentials, possibly including degrees in physical education, adapted physical education, physical therapy, exercise and fitness, recreation, recreation therapy, and sports management. Finally, your organization might also require an applicant to have prior experience working with diverse populations of individuals with disabilities, cross-training in different program areas, and experience with other organizational functions, such as staff development, fund raising, and financial management.

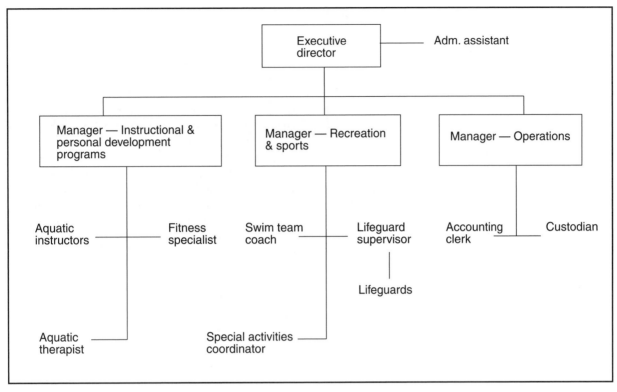

Figure 5.5 Aqu-Achievements table of organization for paid staff.

Staff Development

Effective recruitment provides staff who "best fit" their jobs. Then training creates staff with the skills and competencies tailored to job specifications. Naturally, keeping the same staff over time helps ensure program continuity and stability. Indeed, your organization makes an investment in its success by retaining staff who are well-trained and appropriately qualified. Finally, evaluating staff performance and motivating staff are vital. Implementing the components of staff development effectively requires a range of inter-related organizational activities (see figure 5.6).

Recruitment

After completing the job analysis, the next task is to recruit candidates for the position. Typically, the administration places ads in newspapers, newsletters, and professional journals and through colleges, universities, and community organizations. Then, the administration reviews resumes and screens, interviews, and selects candidates. Although each of these activities is routine to organizational operations, management must generally devote much time and effort to staff recruitment.

Other recruitment alternatives exist that result in qualified and competent placements for staff positions. For example, volunteers can contribute significantly to the human resources of an adapted aquatics program while meeting the constraints of a limited budget and supporting the organization's mission and management and program philosophies. Who might be willing to volunteer?

- High school and college students, particularly schools that require students to complete community service projects
- Relatives of program participants
- Businesses that encourage community participation
- Community-based organizations with similar missions and programs, such as the American Red Cross, United Way, United Cerebral Palsy Association, Multiple Sclerosis Society, Association for the Rights of Citizens With Mental Retardation
- Professional groups and organizations for teachers, physical therapists, and the like
- Local- and state-sponsored volunteer programs such as RSVP (Retired Senior Volunteer Program)

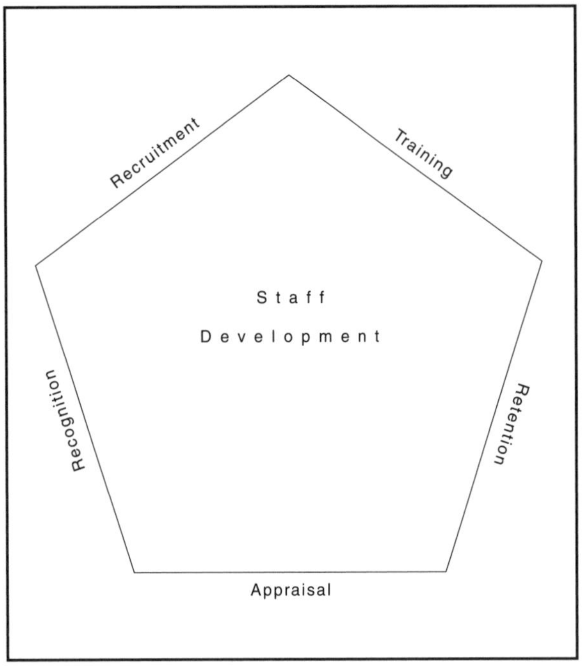

Figure 5.6 Staff development functions.

Volunteer participation and other alternative recruitment strategies can create diversity among staff, demonstrating appropriate sensitivity to customers and representing the community. Programs such as college internships and community work-study provide low-cost ways to recruit temporary staff but may require a greater focus on training and supervision. Each of these considerations may impact the table of organization, thereby influencing decisions about staff recruitment.

Training

A structured staff training program can assist with the immediate and long-term maintenance of qualified staff. Preservice training provides new adapted aquatics staff with the knowledge and skills to start their positions. This training might include an orientation to the facility and equipment, review of operational procedures, description of staff roles and responsibilities, review of program objectives and methods, and an overview of the customer population.

Inservice training provides more comprehensive development of job skills and competencies. Such training for adapted aquatics staff might include practice of program methods for participant skill development, supervisory

practices, medical and emergency protocols, specific characteristics of client population, and program methods for a specific disability. Through cross-training, your organization might do a better job of ensuring the continuity and stability of program delivery. Swim instructors, for example, might cross-train to provide fitness programs or to assist with therapy regimens. A final training component, which will strengthen your organization's ability to retain qualified staff and provide staff with opportunities for personal development, is career development. Through such a program, staff have the opportunity to pursue training that prepares them for higher-level technical, supervisory, and management positions.

Appraisal

Although effective staff training contributes significantly to the delivery of quality programs, other performance management processes impact programs as well. Performance appraisals provide opportunities to more objectively assess if individual staff members have successfully achieved performance standards based on organizational objectives. Lack of achievement may indicate a need for more supervision, training, or appropriate resources for completing the job.

Recognition

At the same time, recognition of excellent performance energizes and motivates staff to continue meeting performance standards, take initiative, and strive to achieve the organizational mission. Administration may provide recognition in a variety of standard and creative ways, including informal verbal and written praise, opportunities to attend training programs and conferences, formal staff recognition programs, and salary increments and promotions. Performance appraisal and recognition are equally important for paid and volunteer staff.

Retention

Of course, many of these components of human resource development are interrelated. Performance appraisal provides feedback for staff recognition, training, and career development. If conducted in a supportive manner, each of these processes may, in turn, increase staff retention, which helps your program maintain continuity and stability.

SUMMARY

You can build an effective and efficient organization by developing and executing strategic plans, securing adequate funding, acquiring appropriate facilities, gaining community support, developing organizational structure, implementing effective programs, ensuring risk management, developing human resources, and communicating effectively internally and externally. Attention to communication and program promotions enhances an organization's ability to receive positive recognition, acquire resources, and improve program participation. Program development and evaluation parallels the process of organizational development by generating program content based on the needs of participants and input from individuals associated with the program. Human resource development increases the ability of an organization to achieve its mission and deliver quality programs by ensuring effective staff recruitment, development, and retention.

CHAPTER 5 REVIEW

1. Describe the major parts of a strategic plan and how these parts guide an organization to achieve its mission.

2. In what ways might effective program communications and promotions help to increase, improve, and sustain programs?

3. Identify four types of financial development activities and give examples of how they might be applied to the development of an adapted aquatic program.

4. What are some basic measures of a risk management program?

5. Identify an existing adapted aquatics program and describe each of the elements of program design as identified in this chapter.

6. Describe three components of program evaluation and how you might use the results for program development.

7. Describe how each of the functions of staff development could help to ensure the delivery of a quality adapted aquatics program.

FACILITIES, EQUIPMENT, AND SUPPLIES

Thus far in this book, we have introduced you to the history, legislation, theories, and typical practices of adapted aquatics. In this chapter, we will explain then show you how to apply specific information so that you can ensure that your facilities, equipment, and supplies are adequate. As you read and study this chapter, keep in mind that the environment of your program must be safe and accessible as well as lend itself to successful and satisfying experiences for participants and instructors alike. You must be familiar with guidelines for accessibility, state and local health codes for aquatic facilities, resources for equipment, and supplies that facilitate aquatic participation.

As we discussed in chapter 1, the Americans With Disabilities Act has mandated that facilities be accessible to individuals with disabilities, and you must follow federal guidelines to make sure your facility complies with the law. Some requirements are very specific, such as standard minimum requirements for widths of doorways and halls, and some are somewhat vague, such as the need for one form of access into the pool. The Access Board of the U.S. Architectural Barriers Compliance Board (ATBCB) is the federal agency responsible for the development of design guidelines for accessibility. The Recreation Access Advisory Committee was appointed to provide advice to the Access Board on accessible recreation environments. Following the publication of the ADA Accessibility Guidelines for Buildings and Facilities (Federal Register 1991), the Recreation Access Advisory Committee published its recommendations for recreational facilities and outdoor-developed areas (Recreation Access Advisory Committee 1994) which included four pages on aquatic facilities. In September 1995, the ATBCB awarded a research contract to the National Center on Accessibility to identify and evaluate methods of access to swimming pools by individuals with disabilities (NCA 1996). In September 1996, the NCA committee submitted its recommendations to the ATBCB.

The recommendations for swimming pool accessibility in this chapter are based on this report. Key specifications are referenced throughout this chapter. Additional specifications may be referenced from the report, National Center on Accessibility—Swimming Pool Accessibility (see appendix E for the address). But although there are standards for access, recognize that no single pool design will satisfy all the demands of a community. There are facilities designed around competitive, therapeutic, portable, recreational, freestanding, sunken, partially sunken, and deck level pools. More challenging areas of accessibility—lakes, rivers, and ocean front—play an important role when providing individuals with disabilities the opportunity to make the transition into the broader world of aquatics that naturally exist in society.

Flotation devices, lifts, transfer equipment, and motivational supplies, such as toys, rafts, and tubes, give you more instructional strategy options, but cannot replace quality instruction. Indeed, don't let availability of equipment be the determining factor when placing an individual in a segregated or integrated program. Good pedagogical practices mandate that individuals with disabilities are entitled to appropriate equipment and supplies in an aquatics setting just as they are in a more traditional classroom or recreational program. Of course, equipment and supplies needed for individuals with disabilities vary with the abilities of each participant.

FACILITIES

The types of facilities available for adapted aquatic programs vary as much as program purposes, goals, and participants do. Facilities come in all shapes and sizes, from 10-yard therapeutic pools to 25-yard pools, 3-foot-deep pools for water-walking, to 16-foot-deep diving wells. While the various purposes of an aquatic program may lend themselves to a specific facility design, most aquatic facilities have locker rooms or changing areas, a pool deck and pool, means of entering and exiting the pool, and storage areas.

Community facilities operated by local governments and agencies, such as the YMCA, serve a variety of uses from competition to water-walking and may be accessible, but not usable or desirable. Therapeutic facilities, operated by rehabilitation hospitals, private therapists, and residential agencies are generally built with a single purpose and may have greater accessibility, utility, and desirability for individuals with disabilities but may not be open to the general public. Current design

trends for most facilities are for multiple uses, combining recreational, instructional, competitive, and therapeutic needs into a single facility design. Unfortunately, however, conditions for every one of the uses may be compromised.

The Americans With Disabilities Act (ADA) is arguably the most significant piece of legislation to affect facility construction in the last 25 years. It asserts that accessibility features should allow independent use by people with disabilities but should interfere as little as possible with nondisabled swimmers using the pool (Mace 1993).

Accessibility

What, then, is accessibility? Accessibility removes architectural barriers, ensuring the participant's ability to gain easy access to the outside of the venue. Close parking with sufficient room for vehicles, visible and safe flow of pedestrian traffic, curb cuts, and generally easy movement outside the facility, and access and movement inside the facility enhance accessibility. Adequate parking, user-friendly entrance-exit doorways, proper signs, ramps, elevators, open meeting areas, and braille on doorway entrances to offices, activity areas, and bathrooms are other examples (see table 6.1). Remember, the Americans With Disabilities Act requires all places of public accommodation, such as camps, playgrounds, auditoriums, fitness centers, community recreational facilities, and gymnasiums, to provide the same goods and services, in the most integrated setting appropriate, to individuals with disabilities as they do to nondisabled individuals. Another important concept of this law includes the providing reasonable accommodations in communication, transportation, and programming.

In order to ensure accessibility, your aquatic facility should have an Americans With Disabilities Act (ADA) committee that is familiar with standards and federal guidelines conduct a compliance check by applying these guidelines. Individuals with disabilities from the community and participants in the program should be on this committee. General aquatic instructors and adapted aquatic instructors should have representatives on the committee to provide input regarding accessibility issues. You can find other practical ideas for implementing the requirements of the ADA in the book *Leisure Opportunities for Individuals With Disabilities*, edited by Grosse and Thompson (1993), including the following:

Table 6.1

Examples of Accessibility Guidelines for Buildings and Facilities

Required minimum number of accessible parking spaces	1-25 spaces in lot 26-50 spaces in lot 501-100 spaces in lot	1 2 2% of total
Access aisles adjacent to accessible parking spaces	60 in. minimum	
Curb ramps	Minimum width=36 in.	
Slope and rise	Least possible, but maximum slope of ramp in new construction is 1:12 ratio.	
Handrails	If ramp has a rise of 6 in. or more or a horizontal projection of 72 in. or more, handrails must be on both sides.	
Wheelchair passages	32 in. at a point (such as a doorway) 36 in. at a continuous area (such as a hallway, accessible route, or deck) 60 in. for 2 wheelchairs to be able to pass 60 in. for a 180-degree turning space	
Thresholds at doorways	Not to exceed 3/4 in. for exterior sliding doors or 1/2 in. other types	
Toilets	17 in.-19 in. to top of toilet seat	
Showers	Seat shall be provided 17 in.-19 in. from floor and extend full depth of stall. Grab bars are necessary. See ADA guidelines for specifications. Controls operable with 1 hand and not requiring tight grasping, pinching, or twisting of wrist. Shower unit with a hose at least 60 in. that converts to handheld and stationary. Curbs in shower no higher than 1/2 in.	

Adapted from Department of Justice, Office of the Attorney General, 1991.

1. Review current policies for admission to programs, registration procedures, health information forms, and other documents to guarantee that the language in the forms or admission requirements do not discriminate in any way.
2. Review the training program for new employees. Disseminate information regarding nondiscriminatory language, procedures, and ways to assist individuals with disabilities in a respectful manner.
3. Develop resources in the community and on staff for using communication aids, sign language, and lifts and for assisting with wheelchairs and transfers. Keep names and phone numbers of advocates in the community as well as interpreters for people who are deaf in a convenient location. Call on these resources immediately in the event of communication or physical accessibility issues.
4. Review safety procedures and considerations for individuals with a variety of disabilities and have a "walk- and wheel-through" of your facilities with people who have a variety of disabilities to ensure that your organization has addressed all aspects of safety.

Administrators of aquatic facilities should know what the terms "readily accessible" and "readily achievable" mean in relation to the ADA (see chapter 1). Along with accessibility issues, the committee must address usability, which is the ability of participants with disabilities to participate in the general programs of the facility, not simply to move through the building. To create a high degree of usability, ensure that your program accommodates participants with disabilities by adapting instruction, activities, and equipment and modifying supplies.

Making your program accessible and usable means that you provide individuals with disabilities the aquatic services you offer to individuals without disabilities. Make it your goal to adapt existing programs or create new programs that are as close as possible to regular circumstances in society. Then, ensure that staff members are made aware of the needs of disabled consumers, trained to meet those needs in a personable and respectful manner, and made aware of the need to treat individuals with disabilities as valuable consumers of your organization's services. What else can you do? Work to make the general conditions more usable. For example, keep air and water temperatures adequately warm, offer times to swim that are not overcrowded, and provide appropriate safety and supervision in an environment without attitudes that create barriers. Your efforts will pay off as you create a program more desirable to consumers with disabilities.

Locker Room

The locker room can be a place of great frustration for individuals with disabilities. Factors such as inadequate lighting or combinations on lockers that impede independence for those with arthritis, poor fine motor control, or upper body amputations do not motivate individuals with disabilities to use a facility. Many other factors may inhibit independence as well, including benches cemented into the floor in front of lockers, shower area ledges or lips that limit access for participants in wheelchairs, and lack of braille signs on lockers and entrances and exits. Because this is the first area a participant must conquer in the aquatic experience, it is imperative that your organization adapt its locker rooms to increase independence, safety, and success. Fortunately, since ADA guidelines in relation to physical education, recreation, and aquatics facilities have

been published, it is easier to know exactly what to do (Grosse and Thompson 1993).

Entry and exit doors shall have a minimum clear opening of 32 inches wide with doors opening to 90 degrees, a minimum five-foot-long level clearance in the direction of door swing, and easy-to-open doors needing less than five pounds of pressure to open (Federal Register 1991). Pathways to the locker area should be wide enough for two wheelchairs to pass each other and clear of protruding objects and should not have benches in front of every locker. Adequate room for storage of wheelchairs is necessary if participants transfer out of their chairs into aquatic/shower chairs.

Post braille maps and signs as to shower, locker, bathroom, and pool direction on the wall outside the doors, not on the doors themselves, so that no one gets injured by an opening door while reading the braille. Nonslip floor surfaces are preferable, such as indoor-outdoor carpeting strips or rubberized matting. Handrails are recommended for those ambulatory participants who may have poor balance when their feet or crutches are wet.

Lockers should have handles that are large, thick, and, easy to manipulate. Key or touch pad locks may be easier than combination locks. Locker hooks and shelves should be about 34 inches high. Some horizontal locker space approximately three feet off the ground is a nice addition to conventional vertical lockers (Canadian Red Cross Society 1980).

Hair dryers should be placed at varying heights to enable those in wheelchairs to use them. Soap dispensers and towels should be no more than 34 inches from the floor and mirrors no more than 40 inches from the floor (Grosse and Thompson 1993). A toilet stall must be large enough for transfers, a minimum of 51 inches wide. Showers should have nonskid floors and be void of lips to cross over. A shower bench, handrails, and handheld shower heads are the most convenient features. A stall whose shower head is stationary should be four feet high with the controls about three feet high. Water should be thermostatically controlled by easy-to-turn valves with long handles and brightly colored raised numbers to indicate temperatures around the valve. A seat shower system is commercially available that caregivers and aides can use to help shower an individual who is dependent, without the caregiver getting wet. In addition, this system incorporates water jets attached to a mobile shower seat that surround the participant and can be placed over any water drain (in appendix E, see Hospital Therapy Products, Inc.). Standard shower chairs should also be available for those who want to wheel into the shower or down an in-pool ramp. Wide benches, changing tables (at wheelchair-seat height), or mats should be available for dressing. Overhead heat bulbs and changing areas that are not drafty are a plus.

If your facility cannot provide accessibility, usability, and desirability in the general locker room, it must provide a separate or private area, such as a family changing room, an area in which caregivers of the opposite sex can give assistance to individuals with disabilities.

Pool Area

Unique architectural design can help a multipurpose aquatic facility meet the needs of many diverse groups. Although the uses and purpos-

Figure 6.1 A transfer wall facilitates easy transfer from pool to wheelchair.

es of a pool should drive its design, unfortunately, it is often the dollars budgeted for the project that dictate the size, shape, and amenities. Often aquatic instructors are not included as part of the aquatic facility construction project team and therefore must work with what is there. In this section, we'll describe ideal pool decks, access components of a pool, and the ideal pool itself. For more information regarding planning, design, and construction of a therapeutic pool facility see Dieffenbach (1991).

Pool Deck

A pool deck may be flush with the gutters or several inches higher than the gutters and water. If not flush, it should not be more than 12 inches above the waterline (American Red Cross 1977a) for safe and easy entry. Individuals with disabilities require pool decks that are wide enough and free from clutter in order to accommodate wheelchair storage, additional shower chairs, crutches, transfer equipment, flotation devices, seizure mats, and pedestrian traffic.

At any given time, multiuse facilities have a lot of equipment and supplies on the pool deck, therefore, if you are a pool administrator, consider the following suggestions as a minimum for deck safety. Floors around the pool should be nonslip but nonabrasive. Surfaces should slope down slightly to facilitate drainage (Golland 1981). Decks should be kept clean and safe by banning outdoor shoes on the deck. Consider placing rubberized flow-through safety mat tiles or other sanitary, slip-resistant tiles pieced together over the deck, especially along high traffic areas from shower to pool edge. Mop-on products can create antiskid surfaces on wet areas as well.

The point at which the deck meets the pool edge should have depth markings and contrasting colors and textures. Contrast is especially important if the deck is flush with the gutter system. For pools constructed with a transfer wall, the top surface should be 12 to 15 inches wide, allowing participants to transfer directly from their wheelchairs to the wall and into the pool. In these types of pools, shown in figure 6.1, the wall is raised 17 inches above the deck (NCA 1996), about the height of a wheelchair seat. The deck in this case is below the level of water as accessed by **a dry ramp** or the pool deck may have been dug lower than the ledge. To further enhance pool entry, water level should be as close as possible to the top of the transfer wall.

In addition to clutter problems, narrow decks pose difficulty for individuals with visual and orthopedic mobility concerns who use crutches, canes, walkers, or wheelchairs. Especially at risk are those individuals with neuromuscular disorders that require the use of a power wheelchair or crutches. The anxiety caused by being on a pool deck is enough to elevate already abnormally high muscle tone. Fears of running into an obstacle course or maneuvering through narrow spots on a narrow deck, close to the water's edge, add to the tension. Such trepidation, compounded by poor deck maintenance, could cause an accident, such as an individual inadvertently driving the wheelchair into people, obstacles, or the pool or slipping and falling.

Pool

The pool itself consists of components that deal with entry and exit, the depth, width, and length of the pool, and water temperature and quality.

Entry and Exit. First, your facility must enable participants to make transitions between the pool deck or wheelchair and the water safely, especially for individuals who harbor some anxiety of the water. In addition, individuals with severe cognitive involvement may not recognize that a change from land to water is necessary; thus, you must ensure that such participants are conditioned to enter and exit at the appropriate location. The first objective is to get the individual safely into the water by offering encouragement and clear explanations of what is happening (Boulter 1992; Bradtke 1979). Provide a facility that offers maximal independent entrance, use, and exit for all participants, while drawing as little attention as possible to the process (Osinski 1993). Because of differing abilities among participants, however, your program may require more than one mode for safe and dignified entrances and exits.

A variety of facility designs lend themselves to safe access. Wet ramps, dry ramps, and gradual steps with handrails are examples of built-in methods of transferring into the pool. Dry ramps are constructed into the pool deck outside of the pool, and a wet ramp connects the deck directly to the water. Regardless of which model, the National Center on Accessibility (1996) recommends that a ramp should meet the following specifications:

- Maximum slope of the pool ramp shall be 1:12 (1 inch rise per horizontal foot).
- Minimum clear width of the ramp shall be 36 inches.
- Handrails shall be provided at heights of 16 to 26 inches and 34 to 38 inches on both sides of the ramp.

Wet ramps (figure 6.2) should be located in shallow water away from swimming lanes and have a nonslip, nonabrasive surface that uses color and texture or curbing to indicate the edges (Mace 1993). To use a wet ramp, participants can walk, crawl, scoot, or use a shower chair to gradually enter the water.

Dry ramps (figure 6.3) provide a gradual slope on the outside of an in-ground pool, bringing the pool deck below the water surface. They provide a transfer point for those who use

Figure 6.2 Wet ramp.

wheelchairs and for participants who have trouble bending down to sit on a pool deck or using a ladder or steps.

Avoid inset ladders as much as possible. These ladders, with their steps in the wall of the pool, are difficult to navigate for individuals with poor strength, visual-motor coordination, or balance, those with arthritis or other joint dysfunction, and children. Gradually sloping steps (figure 6.4) are a helpful adaptation for many participants using the pool, including senior citizens. Although used extensively in in-ground backyard pools, sloping steps are rarely built into indoor community pools because they take up almost one lane of space. But you can purchase portable stairs, ramps, and transfer tiers as movable access modes (see equipment section of this chapter).

Shape, Depth, Width, and Length. Pool shape, depth, width, and length should be of primary concern. Multiuse pools will have a variety of structural shapes, such as rectangular, oval, round, square, L-shaped, and Z-shaped. Depths,

Figure 6.3 Dry ramp.

Figure 6.4 Built-in gradual slope stairs.

lengths, and widths vary even more than shapes. Teaching pools generally have about 40 percent shallow water and 60 percent deep, using an evenly sloping bottom. "Slopes in the shallow end should not exceed 1 in. per horizontal foot. A more gradual slope of 1 in. for each 18 or 20 in. horizontal measure is preferred" (American Red Cross 1977a, p. 113). The depth may vary by a sloping floor, by lanes of differing depths, or actual four- to six-inch steps as wide as the entire bottom of the pool up to the five-foot area. Shallow water pools, two to four feet deep, are ideal for teaching children. Pools adapted for individuals with disabilities, in which caregivers and aquatic instructors must provide support, should have a surface area of which two-thirds of the water depth is four and a half feet or less (American Red Cross 1977a). If your pool is less than four and a half feet deep, however, you may need to limit lap swimming and underwater activities.

Movable pool floors and movable bulkheads are other ways to adapt community and therapeutic pools to multiple uses. Movable pool bottoms, often called hydraulic pool floors, can be installed during pool construction or retrofitted in an existing pool. This feature can be installed so it encompasses the entire pool bottom or only a section of the pool floor. The floor is constructed of reinforced concrete with a nonslip tile finish. A section or an entire pool floor can be raised or lowered by hydraulic cylinders to any water depth for instruction. If only a section of the

floor is raised, various safety design factors eliminate the possibility of entrapment, and the movable floor does, indeed, create a multipurpose pool. Since you can position such a floor at various levels, it is an excellent way to accommodate children, individuals of short stature, those who cannot stand, and inexperienced swimmers. Shower chairs can transfer individuals using wheelchairs directly onto the raised floor and lower them directly into the water where the swimmer can swim or float out of the chair (see figure 6.5). When not in use, you can raise the pool floor to deck level, eliminating the risk of reentry into the water, maintaining pool temperature, limiting water evaporation, and converting the pool area into an all-purpose room available for many nonaquatic events.

Although movable floors offer a great deal of flexibility and accommodation, the initial money outlay is large. Movable bulkheads can shrink very large pools into smaller areas to accommodate various group sizes. The distinct separation that bulkheads afford allow you to safely run multiple activities concurrently. See appendix E for sources of movable floors and bulkheads.

Water Quality and Temperature. Water quality is an issue that, like many aquatic instructors, you may take for granted. As you probably know, pool water treatment disinfects the water to control communicable diseases and balances the water's pH to prevent pool scaling and corroded

Figure 6.5 Movable pool floor.

equipment (Edlich et al. 1988). Water disinfection is important to decrease potential communicable diseases, such as rashes, ear infections, and **conjunctivitis**, which the pool environment may increase the risk of. The most commonly used disinfection agents are chlorine, chlorine compounds, bromine, PHMB (poly hexamethylene biguanide), and copper and silver ions, or ozone. Trained staff members must maintain water balance, controlling water mineral concentration to eliminate pool and equipment damage by monitoring water temperature, pH, total alkalinity, calcium hardness, and total dissolved solids (Edlich et al. 1988).

The water quality of a therapeutic pool is the most difficult to maintain. These pools are normally kept between 84 and 94 degrees, which is higher than multipurpose pools. Unfortunately, water temperature above 84 degrees affects mineral balance (calcium) and the amount of disinfectant needed. Many warm-water pools are using bromine or metal ions, as these chemicals dissipate more slowly than chlorine in warm water. See Vest (1994 and 1995) and Westbrook (1992) for more information about various sanitation materials. If you work in a warm-water pool, you should be concerned with water sanitation and quality since body pores open at high water temperatures, making individuals with low or weak immune systems more susceptible to infection (Osinski 1989). In addition, persons infected with human immunodeficiency virus (HIV) may pass this virus into swimming pools or whirlpools, but dilution (even in the absence of a chemical **germicide**) is adequate to kill the pathology of most viruses—the risk of transmission is so miniscule as to be immeasurable (Edlich et al. 1988). Heat and chlorine help destroy HIV, but hepatitis B and C (HBV and HCV) viruses are more durable (Skaros 1993). Avoiding contact with blood or body fluids is the most effective means of protecting yourself from HBV and HCV; adequate chlorine or other sanitizing agents can ensure that HIV and common communicable diseases that cause skin, eye, and ear irritation will not be problems.

You must clean up the pool after a fecal or vomiting accident. Vest states that a pool should be closed for 24 hours so that four six-hour turnovers may go through the filtration system. In addition, staff should remove the fecal or vomit matter from the pool, shock the accident area with chlorine at a level of 20 to 30 parts per million (1995), superchlorinating the water, and

backwash and clean the filters with a chlorine-based solution. Afterwards, staff should neutralize the high chlorine level with sodium thiosulfate (down to 5 ppm), then backwash and clean the filter a second time. Finally, staff should test the water repeatedly over the next few days to watch for bacteria problems.

EQUIPMENT AND SUPPLIES

Proper equipment and supplies are as important for classes serving individuals with disabilities as they are for the general population. "Equipment" refers to items of a relatively fixed nature, such as portable entrance stairs, hydraulic lifts, and tot docks, while "supplies" are those nondurable items that have a limited period of use, such as kickboards and flotation devices (Dauer and Pangrazi 1986). When planning the budget, consider the life span of each piece, keeping in mind that equipment tends to require more maintenance, periodic replacement, and is higher priced. If your aquatics program is to accomplish its objectives, then you must have enough equipment available for individuals with disabilities to dress, enter, participate, and exit the pool in as independent and timely a manner as possible. Moreover, adequate supplies should be available so that participants do not waste instructional time waiting for equipment or supplies.

Six basic reasons to use adapted equipment and supplies in adapted aquatics include the following: (1) entrance and exit requirements, (2) safety, (3) support, (4) propulsion, (5) fitness, and, when it comes to children, (6) motivation (Crawford 1988; Heckathorn 1980). In the following sections, we'll address these six categories as well as equipment storage.

Entrance and Exit Equipment and Supplies

Lifts, portable ramps, stairs, and ladders are the most important items for transferring into and out of the water when no equipment is built into the facility.

Lifts

Lifts often provide the primary means for individuals with severe orthopedic disabilities to access the pool. In addition, those with acute disabilities, such as postsurgical patients, may also find lifts helpful in providing access. Such equipment varies from hydraulic systems (figure 6.6), water-powered systems (figure 6.7), mechanical lifts, and fully automated lifts. Lifts operate by suspending, pivoting, lowering, and raising the participant. Some lift models require a second party to operate, while others can be operated by the participant, resulting in a more independent aquatic experience. The NCA (1996) recommends that pool lifts should be used that facilitate independent usage. Independent usage is most facilitated when hand controls are located at the front edge of the seat, are operational with one hand, do not require tight grasping, and require five pounds or less of force to operate. Lifts require little space and vary in price from several hundred to thousands of dollars. Most require some type of pool deck modification. Many decks, however, have a permanent sleeve with a portable lift (figure 6.8). When using a removable device, the device must remain in place until all participants have exited the pool. When not in place, a sign must be posted instructing potential users on how to ask for assistance with the lift (NCA 1996).

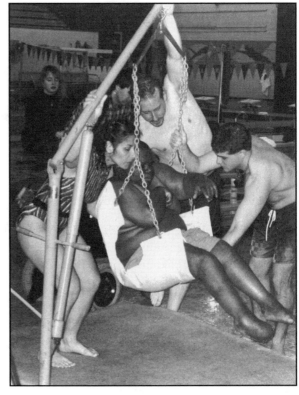

Figure 6.6 Hoyer Lift.

Figure 6.7 Water-powered lift from Aquatic Access.

Figure 6.8 Permanent sleeve for a removable lift is one option for accessability.

Ramps, Stairs, and Ladders

Ramps, stairs, and ladders that are portable are fit to match water depth and deck proportions. Typical materials are stainless steel, PVC, and fiberglass. Figure 6.9 depicts a portable stair that fits flush to the wall and floor in the corner of the pool. These portable steps serve anyone who cannot effectively negotiate a vertical ladder. They should be slip resistant, have a minimum width of 36 inches, and have treads no less than 11 inches deep.

If the pool has a wet ramp, a movable floor, or zero depth entry as the accessible means of entry and exit, an aquatic chair with push rims must be provided. The aquatic chair should measure 17 inches above the deck, be 19 inches wide at the seat, and have foot rests and arm rests that can be moved out of the way (NCA 1996).

Transfer Steps

For individuals who have good upper body use but cannot negotiate stairs or ladders due to lower body involvement, the transfer tier (figure 6.10) can facilitate more independent pool access. Participants transfer from a wheelchair onto the upper step, then lower themselves into the pool step by step. They reverse the process to exit the pool. The transfer tier requires no

Figure 6.9 Portable stairs are easier to use than built-in ladders.

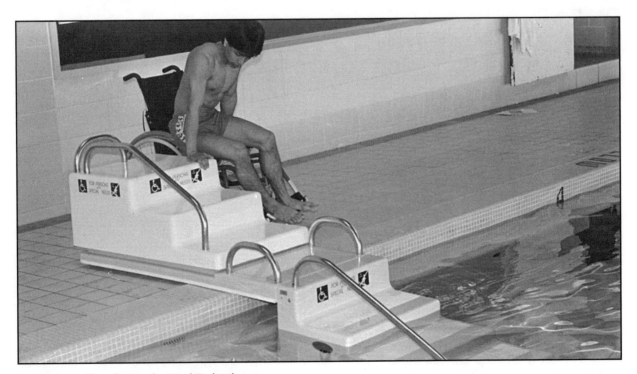

Figure 6.10 Transfer Tier by Triad Technology.

facility renovation, and should feature nonskid tread strips, have no sharp edges, and should be nonabrasive. Clear deck space of 60 x 60 inches should be adjacent to the surface of the transfer steps and the transfer surface should be 17 inches above the deck. The last step into the water should be at least 18 inches below the surface of the water and one handrail should be provided (NCA 1996).

Safety Equipment and Supplies

In addition to typical pool safety equipment and supplies, such as a shepherd's crook or reaching pole, ring buoys, first aid kits, rescue tubes, and backboards, a few gym mats and some water-proof mats might be warranted when individuals with disabilities are patrons. Boosting oneself out of the water with lower body **paralysis** requires an individual to lie face down on the pool deck and drag the lower body over the edge, possibly causing abrasions. Gymnasium mats placed on the deck and slightly overhanging the edge enhance safe transfers (figure 6.11) (Nearing, Johansen, and Vevea 1995). Waterproof aquamats, made of closed-cell foam, are helpful to have around for individuals who are having a seizure or need to rest after one.

Support Equipment and Supplies

A large variety of flotation devices, including PFDs, water wings, pull buoys, wet vests, dumbbell floats, and sectional rafts give you an extra "hand" when you are working with individuals who are dependent on others to stay above the water (see figure 6.12). Flotation devices ensure safety, eliminate fear, provide support, and help participants maintain a level position in the water (Heckathorn 1980). There are flotation devices for head support, especially useful for swimmers with muscular dystrophy; full body flotation devices for swimmers with quadriplegia or severe multiple disabilities; and handheld flotation devices for balance while water-walking. Flotation devices also help keep the ears out of the water for participants with serious ear problems. Specially designed swimsuits by Speedo and other companies provide in-suit inflation bladders to support the swimmer. Because flotation devices help to support, stabilize, and facilitate movement, they may open a new world to individuals with mobility impairments, allowing freedom of movement not possible on land.

While flotation devices are useful, they pose several problems for individuals with disabilities. For example, they may impair independence if swimmers rely on them too long after they

Figure 6.11 A mat placed on the pool deck can alleviate bruises and abrasions during transferring.

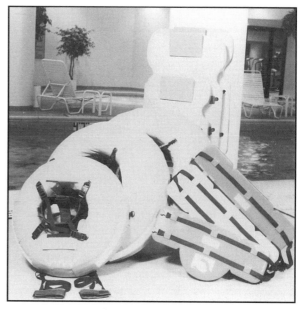

Figure 6.12 Variety of flotation equipment should be maintained for safety, support, propulsion, and fitness.

should have progressed to independent, unaided swimming. Dunn describes more severe problems in the article "PFD's for the Handicapped: A Question of Responsibility" (1981). A research study at the University of Minnesota's Duluth School of Medicine tested **personal flotation devices (PFDs)** on individuals with disabilities and found PFDs difficult to put on and hard to fasten. In addition, they did not help maintain a good surface position due to variations in body buoyancy and density caused by muscle **atrophy**, amputations, and decreased bone density. Researchers found that standard PFDs positioned swimmers with disabilities too far on the back and some did not keep the mouth far enough above the water surface. Unfortunately, however, due to the difference in body types of people with disabilities, it would be very expensive to research this issue, as a tailor-made PFD would have to be made for each person. Therefore, if your participants use flotation devices for support, you must provide proper supervision, even if the PFDs are Coast Guard–approved. The Flotation Suit for the Disabled (not Coast Guard–approved, however) is specially made for the needs of individuals with disabilities. You can add or take off various pieces, depending on flotation needs, body control, and safety issues. "When using floatation aids, most of the flotation must center over the lungs and upper chest, not around the stomach or solely across the back" (Shurte 1981, p. 2; see also discussion of center of buoyancy in chapter 7).

Propulsion Equipment and Supplies

Forward movement in the water is affected by a swimmer's physical ability, body shape, and efficiency of swim stroke (Anderson 1988). The first step to efficient propulsion is to devise flotation or other support to put the body in the most streamlined and balanced position possible. If the participant is still having difficulty with propulsion, try other devices. Thong hand paddles increase surface area of the hands and press against the water for propulsive efficiency as do fins; however, overuse of hand paddles can cause shoulder injuries. **Prosthetics** designed for the water and swim fins that are directly attached to prosthetic sockets can be used by swimmers with lower body amputations (Marano and DeMarco 1984). Those who have part or all of their arms missing may be able to use a

swimming hand prosthesis or Plexiglas paddles attached to the residual stump. For specific ideas for using these devices see Paciorek and Jones (1994) and Summerford (1993).

Fitness Equipment and Supplies

The increase in the number of participants in water fitness classes has increased the number of products available for water fitness training. Underwater treadmills, aquacycles, water workout stations, and aquaexercise steps provide cardiovascular conditioning, muscle toning, and strength training. Water fitness participants also use supportive and resistive equipment and supplies in the water that are handheld, pushed, or pulled, such as finger and hand paddles; balance bar floats; upright flotation vests and wraps; aquashoes; webbed gloves; waterproof ankle and wrist weights; workout fins; buoyancy cuffs; water-ski belts; aquacollars; and water jogging belts (see figure 6.13). Encourage participants to use caution with hand paddles, as they may contribute to shoulder injury if overused or improperly used.

Indeed, companies have developed dozens of pieces of equipment and a variety of supplies over the last few years to facilitate fitness, and many are geared toward water rehabilitation. Peruse equipment and supply catalogs to compare prices and materials (see appendix E).

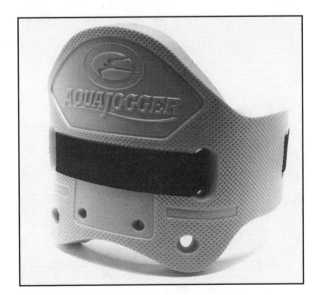

Figure 6.13 AquaJogger.

Motivational Equipment and Supplies

The developmental levels, interests, and attention spans of children require a different approach to aquatic instruction and recreation. Attractive, brightly colored equipment, nontoxic and sturdy supplies, toys, flotation devices, and balls will help you devise instructional strategies that focus on fun. Other devices you might use under close supervision include swim belts, bubbles, and squares, many of which come with modules to increase or decrease flotation. Foam rafts offer kicking fun and relaxation as well as a central place to play in the pool. They are more durable than blow-up rafts and can support more weight. Water logs, also known as water noodles or woggles, are hefty, flexible buoyant logs that encourage water exploration and kicking in a fun way. In addition, hoops, inner tubes, diving rings, sticks, disks, water basketball games, goggles, fins, nose clips, and swim caps are useful (figure 6.14).

The Wet Wrap by D.K. Douglas Co., Inc., is a wet suit vest to wrap around the body for added warmth; it can be used with both adults and children (see appendix E). In multipurpose pools in which the water temperature is less than 85° F, the Wet Wrap and its partner, Wet Pants, are useful for participants with poor internal heat production systems, those with low body fat (as often is the case for individuals with cerebral palsy), and children who don't move enough to keep warm. The Wet Wrap is easy to put on as it does not have to be pulled over the head.

Storage of Equipment and Supplies

You should have sufficient supplies available to safely conduct the adapted aquatics class. Advanced planning by instructors simultaneously using the supplies is critical to instructing without delays and to accounting for equipment at all times. Valuable instruction time is often lost when equipment is in disrepair, sud-

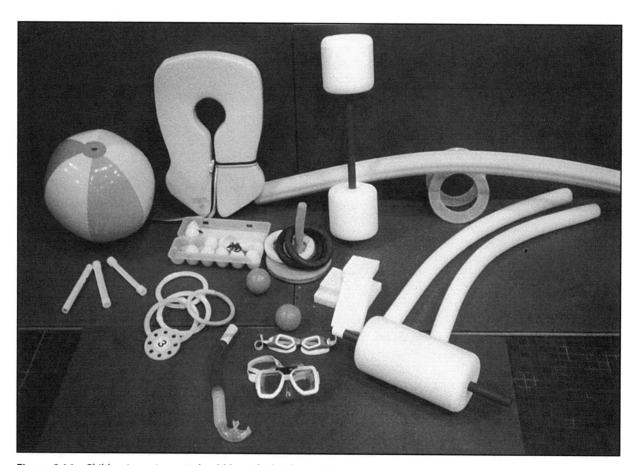

Figure 6.14 Children's equipment should be safe, bright, and have many uses.

denly borrowed by another instructor, or lost in storage.

To prevent these problems, ensure that all equipment and supplies are marked and remarked at regular intervals with an indelible marker. Maintain an accurate inventory of all equipment and supplies in storage and make it available to every instructor. Still, expect a reasonable turnover of equipment, reflecting this in replacement schedules. Restrict use of such equipment to classes and organized recreation programs, avoiding the damage and loss that inevitably result from use in open recreation and outside group activities.

Establish a system for storage, repair, and issuing of equipment and supplies. Label shelves and bins and ensure appropriate ventilation to prevent mildewing. Insist that all instructors and participants accept responsibility for the care and storage of equipment.

Finally, designate an additional area for storage of wheelchairs, crutches, canes, braces, and the like during class times. This will keep the deck free of objects that may further impair the mobility of participants.

SUMMARY

Although the most important aspect of your adapted aquatics program is your knowledge, skills, and attitudes, facilities, equipment, supplies, and storage play a critical role in the comfort, safety, support, and, ultimately, the achievements of your participants. Fortunately, physical barriers to participation in aquatic programs of individuals with disabilities are disappearing as technology develops to better assist and support individual needs. As these barriers disappear and adapted facilities, equipment, and supplies become more widely available, individuals with disabilities are afforded more opportunities to participate with individuals without disabilities. If your program uses equipment and supplies appropriately and wisely and modifies existing facilities, your program will help participants with disabilities make transitions to more natural recreational settings, such as community pools, lakes, oceans, and regular aquatic instructional programs.

CHAPTER 6 REVIEW

1. What architectural issues should your program consider in regard to accessing the exterior of an aquatics facility?

2. What factors should your program address in the locker room for individuals with disabilities?

3. Why would individuals with disabilities and weak immune systems be more susceptible to infections in high water temperatures?

4. What pool procedures should you follow after fecal or vomiting incidents?

5. Discuss the six basic reasons for using adapted equipment and supplies in adapted aquatics programs.

6. Differentiate between "equipment" and "supplies" and state the replacement philosophy for each category.

≋ Part II ≋

FACILITATING INSTRUCTION

PREREQUISITES TO SAFE, SUCCESSFUL, AND REWARDING PROGRAMS

As the leader of an adapted aquatics program, you play a pivotal role in its overall success. In this chapter, we will focus on the essential knowledge and skill competencies that are necessary for conducting programs in which individuals with disabilities learn to feel safe, comfortable, and confident.

The most important skill—and the foundation on which all progress rests—is the ability to communicate. You must know how to connect mentally, physically, and emotionally with participants in order to develop relationships based on trust. For example, the first opportunity to establish trust and rapport may occur when you assist a participant with undressing and toileting. Knowing how to respectfully approach and assist an individual who is struggling with a urine bag, for example, may make the difference between the individual feeling relaxed enough to participate in, rather than watch, the first session.

In addition to communication skills, you must have a thorough understanding of proper participant positioning, guiding, and supporting. Indeed, the art and science of assisting participants during all parts of the aquatic experience are crucial to the learning process and to building confidence. Participants will expect you to give understandable instructions and to provide assistance whenever needed in order to correctly perform the activity or skill. Thus, you must understand hydrodynamic principles in order to appropriately give feedback.

Other fundamentals that are essential in developing successful programs are those regarding participant safety, personal care, and behavior management. It is vital that you be well-trained in each of these areas in order to provide individuals with disabilities the individualized care they require in a safe, secure environment.

ESSENTIAL COMMUNICATION SKILLS

Moving a lesson from paper to pool requires you to interact with the participants and the environment. Interactive skills are especially important when providing aquatic instruction to individuals with disabilities. Awareness of the needs of each individual along with a "no pity" attitude provides the basis for a relationship.

While instructor-participant interaction does not solely deal with verbal communication, words, voice inflection, and tone can greatly enhance or detract from interaction. How do you know if you are using an appropriate approach? Have someone observe you to answer the following questions: Do you use phrases or sentences that are geared below the participants' mental or social ages due to low expectations of individuals with disabilities? Are you aware of other group interactions? If a participant needs constant redirection, can you attend to two events simultaneously? Do you interact with all participants irrespective of disability with the same intensity and motivation? Do you provide an emotionally safe group atmosphere in which you discourage teasing, flippant remarks, and subtle derogatory behavior? Do you encourage the individual with a disability to contribute?

We all send verbal and nonverbal messages through oral, signed, or written language as well as body language, gestures, and facial expressions. Of course, some forms of communication are more effective and positive than others. Effective communication skills are important for safety, learning, and enjoyment. Establishing excellent communication with participants and significant others is important from the very first meeting. Overcoming communication barriers facilitates safe, effective, and relevant aquatic experiences for all involved.

Each aquatic instructor has a unique, distinctive manner in which he or she seeks harmony with a group. When you can pinpoint your own interactive repertoire, you can begin to make changes in your techniques. If participants with disabilities do not receive an opportunity to respond to questions and challenges or to have adequate practice opportunities, they will not take risks to venture beyond their current repertoire of skills, limiting growth of their aquatic skills. So talk frequently to the participants and significant others to become comfortable with each individual's interactive limita-

tions and to learn how to create more positive interactions. In addition to positive interaction skills, implement all the elements of effective instruction in order to make the aquatic session safe, effective, and relevant for an individual with diverse learning needs and abilities.

Establishing Initial Communication

Beginning with the first meeting, never underestimate the importance of effective communication between you and an individual with a disability. Any activity that permits shared planning can promote communication building. Begin by discussing the program, learning about the participant, and going over what you should expect from each other. Foster a strong relationship right from the start by working together as equals to plan a program. If the participant is too young or has a cognitive impairment that limits the ability to plan for the future, then invite significant others to help plan.

Becoming Comfortable With Equipment

To begin developing a positive relationship, become familiar and comfortable with all of the appliances and equipment used by the participant. Clumsily transferring a participant at the first meeting, for example, will not get your relationship off to a good start. Therefore, practice procedures and familiarize yourself with transfers, braces, lifts, ostomy bags, and so on, well in advance of the initial pool session. Naturally, such efforts will lead to more comfortable interactions during initial swim sessions.

Overcoming Hesitation

Initially, an individual with a disability may be hesitant to communicate with you. Lack of aquatic experiences, fear of failure, newness of disability, or apprehension caused by new people and places can all hinder communication initially. To overcome a participant's hesitancy, make him feel welcome. Walk or wheel around the pool area, pointing out interesting people and features of the pool facility. Introduce him to others, show how the lift works, and point out participants who have been successful. Let him chat with one of the program participants who is upbeat; this is a great motivator.

Answering Questions

Be patient with questions that a participant or caregiver has. Give out a typed program information sheet with answers to commonly asked questions. Provide phone numbers of others in the program as well as the pool office and your contact number. Have a pen or pencil handy with a clipboard for the person or caregiver to jot down additional information of interest on your information sheet. If the person cannot use her hands to write or has a poor memory, take a portable cassette player to record the initial tour and orientation with important information so she may review your introduction at a later date.

Showing Respect

No matter how severely physically or mentally disabled the participant is, shake or touch the participant's hand in greeting. Come down to the physical level of the participant and talk directly with the participant, not the caregiver. Speak loud enough for the caregiver to hear but direct conversations to the participant. Stand close to the participant and offer help if necessary during the tour and discussion. Remember, too, that nonverbal language is as important as verbal. Standing far away with hands on hips or arms crossed during a discussion may alienate the participant. Standing over someone in a wheelchair and looking down might convey the nonverbal message that the participant is inferior.

Empowering the Participant

Always remember that each participant is a person—not a disability. Look for ways to empower each individual. After giving the tour, answering questions, and discussing goals, activities, and skills that you should assess, offer a chance to swim. Some individuals may be comfortable getting into the water at this point while some may need to observe a few sessions before actually getting into the water. Be patient; keep in mind that many individuals have not been swimming in a long time and a few may never have been in a pool. Fear of water or of failure, or inability to control oneself in this new environment may make an individual reluctant or even resistant. Respectfully acknowledge these natural emotions and allow the participant to decide when he is ready to enter the water.

In a further attempt to empower a new participant, consider requesting that the participant come to the first or second meeting with a prioritized list of aquatic activities she would like to accomplish. While assessment may dictate that you modify this list, the participant will feel more at ease during assessment, knowing she will be doing some activities she has chosen.

Developing Trust and Rapport

As you show respect for the individual with disabilities, you will begin to develop trust and rapport that should, with careful attention on your part, continue throughout the life of the relationship. Growth in trust and rapport depends on honesty, commitment, and integrity. Therefore, be honest about your experience and abilities in adapting aquatic activities, be committed to the client and the program even when difficulties arise, and demonstrate integrity by following through on decisions and promises. In addition, foster trust by being sensitive in your use of language. Language that is "people first" and up-to-date has a positive impact on rapport. For example, using phrases such as "individuals with cerebral palsy," instead of "those CPs," and "people with disabilities," rather than "handicapped people," shows sensitivity toward participants.

Proper methods of transferring, touching, and supporting participants in the locker room, on the pool deck, and in the pool will also help to develop relationships based on trust. Asking participants or caregivers about successful methods of assisting, rather than just assuming one way is best, can help the participant and caregiver feel in control of the situation. Knowing how to use and work all the adapted equipment, wheelchairs, and flotation devices provides an atmosphere of efficiency and safety that makes everyone feel comfortable. Likewise, holding someone with a firm and balanced grip, as close as safety and comfort allow, communicates care and establishes trust and rapport. For more specific information on positioning and holding, see related sections later in this chapter.

Strategies for Overcoming Communication Barriers

Just as an individual's aquatic skills may vary, so too will the ability to communicate. So, in addition to aquatic assessment, to be effective, you must be able to assess an individual's communication abilities and respond to each person at the appropriate level. Difficulties in communicating may stem from oral muscle dysfunction, scarring from traumatic injuries, mental retardation or other cognitive impairment, and damage to the brain in the areas governing emotion or language. Common deficiencies in speech and language may include apraxia (problems with motor planning of speech), expressive and receptive **aphasia** (impairment of ability to express or interpret language), dysarthria (poor ability to articulate), and problems with tone, inflection, and volume. Participants who have sustained facial injuries, traumatic brain injury, or stroke or who have been diagnosed with pervasive developmental disabilities or severe mental retardation may be unable to speak or affect facial expressions at all. Since facial expressions and intonation are significant elements of communication, it may be difficult for you to determine if such a participant is calm, anxious, fearful, happy, or unhappy.

You can overcome some of these communication barriers by carefully observing participants to determine their preferred method of communication, helping you develop specific strategies for adapting communication in the pool. In addition, ask participants to repeat anything that they say that you don't understand and ask others who spend more time with them to help translate. Some people use hand gestures, pointing, word or letter boards, eye movements, and speech to let others know what they want or need. Alternatives to speech and facial expressions as communication may be necessary, however. Adapt alternative strategies for overcoming barriers to meet the needs of each individual. Use the following list to help you get started.

STRATEGIES FOR OVERCOMING COMMUNICATION BARRIERS

- Give thumbs up or down for "yes" or "no."
- Hang laminated word or letter boards from pool edge.
- Place chalk and small slate near pool edge.
- Use sign language.
- Enhance communication by being patient.
- Have caregiver or significant other stay nearby for translating.
- Never say you understand if you don't.
- Share your goals and plans with the participant, using a simple format with the severely disabled (Lepore 1991).

Good communication enhances safety. You will know, for example, when a participant is cold, uncomfortable, or in pain. Communication with professionals and significant others will help you avoid contraindicated activities and medical emergencies. Significant others may reveal information about behavioral and physical problems that might be potentially dangerous and may share **behavior modification** programs, increasing your effectiveness as a teacher by increasing consistency. So work hard to overcome communication barriers to create an individualized program that is more relevant to and safe for the participant.

TRANSFERRING TECHNIQUES

A transfer is the moving of a participant from one surface to another or from one object to another by means of a specified pattern of safe and efficient movements. Transfer activities include movements from the wheelchair to the pool deck, lifts or hoists, toilet, shower chair, and vice versa. The Americans With Disabilities Act mandates that using manual transfers as the sole means of providing access is unacceptable. However, manual transfers may be appropriate alternatives to accommodate participant preferences or comfort and to implement emergency procedures. In addition, safety concerns, appropriate physical support, and specific functional abilities of the participant may also warrant using manual transfers.

General Rules of Transfer

Transferring in and out of a manual or electric wheelchair is potentially dangerous and therefore requires the maximum efforts of all involved. Safety of the participant and lifters is paramount, and proper use of body mechanics will reduce the possibility of injury. In addition, keep in mind that individuals with disabilities represent an extremely heterogeneous group; therefore, no one generic transfer technique can accommodate all participants and settings. You must properly assess the participant and the environment in light of up-to-date knowledge of transferring techniques and of disabilities. Thus, before undertaking a transfer, analyze the answers to the following questions:

1. Can you teach the participant to transfer independently?
2. Can the participant explain how to perform the transfer?
3. Have you discussed with the participant and caregivers how the participant will help and cooperate?
4. If the participant requires assistance, are competent aides available?
5. Have you informed the aides of their roles and designated who is in charge?
6. Do the aides understand their roles and the group goal?
7. What will be done, and what is the easiest method?
8. What equipment does the participant need and have you checked it for proper function and safety?
9. Is the transfer area set up and have obstacles been removed?
10. Are hands positioned on the participant and equipment properly?

Ask the participant to explain his preferred method or explain the steps required to execute a transfer to a participant, ensuring that he or she understands your expectations. Use commands and counts to synchronize the actions of all participants in the transfer. When the assistance of more than one person is required for the transfer, designate one lifter to give commands. This "head lifter" should explain how the count will be given, for example, "I will count to three and then give the command to lift. When I say lift, we will lift. One, two, three, lift." The lifter giving the commands should always check visually and verbally to ensure that all individuals are ready before the team attempts the transfer. Once the transfer seems to be complete, the head lifter should make sure that the participant is positioned correctly and is comfortable and that all lifters are ready to relinquish their holds.

Basic Body Mechanics

Good body mechanics are essential to performing a task efficiently and safely. The following principles and techniques from Rantz and Courtial (1981) will help promote good body mechanics:

- When lifting and carrying, keep the load close to your body and well-balanced.
- Carry your load at a comfortable height.
- Use your legs and hips for lifting.
- Keep your back straight when working and lifting.
- If possible, roll, drag, push, or pull rather than lift.
- Avoid twisting the trunk of your body when lifting and carrying.
- Plan your actions to best use the leverage provided by your trunk and legs.
- Stand with one foot forward to give a wider base of support.
- Remove any parts that will hinder the transfer, such as armrests, footrests, or abduction pommel.
- Unfasten the participant's seat belt and any other safety straps (e.g. chest straps, foot straps).

Dependent Transfers

Transfers requiring minimal, or no active, participation by the participant are called dependent transfers. Dependent transfers include the two-person standard lift, the two-person through-arm lift (the most dependent transfers), the standing pivot transfer, and the sliding board transfer (less dependent transfers). (See also dependent transfers using a mechanical lift later in this chapter.)

If the participant has limited mobility or is very large, you'll need a minimum of two people for a safe transfer. Participants who have some upper or lower body strength may be willing to assist in the transfer in some way. When this is the case, the standing pivot transfer and the sliding board transfer may be the most successful. The sliding board transfer is also useful in situations in which the individual is too large for the lifters to move safely. When appropriate, make it your goal to gradually reduce the assistance the participant needs until she can perform the transfer as independently as possible.

Two-Person Standard Lift—Wheelchair to Pool Deck (see figures 7.1 a-h)

1. Ask participant about preferences or explain transfer procedure to participant (figure 7.1a).

2. Position wheelchair parallel or at slight angle to transfer spot.

3. Lock brakes on wheelchair.

4. Remove footrests and armrests and place under wheelchair.

5. Lifter 1 (primary/head lifter) and lifter 2 stand on each side of participant, facing each other with feet apart, knees bent, backs straight, and heads erect (figure 7.1b).

6. Participant places one arm around each lifter's upper back.

7. Lifters place one arm under participant's thighs as close to hips as possible.

8. Lifters grasp each other's hands by one of the following methods: (a) single-wrist grip; (b) double-wrist grip; (c) finger grip; or (d) double-hand grip (for individuals with good upper body control).

9. If either single-wrist or finger grip is used, other hand should support participant's back, shoulders, or neck.

10. On command of lifter 1 (head lifter), the lifters straighten their knees and hips (using leg muscles, not back) and then move participant toward transfer spot (figure 7.1 c-d).

11. Lifters carefully lower participant to deck, contacting participant's buttocks squarely on deck, legs parallel to water (figure 7.1e).

12. Lifter 1 continues providing trunk support (figure 7.1f).

13. Lifter 2 enters water and moves participant's legs around so they are hanging over pool edge from the knees.

14. Lifter 2 reaches up, supports participant under shoulders, and lifts participant into water, while lifter 1 prevents head lag (figure 7.1g).

15. Lifter 2 sits participant on lifter's thighs or lays participant on back (figure 7.1h).

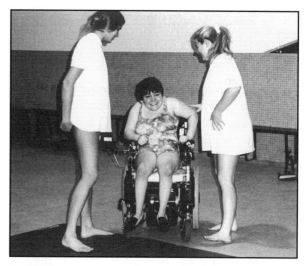

Figure 7.1a Two-person standard lift. Discuss transfer with participant.

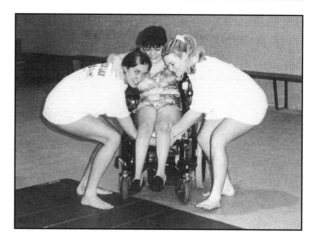

Figure 7.1b Emphasize correct body position of participant and lifters.

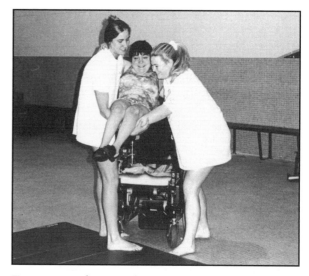

Figure 7.1c Lifters stand in unison using verbal count.

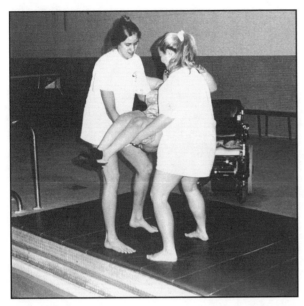

Figure 7.1d Verbally communicate to initiate movement.

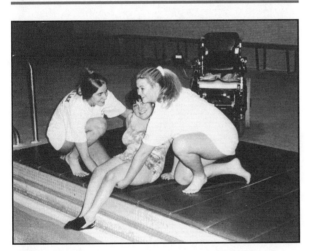

Figure 7.1e Use legs when lowering participant.

Figure 7.1f Continue trunk support.

Figure 7.1g Support participant under arms.

Figure 7.1h Balance participant on lifter's thighs.

Two-Person Through-Arm Lift—Wheelchair to Pool Deck (see figures 7.2 a-d)

1. Begin with steps 1 through 4, as presented in the previous lift.

5. Lifter 1 stands behind, while lifter 2 stands beside participant, facing the transfer spot.

6. Lifter 1 asks participant to sit upright and cross arms in front of trunk.

7. Lifter 1 reaches under participant's arms and grasps opposite wrists (left on right and right on left) (figure 7.2a).

8. Lifter 1 then places one foot on either side of wheelchair's rear wheel, and leans around vertical back frame of wheelchair (figure 7.2b).

9. Lifter 2 places arms under the participant's thighs and calves for support (Turner 1987).

10. On command of lifter 1 (head lifter), lifters lift and move participant to transfer spot (figure 7.2c).

11. Continue steps 11 through 15, as in previous lift (figure 7.2d).

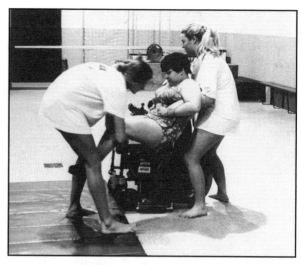

Figure 7.2b Position participant.

Figure 7.2c Verbally communicate and initiate movement.

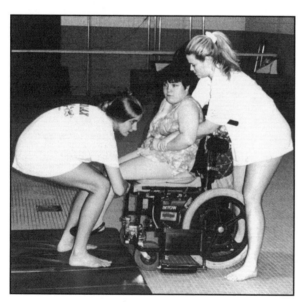

Figure 7.2a Two-person through arm lift. Discuss transfer with participant.

Figure 7.2d Continue sitting support during transition to pool.

Two-Person Through-Arm Lift—Pool Deck to Wheelchair

1. Begin with steps 1 through 4, as in previous lifts.

5. Lifter 1 asks participant to sit upright and cross arms in front of trunk.

6. Lifter 1 (head lifter) squats behind, while lifter 2 squats beside participant, facing the wheelchair.

7. Lifter 1 reaches under participant's arms and grasps opposite wrists (left on right and right on left).

8. Lifter 2 places one hand under the participant's thighs and calves for support.

9. On command of lifter 1, lift participant (using leg muscles, not back) to a height that will clear all parts of wheelchair.

10. Lifters move toward wheelchair and stop once the participant is centered over wheelchair seat.

11. Lifter 2 gently pulls participant away from the back of the wheelchair to clear the vertical wheelchair back.

12. Lifters place participant in wheelchair chair.

13. Lifter 1 could lean participant forward to check spine for red marks or lesions.

14. Lifter should provide towel for warmth, secure seatbelt, and straighten clothing.

15. Lifter never releases contact with participant until balance is secured.

16. Return armrests, footrests, and feet to appropriate positions.

Standing Pivot Transfer (see figures 7.3 a-d)

1. Repeat steps 1 through 4 from previous lifts.

5. Stand in front of participant.

6. Move buttocks of participant forward in wheelchair to facilitate clearing the wheelchair's wheel.

7. Place feet and knees outside the participant's feet and knees while maintaining a comfortable base of support.

8. Stand in a semicrouched position in front of the participant.

9. Place one hand at base of neck if neck support is required and other hand around trunk. Or place both arms around rib cage or waist of participant and lock both hands (figure 7.3a).

10. Synchronize forward and backward rocking motion with participant during count of three.

11. Lean back, straighten legs, and lift participant from chair on count of three (figure 7.3b).

12. Lift only as high as necessary to clear wheel.

13. Pivot toward transfer target, rotating participant toward target (figure 7.3c).

14. Lower participant into sitting position (figure 7.3d).

15. Lifter never releases contact with participant until balance is secured.

16. Have another aide remove wheelchair and components from transfer area.

Figure 7.3a Standing pivot transfer. Position lifter and participant.

Figure 7.3b Lifter supports participant.

Figure 7.3c Comminicate, initiate movement, and rotate toward target.

Figure 7.3d Slowly lower participant, while maintaining balance.

Sliding Board Transfer (see figures 7.4 a-d)

This is to be used when the individual has good trunk and upper body control, but cannot perform an independent transfer, and/or wants to transfer to a spot level with the wheelchair.

1. Follow steps 1 through 3 from previous transfers.
4. Remove footrests and place under wheelchair (figure 7.4a).
5. Ask and help participant to move to front of chair.
6. Remove armrest on transfer side and place under wheelchair.
7. Ask and help participant to lean away from sliding board so that hip and buttock on side of transfer are raised (figure 7.4b).
8. Place sliding board under raised hip and buttock.
9. Ask and help participant to place fist or place palm flat on the sliding board and place other hand on armrest or seat (figure 7.4c).
10. Ask and help participant to perform transfer by performing a series of push-ups, lifting or sliding body while straightening arms and depressing shoulders.
11. Wait patiently while participant slowly moves toward target spot.

12. Spot for balance by maintaining contact with participant's shoulders.
13. Remove sliding board once participant reaches target (figure 7.4d).
14. Never release contact with participant until balance is secured.

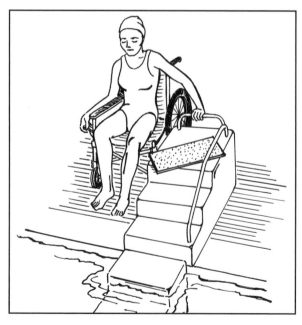

Figure 7.4a Remove wheelchair components and position participant.

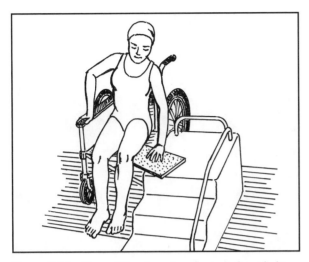

Figure 7.4.b Place sliding board under transfer side hip.

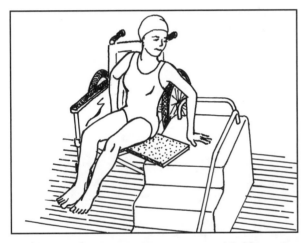

Figure 7.4c Participant initiates movement while lifter spots.

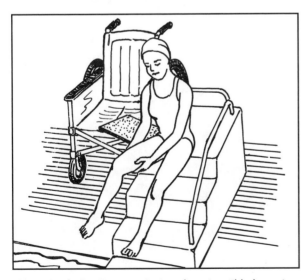

Figure 7.4d Continue contact and spot until balance is secure.

Hydraulic Lift Transfer

1. Repeat steps 1 through 3, as in previous transfers.

4. Remove footrests and armrests and place under wheelchair.

5. Lifter 1 (head lifter) and lifter 2 stand on each side of participant and face each other with feet apart, knees bent, backs straight, and heads erect.

6. Participant places one arm around each lifter's upper back.

7. Lifters place one arm under participant's thighs as close to hips as possible.

8. Lifters grasp each other's hands by one of the following methods: (a) single-wrist grip, (b) double-wrist grip, (c) single-hand finger grip, or (d) double-hand grip (for individuals with good upper body control).

9. If either single-wrist or single-hand finger grip is used, other hand should support participant's back, shoulders, or neck.

10. On command of lifter 1 (head lifter), lifters straighten their knees and hips (using leg muscles not back) and then move participant toward transfer spot.

11. Lifters carefully back participant into lift chair and secure waist belt.

12. Lifter 1 continues providing trunk support.

13. Lifter 2 enters water and reaches up, supporting participant's trunk while lifter 1 activates lift to lower chair and lifts participant's feet so they do not drag on pool deck.

14. Lifter 2 continues supporting trunk while hydraulic lift lowers participant into water.

15. Lifter 2 slides participant into water, sitting participant on lifter's thighs, or lays participant on back.

Sling Hoist Transfer (see figures 7.5 a-d)

1. Repeat steps 1 through 4 in previous lifts.

5. Lifter 1 (head lifter) helps participant stand while lifter 2 places sling in wheelchair seat so participant is safe and comfortable.

6. Lifters should be careful to keep spreader-bar, hooks, and chain attachments with hooks facing away from the participant's flesh (figure 7.5a).

7. Lifters position participant's arms inside of one-piece sling and outside for two- and three-piece slings.

8. Lifter 1 initiates raising the sling seat and swings participant over water (figure 7.5b).

9. Lifter 2 enters water and reaches up, supporting participant while lifter 1 activates the lift to lower the participant (figure 7.5c).

10. Lifter 2 slides participant into water, sitting participant on lifter's thighs, or lays participant on back (figure 7.5d).

Figure 7.5.b Swing participant slowly over water.

Figure 7.5c Lower participant into water with aide waiting.

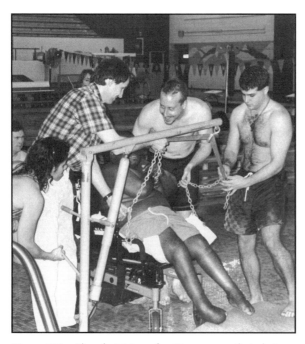

Figure 7.5a Sling hoist transfer. Use care so that chains and spreader bar do not injure participant.

Figure 7.5d Hold participant and detach chains.

Independent Transfers

Independent transfers are those performed as completely as possible by the participant and therefore require the participant to have significant strength, balance, and functional ability. Although these transfer methods may be difficult to learn and require practice to master, they encourage independence, which, in turn, promotes self-esteem. Which transfer should a participant use? Base the answer on (a) participant preference, (b) muscular strength of participant, (c) trunk stability of participant, (d) length of participant's arms, and (e) degree of functional use of hands and arms.

Don't let the participant become discouraged, but rather encourage the participant to continue practicing the chosen transfer. Become highly knowledgeable of the following transfer techniques so that you can help each participant maximize independence, thereby facilitating uncompromised use of community swimming pools during leisure pursuits. Use the following transfer task analyses to direct a participant.

Transfer From Wheelchair to Pool Deck (see figures 7.6 a-f)

1. Instruct participant to position the wheelchair next to transfer spot, not pool edge, and place a mat there for comfort and safety.

2. Instruct participant to lock brakes, or have aide secure wheelchair, and remove footrests.

3. Instruct participant to move buttocks to edge of seat and position feet slightly back.

4. Instruct participant to grasp armrest with one hand or wheelchair seat rail and place the other hand on the floor about where the knees will land (figure 7.6a).

5. Instruct participant to place the other hand on the floor as well (figure 7.6b).

6. Instruct participant to rest on all fours, bearing weight on hands and arms, leaning forward, and preventing knees from contacting the mat too hard (figure 7.6c).

7. Instruct participant to move one hand out to side, controlling hips and lying on the side (figure 7.6d).

8. Instruct participant to swing legs around so they are hanging over pool edge at knees (figure 7.6e).

9. Instruct participant, depending on swimming ability, to either roll onto stomach and slide into shallow water or perform a sitting dive into water of safe depth (figure 7.6f).

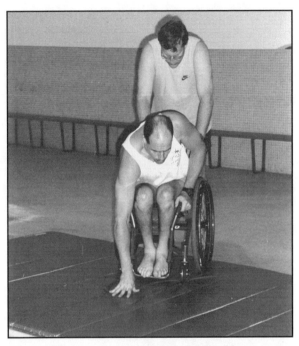

Figure 7.6a Transfer from wheelchair to pool deck. Lifter stabilizes wheelchair and participant positions body.

Figure 7.6b Participant places both hands on mat.

Figure 7.6c Participant lowers self to all fours.

Figure 7.6d Participant moves to side-lying position and uses hand to control legs.

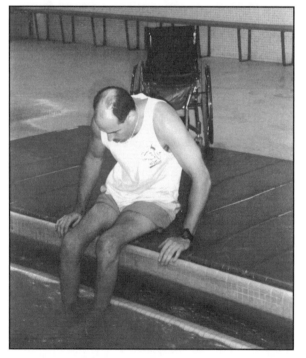

Figure 7.6e Participant swings legs over edge of pool.

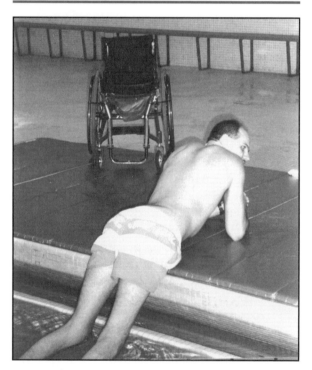

Figure 7.6f Participant enters water from diving or prone position.

Transfer From Wheelchair to Pool Deck Using a Forward Pivot (see figures 7.7 a-c)

1. Repeat steps 1 through 3, as in previous transfer.
4. Instruct participant to place arm on one side on the armrest or wheelchair seat rail.
5. Instruct participant to place the other hand down on the mat far enough out so the hips won't contact wheelchair parts (figure 7.7a).
6. Instruct participant to pivot (lower) hips to pool deck gently, contacting buttocks squarely on the mat (figure 7.7b-c).
7. Repeat steps 7 and 8 from above transfer.

Figure 7.7c Participant slowly lowers buttocks squarely onto mat.

Figure 7.7a Transfer using forward pivot. Lifter stabilizes wheelchair and participant positions body.

Figure 7.7b Participant pivots hips.

Transfer From Pool Deck Into Wheelchair (see figures 7.8 a-c)

1. Instruct aide to position the wheelchair next to transfer spot, not pool edge, and place a mat there for comfort and safety.

2. Instruct aide to remove the seat cushion, reducing height, and to position wheelchair with casters back, lock brakes, remove footrests, and hold wheelchair.

3. Instruct participant to sit sideways, facing the wheelchair. Instruct participant to move up onto knees by pushing up with the hip-leaning side hand (figure 7.8a).

4. Instruct participant to pull and stabilize with other hand on seat by opposite armrest (figure 7.8b).

5. Instruct participant while in kneeling position to rest chest on the seat, while you stabilize hips in kneeling position and, if required, lift at waistband.

6. Instruct participant to place one hand on the lower part of the armrest and one on the upper part of the other armrest.

7. Instruct participant to push down, extending arms, until hips are above wheelchair seat.

8. Instruct participant to not let go or change hand position.

9. Instruct participant to rotate or pivot hips toward the downhill arm (figure 7.8c).

10. Instruct participant to lower self and position self in wheelchair.

Figure 7.8b Participant faces chair in kneeling position and stabilizes wheelchair.

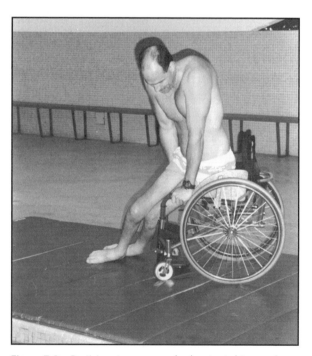

Figure 7.8c Participant presses up body, pivots hips, and positions self in wheelchair.

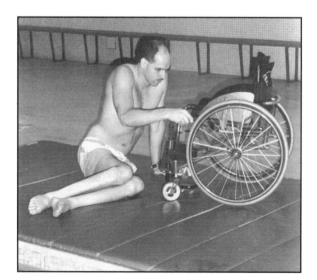

Figure 7.8a Transfer from pool deck to wheelchair. Participant faces wheelchair in side-sitting position.

Transfer From Pool Deck Into Wheelchair With Backward Movement (see figures 7.9 a-b)

1. Repeat steps 1 and 2 from previous transfer.

3. Instruct participant to position back of trunk in front of wheelchair with hips slightly to the side and legs stretched out in front.

4. Instruct participant to cross legs so that the chair-side leg is on the outside or top.

5. Instruct participant to place chair-side arm on the seat next to the armrest and the other hand as close as possible to the hip or to place both hands on the seat if shoulder flexibility allows (figure 7.9a).

6. Instruct participant to lift the hips up into wheelchair to avoid hitting the sacrum or the hips on the wheelchair front assembly or catching under the seat (figure 7.9b).

7. Tell participant that once the hips are in the chair, participant must extend upper body (without excessive pushing on the legs to get up, as dislocation of hip or knee may occur).

Figure 7.9b Participant extends arms, lifting buttocks into wheelchair.

Figure 7.9a Transfer with backward movement. Participant positions body in front of chair.

HYDRODYNAMICS: PROPERTIES OF WATER AND IMPLICATIONS FOR MOVEMENT

In order to develop effective and relevant activities and provide appropriate feedback to individuals in adapted aquatic programs, it is important to understand the basic principles of how the human body is affected by the aquatic environment and the consequences of movement in this medium.

As you already know intuitively, water has several properties that make it a versatile and practical medium in which individuals with disabilities may move more effectively. Water acts upon the body in two different ways at once: buoyant forces, known as upthrust, and gravity, known as downthrust (Reid 1979). When movement in the water creates resistance, the aquatic medium produces a three-dimensional response as no other medium can. You can increase resistance for strengthening and conditioning purposes by simply increasing movement speed and therefore turbulence or you can reduce it for individuals with poor strength simply by decreasing the speed of the movements (Genuario and Vegso 1989; Moran 1979).

Keep specific gravity, buoyancy, hydrostatic pressure, and temperature in mind when designing adapted aquatics programs for individuals who may have atypical body postures and variations in percent body fat and its distribution. A thorough understanding of how water can assist, support, and resist participants' movements will help you more successfully adapt body positions for swim strokes and other aquatic activities.

Specific Gravity

Specific gravity relates to the ability of an object to float or sink. The specific gravity of the water (relative density) is one (1). An object with specific gravity less than one will float, while an object with a specific gravity more than one will sink. As this pertains to the human body, three factors come into play: bone to muscle weight, the amount and distribution of fat, and the depth and expansion of the lungs. In general this means that the more muscle (and density of bones) that a person possesses, the more likely he is to sink. When muscle mass has not developed or has decreased due to atrophy, a higher portion of the body mass may be fat and the person may be more likely to float. The body's center of mass, a point around which its mass is evenly distributed, is usually in the pelvic region. Due to paralysis, atrophy, dystrophy, or bone density irregularities, the weight of each body part and percent body fat and the distribution of fat may cause the center of mass to be different from the norm. The center of buoyancy, the point around which the body's buoyancy is evenly distributed, may be affected not only by structural differences of individuals with disabilities but also by lung irregularities in individuals with asthma, cystic fibrosis, chronic pulmonary obstructive disorders, and other chronic respiratory dysfunction.

Bouyancy: Support and Assistance

It is necessary during the initial water session to carefully determine the floating ability of each individual in various positions (figure 7.10). In the **prone** position, the jellyfish float is an easy test of buoyancy. In chest-deep water, have the individual take a breath, bend forward at her waist, put her head in the water, and flex her knees slightly. Her arms should hang toward the bottom of the pool, her feet slightly off the bottom of the pool, and her back slightly rounded. If the person sinks, the specific gravity is likely to be greater than one, and if a portion of the back remains above the surface, there is a good chance that the individual will float on the back with at least the face out of the water. At this time, you can also check for ability to maintain a stable body position without tipping to one side or another. During floating, the center of mass is below the **center of buoyancy**. Extreme variations to body posture, center of mass, or center of buoyancy may cause an individual to rock to one side, float in a vertical position, or fail to maintain a floating position at all. If a person cannot maintain a balanced position and shifts to one side, you may need to help her adapt strokes so that she will be able to maintain body position during propulsion.

In contrast to those with a specific gravity greater than one, some individuals possess excessive floating potential in the lower extremities, such as those with spina bifida. A person with paralysis or paresis affecting the legs and hip area may have no trouble floating but may

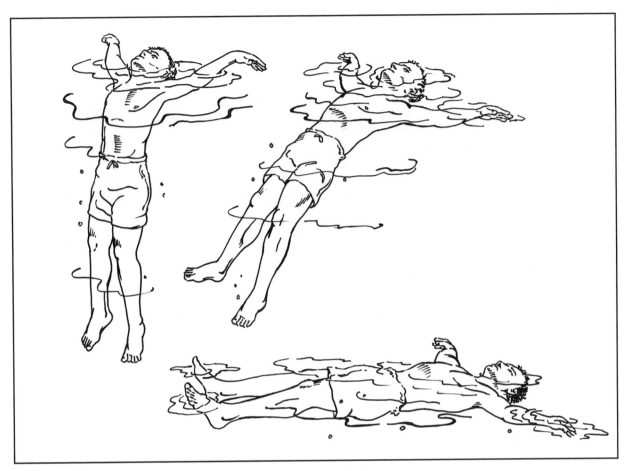

Figure 7.10 Various floating positions of people with varying body density.

not be able to return to a vertical position easily due to excessive buoyancy in the hip and buttock area. Thus, as a safety precaution, remember to observe for ability to recover from floats during initial evaluations.

Buoyancy is the force that exerts upward thrust in the opposite direction to the force of gravity. Thus, the buoyant force assists movement toward the water surface and resists movement away from the surface (Selepak 1994). Buoyancy is explained scientifically by Archimedes' Principle, which states that a body in water is buoyed up by a force equal to the weight of the water displaced (American Red Cross 1992a). When a person enters the water, his body displaces a certain amount of water. When the weight of the water displaced is more than his weight, he will be able to float in the correct positions.

On land a person is greatly affected by gravity, and when moving, balance is around the center of gravity. But in the water, a swimmer must learn to balance around the center of buoyancy, located in the chest area and usually higher than the center of gravity. This may not seriously affect a nondisabled swimmer, but the swimmer with a disability may have adapted her own body balance to fit the needs on land. Thus, such a swimmer will need time to find her own balance in the water. Moreover, flotation devices will require additional adjustments, because, naturally, if the support is not in the right place, it may be more difficult to balance (see also discussion of flotation devices under "Equipment and Supplies" in chapter 6).

The support and assistance buoyancy provides allow an immersed body to overcome most of the effects of gravity (Moran 1979), making it feel lighter in the water. Up to 90 percent of bodyweight is "lost" in the water; therefore, moving the body in ways that may be painful, difficult, or impossible on land becomes possible in the water. As a result of the near weightlessness in the water, the participant can move more freely while controlling stress on weight-bearing joints.

By changing the depth of water the participant is moving through, you can adjust the amount of work the individual does. When a body is submerged to the neck (cervical vertebrae C7), an individual will only bear approximately 8 percent of bodyweight, whereas, when submerged to the xiphisternal line (about chest high), a male bears 28 percent and a female bears 35 percent of bodyweight (Selepak 1994). The percentages increase as more of the body is held out of the water. Differences in body mass distribution and therefore different centers of gravity and buoyancy affect the male and female weight-bearing percentages. Males tend to have a higher percentage of weight in the upper body as opposed to women, who carry most of their weight in the lower body.

When an individual is submerged in water, he can focus energy on functional movements, rather than on carrying or supporting the bodyweight. This allows individuals who usually can't maintain an upright position to walk or stand on their own. Individuals who have difficulty moving body parts against gravity on land may be able to use the effects of buoyancy to move more freely and effectively in the water.

Resistance

In addition to support and assistance, water can provide resistance. Any object that attempts to move through the water will meet with resistance. Some knowledge of form drag and wave drag can help you grade exercise difficulty or improve stroke potential.

Form drag is the resistance that occurs at the front of an object passing through the water and its subsequent resistance as water passes around the object (American Red Cross 1996). As you know, when a person glides through the water, it is more advantageous to present a streamlined position in order to decrease form drag. As the surface area that the water must pass around increases, as in the case of someone with a body part out of alignment, the form drag increases, and the person cannot glide as far. In addition, the less streamlined the person is, the more turbulence her movements create behind her. This water turbulence can impede forward momentum by creating eddies or small whirlpool turbulence, which in turn creates a drag force called wave drag.

Using Buoyancy and Resistance

By using a combination of fast or slow movements, streamlined or nonstreamlined movements, and variation of water depth, you can control the effects of water assistance or resistance. For individuals who are weak, slow streamlined work will be the most manageable. As a person gets stronger, increase resistance for improved muscular strength and endurance by natural turbulence through faster movements and using equipment to increase surface area of the body (e.g., fins or hand paddles) and artificial turbulence, created by you or other people in the pool churning up the water. (See also chapter 12.)

Water Temperature

Another property that affects an individual's ability to perform aquatic activity is water temperature. Variations in water temperature can cause different physiological effects, including changes in heart rate. Cooler water (80°F or less) is recommended for strenuous exercise in the pool. But most individuals who participate in adapted aquatic programs do not participate in strenuous activity that would require a cooler water environment; quite the contrary, most of the participants will need a warm water environment in which to perform to the best of their abilities. In general, water that is 85°F or warmer aids in relaxation, which will facilitate greater freedom of movement. Moreover, it is easier to concentrate on the task at-hand if an individual is comfortable and relaxed. Certainly, it won't matter if buoyancy makes the body parts feel lighter if a person with **spasticity** cannot reap the benefits of water's properties because the water is too cold or the air temperature is cooler than the water! While you will find very few exceptions to this "warmth rule of thumb," keep in mind that evidence has clearly shown that individuals with multiple sclerosis have a negative reaction to warm water due to nerve transmission dysfunction and fatigue following exercise in warm environments (National Multiple Sclerosis Society 1993).

POSITIONING AND SUPPORTING PARTICIPANTS

Once an individual is in the water, you will often need to provide support and assistance to maximize relaxation, learning, and mobility.

Touch, hold, assist (move), and position the participant and his body parts in order to provide a comfortable, safe, and effective learning and performing environment. A respectful and appropriate approach will meet your participants' most basic needs for safety and feeling safe.

Touching Participants

In order for participants with disabilities to feel safe in an aquatic environment, you may need to touch them many times during instruction, practice, and dressing. Use the fundamental skills we'll discuss in this section with individuals who need help with support for safety, learning, practice, and mobility.

The art of touching has many implications in the aquatic environment. Touch has been used as part of the healing process, as a way to channel energy, as the medium for massage, and as a necessity for healthy emotional growth. **"Therapy hands"** is a term that denotes the effective use of touching, supporting, positioning, and handling of people to facilitate greater movement potential (Cratty 1989). Good therapy hands are important, whether or not water is used for therapeutic, recreational, or educational means. Knowing where to place your hands and body so that a participant has the best chance to practice skills is as important as a verbal explanation or visual demonstration. Some individuals will need full support and hands-on, or tactile, teaching in order to accomplish aquatic skills. Individuals who are deaf-blind, quadriplegic, or those with cerebral palsy will most likely need you to manually guide them through skills as well as hold them in the proper positions for executing the skills. This will help these and other participants feel the movement kinesthetically (Cratty 1989).

Tactile teaching is also good for individuals with body image problems and difficulty with proprioceptive input, conditions that result in not knowing where the body is in space. Tactile teaching may have a positive effect on sensory input and give individuals with body awareness problems a channel for learning.

Trust and Abuse

Good touching, holding, and guidance will improve rapport and enable a person to try more difficult skills due to the increased trust felt between you and the swimmer who needs physical cues and emotional and physical support. You should, however, use the lightest and briefest touch that is still effective. For example, you might gently prompt a participant to complete the action. But pulling, tugging, and dragging the participant through various motions does not represent therapeutic touching and handling.

The relationship between participant and instructor or aide is one requiring close physical contact. Because the tactile approach requires close physical contact, participants and their caregivers may be concerned about what constitutes necessary touching and what constitutes abusive or negligent touching. Child abuse, molestation, and other perverse uses of touch have created negative attitudes toward touch in society at-large. Children, young adults, and people who are mentally retarded are cautioned by their parents and caregivers about the dangers of people touching them. Since as an aquatic professional, you are in situations in which you are touching people wearing little clothing, you must directly address this subject with participants, parents, and caregivers. Talk openly with them about the kinds of touching and holding that you will need to use. Demonstrate the specific holds and positions. Encourage caregivers to don their bathing suits and feel what each hold entails. In addition, videotapes of swimmers in past programs are helpful to provide examples of actual touching techniques.

Beyond the concerns raised by fears of abuse, you must take into account the particular conditions and disabilities affecting participants, then observe appropriate cautions to protect both participants and yourself. These may include brittle bones (osteogenesis imperfecta), fragile skin (those with skin lesions, the frail, and the elderly), poor circulation (diabetics and those with paralysis), dislocation and **subluxation** of joints (cerebral palsy, spina bifida), and tactile defensiveness (hypersensitivity to touch such as those with pervasive developmental disabilities). For more specific information about each of these conditions, see chapter 9.

Ultimately, your interest in adequately briefing participants and their caregivers regarding your tactile approach as well as interviewing them regarding relevant medical conditions will demonstrate your respect for each individual in a positive, proactive manner.

Holding Participants

Various ways to successfully hold participants in water are also important fundamental concerns. When a participant is in the **supine** position (see figure 7.11), you can stand behind the swimmer and hold her under the armpits. The swimmer may then rest her head on your forearms. If more support is necessary, you can move closer and slide the whole forearm under the swimmer so that the armpit is in the crux of your elbow. The swimmer may then rest her head on your shoulder. You should be in deep enough water; if not, bend down so that your shoulders are even with the participant's head. If eye contact is necessary while participant is on her back, you can stand next to the swimmer and put one hand under the swimmer's hips and the other under her shoulders, neck, or head, depending upon the level of support needed (see figure 7.12). Although this position may be necessary for individuals with hearing impairment (for lip reading, signing) or for frightened swimmers (for security in seeing you), it limits mobility and freedom because the swimmer cannot move the arm closest to you in this position.

If the participant is lying on her side, its best to support the head, if needed, or under one arm and at the hip from behind. A swimmer, especially an adult, lying prone is hard to support. If necessary, face the swimmer who is prone and support under the chest or armpits (see figure 7.13). A good resource for various holding positions, especially for children, can be found in the American Red Cross manual Infant and Preschool Aquatic Program (American Red Cross 1988).

Assisting Ambulation

Mobility in the water is not limited to swimming positions. Walking is a skill most individuals like to use when talking to others, warming up, or getting from one part of the pool to another. Since participants with disabilities vary in ability to walk, you should devise numerous ways to assist. When walking with a participant who uses a wheelchair for mobility or has a great deal of difficulty walking in the water, place yourself (or an aide) in front facing the participant. Support the participant's rib cage or underarms while the participant's hands rest on your shoulders. If additional help is available, have an aide or another instructor stand behind the participant, giving support at the hips (see figure 7.14). Encourage the person to stand erect.

Participants who use walkers, crutches, or canes will need two-person support only if they have severe posture problems or if they are very frightened. They may only need the support of your hands held out in front of them, an arm to lean on, the use of the pool gutter, or no support at all. Remember, the deeper the water the par-

Figure 7.11 Supine hold from behind.

Figure 7.12 Supine hold to the side allows for eye contact while on back.

ticipant stands in, the more buoyancy will support independent walking.

In contrast, often a participant who is an independent walker on land will have difficulty in the pool due to impaired sense of depth, poor spatial awareness, or frequent seizures and so will also prefer assistance in the pool. In these situations, you, an aide, or a significant other could act as a spotter, providing assistance when necessary. Individuals with cognitive or behavioral disabilities may also need someone in the water with them in order to keep them on-task and to ensure the safety of themselves and others.

The pool deck and the locker room are also places where you need to know various holds, supports, and other assistance positions. Brainstorming with the participant and significant others will help provide viable options for assisting with walking on deck and in the locker room. For example, you may find that when walking on deck with a person who has balance problems, it is better to have one spotter on each side, each with one hand near her waist and one hand supporting her elbow.

Positioning Participants

Not surprisingly, a participant's position during transfers and skill development may affect the participant's ability to perform the skill or be safe in the water. Individuals with physical disabilities

Figure 7.13 The prone hold provides support and face-to-face communication.

Figure 7.14 Assisting ambulation.

who cannot support themselves during explanations and demonstrations need you to be sensitive to the way you are holding them. For example, lying prone with the head held up is not a comfortable way to view demonstrations or any other interaction in the pool. Some individuals need specific positions in order to have more freedom of movement. In particular, individuals with spasticity or abnormal posture and reflexes need special attention to positioning. The most common population with spasticity are those with cerebral palsy, traumatic brain injury, spinal cord injury, multiple sclerosis, or stroke. Individuals with cerebral palsy, traumatic brain injury, or profound mental retardation may also exhibit abnormal reflexes and postures (Harris 1978).

Since inhibition of abnormal reflexes and postures and facilitation of proper body movements are in the realm of **physical therapy (PT)**, it is important that as an aquatic instructor you seek the advice of the participant's physical therapist while setting up a program. You may learn, for example, that placing the participant in a supine position and performing lateral swaying decrease spasticity in a participant. In addition, you may learn that adding a rotational motion at the end of each sway is helpful. (You need two instructors or one instructor and a flotation device near the swimmer's head for this action [Campion 1985].) The physical therapist may also recommend symmetrical activities, which force the participant to use both sides of the body

simultaneously, to promote more normalized muscle tone and more control. So don't hesitate to use the physical therapist as a resource.

As in all swimming, the position of a participant's head may dictate what the rest of the body does. Be aware and facilitate a position that promotes a neutral or slightly tucked chin position with the head aligned with the midline of the rest of the body. This has been shown to facilitate better quality movement.

PARTICIPANT CARE AND SAFETY

Although the participant is most likely concerned about fun, swimming, and fitness, these aspects should never supersede safety issues. You must be aware of and implement fundamental safety procedures from the time that participants enter the locker room until you return them to the care of their families or caregivers.

Locker Room and Shower Area Care

For all staff members, the locker room may be the place where apprehension levels run high as you all confront the task of getting numerous participants with various mental and physical disabilities undressed and into their swim suits, toileted, their clothes organized and stored in lockers, and safely moved to the pool. Two ways to reduce the stress is to prepare for the participants' arrival and to schedule enough time for them to get ready for class. Before participants arrive, be sure the locker room has enough changing space for each person and that it is equipped with changing tables, benches, or mats for those who change in the supine position. In addition, be sure to have adequate supplies of gloves, diapers, wipes, sanitary pads, first aid kits, and cleaning agents.

When participants arrive, make the time spent in the locker room a positive, productive experience that will enhance trust and rapport. Use appropriate verbal and body language to project a professional but low-key attitude to minimize the risk of embarrassing participants or otherwise damaging their self-esteems. Introduce participants to locker room facilities and briefly explain how to use equipment they need. Ensure that everyone has adequate locker space at appropriate levels. Label the lockers of those participants who may be unable to recognize their own clothes.

Because it is often the participant's first and last contact with the facility and its staff, its ambiance, accommodations, and condition will make an important contribution toward the overall aquatic experience; in fact, the locker room can be a determining factor in an individual's return. Many organizations have made changes to implement the requirements of the Americans With Disabilities Act, ensuring that locker rooms are accessible (see chapter 6 for more specific details).

The locker room also presents an opportunity to build confidence and self-esteem through practicing activity of daily living (ADL) skills, such as dressing and personal hygiene in a naturally reinforcing environment. Thus, you should allow participants as much time as possible to get ready on their own. To increase efficiency and success, request that participants arrive in clothing that has uncomplicated closures, such as shoes with Velcro instead of laces. Encourage independence in those who have greater abilities so that you can turn your attention to those who require more assistance.

Dressing

All staff should be ready to offer participants assistance in dressing, undressing, washing, and other matters of personal hygiene. Sometimes assisting individuals with severe disabilities can be a real challenge. Consulting with caregivers, parents, and therapists to learn their "tricks of the trade" may help when working with individuals with multiple disabilities.

Position as comfortably as possible individuals who require assistance or must be completely dressed by you. Whenever the situation allows, place such individuals in a sitting position so that they can see what is happening, as this will help them to feel less frightened and more secure. If the individual's age, disability, or weight won't permit sitting, try a side-lying or supine position. A firm pillow placed under the head will help raise the head and shoulders to inhibit abnormal postures and facilitate movement. Do not, however, place individuals with spasticity and abnormal reflexes in the supine position, as in this position they tend to extend the neck and shoulders back, stiffen the hips and legs, and cross the legs. Finnie (1975), French, Gonzalez, and Tronson-Simpson (1991) suggest the following tips in dressing participants with spasticity or hemiplegia (due to stroke, brain injury, or cerebral palsy):

1. Place clothes within easy reach.
2. When pulling clothing over an individual's head, position his head with his neck flexed and his chin tucked, rather than letting his neck go into extension.
3. Try to keep the individual's head aligned with the midline of his body.
4. Dress the least functional extremity first.
5. Remove clothing from the most functional extremity first when undressing.
6. Do not try to pull the participant's arm though his sleeve by pulling on his fingers, as this will immediately make his elbow bend.
7. Insert his arm into the sleeve as far as you can, then reach into the sleeve and help the individual straighten his arm while pulling up the sleeve.
8. Have participant sit symmetrically either cross-legged, sitting sideways with both legs to one side, or sitting with both legs stretched out front.
9. Bend the participant forward at the hips making it easier to bring his arms forward.
10. If a participant's toes curl as he tries to put on shoes and socks, bend his hip and knee, crossing one leg over the other.

Bathing and Grooming

Encourage showering after pool activity. This is another opportunity to practice an ADL skill, thereby fostering independence. Staff may need to model correct showering behavior as some students are frightened or unaware of a shower. This is also a good time to check each participant's skin for signs of irritation or poor circulation. Report all suspected lesions to the appropriate personnel. To make a shower facility easier and safer to use and to encourage independence, provide a sponge or bath mitt with a soap pocket so the participant can reach with one hand and a terrycloth bathrobe or poncho to keep participant warm and begin the drying process (Hale 1979); see also recommendations in chapter 6.

Urinary and Bowel Management

The care and management of individuals who have impaired urinary or bowel function or both is a concern to participants and instructors alike. Those participants who are incontinent or lack control of defecation may feel anxious and avoid social interaction because they fear the embarrassment of having an accident. You must respectfully assess each individual's needs and respond accordingly.

As with other conditions, the methods for urinary and bowel management depend on the severity of the impairment. For some it will be an issue of bladder and bowel training, which will necessitate reminding them to use the facilities before and after class. Resources by Snell (1987) and Foxx and Azrin (1973) provide excellent suggestions for toilet training individuals with severe disabilities. You need to be part of the team that reinforces responsible behavior in this self-care area. For those individuals who have partial or total loss of bladder and bowel function due to more severe mental or physical disabilities, diapers, protective pants, catheters, and external waste collection devices may be necessary.

Speak privately to the individual and caregivers to become knowledgeable in the care of various types of catheters and external waste collection systems used by your participants. Be sure to ask about what to do if the stoma appears to be inflamed, starts to bleed, or breaks down, and report any abnormalities. Waste collection pouches should be emptied and reattached before entering the pool and after activity as part of the grooming process. Before leaving the locker room be sure that the pouch

is correctly attached to the **stoma** and is watertight. Wear protective gloves whenever you give care that involves exposure to body waste or fluids. Whatever system is employed, be sure to give the participant the privacy and time to attend to her personal needs.

Regardless of the precautions taken, accidents are bound to happen. When they do, remember to respond in a calm, professional manner to preserve the dignity of the individual. Help the participant out of the pool and take him immediately to the locker room to get cleaned up. Follow pool rules to ensure that the pool is properly sanitized for the protection of all participants (see chapter 6).

Safety and Injury Prevention

The aquatic environment introduces a host of potential hazards that may cause accidents or injuries. Adapted aquatics programs have other inherent safety concerns resulting from specific instructor-student interactions, special equipment, skill development, and instructional methodology. In addition, many professionals who conduct recreational, therapeutic, or educational programs are not trained in principles and practices for ensuring the safety of aquatic program participants and personnel. Thus, your program must develop and teach preventive and standardized safety practices for supervision, lifeguarding, program implementation, class organization, and instructional design.

Supervision

The level of swimmer supervision should be specific to the design of the pool, the number of swimmers, the characteristics and abilities of the swimmers, and the types of activities being conducted at the pool. State and municipal regulations may set minimal standards for lifeguarding requirements and facility occupation, but aquatic personnel should not limit the establishment of safety practices to these regulations. Swimmer supervision should include the use of lifeguards as well as instructors, aides, other facility staff, volunteers, and even significant others. Organize these individuals appropriately to maximize safety. An extra set of eyes during peak activity and an extra set of hands to assist a swimmer across a slippery deck can help prevent injuries. Instructor-to-student ratios should reflect the ability to provide a satisfying educational or recreational activity in a safe environment. All program staff should receive a proper orientation to make sure that they understand roles, responsibilities, and duties.

Emergency Plans

Preparation is a key to ensuring safety. Thus, your program should develop emergency action plans for the variety of accidents, injuries, behavioral problems, or other events that may occur. Your program director should document these action plans and discuss them with all staff during orientations and inservices. Lifeguards and ancillary personnel should practice the emergency rescue procedures, including using any equipment needed in a rescue. Swimmers should also practice the appropriate responses to emergencies by participating in safety drills. Such drills might include evacuation procedures or simply moving to other parts of the pool. Don't underestimate the value of preparedness and the need for emergency action plans. Consider, for example, a fire situation in which nine participants must be removed from a pool via a mechanical lift and transported by wheelchairs outside the building.

The arrangement and availability of equipment are critical to emergency preparedness. Identify rescue and first aid equipment specific to the conditions, emergency situations, and swimming population of your pool. A ring buoy is of no use if the swimmers don't have the ability to grasp it, but a rescue tube could be used for swimmers to drape their arms or body across. Foam pads or mats are very appropriate if several of the swimmers are prone to seizures. Of course, equipment should be easily accessible to all trained personnel. Proper orientations and drills will ensure that everyone is prepared.

Rules

Many aquatic facilities have general rules to ensure safety and prevent injuries. However, general rules may not account for the needs of specific groups or activities around which the aquatic program is designed. For example, an individual may need a flotation device that has been prohibited to maintain a stable and safe body position for instructional or recreational swimming. You must establish rules based on the needs of the individuals using the pool, and the purpose and type of program activity. Then you must effectively communicate and enforce these rules.

Posting rules in a visible or common area such as the pool entrance is the usual way to communicate them. However, this method does not ensure that program participants are truly aware of the rules nor that they have understood and learned them. You may need to post rules in alternate forms, such as in pictures, braille, or an audio recording. Reinforce rules through periodic orientations and reviews. Routinely discuss the purposes of the rules as well as what specific behaviors violate the rules with the swimmers.

The key to enforcing rules is consistency. Thus, all program personnel should enforce the rules in the same manner as soon as a rule is broken. Consider explanation, discussion, modeling, and simple role-playing, instead of the usual "time-out" or punishment approach. Keep in mind that the purpose of the rules and correcting individuals when required is to ensure safety, not to assert authority.

Other Basic Safety Principles

You can further improve the safety of any instructional or recreational activity if you adhere to some basic principles. First, always be in positions that permit you and your participants to see and hear each other. Effective class organization and appropriate demonstration and practice formations can also prevent injuries. Before allowing other classes to take place at the same time or in rapid succession, predict and analyze any confusion or hazards that might result from the interaction of various groups and the use of different types of equipment. Facility design, for example, may limit the number of wheelchairs having access around the pool and locker room and people who can fit in the shallow water area during a beginner swimming class.

A consistent regimen is always helpful in maintaining safety because it reduces the discomfort and fear that participants might feel when asked to perform unexpected activities. Provide an overview of activities at the beginning of class and preview the next lesson at the end of class. Be sure that participants understand directions. Follow a standard lesson plan so that participants become accustomed to the sequence of class activities.

Recognize additional, potential safety measures that you may need to implement to protect those with special physical, cognitive, or behavioral needs. The following highlights some difficulties experienced by persons with disabilities and some safety measures you can take to effectively respond.

SAFETY MEASURES

- Slips and falls caused by poor balance and use of canes or crutches.

  Safety Measures: When necessary, provide appropriate support staff for escorting participants. Identify wet or slippery areas. Use broom or squeegee to get rid of puddles. Install rubber matting with drainage capacities. Encourage participants to wear aquashoes or aquasocks. Install grab bars and handrails to and from pool area.

- Injuries and dangers caused by an inability to distinguish water depth.

  Safety Measures: Post signs to indicate deep and shallow ends that include pictures as well as words and numbers. Communicate rules about swimming in areas appropriate to skill level. Verbally remind participants who cannot read.

- Skin lesions from pressure sores prohibiting swimming until healed.

  Safety Measures: Encourage self-examination and instructor assistance to identify sores early. Communicate health rules to participants. Prohibit participants with open sores from participating.

- Visual perception problems causing participants to fall.

  Safety Measures: Paint steps in contrasting colors or paint contrasting color stripe at edge of each step to denote end of step. Use texture strips, such as raised rubber or sand-embedded, on each step to improve footing. Provide spotter at steps.

- Aggressive behaviors.

  Safety Measures: Remind participants of overall pool rules. Provide copies of rules for reinforcement at home, school, or residential facility. Enforce rules and discipline procedures promptly and consistently. Ask caregivers and teachers for suggestions as to what behavior management techniques work with the participant.

- Impulsive behaviors, such as running on deck, diving at the shallow end, or irrational actions.

  Safety Measures: Follow measures used for aggressive behavior. Use appropriate number and quality of trained staff. Collaborate with significant others and professional caregivers as to proper methods of reinforcing correct behavior and decreasing inappropriate behavior (see next section on behavior management).

- Sensory and proprioceptive difficulties.

  Safety Measures: Identify problem areas. Add additional staff as needed during activities that may compromise safety. Consult with occupational therapist about sensory difficulties, asking for suggestions for intervention.

- Inability to follow directions.

  Safety Measures: Present directions in small increments. Remind participants at regular intervals about rules. Use preventive measures and try to project what might happen if the directions are not followed.

Mobility

Once participants are dressed for swimming and have used the restroom, movement to the pool area should follow a preplanned and systemic procedure. Adherence to a few rules can prevent many accidents and increase instructional time (Mori and Masters 1980). Follow these tips to move groups or individuals safely from locker room to pool, and vice versa.

- Assemble students in pairs, lines, or small groups when moving to the pool area.
- Have aides and volunteers walk beside participants, between pool and participants.
- Avoid wet spots and remove all obstacles.
- Do not stop along the way to the pool.
- Once in the pool area, seat all students on assigned mats or bleachers.
- Do not allow engaged motorized wheelchairs within three feet of the pool edge.
- Disengage motors upon arrival at wheelchair storage area or lift.
- After class, never leave the pool area until you have accounted for everyone.
- Always post someone on the pool deck while participants are changing in case someone comes back into the area.

You can use aides and volunteers during locker room activities, travel to the pool area, and aquatic instruction. Beware, however, that in their willingness to help, they frequently carry the slower participants, often more than necessary. In the case of ambulatory students, instruct aides and volunteers to encourage walking or crawling whenever possible. Have them closely monitor students who have a tendency to run.

Seizure Management

Since seizures may be exhibited with increased incidence among individuals with certain disabilities, you and other aquatic personnel should have the skills and knowledge to respond appropriately to such an emergency. As we have discussed, your aquatic facility should have an emergency action plan to guide the actions of personnel.

Some people have many seizures a day but do not require medical treatment. Individual seizure patterns will determine if an occurring seizure is normal or abnormal for a given person. For safety reasons, request a participant who is subject to seizures to list specific information about her medical condition on a medical form. (See "Seizures" in chapter 9 for description of possible seizure behaviors.)

A medical emergency exists if a seizure lasts more than a few minutes or if seizures continue in rapid succession (status epilepticus). Some short seizures may also require medical treatment, such as when the person has never had a seizure, or when seizures recur during the session and are unusual for the individual. Regardless of the type of seizure, always take steps to ensure that the person has an open airway and is protected from physical injury caused by contact with other people or objects or physical restraint. When in doubt, always activate EMS, the emergency medical system.

The following suggestions will help you manage a seizure effectively during and after an incident:

- Time the seizure. Notice what is physically happening to the person. Give this information to caregivers, emergency technicians, and, if appropriate at a later time, the participant.

- Have foam or gym mats available. These cushion hard decks when the person is removed from the pool. Drape mats, towels, or blankets along the pool edge when lifting the individual out of the pool.

- After checking for breathing and heartbeat and, if necessary, starting rescue breathing or CPR, maintain an open airway and make sure help is called. Next survey the person's body for additional injuries, such as bleeding, cuts, and broken bones.

- If necessary, maintain body temperature with blankets or towels.

- Position the person on his side so blood, saliva, or vomit can drain from his mouth.

- After stabilizing the person, let him rest.

- Fill out an incident report, and let caregivers know what happened.

You can receive additional information and training to prepare for and cope with such situations through American Red Cross first aid, CPR, water safety, and lifeguarding courses.

Seizures in the Pool. Although a seizure may be frightening to witness, you and other personnel should be prepared to provide immediate assistance, especially for participants having seizures in the water. The natural qualities of the water provide buoyancy and support during a seizure if the individual is kept away from the pool edge, equipment, and others. The first aid objectives for assisting an individual having a seizure in the pool are to keep the individual's face above the water, to maintain an open airway, and to prevent injury by providing support with a minimal amount of restraint. One position that meets these objectives is to first stand behind the individual's head, low in the water, and place the individual in a supine position. Then support the individual under her armpits and shoulders and head (figure 7.15). This position can also help protect the rescuer from being hit if the individual's arms or head are flailing during a seizure. Remember to provide only the support needed to keep the individual's face out of the water, as unnecessary restraint may cause injury to both individual and rescuer. Do not attempt to remove the individual from the pool until the seizure has subsided. However, do not allow the individual to remain in the pool if the seizure lasts for more than several minutes, continues in rapid succession, if injury or **hypothermia** occurs, or the person needs CPR.

If the individual must be removed from the pool, several rescuers or aides can lift him from the water. You can direct a simple lift by having several rescuers standing on one side of the individual, rolling the individual toward their chests, and laying the individual on a mat or towels on the side of the pool (figure 7.16a-c).

Figure 7.15 Hold for seizure management.

Render first aid for any injuries and contact the emergency medical system, if necessary. The individual's medical or participation form should indicate the exact protocols for care in the event of a seizure. Be familiar with this paperwork before an incident occurs.

Seizures in the Locker Room or on the Pool Deck. The hard surfaces of the locker room floor and the pool deck do not offer the same cushioning effect as the water. Therefore, additional first aid care may be necessary to guard against physical injury that a person may sustain during convulsions. Do not attempt to hold the individual still during convulsions; instead, use gym mats (if available), towels, or blankets to cushion the individual to reduce physical injury. (Ensure that adequate padding is available whether par-

ticipants are known to have seizures or not—emergencies happen and you must be prepared.)

When the Seizure Is Over. An individual may experience a variety of physical and emotional effects once the seizure has subsided. Some individuals seem drowsy or complain of headaches. Others may appear confused or feel uncomfortable, embarrassed, or frightened. At this time it is important to offer the individual psychological first aid. Indeed, emotional support and reassurance are essential components of seizure management, as they reduce anxiety and let the individual know that she is receiving appropriate care. If warranted, take the individual out of the pool to a quiet, comfortable room where recovery can progress. Calmly communicate the individual's health status to other program participants and personnel to allay their concerns. The incident may also provide a teachable moment—an opportunity to discuss seizures and how to be of help when one occurs. However, be sure to maintain the individual's privacy.

ADDRESSING PROBLEM BEHAVIORS

A successful and effective aquatics program should employ appropriate behavior management techniques. Managing an individual's behavior keeps the person on-task, thereby increasing learning time. Managing group behavior prevents injuries, facilitates positive social interaction, and creates an environment in which all participants can learn.

Formal Behavior Modification

As part of an interdisciplinary treatment team, aquatic personnel may be involved in, not originators of, an individual's behavior modification program. Some individuals may be involved in a systematic treatment program to modify or reinforce targeted behaviors. Such a behavior modification program is designed by a professional trained in behavior management and must be consistent with what others (e.g., classroom teachers, therapists, family members) are doing. Consider behavior modification as a treatment intervention in contrast to other, less formal behavior management techniques, which we'll describe in the next section.

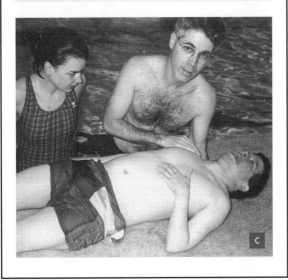

Figure 7.16 Lift for seizure management. Staff stands facing client's side, puts arms under his back and legs (a); roll client toward you, take a step toward the wall (b); place client on mat in pool or on deck (c).

ADDRESSING PROBLEM BEHAVIORS

The following information, taken from Physical Education for the Severely Handicapped (Dunn, Morehouse, and Fredericks 1986), is one model of behavior management and instruction that you can apply directly to the physical activity setting. This model, entitled the Data-Based Gymnasium (DBG) Program, can help you understand the kind of consistency necessary when working with a person who has been brain injured, has mental retardation, or has a behavior disorder.

Example of a Correction Procedure From the DBG Program

- Give verbal cue: "Jim, kick your legs."

  If proper response, give strong positive reinforcement and move on. If improper or no response, give a mild negative statement such as, "No, Jim." Then say, "Watch me," and go to next step.
- Model desired behavior (give visual cue), then give same verbal cue again.

  If proper response, give mild positive reinforcement and move on. If improper or no response, give mild negative statement such as, "No, Jane." Then say, "Let me help you," and go to next step.
- Give verbal cue and physical assistance.

  Give mild positive reinforcement if cooperative. If person is displaying poor behavior, deal with that before correcting motor skill.

Rules for cues:

- Don't repeat cue unless person doesn't hear or see it.
- Give the person time to process the cue before moving on.
- Don't change the wording of a cue.

Rules for applying consequences:

- Each time you give a cue and person makes a response (or makes no response), immediately (within two seconds) let him or her know if response was correct or incorrect.

- Use any form of communication to reinforce (e.g., signing, speaking, body language).
- If you use primary, or tangible, reinforcers, always pair with verbal praise.

In the DBG Program, you identify a behavior to be changed, count its rate of occurrence, and devise a systematic plan of action. Then you put rewards, reinforcement schedules, and, if necessary, punishment into effect. A behavior modification program may be as strict as one positive, tangible reinforcement (food or tokens) for each on-task behavior paired with social praise, to a less strict plan involving a certificate at the end of a four-week session. To be the most effective, the program requires the same consistent treatment in other areas of the swimmer's life.

Aquatic personnel untrained in behavior modification programs may not feel prepared to participate in a treatment program. A few questions to consider before implementing a specific behavior modification program include the following: (1) What behavior will you target? (2) What are the antecedent (preceding) behaviors? and (3) What consequence, in terms of reinforcement or punishment, will you provide following the behavior? Remember, the key to behavior modification is consistency: the participant must learn that the consequences of certain behaviors will always be the same.

Informal Behavior Modification

It may not always be possible to implement a formal behavior modification program when participants exhibit inappropriate behaviors during an aquatic program. But you can intervene in simple and practical ways to encourage more appropriate behaviors. In short, ignore, redirect, reinforce, and when absolutely necessary, remove. Yet, understanding these interventions is much easier than internalizing the attitudes and skills you need to implement them. So we will look at each tool more closely.

Ignoring Inappropriate Behavior

A great deal of patience and compassion is required to ignore behaviors that interrupt the continuity of an aquatic program. But, unfortunately, the alternative is usually to engage in a confrontation, which only aggravates a situation. While it is true you cannot ignore unsafe

behaviors, whenever possible, focus on appropriate or positive behaviors rather than inappropriate or negative behaviors.

Redirecting Inappropriate Behavior

Redirecting involves providing an individual with an alternative to the inappropriate behavior. For example, during a swimming lesson a child might shout and splash with another child in an effort to gain attention. You could intervene by engaging both children in a pleasant conversation while having them hang on to a flotation device and practice kicking across the pool. Explain or demonstrate alternative behaviors that will meet the needs of the participant as well as positively reinforce appropriate behavior. Changing to another activity is another good way to redirect behavior. Sometimes, however, nothing short of direct one-on-one instruction and supervision may be effective in redirecting a child.

Positively Reinforcing Appropriate Behavior

When the participant exhibits an appropriate behavior after being redirected, offer positive reinforcement. Use words, body language, and participation in desired activities. In the preceding example, you could say to the child, "You did a great job kicking across the pool and swimming with the rest of the group and thanks for helping everyone to have a good time by not splashing them." Note that the comment is specific as to what it is praising, as opposed to "Good job!" Stated with a sincere, rather than sarcastic, tone, such a comment helps the child focus on appropriate behaviors and the impact of appropriate behaviors. Make other personnel aware of any specific behaviors you are trying to reinforce with particular participants. Maintain the reinforcement until the participant has internalized the new behavior. Keep in mind that only continuity and consistency maintain a behavior.

Removing a Participant

Behavior disorders, such as hyperactivity, impulsivity, aggression, and withdrawal, can become safety issues if you do not manage related behaviors properly. Sometimes a participant may exhibit a behavior that is so extreme that removal, or time-out, becomes necessary. Removal of a participant becomes necessary for the safety of anyone in the program, including that of the participant being removed, other participants, or instructional personnel. Another reason for removal besides aggressive behavior is when a participant might become so fearful and withdrawn that temporary removal is the only way to calm her. Before removing a participant, however, determine if other options are possible, such as providing direct one-on-one supervision and instruction.

Structuring the Learning Environment

You can structure learning environments so individuals with behavior disorders can safely focus on the tasks at-hand and become more successful in swimming activities and ADL skills. The following suggestions (Lepore 1991) offer some tips for managing various behaviors (see also "Teaching Tips" under related disorders in chapter 9).

Suggestions for Assisting People With Attention Span Difficulties, Restlessness, and Disorientation

- Keep structured swim lessons short (no more than 30 minutes).
- Limit crowds, noise, and other distractions to help decrease time off-task. Keep in mind that some participants can only function in minimal distraction settings.
- If possible, maintain a one-on-one ratio, but you should be able to manage two or three swimmers who are not agitated and do not have severe behavior disorders.
- Try having a participant swim toward the wall or face away from the rest of the pool to improve attention during a lesson.
- Arrange to have lap counters help participant keep track of laps.
- Use kitchen timers to help a person remember about when to leave or how much time he has spent on a task.

Suggestions for Developing the Ability to Self-Monitor

- Teach people how to take their own pulse.
- Use journals, worksheets, or logs so that individuals can see what they have done session to session.
- Ask questions so that they can recall and verbalize their activities and progress.
- Give verbal feedback continuously; this acts as an external monitor, validating the individual's internal experience.

Suggestions for Working With People Who Are Easily Frustrated, Quickly Irritated, or Lack Patience With Themselves and Others

- Use logical progressions of skills during each lesson.
- Build success into every lesson.
- Task-analyze each motor skill, because presenting one small part of the skill will increase success versus the frustration of trying to do the entire skill at once.
- Offer sincere positive reinforcement for each accomplishment.
- Arrange to send the lesson plan to the participant or caregivers a day before swimming class as this practice has alleviated problems with participants who don't deal with changes very well. The extra day helps them to prepare psychologically for a new and often frightening skill. This plan is not for everyone, however! Some individuals might worry about new skills and then not want to come to the session.
- Set the tone for sessions that are free of misunderstandings and therefore free of frustrations by consistently applying rules, following procedures, presenting tasks, and reinforcing or punishing behavior.
- Incorporate five-minute free swims into your sessions as a fun and motivating way to vary structure.
- Keep structured lessons 5 to 30 minutes long, according to the swimmer's attention span.
- Talk with the swimmer's psychologist for a behavior modification program.
- Talk to client while she is exhibiting poor behavior and explain how the behavior is not appropriate.
- Frequent change in activities and provision of contained choices helps to decrease restlessness and increase motivation.

SUMMARY

Review often the fundamental skills we have discussed in this chapter that you must possess in order to provide safe and comfortable aquatic environments. Remember, developing trust and rapport is the first step to establishing a relationship and overcoming communication barriers. Look carefully at your verbal and non-verbal language to ensure you are communicating positive and caring messages. Beyond communication, work on developing positive interactions with participants as you provide hands-on respectful support, positioning, dressing, and hygiene care, and, when necessary, behavior management.

Quality aquatic programs that include participants with disabilities require you to know how to apply hydrodynamic principles, use transfer techniques, provide locker area care, and plan for safety to ensure that you meet the basic needs of participants and their families. With proper communication, a consistent learning environment, and preestablished plans for transferring and assisting participants, your aquatic program will be on its way to meeting the needs of your participants with disabilities.

CHAPTER 7 REVIEW

1. List three examples of nonverbal communication.

2. What may be some barriers to initial communication between you and a participant with a disability?

3. List questions that you must answer before transferring an individual.

4. List general techniques of lifting and transferring safely.

5. What are the types of dependent transfers?

6. List three general guidelines to use when selecting an independent transfer.

7. Compare different types of independent transfers.

8. What does the term "therapy hands" mean?

9. Why is physical contact between instructor and participant an important issue?

10. How can you facilitate independence in the locker room and shower area?

11. What additional safety precautions should you exercise in an aquatics setting for individuals with disabilities?

12. What procedure should you follow if someone has a seizure?

INSTRUCTIONAL
STRATEGIES

A successful aquatics program does more than simply offer individuals with disabilities the chance to learn swimming and water safety skills: It actually teaches those skills. If you have the ability to manipulate variables within various placements, you can provide effective instructor-learner interactions, thereby enabling learning to occur. Understanding the process of learning and factors that affect learning will give you more insight into how to effectively design and deliver instruction—whether you apply these ideas to instruction in general or specifically to adapted aquatics.

Indeed, the acute needs of some participants with disabilities demand that you develop unique strategies, forcing you to examine the processes of learning that may be atypical in some individuals with disabilities so that you can appropriately adapt traditional instructional design and delivery. In this chapter, we will address the issues of teaching and learning you need to understand to appropriately adapt aquatic instruction to individuals with disabilities.

THE PROCESS OF LEARNING

If your approach to teaching reflects knowledge of the general principles of the way people learn, you will be more effective (American Red Cross 1992b). Beyond this, an understanding of the limitations participants with disabilities may bring to your class will help you improve the teaching-learning process (Canadian Red Cross Society 1989).

Theoretically, according to Fitts and Posner (1967), individuals go through three stages of learning new motor skills. The first, or cognitive, stage consists of the participant thinking about what to do before moving. Movements are usually awkward and slow, with many errors. The swimmer enters the second, or associative, stage as he gains more experience. Here, the swimmer has a better understanding of the movement and objectives and spends less time on gross motor aspects. The swimmer tries to associate some part of the aquatic movement with other movements in his repertoire to perform the stroke more automatically and rhythmically.

In the final, or autonomous, stage the swimmer thinks very little of the specific movements, can correct herself when she does not perform the skill well, and is no longer instructor dependent (American Red Cross 1992b). In order to become an efficient swimmer, an individual must move to the autonomous stage. Some individuals with disabilities, however, may never get to this stage for many reasons, including impaired sensory input, memory, organization and interpretation of input, motor planning, motor output, or internal feedback systems.

Physiological Factors That Affect Learning

Aquatic skills do not simply emerge, you must present them and give learners appropriate practice activities to develop them. Acquisition of aquatic skills is based on the learner's readiness to receive the skill, the ability to understand the goal, and the opportunities to practice the skill at a challenging but manageable level and receive feedback. Readiness of the learner takes into account psychological and physiological factors (Auxter, Pyfer, and Huettig 1993). Physiologically, as neurological maturation takes place, the more the participant can learn. Physiological factors are those in which anatomical and physiological variations in an individual's body (figure 8.1) affect how and what a person learns, including (1) how pathology, disease, disuse, or environment impact the body systems' abilities to function and (2) how medications alter function (see table 8.1). You must ascertain a participant's approximate neurological maturity level or you may, for example, spend five days a week for five months teaching rhythmic breathing to the side in coordination with the front crawl arm stroke, but if the individual is not neurologically mature enough to achieve coordination, you have wasted time that you should have devoted to a more developmentally appropriate skill.

Body Systems

Learning motor skills so that they are permanent depends on intact sensory input systems, general functional abilities (such as physical fitness and motor ability), and the acquisition of skills that are motor behaviors specific to a culturally determined form of movement, such as swimming and aquatic skills (Auxter, Pyfer, and Huettig 1993). Many constraints like arthritis affect learning or execution of an aquatic skill.

Other constraints to functional ability may be due to limitations in body structure and function (achondroplasia–short stature), abnormal posture (kyphosis), poor reflex integration (cerebral palsy), abnormalities in muscle structure (muscular dystrophy), amputations, and obesity (Sherrill 1993). Naturally, if one or more body systems are impaired, learning to swim can be quite a challenge.

For example, cardiorespiratory problems, as in asthma or cystic fibrosis, may limit the amount of work that the participant can safely perform in a single session. Joint and bone disorders, such as arthritis, juvenile rheumatoid arthritis, osteogenesis imperfecta, short stature, and lupus, may alter body shape and size. Those with one of these disabilities, as well as individuals with amputations or posture disorders, are at a disadvantage when it comes to propulsion. As we have discussed throughout this book, some individuals require specific water temperature, adapted strokes, and unique aquatic activities. The list of disabilities and unique manifestations and needs of each disability goes on and on.

Simply put, no matter how well you plan your lessons, no matter how creative your instructional strategies, and no matter how powerful your teaching methods, if you do not first assess and then plan for an individual's motor and cognitive capabilities, you're wasting everyone's time and energy. In other words, don't spend instructional time on the breaststroke kick, for example, if the individual has total muscle paralysis and no movement and sensation in the legs!

Medication

In addition to congenital and acquired disabilities, medication can play a positive or negative role in aquatic learning. As a positive measure, drug therapy can produce substantial behavioral changes in individuals with mental illness, emotional and behavioral disabilities, and attention deficit disorders. In children, **stimulants** can actually lessen hyperactivity and improve short-term memory. Unfortunately, you will find that some people are overmedicated; this is especially likely in people who have unstable conditions, who are just beginning drug therapy, or whose body chemistry changes as a result of puberty. Other drug side effects may cause difficulty developing and maintaining physical and motor fitness. In addition, nausea, vomiting, increased appetite, weight loss,

Figure 8.1 Physiological characteristics such as hemiplegia can limit acquisition of aquatic skills.

anemia, visual and hearing disturbances, hyperactivity, fainting, and inability to concentrate are possible side effects of medication.

If an individual uses medication, use the Physicians' Desk Reference (Mehta 1996) to learn about its use, indications, and possible side effects. Discuss with a pharmacist possible behavioral and physical signs caused by the drug and ask caregivers if they have noted any side effects. Use your knowledge of possible side effects to work with the participant and significant others to develop emergency procedures and to adapt fitness swims and activities to meet the needs of the medicated individual.

Not only must you be aware of the possible effects medication may have on learning and aquatic performance, you must also be sensitive to medication timetables, as missing or delaying a dose may significantly alter an individual's behavior. In addition, be sensitive to individuals with disabilities who have an indwelling or intravenous catheter (usually in the arm) through which medications are injected. Avoid placing pressure on such areas and ensure that plastic wrap covers the area during class time. You will find a review of the major drugs used by individuals with disabilities, their side effects, and implications for aquatics in the table at the end of this chapter.

Psychological Factors That Affect Learning

Psychologically, each person is unique and learns at his own rate, depending on a number of psychological factors. As an aquatic instructor you can facilitate change, but the learner controls it (American Red Cross 1992b). Individuals with disabilities may have psychological characteristics that hinder the acquisition of aquatic skills. Some psychological factors, such as anxiety, motivation for learning, cognitive readiness, social ability, and preferred learning modality, are factors to examine before developing instructional strategies.

Anxiety

Anxiety stems from fear and inhibits mental adjustment to the aquatic environment. Although mental adjustment generally takes time for new or frightened swimmers, it may take a greater amount of time when coupled with physical, emotional, or mental disabilities. Individuals with poor breath control due to oral muscle dysfunction or asthma and individuals with high or low muscle tone, limiting the ability to stand or hold the wall, are at a high risk of having fear and anxiety control their openness to learning (see figure 8.2).

Figure 8.2 Fear affects the ability to acquire skills.

Some fears that may cause a swimmer to be anxious include fear of drowning, past frightening water experiences such as inappropriate instructional techniques, submerging unexpectedly and choking on water, fear reinforced by warnings (e.g., "Don't go near that water or you will drown"), capsizing in a boat, being knocked down by a wave, or feelings of insecurity caused by poor physical ability or unfamiliar surroundings. Children sometimes fear that their caregiver will not return for them after class, and those with mobility problems may fear that they will not be able to recover if they slip underwater.

Fear stimulates physiological responses, such as heightened muscle tone, increased involuntary muscle movements, and inability to float. Fear is a powerful emotion that may lead to poor self-respect and insecurity, preventing participation in aquatics (Moran 1961). The following suggestions for eliminating fear from the process of learning to swim come from an article by Moran (1961) on fear and aquatic instruction. In addition to this article, we encourage you to read "Systematic Desensitization of Aquaphobic Persons" by Hicks (1988).

You must help participants get past fear and anxiety in order to practice the skills that will make them water safe. Simply put, when partic-

ipants are free of fear, they are free to learn. So consider implementing a formal or informal fear-reduction program. Use the following tips to help you get started:

- Do not ridicule or exhibit impatience with fearful reactions.
- Use patience without pampering.
- Gently guide, don't force.
- Explain everything in a calm, sympathetic, matter-of-fact voice.
- Progress from step to step gradually.
- Use noncompetitive activities.
- Encourage practice of breath control at home.

Motivation for Learning

Motivation, the ". . . internal state that directs us toward some goal" (Sherrill 1993, p. 62), can be intrinsic or extrinsic. Individuals may participate in aquatic classes for any number of reasons, including to improve skills, achieve personal goals, compete against others, have fun, find excitement, meet a school requirement, make friends, or please significant others. You must seek out the actual reasons that individuals are in your class and help them to set goals accordingly. Beware that when individuals do not choose aquatic participation of their own accord, motivation to learn may be nonexistent.

Cognitive Readiness

Cognitive readiness combines several factors, including (1) the ability to understand directions relating to aquatic instruction, (2) mental adjustment to the aquatic environment, (3) preconceived ideas about the class or swimming, and (4) selective attention. Understanding directions is based on the cognitive level of the learner and the cognitive level of the directions you give. Thus, you must know the mental age of the participant in order to appropriately gear instructions. Using pictures, shorter sentences, and key words are important strategies for lower mental ages. Make sure the learner understands the words you are using as his movement vocabulary may be limited—words such as bend, straighten, twist, roll, and so on may be foreign to a participant with low cognitive ability.

The degree of mental adjustment determines whether or not the individual is ready to learn. Not surprisingly, fear and motivation play large roles in mental adjustment. The ability to relax in the aquatic environment depends on cognitively being aware of safety and knowing when it is appropriate to be afraid. For example, developing breath control often plays a major part in mental adjustment, as good breath control decreases fear.

The nature of the total teacher-learner environment is vital to overcoming difficulties (Campion 1985). If you bring to the experience a consistent personality, discipline methods that remain flexible but consistent, caring verbal assurances, and balanced, controlled physical handling to promote stable body position, you will help promote trust, security, and mental adjustment over time.

Negative preconceived ideas about the class or swimming can render a learner helpless. Individuals may have heard previous participants complaining or criticizing a particular instructor or program or facility and may have carried such notions into the class with them. Participants may also bring with them the burden of horror stories they've heard about swimming in general. "It increases body fat, promotes ear infections, and spreads infectious diseases" are some of the more common pieces of gossip passed from one reluctant swimmer to the next. But being "on your guard" for one reason or another is hardly conducive to learning. Honest answers to questions that may appear ridiculous is the best method of putting everyone at ease and letting preconceived ideas die.

Selective attention can shape an individual's ability to be cognitively ready for learning. You might give clear directions at the correct mental age, but if the participant cannot attend to the important information, learning will be hampered. Extraneous noise, people, and activities in the environment can cause individuals with deficits in selective attention to look and listen elsewhere. Often, you will not have the luxury of a quiet area free of others. To cope with this, give extra attention to cue words, offer praise for being on-task, and make activities exciting so the participants with selective attention disorders can remain focused on important teacher-learner interactions (see also "Teaching Tips" sections in chapter 9 for related disorders).

Social Ability

Social ability, the skills necessary to interact with others, can play a role in learning aquatic skills, especially if the participant attends class in a group setting. Many individuals may have the physical skills to participate within inclusive aquatic classes but lack appropriate social competence. The ability to function within a group demands a social age of approximately five years old. If an individual cannot, for example, wait for turns, follow rules, start and stop on command, or share, he will have a difficult time acquiring aquatic skills within a group. The abilities to initiate contact with others and make friends are also important in an adapted aquatic group—as they are in any other social setting. Individuals who experience difficulty judging their personal best, who feel their own abilities don't measure up to that of others', or who are egocentric may have great difficulty learning in group settings.

Some people cannot establish a bond with a group, lack concern for others, are manipulative, or exhibit aggressive behaviors. Such conduct disorders interfere with a positive learning climate and may decrease the amount of learning that all participants achieve. Thus, participants who persistently exhibit behavior that interferes with the learning process of themselves and others will need specific behavior intervention, a learning support aide, or removal to a more restrictive environment (see also discussions of informal and formal behavior modification in chapter 7).

Preferred Learning Modality

The way participants process and use information can affect how much they learn. You should match the instructional method that best suits a person's distinct characteristics in order to have a more effective outcome (Snider 1990). This theory is called learning style matching. There are two considerations to be made. First, what is the student's preferred learning modality. While we all process information visually, auditorily, and kinesthetically, we each prefer one over the other two. Second, we must choose a teaching style that best facilitates the goals of the lesson we are presenting (Mosston and Ashworth 1986).

The general tenet of matching instructional strategies to learning styles recommends that you seek to recognize and accommodate individual differences in learning. Present materials in a variety of ways designed to address all learners, then stick with the style that works. Placing learners into one category of styles, depending on disability or mental age, however, is unreasonable. You should create a myriad of opportunities for participants to learn by enhancing instructional presentations with more visual, verbal, tactile, and kinesthetic input, as well as using direct, indirect, small group, one-on-one, structured, or less structured methods. Using a variety of teaching strategies gives all participants the chance to develop the ability to receive information in a variety of ways, whether or not it is their preferred style.

Cultural values can also impact a learner's style (see figure 8.3). While learning swim skills is considered valuable in the American culture, other cultures might value other culturally determined forms of movement, such as soccer, ice hockey, and wrestling. Cultures that do not permit extensive eye contact or "staring" may have problems with visual demonstrations. Those that mandate wearing headdresses in public may not be able to participate fully in swimming. As a culture, people who are Deaf require your using American Sign Language, rather than signed English. Individuals who are Orthodox Jews may need separate gender classes. "The key issues are people are different,

learners will respond differently to a variety of instructional methods, and we need to respect and honor the individual differences among us" (Brandt 1990, p. 12).

THE PROCESS OF TEACHING, FACILITATING, AND GUIDING PARTICIPANTS TO GOALS

We cannot stress enough that successful adapted aquatics instructors not only provide the opportunity to learn but also help participants acquire aquatic skills. You must know the content involved in swimming and water safety instruction and be able to design lessons and implement a delivery system that leads to learning (Arreola 1966). In writing this section, we have assumed you have expertise in water safety instruction and its content. Instead, we'll focus on designing and delivering more creative, comprehensive, and thoughtful instruction when a group includes individuals with disabilities.

Instructional Design

You must properly plan, sequence, and organize instructional experiences to meet the needs of the participants in the aquatic group, using strategies that meet the needs of all students. As an adapted aquatics instructor, you can help regular aquatics instructors modify traditional strategies to be more individualized and inclusive. In this section, we'll look at several successful modifications and workable strategies you can use.

In teaching aquatic skills to individuals with disabilities, especially in a group situation, you must make decisions before, during, and after every lesson (Mosston and Ashworth 1994). As mentioned in chapter 4, instructional design begins with determining assessment criteria and procedure. Following the assessment, you must outline learning objectives and prepare an individualized plan before beginning instruction. The third part of the design phase is when you prepare the instruction itself, including selecting teaching style, developing strategies for lessons (individual or group), modifying activities, and sequencing the learning experiences to maximize learning.

Figure 8.3 Cultural aspects may affect learning.

Teaching Styles

In their 1994 edition of Teaching Physical Education, Mosston and Ashworth delineate eleven different teaching styles: command, practice, reciprocal, self-check, inclusion, guided discovery, convergent discovery, divergent production, individual program, learner-initiated, and self-teaching styles. Each style has a specific role for teacher and learner and, depending on what you wish to accomplish in a given lesson, you must choose a style to facilitate that process.

We'll examine each of these styles in relation to adapted aquatics to provide you with a variety of ways to introduce skills so you may find what works best with each participant. If something you try doesn't work, simply try one of the other styles. As space limitations mandate that we only summarize this spectrum of teaching styles here, we encourage you to read Mosston and Ashworth's 1994 book. We took this summary from the article "Tug-o-War No More" by Mosston (1992).

Command Style. The purpose of this style is to learn to do a task accurately and within a short period of time, with all decisions made by the instructor. The nature of this style involves an immediate and accurate response to a stimulus by the learner. Learners replicate models. Use this style when you want all participants to do the same and look the same as, for example, in drills in which you ask the swimmers to concentrate on a particular aspect of a stroke and have everyone perform that stroke in the same manner ("with elbows like this"). Adapted aquatic instructors have used this style successfully with individuals who are severely mentally retarded, learning disabled, emotionally disturbed, pervasive developmentally delayed, hyperactive, and distractible because the teacher maintains control in a uniform and consistent way.

Practice Style. This style allows you time to offer each learner private practice and one-on-one feedback. This style may be less stressful for the learner than the command style because it avoids situations in which the learner may compare himself to others. In this style, you shift the responsibility for making certain decisions to the learners, especially how to use practice time. But a learner in a practice style lesson must know how to stay on-task and must value practice time as he begins to feel some independence. You can use laminated 5" x 7" index cards with words on one side and a picture of the skill on the other side to guide the participant during practice. You can give easier and harder directions on the card as well. You may need to demonstrate all the skills on the cards at first to ensure the swimmer understands the directions. You can use this style effectively with individuals who can interpret words or pictures, for example, those with memory loss due to traumatic brain injury.

Reciprocal Style. In this style, learners work with a partner and offer feedback to the partner, based on criteria prepared by the aquatic instructor. The substance of this style is that the learners work in a partnership, receive immediate feedback, follow criteria for performance designed by the teacher, and develop feedback and socialization skills. Individuals who are to be included in this style must be knowledgeable enough to compare peers' performances to criteria, have the ability to communicate, and have some patience with and tolerance of others. Laminated skill sheets with task-analyzed swim skills and grease pencils to write on the lamination help facilitate this process, as do clipboards or other hard surfaces to lean the skill sheets on. You can use the reciprocal style effectively with individuals who can understand communication, give and receive feedback, have enough comprehension skills to compare partners' performances to a list of performance criteria, and who are able to properly socialize with others.

Self-Check Style. The purposes of this style are to learn to do a task independently and to check one's own work. The learner does the task individually and privately, then gives herself feedback by using criteria developed by you. Thus, this style encourages independence. The individual must be able to accept her own limitations, be honest and objective about her performance, and be able to use a self-check sheet. You can design each self-check sheet, altering performance criteria to meet specific needs. To do this, observe the swimmer, task-analyze the stroke including deciding what you should modify, and type or write this out on an index card. Laminate or place this card in a plastic zip-style bag, hung by the starting blocks with tape or laid over the gutter of the pool. While this style is not appropriate for learners with low cognitive ability or poor sensory integration, kinesthetic sense, or judgment, it is useful for learners with good cognition who prefer social isolation.

Inclusion Style. The purposes of this style are to help the learner learn to select a level of a task he can perform and to offer a challenge by which he may check his own work. To use this style, you must design a task to include different degrees of difficulty. Then you allow the learner to decide his entry point into the task and when to move to another level. This style is especially effective with an integrated (inclusion) aquatic class. For example, you could present a task such as swimming underwater through hoops submerged at various depths. The learner picks the hoop that he will be successful with but challenged by. Participants must already have some degree of independence and be able to make decisions about which level to work at. The difficulty with this style is that you must allow the participant to choose the level for himself, resisting the urge to impose what you would choose for him.

Guided Discovery Style. The purpose of this style is to discover a concept by answering a sequence of questions you present. The main focus of this style is that you, by asking a specific sequence of questions, systematically lead the learner to discover a predetermined "target" previously unknown to the learner. This style is good for students who will not be able to perform to a particular performance standard, but who have the cognitive ability to explore alternative ways of answering a question. Examples of questions might include "In what ways can you swim to the bottom of the pool with your hands leading you to pick up the diving rings?" or "How can you swim the breaststroke without letting your feet come out of the water on the kick?" The problem-solving method of the guided discovery style lets learners discover movement patterns most efficient for themselves. Participants must have sufficient cognitive ability to follow directions and attempt the task at-hand. This style is good for inclusion of students with mild physical disabilities, mild cognitive delay, as well as some health impairments that would prohibit exact replication of a specific performance criteria. In addition, the guided discovery style is very good for the discovery of balance, buoyancy, stability, and initial propulsion in aquatics.

Convergent Discovery Style. In the convergent discovery style, learners discover the solution to a problem and learn to clarify an issue and arrive at a conclusion by employing logical procedures, reasoning, and critical thinking. First, you present a question that requires a single correct answer. Questions such as "Where is the best place for my hand to be in order to cut down on drag?" or "When is the best time for breathing to begin in the crawl stroke?" Learners must have a high degree of independence, skills in problem solving, and high intelligence, must be able to work with little feedback, and be motivated to find the solution. Use this style with groups of individuals learning safety information, synchronized swimming, competitive swimming, or water aerobics routines.

Divergent Production Style. In contrast to the convergent discovery style, the purpose of this style is to produce multiple responses to a single question. In this style, you set the scene, making sure that the emotional climate is OK for learners to take risks and come up with solutions; then learners make responses based on the parameters you have set. This style is useful when presenting water safety information to groups and safety rules for individuals with mild cognitive delays or normal cognition. Questions such as "What are some pool rules we should follow?" and "What are ways we could go across the pool with a partner that are not standard swim strokes?" It is useful for learners who can come up with novel ideas, such as creating movements in the water for the simple pleasure of moving. This style is too open and too dependent on high cognitive skills and awareness to be useful for learners with little initiative, poor judgment, severe cognitive problems, or hyperactivity.

Individual Program Style. The purpose of this style is to design, develop, and perform a series of tasks organized into a personal program in consultation with you. You select the general subject area (e.g., cardiorespiratory health) while the learner selects the topic (e.g., aerobic work), identifies the questions (e.g., What aquatic moves produce high heart rates?), collects data (e.g., experiments with different moves and writes down heart rate following each), discovers answers (e.g., compares heart rates and moves), and organizes the information. This style requires highly disciplined, highly motivated learners with high cognitive ability, especially in fitness or competitive programs. Participants must be relatively skilled, able to make long-range plans, and willing to take on a challenge. The learner may need to do some research on physical training or review other training routines to collect data about the topic and organize information to achieve his goal.

Learner-Initiated Style. The purpose of this style is for the learner to initiate a learning experience, design it, perform it, and evaluate it, together with you, based on agreed-upon criteria. In this style, a learner comes to you and states her willingness to design a program for self-development. Your job is to give feedback about whether or not the learner's actions are matching her intentions. For example, the learner might be coaching herself, but may need some feedback once a month about stroke technique, turns, and timing of swim strokes. This style will work with individuals with a disability who have their own goals, usually in the fitness or competitive category, and need only occasional checks by you.

Self-Teaching Style. This style allows the learner to make all the decisions without any involvement on your part. The learner initiates his learning experience, designs it, performs it, and evaluates it. Although it is possible for a learner to choose this style, it usually does not occur in the aquatic setting, unless the participant is a long-time swimmer who decides to begin training on his own.

Developing Strategies

When you develop strategies for group and individual lessons, you must focus not only on the appropriate teaching-learning style but also on the interaction of the participant with the environment. Figure 8.4 provides an example of some of the different environmental influences that include physical and learning environment issues.

When making decisions, you must keep in mind that the more time the student is appropriately engaged in the content you are teaching, the more the participant will learn. Strive, then, for high academic learning time (ALT) with all students, but particularly those with intense learning or physical needs. ALT is ". . . the amount of time that a student spends engaged in an academic task and that s/he can perform with high success. The more ALT a student accumulates, the more the student is learning" (Fisher et al. 1980, p. 8). When you include individuals with disabilities into regular group instruction, you must be especially aware of the time you allot for instruction and the time the participants are truly and fully engaged in practicing the objectives. Thus, you must use effective strategies to ensure the individual with a disability is on-task at the appropriate level

with the support necessary to be successful. In other words, practice that is too easy or too hard does not enhance learning of aquatic skills.

You can use a variety of instructional strategies when participants cannot perform a skill the same way or at the same level as others in the group. Finding ways to teach aquatic skills while incorporating individuals with varying needs requires you to focus on several factors, including age of participants; instructor-participant ratio; cognitive, social, and physical abilities of participants; your experience with group management; and safety issues (Auxter, Pyfer, and Huettig 1993).

When designing an aquatic lesson plan for a group or individual, you must sequence instructional strategies and presentation of skills from general to specific (full body feedback to feedback on hand and wrist position) and from simple to more complex (front glides to front glides with kick and arm motion), building on any necessary prerequisites. You also need to include in your lesson plans alternative activities, cue words, and presentations as needed. The following sample demonstrates the relationship of a participant's individualized program plan to a group lesson. Raquel has spina bifida with paraplegia, is 20 years old, and is participating in a college's basic swimming class.

SAMPLE OF INTEGRATION OF IAPP AND GROUP LESSON

≈

Raquel's Individualized Aquatics Program Plan

Present Level of Performance

Raquel is a young adult with good upper body strength and endurance and no use of her lower trunk and lower extremities. She is in a basic swim and fitness class at the university and functions at level four ("Stroke Development") of the American Red Cross progressive swim program.

Long-Term Goals

1. To use swimming as the means to improve cardiorespiratory fitness

2. To develop competitive, fitness, and relaxation strokes

3. To improve water safety skills and knowledge

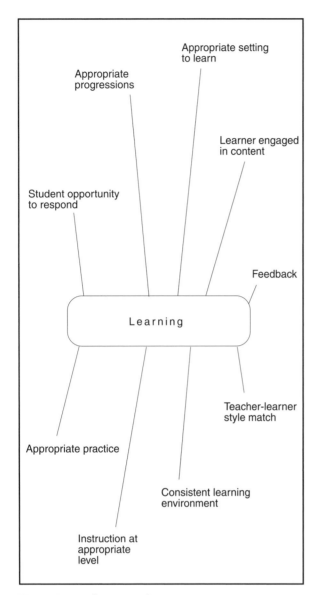

Figure 8.4 Influence on learners.

4. To maintain current range of motion in lower extremities

5. To increase trunk rotation and upper body range of motion

≋

Example of a Group Lesson

Lesson will be led by an aquatics instructor with an adapted aquatics instructor as a co-instructor. After a few weeks' guidance from the adapted aquatics instructor, the aquatics instructor should be able to operate alone.

Group Lesson Goals

To improve fitness and swim stroke efficiency

Group Lesson Objectives

- Wall stretches, 3 minutes
- Treading water, 5 minutes
- Open turns on front, three correct in a row
- Kickboard presses, 2 minutes consecutively during fitness routine
- Aerobic fitness routine, 12 minutes
- Continuous swimming, 5 minutes
- Improving swim strokes to level five efficiency
- Water-walking, two lengths of pool

Group Lesson Timetable

University Swim 101 Tues. and Thurs. 12-1

12-12:05 Water-walking, using arms to pump as warm-up for fitness routine.

Raquel will use the water bench to perform continuous trunk rotations while alternately punching arms out in front of her; will need assistance to maintain balance.

12:05-12:10 Treading water.

Raquel will use the Wet Vest and her arms for sculling motion of treading water.

12:10-12:15 Stretching lower legs and arms.

Raquel will perform arm stretches while sitting on the water bench with assistance for balance. Also, adapted physical educator or adapted aquatics instructor will come in to assist with lower body flexibility exercises. Or Raquel will continue treading water, concentrating on large arm movements, or will use inner tube to perform stretching exercises.

12:15-12:20 Fitness swim.

Raquel will perform modified breaststroke and elementary backstroke at her own pace.

12:20-12:32 Fitness routine.

Raquel will perform a modified routine while using a ski belt to keep vertical. Raquel can do some leg work by manipulating her own legs, for example, using her hands to push down her legs. She may substitute arm actions for leg actions of a similar nature. Instructor should brainstorm with Raquel and adapted aquatic instructor before modifying the routine.

12:32-12:55 Stroke work.

Raquel will be given feedback by the adapted aquatics instructor on compensation for leg action.

12:55-1:00 Water-walking and stretching.

Raquel will be encouraged to cool down by using the elementary backstroke and then stretching similar to the earlier stretching, emphasizing shoulder and upper trunk stretching. Since she is able to do some weight bearing, the instructor can assist her in the pool by providing support or Raquel can use a floatation device.

In this example, Raquel participates with the group while still working on her goals through modified activities and related adaptations. (See also chapter 3 for more detail as to how to include participants with disabilities and chapter 9 for teaching tips specific to a variety of disabilities.)

Instructional Delivery

In this section, we'll offer suggestions for how to move instructional strategies and creative solutions from the planning (preimpact) stage to the implementation (impact) stage through instructional delivery skills.

Your actions influence what learners will do, which, in turn, will influence their learning (Randall 1992). When a gap exists between instructional planning and instructional delivery, it is most likely wider for individuals with disabilities in aquatic classes than for their nondisabled peers. For example, if you plan to use water baseball as a strategy for increasing participants' comfort with moving around in shallow water but do not identify all the social, cognitive, and physical skills necessary to play, you will most likely fail to engage several students for a variety of reasons. The students without disabilities who can walk in the water may not have any catching or striking skills but will at least be able to run or walk to the water bases. In contrast, the individual with a disability, such as severe cerebral palsy, may not be able to perform any of the skills at all. To help you close the gap between design and delivery, we must first examine the elements of effective instruction.

In addition to interaction skills, basic elements of effective instruction must be present in order to enhance learning opportunities for individuals with disabilities. These elements include selecting objectives at the appropriate level of difficulty, teaching to those objectives, monitoring participants' progress, modifying instruction when nec-

essary, using principles of learning to direct lessons (Hunter 1982), giving clear directions, engaging all in active participation, giving continual feedback, and managing behavior. See chapter 4 for information regarding selecting appropriate objectives, teaching to those objectives, and monitoring participants' progress. See earlier in this chapter for using principles of learning to direct lessons and chapter 7 regarding managing behavior. The following section addresses the other elements of effective instruction

Modifying Instruction

Many times will arise when you'll have to modify your lesson plans, whether you're teaching in a segregated or integrated setting. Although we have discussed in-depth ways to modify program plans, we must now focus on modifying lessons in progress. This skill is sometimes called "thinking on your feet" in pedagogical circles. The best way to be ready to shift gears on the spur of the moment is to have alternative plans you can implement immediately when necessary, including adjusting your style and strategies. When the lesson is not going well, don't fall into the common trap of muddling through the lesson as planned; instead, identify problems and make quick, but helpful, modifications. Keep in mind that while aquatic classes without individuals with disabilities might proceed satisfactorily (but not succeed) without changes in plans, individuals with behavior problems, physical comfort and safety needs, or disorientation will be at a high-risk for injury if you don't promptly modify the lesson to suit their needs.

How will you know when to change course? Your participants will tell you! Try a new strategy when a participant or equipment is being mistreated; when emotional comfort is low as demonstrated by participants teasing, ignoring, yelling, criticizing, or controlling others; when participants are practicing but not doing their best; when parents or caregivers are intervening; when the group is too spread out; when individuals are climbing out of the pool; or when participants are crying or whining. When these things happen, quickly judge the situation and correct it. Ask yourself "Was the teaching style too learner-driven for the group or individual to handle? Was the equipment too large or too small? Are participants spending too much waiting for turns and attention? Is the class size too large for the abilities of the students? Are the participants working at their own levels or trying skills too easy or too hard for them?"

"Now what?" you may ask. Calmly bring the group in close, redirect them, and move on to another part of the lesson or substitute another more appropriate activity. Setting a prearranged signal for respectfully regathering the class during the first meeting with the group is a positive and proactive way to deal with problems. Use signals such as: (1) "When I am sitting on the pool deck that means come over quickly." (2) "When I wave both hands over my head, please swim in to me." (3) "When I shout 'icebergs,' stand still for directions." Or (4) "When I shout 'Marco Polo,' please swim to me." Often merely changing to the next activity will get your class back on track, but after the lesson (postimpact), examine what went wrong and plan the next lesson with new insight!

You may also need to adapt your verbal and visual demonstrations on the spot. Learn sign language to use with individuals who have impaired or no hearing or who have language disorders. Visual demonstrations are useful in communicating information as long as all can see, all are focused, and as long as you demonstrate slowly enough. Individuals with attention problems often need help refocusing many times during demonstrations. Individuals who have physical disabilities may find it difficult to maneuver to a spot from which they can view the entire demonstration, and individuals who have visual impairments may need alternative (tactile, kinesthetic, auditory) methods of receiving directions. Figure 8.5 gives an example how to modify demonstrations.

Giving Clear Directions

Giving clear directions will help a group or individual to stay focused on the activity at-hand. The following hints will help you deliver your instructions more clearly:

1. Use a person's name (respectfully) if you are directing a comment to him or her.

2. When telling participants where to go in the pool, mention landmarks such as "Swim to the ladder" instead of "Swim over there."

3. Use simple sentences that tell what the person needs to do without added verbiage.

4. Give one set of directions at a time.

5. Repeat key points of directions for those who need it.

6. Check for understanding by asking participants questions such as "Where will you stop?" or "How many lengths will you do?"

7. Provide signed or tactile directions for those who need it.

Engaging All in Active Participation

No matter how well you demonstrate and explain, if the learner does not have enough time to practice the skills necessary for learning the objective, he will not learn to his potential. In an inclusion group, learners with disabilities may not participate actively very much because of behavior problems, a lack of appropriate physical support, or because they do not possess adequate prerequisites for the skill or experience. You must clearly see the big picture, make accurate placements to start with, plan lessons effectively, and deliver them so that all participants are successful. You must be patient and caring to carry out the elements of effective instruction, applying both your knowledge of safety issues related to individuals with disabilities and creative methods of adapting activities and instruction.

Figure 8.5 Swimmers who are blind need to feel a demonstration.

Giving Continual Feedback

Give timely, appropriate, and specific feedback to let participants know how they are doing. This feedback, both positive and negative, may be in response to social behavior or physical performance. Social feedback can be given for waiting, listening, following directions, trying hard, being on time, not crying or whining, or appropriate group interaction.

Physical performance feedback falls into two categories: knowledge of results and knowledge of performance. Knowledge of results refers to information given to the learner following performance of a skill, concerning whether or not the learner achieved the set goal (Canadian Red Cross Society 1989). Examples of this include "Great, Nisha, you walked across the width of the pool!"; "Terrific, Tristen, you've completed five laps"; and "Nice work, Courtney, you were able to meet your goal of jumping into the deep end four times today!" Giving feedback can also be corrective to help spur a participant toward a goal, such as, "Almost, Michael, you treaded water four seconds; now let's try to tread water five seconds and don't forget to keep your hands in the water as you move them back and forth." Note that even the corrective feedback starts with a compliment, encouraging the learner.

Feedback that includes comments, gestures, or signs about how the movement was performed falls into the category of knowledge of performance. Reference made to the quality of the movement, position of the body or body parts, coordination of the movements, or efficiency of the movement are examples of knowledge of performance (KOP). Work on the most crucial aspects of the movement first, one that will make a large difference if corrected. For example, correction of body position would be of greater concern than correction of the angle of the wrist. Examples of KOP statements include "You were much faster because you kept your body horizontal that time" and "Great arm stroke, but keep your head turned more to the side instead of lifting it in front when you breathe."

KOP comments are much more difficult to give, but individuals with poor sensory feedback, low cognitive awareness, or limited experience in the water need specific feedback, given immediately, in order to progress. Finally, remember to give feedback in the learner's preferred communication mode and at her level of understanding.

SUMMARY

Developing instructional strategies for teaching aquatic skills to individuals with disabilities requires that you examine the process of learning and factors that affect learning. Indeed, no aquatics program that serves the diverse needs of learners with disabilities can be successful without attention to the personal needs of each learner. A single approach to aquatic instruction does not work. You must consider the forces of physiological conditions within the learner, such as anatomical and physiological parameters and medication, in the learning process. Psychological conditions, such as motivation, trust, readiness, previous learning in aquatics, cognitive and social ability, and teaching-learning style preference are also factors to consider when planning. Once you accommodate the psychological functioning of your participants during instruction, you can establish realistic goals and set up an effective and fun learning environment.

As you try to bridge the gap between planning and implementation of programs and classes that serve individuals with disabilities, you must recognize that environmental, emotional, physiological and psychological elements may have a greater impact on individuals with disabilities due to different and sometimes more pronounced needs. Then you must identify the effect of each element on your participants so that you can plan, deliver, and adapt appropriate instructional strategies in a competent, sensitive, and effective manner. Remember, individuals who face cognitive, emotional, and physical challenges in the aquatic realm need you to plan carefully, then to adapt strategies and styles as often as necessary during each lesson. We do not, however, intend the suggestions and general strategies for adapting instructional design and delivery in this chapter as a cookbook of recipes with stringent formulas for success, but rather as a resource of guidelines to help you modify your existing strategies as needed.

CHAPTER 8 REVIEW

1. Explain the three stages of learning new motor skills.

2. What are physiological factors that impact the ability to learn aquatic skills?

3. How can medications affect an individual's behavior?

4. How can you accommodate various learning styles in an aquatics setting?

5. Explain how psychological conditions can inhibit the acquisition of aquatic skills.

6. List five teaching styles as described in this chapter.

7. What are the basic elements of effective instruction that should be present in order to enhance learning opportunities?

8. Explain how you can help a participant improve performance through knowledge of results and knowledge of performance.

Table 8.1

Pharmacological Agents: Effects on Heart Rate and Blood Pressure During Rest and Exercise

Key

Possible effects in therapeutic doses:

+	Increase
–	Decrease
0	No change
RHR	Resting heart rate
EHR	Exercise heart rate
RBP	Resting blood pressure
EBP	Exercise blood pressure

Note: Lower case notation refers to actions of a specific drug only. Drugs may also exert no effect. Absence of information indicates unknown or no known effect.

Exercise precautions:

DE	Dehydration
DI	Dizziness or lightheadedness
EH	Exercise or postexercise hypotension
HI	Heat intolerance
MI	Muscular incoordination
OE	Overexertion

OH	Orthostatic hypotension
UN	Unsteadiness
VI	Vision disturbances
WE	Weakness

The following information summarizes general effects that specific classes of drugs may have on cardiovascular function at rest and during exercise (if known) as well as precautions with their use. Remember that in addition to causing different responses among individuals, pharmacologic agents induce dose-related responses. Furthermore, within each major class of drugs, specific agents may have differing or even opposite effects.

This is not intended to be a comprehensive list of pharmacologic agents. A discussion of the specific effects of each available drug is beyond the scope of this text. It is essential that you discuss any medications used by your clients with their physicians to determine the safe limits for exercise and expected responses with exercise.

Drug		Angina, arrhythmia, hypertension	
Generic name	Brand name	Possible cardiovascular effects	Exercise precautions
Ace inhibitors		R/EBP –	DE, DI, HI
Benazepril	Lotensin		
Captopril	Capoten, Capozide*		
Enalapril	Vasotec, Vaseretic*		
Fosinopril	Monopril		
Lisinopril	Prinivil, Prinzide*, Zestril, Zestoretic*		
Quinapril	Accupril		
Ramipril	Altace		
Alpha adrenergic blockers		R/EHR +/0	DI, EH, OH
Prazosin	Minipress, Minizide*	R/EBP –	HI
Terazosin	Hytrin		
Antiadrenergic agents		R/EHR –/0	DI, EH, OH, HI
Centrally or peripherally acting:		R/EBP –	
Clonidine	Catapres, Combipres*		
Doxazosin	Cardura		
Guanabenz	Wytensin		
Guanadrel	Hylores		
Guanethidinel	Ismelin, Esimil*		
Guanfacine	Tenex		
Methyldopa	Aldomet, Aldoril*		
Reserpines	Diupres, Regrotan, Hydropres, Salutensin		

(continued)

Table 8.1 *(continued)*

Generic name	Brand name	Possible cardiovascular effects	Exercise precautions
Antiarrhythmic agents (Class I)			
Disopyramide	Norpace	r/ehr +/0 rbp +/0	DI, HI, OH, VI
Procainamide	Procan, Promine, Pronestyl	rhr +	DI
Quinidines	Cardioquin, Quinidex	r/ehr +/0 rpb +/0	DI
Beta adrenergic blockers		R/EHR −	DI, OE, HI
Acebutolol	Sectral	R/EBP −	
Atenolols	Tenormin, Tenoretic*		
Betaxolol	Kerlone		
Bisoprolol	Zebeta, Ziac*		
Carteolol	Cartrol		
Labetalol	Normodyne, Trandate, Normozides*, Trandate HCT*		
Metoprolol	Lopressor, Toprol XL		
Nadolol	Corgard, Corzide*		
Penbutolol	Levatol		
Pindolols	Visken		
Propranolols	Inderal, Inderide*		
Timolol	Blocadren, Timolide*		
Calcium channel blockers		R/EHR +/−	OE
Amlodipine	Norvasc	R/EBP −	
Bepridil	Bepadin, Vascor		
Diltiazem	Cardizem, Dilacor XR	r/ehr −	
Felodipine	Plendil		
Isradipine	DynaCirc		
Nicardipine	Cardene		
Nifedipine	Adalat, Procardia	r/ehr +	
Verapamil	Calan, Isoptin, Verelan	r/ehr −	
Digitalis glycosides			
Digitoxin	Crystodigin		
Digoxin	Lanoxin, Lanoxicaps		
Nitrates		RHR +	EH, OH
Erythrityl tetranitrate	Cardilate	EHR +/0 RBP−	
Isosorbide dinitrate	Dilatrate, Isordil, Sorbitrate	EBP −/0	
Nitroglycerine	Nitrogard, Nitrol, Nitr-Dur, Nitrocap, Nitrolin		
Pentaerythritol tetranitrate	Duotrate, Peritrate, Pentritol		
Vasodilators		RHR +	
Hydralazine	Apresoline, Apresazide	EHR +/0	
Minoxidil	Loniten	R/EBP −	

*diuretic

Drug		Anxiety, depression, psychotic disorders	
Generic name	Brand name	Possible cardiovascular effects	Exercise precautions
Benzodiazepines			DI, MI, UN
Alprazolam	Xanax		
Chlordiazepoxide	Librium, Libritabs		
Clorazepate	Tranxene		
Diazepam	Valium, Valrelease	ehr/bp −	
Halazepam	Paxipam		
Lorazepam	Ativan		
Oxazepam	Serax		
Prazepam	Centrax		
MAO inhibitors		RBP −/0	DI, OH
Phenelyzine	Nardil		
Phenothiazines		EHR +	DI, HI, OH, VI
Chlorpromazine	Thorazine	EBP−	
Fluphenazine	Permitil		
Perphenazine	Trilafon		
Prochlorperazine	Compazine		
Thioridazine	Mellaril		
Trifluoperazine	Stelazine		
Seratonin uptake inhibitors			
Fluoxetine	Prozac		DI, MI, OH,
Paroxetine	Paxil		impaired judgement
Sertraline	Zoloft		
Velafaxine	Effexor		
Tricyclic antidepressants		R/EHR +/0	DI, OH
Amitriphyline/Chlordiazipoxide	Limbitrol	R/EBP −/0	
Amitriphyline/Perphenazine	Triavil		
Amitriptyline	Elavil, Endep		
Amoxapine	Asendin		
Clomipramine	Anafranil		
Desipramine	Norpramin		
Doxepin	Sinequan		
Imipramine	Tofranil		
Nortriptyline	Aventyle, Pamelor		
Protriptyline	Vivactil		
Trimipramine	Surmontil		
Others			
Bupropion	Wellbutrin	RHR +	DI
Buspirone	BuSpar	RHR +	DI
Chlormezanone	Trancopal		DI
Clozapine	Clozaril	R/EHR + R/EBP −/0/+	DI, OH, VI
Maprotiline	Ludiomil		DI, OH, WE
Meprobamate	Equanil, Miltown		DI, MI, UN
Trazodone	Desyrel	RHR +/− RBP −	DI, OH

(continued)

Table 8.1 *(continued)*

Asthma, bronchospasms, pulmonary disease

Drug		Possible cardiovascular effects	Exercise precautions
Generic name	Brand name		
Antihistamines			
Astemizole	Hismanal		
Loratadine	Claritin		
Terfanadine	Seldane		
Bronchodilators—adrenergic		R/EHR +/0	
Albuterol	Proventil, Ventolin, Volmax	R/EBP +/0/–	
Bitolterol	Tornalate		
Isoetharine	Bronkosol		
Isoproterenol	Isuprel	ehr/bp +	
Metaproterenol	Alupent, Metaprel		
Pirbuterol	Maxair		
Terbutaline	Brethair, Brethine, Bricanyl		
Bronchodilators—xanthine derivatives		R/EHR +/0	
Aminophylline	Somophyllin	R/EPB +/0	
Dyphylline	Dilor, Lufyllin		
Oxtriphylline	Choledyl		
Theophylline	Aerolate, Bronkodyl, Slo-bid, Theo-bid, Theo-Dur, Uniphyl		
Corticosteroids			
Beclomethasone	Vanceril, Beclovent		
Flunisolide	AeroBid		
Triamcinolone	Azmacort		
Others			
Cromolyn	Intal		
Isoproterenol and phenylephrine	Duo-Medihaler		

Convulsions, seizures, epilepsy

Barbiturates			For all classes:
Mephobarbital	Mebaral		DI, WE, MI, OH, UN
Benzodiazepines			
Clonazepam	Klonopin		
Clorazepate	Tranxene		
Diazepam	Valrelease, Valium	ehr/bp –	
Lorazepam	Ativan		
Carbonic anhydrase inhibitors			
Acetazolamide	Diamox		
Hydantoins			
Phenytoin	Dilantin		
Others			
Carbamazepine	Tegretol		
Felbamate	Felbatol		
Gabapentin	Neurontin		
Primodones	Mysoline		
Valproic acid	Depakene, Depakote		

Inflammation, pain with arthritis

Drug		Possible cardiovascular effects	Exercise precautions
Generic name	Brand name		
Nonsteroidal anti-inflammatory drugs			DI, VI
Diclofenac	Voltaren		
Diflunisal	Dolobid		
Etodolac	Lodine		
Fenoprofen	Nalfon		
Flurbiprofen	Ansaid		
Ibuprofen	Advil, Motrin, Nuprin		
Indomethacin	Indocin		
Ketoprofen	Orudis, Oruvail		
Nabumetone	Relafen		
Naproxen	Aleve, Naprosyn, Anaprox		
Oxaprozin	Dapro		
Phenylbutazone	Butazolidin		
Piroxicam	Feldene		
Sulindac	Clinoril		
Tolmetin	Tolectin		
Corticosteroids, cortiocotropins			
Betamethasone	Celestone		
Cortisone	Cortone Acetate		
Dexamethasone	Decadron, Haxadrol		
Hydrocortisone	Cortef		
Methylprednisolone	Medrol		
Prednisolone	Prelone		
Prednisone	Deltasone, Meticorten, Orasone		
Triamcinolone	Aristocort, Kenacort		
Gold compounds			
Auranofin	Ridaura		
Salicylates			
Aspirin	many brands		
Choline Salicylate	Athropan		
Choline and Magnesium Salicylates	Trilisate, Tricosal		
Magnesium Salicylates	Magan, Mobidin		
Salsalate	Amigesic, Disalcid		
Others			
Capsaicin	Zostrix (cream)		Heat and sweating may increase stinging on skin
Hydroxychloroquine	Plaquenil		
Methotrexate	Rheumatrex		Bruising or injury may occur from contact sports
Penicillamine	Cuprimine, Depen		

(continued)

Table 8.1 *(continued)*

Spasticity, muscle spasms			
Drug		Possible cardiovascular effects	Exercise precautions
Generic name	Brand name		
Benzodiazepines			
Diazepam	Valrelease, Valium	ehr/bp −	For all classes: DI, MI, WE, UN, VI
Lorazepam	Ativan		
Skeletal muscle relaxants			
Carisoprodol	Soma	RHR +	
Chlorzoxazone	Paraflex		
Metaxalone	Skelaxin		
Methocarbamol	Robaxin, Robaxisal		
Orphenadrine Citrate	Norflex, Norgesic		
Others			
Baclofen	Lioresal		
Cyclobenzaprine	Flexeril		
Dantrolene	Dantrium		

Reprinted from Miller 1995.

SPECIFIC NEEDS OF ADAPTED AQUATICS PARTICIPANTS

In this chapter, we focus on common difficulties of functional, movement, and behavioral diagnoses versus medical diagnoses. Specifically, we examine common attributes that pose obstacles to achieving swim skills or creating safety in the aquatic environment. We look at how these attributes affect some aspect of the aquatic experience and offer teaching tips, safety factors, and goals you should target. Finally, we list the disabilities in which this attribute is common at the end of each area of concern. If you need additional information about specific disabilities, we offer a brief explanation of common disabilities in the Glossary of Common Disabilities in the back of the book. If you want to find certain attributes that may be common in a specific disability, locate the disability in table 9.1.

Note, however, that you should not assume that the characteristics table 9.1 lists will be manifested in each person. Instead, discuss the challenges related to each individual with him and his caregivers, assess the individual on land and water, and then make a list of attributes to review in this chapter.

We cannot stress enough that to meet the needs of a variety of individuals, it is necessary to know certain unique attributes or characteristics of the learners in order to provide safe, effective, and relevant aquatic opportunities. Therefore, you do need information pertaining to common disabilities and implications for the aquatic setting. Refrain, however, from looking at a person as a disability with the characteristics listed; instead, ascertain what the person can do. Labeling the individual with a certain diagnosis is counterproductive: it has little to do with what that particular individual will be able to do in and around the pool.

Labeling individuals with disabilities emphasizes diagnosis of a person's "condition" or disability area, resulting in statements of what an individual *has* rather than what the person *does*, for example, "Linda has CP," "John is retarded," or "Tisha is learning disabled." The social complexities of focusing on an individual's primary disability area or diagnostic category can cause negative attitudes and low expectations. It leads to "helping" professionals not seeing the individual, but programming

Table 9.1

Disability Reference Sheet

	Attention deficit	Atlanto-axial instability	Auditory perception disorders	Circulatory disorders	Contracture; limited ROM	Hearing problems	Poor head control	Hyperactivity	Interaction problems	Joint dysfunction	Kinesthetic disorders	Memory problem	Understanding problems	Multisensory deprivation	Oral motor dysfunction	Paralysis or paresis	Atrophy	Posture problems	Primitive reflex retention	Respiratory dysfunction	Language disorder	Seizures	Tactile system disorder	Temperature regulation disorder	Vestibular disorder	Visual impaired	Visual perception disorder	Cardiovascular disorder	Brittle bones
Amputee				•	•												•	•								•			
Alzheimer's			•	•		•			•			•	•	•		•	•	•			•				•		•	•	
Asthma																				•									
Arthritis					•					•							•	•											
Autism	•		•						•	•		•		•							•				•		•	•	
AIDS																													
ADD	•		•						•			•									•				•		•	•	
ADHD	•		•					•	•			•									•				•		•	•	
Ataxia																											•		
Blind											•							•								•	•		
Behavior disorder																													
Cerebral palsy					•		•		•		•				•	•	•	•	•	•	•	•	•	•	•	•		•	
Deafness						•																							
Down syndrome	•	•	•			•			•	•		•	•	•		•	•	•			•				•		•	•	•
Diabetes				•																									
Fetal alcohol syndrome																													
Impaired hearing						•																							
Hemophilia				•					•	•																			
Heart defects				•																								•	
Legally blind																										•			
Learning disabled	•		•						•	•		•	•	•					•		•				•		•		
Mental retardation	•		•						•	•		•	•	•	•														
Multiple sclerosis					•											•	•	•						•	•	•	•		
Muscular dystrophy					•		•									•	•	•											
Myelomeningocele					•											•	•	•											•
Obesity				•						•								•										•	
Osteogenisis imperfecta					•					•						•	•	•											•
Paraplegia					•											•	•	•											
Polio					•											•	•	•											
Postpolio syndrome										•						•													•
Kyphosis					•													•		•									
Lordosis					•													•											
Scoliosis					•													•											
Quadriplegia				•	•											•	•	•							•			•	•
JRA					•					•						•	•	•											
Spinal cord injury				•	•													•							•				
Spina bifida					•											•	•	•											•
Stroke					•				•		•	•	•		•						•	•	•	•	•	•		•	
Traumatic brain injury					•				•		•	•	•		•	•	•	•	•		•	•	•	•	•		•		
Deaf-blind				•					•					•				•			•					•	•		
Prenatal drug exposure	•							•	•			•		•							•			•		•	•		

and planning for the disability. The label of "mental retardation," for example, can burden a person her entire life, lowering self-esteem, separating her from others, probably reducing social opportunities.

Yet, a list of common characteristics may be helpful in order to plan for possibilities in certain situations and provide necessary precautions. For example, not knowing about atlantoaxial instability found in some participants with Down syndrome is neglectful and dangerous. Moreover, categorical methods provide opportunities for special services, individualized programs, and finances for therapeutic equipment. You and the treatment team must, however, clearly understand the issues involved in labeling individuals with disabilities. Such identification should be for the purpose of access to services, not for categorically placing certain characteristics on people or subjecting them to segregated programs. With this in mind, we have structured this chapter as noncategorically as possible. Finally, to help you find what you need to know quickly, we have arranged the attributes in alphabetical order.

ATLANTOAXIAL INSTABILITY

Atlantoaxial instability syndrome (AAIS), also called atlantoaxial dislocation syndrome (ADS), is an instability due to pathology within the first (atlanto) and second (axial) cervical vertebrae, potentially resulting in dislocation of the atlas vertebrae causing spinal cord injury or death. This orthopedic problem may occur in 17 percent of individuals with Down syndrome and is said to occur due to lax ligaments and muscles surrounding the joints (Sherrill 1993). Although this is not a majority, for safety reasons, you should treat all individuals with Down syndrome (see figure 9.1) as though they have atlantoaxial instability unless there is a specific medical diagnosis to the contrary.

Teaching Tips

• Seek information from physician as to the status of swimmers with Down syndrome.

• Consult with medical personnel as to specific movements to stress or avoid.

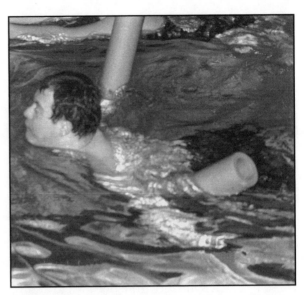

Figure 9.1 Individuals with Down syndrome may have atlantoaxial instability.

Safety Issues

• An X-ray report of AAIS would cause a physician to prohibit forcefully bending the neck forward (flexion) and backward (hyperextension).

• Participants with AAIS should not participate in diving, butterfly stroke, or warm-up exercises that place pressure on the neck and head.

Goals to Target

Plan activities that avoid forcefully bending the neck forward and backward and attempt to improve swim skills that do not put pressure on head or neck; instead, emphasize participation in safe aquatic activities.

Common Related Conditions

Atlantoaxial instability syndrome may be secondary to individuals with Down syndrome and Morquio syndrome.

ATTENTION DEFICIT

The ability to initially attend to and then maintain attention to complete a task greatly improves the chances of learning the task. Individuals with chronic and intense difficulties addressing and sustaining attention on demand, persisting in tasks that are developmentally appropriate, following rules, and concentrating tend to have trouble improving the quality of their skills. They may perform the task once or twice, then be ready to move on. Their lack of attention and persistence often leads to skills that are immature.

Teaching Tips

- Use participant's name when providing feedback.

- Provide only one aspect of feedback at a time and make it frequent and specific.

- Place participant close to you.

- Warn a participant of upcoming changes to routine or when moving from one task to another, as transitions to other activities may be difficult.

- Decrease competition, stress, and fatigue.

- Encourage self-monitoring of activities because self-control is an important goal.

- Provide appropriate amounts of work to complete in a work period.

- Assign one task at a time.

- Provide learning support such as cue cards or a teacher aide or peer tutor for longer or harder tasks.

- Maintain eye contact when providing verbal directions.

- Use positive reinforcement for correct behavior.

- Use calm voice during discipline.

- Apply less obtrusive discipline initially, such as short time-outs.

- Use preestablished cue words or motions to decrease unwanted behavior.

- Follow through with preestablished consequences that are as natural as possible.

- Structure swim lessons no more than 30 minutes long.

- Schedule pool times during which crowds, noise, and other distractions are at a minimum to help decrease time off-task.

- Use a one-on-one ratio when appropriate and available.

- Arrange for participant to swim toward a wall or face away from the rest of the pool while practicing.

- Supply lap counters to help participant keep track of laps.

- Provide kitchen timers to help participant visualize how much time he has spent on a task.

Safety Issues

- Use additional lifeguard coverage to enhance supervision of impulsive participants.

- Repeat rule explanations often and ask participant to repeat rules when distractions are present.

- Hyperactivity may accompany attention deficit in some students, therefore, keep pool decks dry and free of equipment.

Goals to Target

Strive to increase ability to follow multitask directions, time on-task, and quality of aquatic skills and to decrease impulsive behaviors.

Common Related Conditions

Attention deficit is often associated with secondary disabilities including ADD (attention deficit disorder), ADHD (attention deficit–hyperactivity disorder), cerebral palsy, learning disabilities, mental retardation, traumatic brain injury, and stroke. Attention deficit is common in individuals who were prenatally exposed to drugs.

AUDITORY PERCEPTION DISORDERS

Sound entering the ears may be hindered due to damage within the structural mechanisms for auditory input, as in those who are deaf or hard of hearing, or due to the inability of the brain to translate what is heard into information that is meaningful, as in auditory perception problems. Deafness and hard of hearing are different than auditory perceptual difficulties. Deafness and difficulty hearing are problems with auditory acuity, while picking out important auditory information from a complex sound background is a problem with auditory perception.

If a participant has trouble with hearing due to auditory perception problems, find out the participant's level of sound identification and discrimination in addition to auditory memory and sequence skills. Acoustics in the pool area do not provide a good background for auditory discrimination and often participants with auditory perception problems cannot focus on the primary components of a message. Another area of difficulty for these participants is that they may not be able to move rhythmically to music or to a beat.

Teaching Tips

- Use written or pictorial cue cards in conjunction with verbal directions.
- Repeat verbal directions to the challenged participant, using as few words as possible.
- Use games that focus on sound identification such as "What do you hear?"
- Attend to and name environmental sounds.
- Use voice inflection to focus attention on important points.
- If age-appropriate, use songs or rhythms to imitate the rhythmic breathing used in the front crawl, such as "Row, row, row (breathe) your boat, gently down the stream (breathe). . . ." Put the pronunciation on the breathing word as appropriate.
- Provide a steady tempo, such as a drumbeat, for students who have difficulty with rhythmic patterns due to lack of auditory rhythmic ability. Have students stand in place to perform arms in correct rhythm, using a bigger bang on the drum for the breath.

Safety Issues

- Provide extra assistance for verbal explanations to be sure the participant knows the rules. Have them repeat what was said or answer questions about the rules or explanations.

Goals to Target

Provide activities that improve auditory memory, sequencing, and discrimination.

Common Related Conditions

Disabilities commonly associated with auditory discrimination problems include learning disabilities, traumatic brain injury, and stroke.

AUTONOMIC DYSREFLEXIA OR HYPERREFLEXIA

Autonomic dysreflexia or hyperreflexia is a phenomenon that may occur in individuals with spinal cord injury above T6 and is a medical emergency. It is a medical condition with signs such as pounding headaches, goosebumps, sweating, or vomiting that may result from overextension of the bladder or colon which in turn may be caused by a blocked catheter, disturbance of bowel and urine schedules, or purposely keeping the bladder full. Other infections and irritations may also cause this phenomenon, such as pressure sores and kidney stones.

Teaching Tips

- Remind participant to empty waste collection bags or pouches before swimming.
- Be sensitive about dressing room privacy and personal space.
- Occasionally, assist participant in checking catheter tubing for kinks.
- Remind participant of the need to urinate before and after swimming.

Safety Issues

- Signs such as pounding headache, goose bumps, vomiting, and extreme sweating indicate a medical emergency, and you should summon appropriate medical personnel immediately.
- First aid involves raising the head and upper body to sitting position, emptying the bladder or colon or both, taking blood pressure, and activating the Emergency Medical System.

Goals to Target

Provide support for the participant to increase awareness of healthy habits, improve fitness, and increase or maintain physical activity for improved bladder drainage.

Common Related Conditions

Autonomic dysreflexia may occur in individuals with a T6 injury or above.

BALANCE DISORDERS

See "Vestibular System Disorders."

BRITTLE BONES

Imperfect bone growth is typically a congenital impairment but can be caused by trauma, lack of weight-bearing activity, or mineral deficiency. Bones that are weak in structure will not grow properly and may be brittle. Repetitive fractures may result from walking, bumping, jarring, transferring, or high-impact or stationary weight bearing.

Individuals with congenital osteogenesis imperfecta (OI) may have excessively mobile joints (hypermobility) as well as thin (atrophic), fragile skin. Most with congenital OI use wheelchairs for mobility. Bone fractures may decrease after age 15, but chest deformity and posture problems may lead to decreased vital lung capacity and permanent disability. Individuals with congenital or late-developing bone growth deficiencies most often have posture deviations, such as kyphosis, scoliosis, and bowed legs (see posture disorders). Swimming is an especially appropriate activity because an individual can participate with a minimal risk of injury.

Teaching Tips

- Adapt aquatic activities to individuals with mobility impairments.
- Use water tables or tot docks for individuals with congenital OI who have short stature.
- Use soft equipment such as beach balls to limit risk of contact injury.
- Treat individuals with OI in an age-appropriate manner despite that fact that their small stature tends to make them appear younger.
- Develop a sense of trust, as individuals with brittle bones may be totally dependent on you for safety.
- Adjust cardiorespiratory activities to accommodate decreased vital lung capacity due to chest deformities.
- Adapt activities for range-of-motion difficulties. Although people with congenital OI may have hypermobile joints, weak muscles may limit their functional ranges of motion.
- Use isometric exercises underwater in the pool, tightening and relaxing without resistance and without using a range of motion.
- Use continuous rhythmical activities instead of ballistic or jerky movements.

Safety Issues

- Make prevention of injury a priority, providing protection as needed.
- Distribute pressure over the trunk to support during transfers, applying little pressure on limbs.
- Avoid crowded areas in the pool.
- Obtain medical clearance for contraindicated activities.
- Hold brainstorming sessions with caregivers, participants, and medical personnel to learn precautions you should take in transferring and pool entry and exit.
- Avoid risky activities, such as jumping, high-impact activities, bumping, and contact with others, equipment, walls, and floors.
- Avoid twisting and turning.
- Report redness, swelling, and heated skin areas to participants and caregivers.

Goals to Target

Physical goals include improving body awareness through carefully designed movement exploration, muscle strength, and functional range of motion; improving or maintaining vital capacity; increasing physical comfort level; and decreasing posture deviation progression. Psychological goals include improving the quality of life through fun, normalized activities and increasing independence through recreational activities. Focus on increasing awareness of how to keep oneself safe in the aquatic environment.

Common Related Conditions

Disabilities commonly associated with brittle bones include osteogenesis imperfecta (in various categories), osteoporosis, spina bifida, traumatic spinal cord injury, and any progressive neurological or orthopedic condition in which weight bearing is compromised.

CARDIOVASCULAR DISORDERS

Cardiovascular disorders can be congenital or acquired, progressive or nonprogressive, temporary or permanent, or primary or secondary. Although not visible, disorders of the heart and circulatory system can be as limiting or more limiting than neuromuscular or orthopedic disabilities, because the cardiovascular system is responsible for transport of oxygen and nutrients to the body.

Examples of primary cardiovascular disorders are rheumatic heart disease and valvular stenosis. Secondary disorders include congenital heart defects accompanying Down syndrome or peripheral vascular disease caused by diabetes. Research the limitations of those cardiovascular challenges that are evident in your participants.

There are many forms of cardiovascular (CV) disease, including congenital heart disorders, acquired inflammatory heart disease, valvular disorders, degenerative heart disease, and vascular disorders (Surburg 1995). In general, CV disorders that limit function result in decreased oxygenation of the blood, insufficient cardiac output, and (or) abnormalities in transporting blood supply. Total performance suffers because of low endurance. Fatigue, tingling of extremities, dizziness, and blurred vision may be problems that force individuals to be sedentary (Miller and Sullivan 1982).

Teaching Tips

• Activities done in a horizontal or recumbent position are the least strenuous with sitting positions more strenuous and standing most strenuous.

• Control vigorous, sustained aerobic activity.

• Monitor **target heart rate** zone and blood pressure closely.

• Communicate frequently about exertion level. Use the perceived exertion scale (Borg 1982) to monitor participant's fatigue level.

• Have physician designate the level of restriction using a MET equivalent chart.

• Reduce intensity in hot, humid surroundings.

• Refer to the Physicians' Desk Reference (Mehta 1996) regarding medications and exercise.

• Incorporate frequent rest periods during aquatic sessions.

• Encourage calorie-burning, low-intensity swimming.

• Lower the intensity of swimming by proposing an underwater recovery of the arms during swim strokes.

• Lower the intensity of exercise by not raising arms out of the water above the head during vertical exercises.

Safety Issues

• Be aware that water pressure affects elasticity of the lungs, causing difficulty in expansion and contraction. Individuals with heart failure or mitral valve obstruction may have aquatic activities contraindicated due to breathlessness resulting from water pressure.

• Monitor pulse rate (before, during, and after) and blood pressure (before and after) to make sure they comply with physician-approved target zones.

• Check with physician for contraindications, such as isometric exercises (due to possible increase in blood pressure).

• Move slowly when changing positions (e.g., lying on back to standing) as the heart needs time to compensate for the new position (Daniels and Davies 1975).

Goals to Target

Programs for individuals with cardiovascular disorders should focus on increasing cardiovascular endurance, relaxation, and knowledge of physical strengths and limitations. Individuals should strive to increase safe participation in lifetime aquatic fitness activities.

Common Related Conditions

Disabilities commonly associated with cardiovascular disorders include pulmonic or aortic stenosis, coarctation of the aorta, atherosclerosis, tetralogy of Fallot, transposition of the great vessels, rheumatic heart disease, ventricular or atrial septal defect, valvular defects, coronary artery disease, stroke, congestive heart disease, and dysrhythmia.

CIRCULATORY DISORDERS

Circulatory disorders involve pathology to the veins, arteries, or blood traveling through the body. Such a condition may be due to irregularly shaped cells, hardening of the arteries, fat deposits forming plaque, high blood pressure, inability of the blood vessels to repair themselves (to clot), aneurysms, or insufficient oxygen-carrying capacity. In general, insufficient circulation may result in poor aerobic capacity, heart attacks, or stroke as well as poor sensation in the extremities and fatigue.

Teaching Tips

• Be aware that although warm water increases circulation, water temperatures over 98°F may be contraindicated for people with heart problems.

• Encourage individuals with poor muscle tone in their lower bodies (where blood pools in legs and feet) to kick, or move their legs. Having someone passively move or massage their legs for them may be contraindicated due to the possibility of dislodging blood clots.

• Keep in mind that decreased blood flow to the extremities causes feet and legs to bruise easily.

• Use caution in walking, transferring, stair climbing, and swim strokes.

• Be aware that decreased blood flow to the extremities may cause hands and feet to be cold. After swimming, encourage participants to dry their hands and feet well and cover themselves in dry towels.

• Keep in mind that pain, aching, and cramping are also problems caused by inadequate blood supply to extremities. Encourage participants to rest for about two minutes when this occurs (Sherrill 1993).

Safety Issues

• Due to insufficient blood supply in the extremities, cuts and bruises may heal poorly, which may lead to chronic skin ulcers and gangrene.

• At high risk for circulatory disorders are the elderly, severe diabetics, and individuals with lower body paralysis.

• If edema (swelling) is present in feet and ankles, report this to the individual and/or to caregivers.

• If hypertension is uncontrolled, strenuous activity may cause headache, blurred vision, nosebleeds, or convulsions.

• Monitor blood pressure before and after exercise.

• If blood pressure is high or any symptoms have occurred, reduce duration or intensity or both and urge participant to contact physician.

• If resting blood pressure exceeds 200/120 or resting rate is different than typical pattern, participant should not engage in physical activity.

• Isometric exercises (like pushing against an immovable object) should be used with extreme caution by individuals with hypertension.

• Individuals with sickle cell anemia may need medical attention if they display symptoms, such as jaundice, pain, aching bones, swollen joints, or fatigued and labored breathing (Surburg 1995). Physicians must approve activity intensity in individuals with sickle cell anemia.

• Individuals with hemophilia will need medical attention if injuries to the head, neck, and chest occur or if swelling of the joints or bleeding will not cease. Individuals with hemophilia should not take aspirin and should also avoid jumping and high-impact and contact sports.

• Staff should be prepared for emergencies, including having access to medical emergency numbers and training in first aid and CPR. Staff should also be knowledgeable of medications the participant is taking and the possible side effects.

Goals to Target

Improve cardiovascular function within limitations. Develop an aquatic fitness routine that is safe, successful, and satisfactory to the participant.

Common Related Conditions

Circulatory disorders may occur in people who have had a stroke, spinal injury, traumatic brain injury, orthopedic injury, lead poisoning, or an amputation; or in people with peripheral vascular disease, hemophilia, or sickle cell anemia; or in those who are elderly.

CONTRACTURES AND LIMITATIONS TO RANGE OF MOTION

A contracture develops when muscles and connective tissue around a joint become abnormally short, severely limiting the range of motion (ROM). The joint often becomes rigid, flexed, and resistant to stretching and relaxation exercises. Contracted joints limit mobility, flexibility, and functional skills necessary for work, play, and self-care (figure 9.2). If you notice a contracture developing in a young child or someone recently injured, immediately refer the person to an orthopedic physician or physical or occupational therapist. You can tell a joint is developing a contracture when you notice a progressive decrease in range of motion over time.

Contractures may develop as a result of neuromuscular pathology (e.g., multiple sclerosis), nervous system dysfunction (e.g., spinal cord injuries), joint damage (e.g., hemophilia, arthritis, trauma), brain injury (e.g., cerebral palsy, traumatic brain injury, cerebrovascular accidents), or anything that causes muscular weakness on one side of the joint or pathological muscular hypertrophy. Muscles used against

gravity, such as the muscles in front of the leg (shin) to help keep feet dorsi flexed, may be damaged, permitting gravity to cause the foot to drop (plantar flexion).

Many individuals do not experience pain from contractures, but some individuals with arthritis or other joint degeneration disorders may. Warm water aids in relaxing contractured joints, thereby making swimming an activity of choice for those with contractures. Moreover, aquatic activities and swim strokes done underwater can increase range of motion in joints due to the ease of movement and decreased pain in the water (Dulcy 1983a). Thus, very often a person with joint pain can use fun aquatic activities instead of land exercises that may be painful and less effective due to gravity. Another benefit that can assist individuals with contractures or poor ROM is that the water affords a wider range of positions on many different planes (Dulcy 1983a).

Teaching Tips

The National Multiple Sclerosis Society Aquatic Exercise Program handbook (1993) describes these and other tips given below.

- Appropriate aquatic activities for individuals with plantar flexion contractures include

Figure 9.2 Contractures limit range of motion.

walking with good heel strike; walking downstairs backward to get into the pool; and leaning forward facing the pool wall about three feet from the wall, with heels on the ground and hands on the wall.

• Perform activities especially slowly during initial warm-up phase.

• Encourage participants to move through a full range of motion.

• Ask permission before helping participants move.

• Never force movement in a joint or extremity.

• Let movement be facilitated by the effects of the water and the participant's actions, providing support and stabilization to other body parts as needed.

• Perform exercises and activities in a standing position with feet flat.

• Encourage a three-to-five minute swim or walking warm-up before stretching.

• Make stroke adaptations based on limited ROM. Individuals with forward shoulders who have tight chest muscles (pectorals) and weak (lax) upper back muscles (upper back extensors) will have trouble with the recovery in the front crawl, full extension during the glide in breaststroke, and full shoulder circumduction in the back crawl. (See chapter 12 section on enhancing flexibility for more information on ROM.)

• Try having the individual use an underwater recovery as this may be beneficial for the front crawl.

• Try encouraging the individual to exaggerate the body roll to achieve a recovery with rhythmic breathing to one side, to breathe when the recovery arm is lying on the hip along the body, to breathe to the front, or to roll over to the back to breathe. Encourage the participant to find what works for him or her, but do not allow participant to lift the head in order to raise the arms. Place a flotation device at the hips or between the knees to keep the body horizontal.

• In the breaststroke, let the arms spread slightly in front, instead of keeping hands pressed together. People with limited ROM in shoulders due to contractures may not be able to streamline themselves during the glide portion of the breaststroke.

• Modify the back crawl for decreased ROM in shoulders by creating more body roll, which allows the participant to place the arms in the water without as much ROM needed.

• Use a snorkel to enhance breathing when neck ROM is limited.

• Use fins to facilitate hip extension in supine position for participants with hip extension limitations. But don't try to add resistance to anyone with an injury or joint replacement.

• Stress the downward motion of the legs in the back crawl.

• Emphasize hyperextending the hip, not rotating the trunk when performing the back crawl kick.

• Warm up hip extensors by walking backward.

• Be aware that the breaststroke kick may be hard for those with problems of internal and external rotation of the hips. Internal rotation is needed for the beginning of the whip in the elementary backstroke and breaststroke kicks and external rotation of the feet is necessary for the catch.

• Be aware that range of motion limitations and contractures of the knee and ankle may be common in wheelchair users, those who use crutches, and those who experience other orthopedic difficulties, such as muscle weakness or arthritis. To improve knee extension, have the participant sit on the edge of an inflatable raft with knees bent, then extend the knees and push forcefully with shins to move raft backward. When the participant has enough strength to move the float 25 yards during a session, have him or her wear light fins if the physician agrees. But remember: don't try to add resistance to anyone with an injury or joint replacement.

• Use hand paddles for participants whose wrist contractures prevent adequate water catch due to decreased surface area and sculling in preparation for the power phase of the stroke, with physician approval.

• Allow participants with contractured wrists to use a modified back crawl or a double-arm backstroke.

• Be aware that ankle limitations may prevent functional walking. Participants with plantar flexion contractures (toes pointed away from head, toward floor) will have problems with leg propulsion in the breaststroke, elementary backstroke, and sidestroke.

Safety Issues

Contractures generally limit the ability to move, which may cause problems with recovery from a prone position or in transfers. Therefore, have participants roll to the back and stand from a supine position.

Goals to Target

Direct efforts to improve or maintain range of motion, increase independent activity, and improve functional swim skills.

Common Related Conditions

Contractures are commonly found in participants with scar tissue from burns or traumatic injuries, amputees with a stump close to a joint, individuals with cerebral palsy, multiple sclerosis, spinal cord injuries, traumatic brain injuries, arthritis, hemophilia, joint replacements, sports injuries, osteoporosis, osteogenesis imperfecta, or any type of paralysis or paresis, or in individuals who have had polio or a mastectomy or who have been in a coma.

DEAFNESS AND HARD OF HEARING

Individuals who are unable to process linguistic information with or without hearing aids are classified as deaf. There are distinctions made between levels of hearing loss based on performance on an audiogram. Individuals with a moderate hearing loss have difficulty but can usually understand speech through the ears alone with or without hearing aids.

Many individuals with a hearing loss do not consider themselves disabled but as belonging to a linguistic minority as a separate culture. You should read about the Deaf culture, learn American Sign Language, and communicate with individuals who are Deaf to learn the issues surrounding their culture. As members of a swim class, Deaf participants need aquatic instructors who either sign or make provisions for an interpreter. Although interpreters are important for communication during class, you should learn to sign so that you may develop personal relationships with students. In general, Deaf participants are integrated into regular

programs, but if deafness is secondary to a physical or mental disability, other placements may be warranted.

Teaching Tips

• When using an interpreter, remember to look at the participant while speaking.

• Determine what the person needs in order to maximize communication.

• Keep in mind that short sentences are easier to speech-read.

• Don't have participants face into the sun during directions.

• Be aware of the glare of the light on the water, which reduces visibility greatly.

• If someone speech-reads, make provisions for them to be able to see, such as placing him or her in the front of the group during demonstrations.

• Avoid placing your hands in front of your mouth, speaking with your back to participants, and having someone demonstrate at the same time you are talking as it is hard to watch the

Figure 9.3 Sign directions for swimmers who are deaf.

demonstration and the interpreter at the same time.

- Provide a dry place to store hearing aids.
- Employ many visual aids.
- Use hand signals to stop and start activities.
- When using water safety videos, inquire of the participant and interpreter about where to find a closed caption decoder.
- Use E-mail for quick, visual information distribution.
- Stand still while instructing.
- Rephrase any sentence the participant does not initially understand. Develop a private signal for the participant to use to let you know that he didn't understand to reduce embarrassment.
- When addressing a hard-of-hearing participant, make sure you have his or her full attention before giving directions.
- Each state has an 800 number that connects you to a relay system, allowing you to communicate with a Deaf person who uses a TDD if you don't.

Safety Issues

- If the vestibular mechanisms in the inner ear are damaged and if deafness is a result of a sensorineural loss, balance problems may result. Remember to be aware of balance issues.
- Since auditory emergency signals are not useful, establish a visual sign to get attention. Encourage facility to provide visual signals (flashing lights) in addition to auditory fire alarms.

Goals to Target

Appropriate goals include improving balance (if necessary) and improving self-confidence in mainstreamed programs. Develop or maintain social skills. Develop rhythm during swim strokes.

Common Related Conditions

Common conditions resulting in deafness or hearing impairment include meningitis, congenital deafness, acquired deafness, and hearing loss due to traumatic brain injury; secondary condition to cerebral palsy.

HEAD CONTROL DIFFICULTIES

Individuals with limited strength in the neck (cervical) flexors or extensors, such as the sternocleidomastoideus, trapezius, or splenius capitis, will have poor head control. As you well know, however, head control is a necessity in aquatic activities for tasks such as rhythmic breathing, keeping the head above the water in sidestroke, and correct body position in the backstroke and in vertical positions, such as treading water and water-walking. Independent swimming cannot be achieved by participants who lack head control; they must have the assistance of another person or a flotation device. Some individuals with poor head control will not be able to increase strength in the neck muscles due to deterioration, such as that found in people with muscular dystrophy, or will not be able to increase functional strength due to high muscle tone, as in people with spastic cerebral palsy. Other reasons for poor head control may be inadequate development of righting reactions. The development of these reactions as an infant and young child help the individual right the body and head in relation to gravity. Individuals with damaged vestibular systems may have a poor ability to right the head.

Teaching Tips

- Develop strokes on back, eliminating need for head control with rhythmic breathing.
- Use face mask and snorkel for swimming on the front, eliminating the need for rhythmic breathing (see figure 9.4).
- Assist breathing to the front by walking or swimming in front of participant and pushing up on chest or giving support on chin or underarms to lift head and face.
- Do not encourage participants with cerebral palsy who have poor neck and head control to breathe by lifting the head as this action causes neck extension and possibly primitive reflex patterns that affect arm and leg control.
- Assist breathing to side by pushing down on shoulder of nonbreathing side to rotate participant onto side for breathing.
- Try having the participant wear a ski belt or rescue tube across chest and under armpits (with closing clip on back) to elevate chest and face area (see figure 9.5).

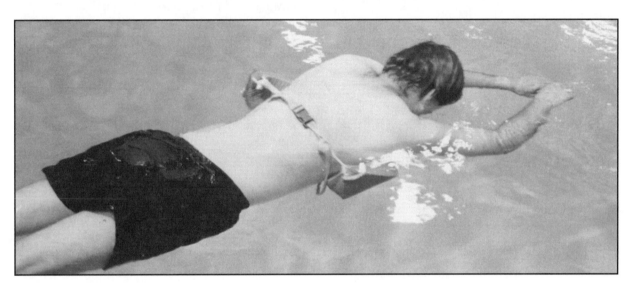

Figure 9.4 Using a face mask and snorkle can aid a swimmer with a limited range of neck motion.

Figure 9.5 Using a rescue tube under chest and armpits helps elevate face for easier rhythmic breathing.

• Consider allowing participants to wear a flotation collar to hold head above water.

• During activities, maintain a position at or near the participant's head to prevent sudden submersion due to lack of head control.

Safety Issues

• When in a prone position, individual must have one-on-one assistance.

• You must know how long the person can hold his or her breath and establish signals for when to help the participant breathe.

Goals to Target

Increase awareness of movements used to breathe in addition to rhythmic breathing. Improve ability to right the head and otherwise control the head. Increase comfort when wearing various flotation devices. Improve body position while swimming.

Common Related Conditions

Poor head control occurs in people who have had a stroke or traumatic brain injury and in people with cerebral palsy, muscular dystrophy, multiple sclerosis, cervical fusions, amyotrophic lateral sclerosis (ALS), or other neuromuscular or muscular disabilities.

HIGH MUSCLE TONE

High muscle tone (spasticity, **hypertonicity**) is caused by damage in the motor areas of the brain. Strong muscle contractions may occur spasmodically or repetitively to interfere with voluntary motor control. In individuals with cerebral palsy, spasticity and the hyperactive stretch reflex are related. "Receptors in the muscles that control tone in the stretched muscles overreact, causing the stretched muscles to contract" (Winnick 1995, p. 168). Spasticity results from these abnormal contractions and contributes to contractures and limitations in ranges of motion. Spasticity is also a frequent problem for individuals with hemiplegia, paraplegia, or quadriplegia.

Teaching Tips

• Maintain water 86 to 92°F so as to reduce spastic reaction of muscles by increasing the tendency to relax. Air temperature should be 4 degrees higher than water temperature.

• Be aware that sometimes spasticity causes internal rotation and **adduction** of legs, commonly referred to as "scissoring," which prevents walking and promotes sores between the knees. Place a comfortable piece of cushioning between the knees during swimming. Use partially inflated swimmies (arm floats), pull buoys, a half-kickboard, or a small black tube used by the swim team to work on arm strokes. But if a flotation device makes it difficult for the individual to recover to a vertical position, try using long tube socks (with the feet cut out) around the knees.

• Act as a spotter near the swimmer's head whenever spastic movements of the participant are sudden and involuntary, because these movements might cause the swimmer to submerge unwillingly or splash herself or others.

• Plan warm-up activities, such as slow gentle movements, gentle stretching, rotational movements, walking, easy kicking, or slow swimming as these have been shown to reduce spasticity. Consult with the participant's physical therapist about muscle tone management and appropriate range of motion.

• Avoid quick movements and sudden hands-on and hands-off movements; slow movements and steady touch are best with persons who have high muscle tone.

• Be aware that tactile teaching, or moving a person's body the way you want him to move it, may be necessary. Frequently a participant with high muscle tone cannot move the way desired. A participant may also have problems with body image and proprioceptive input, resulting in not knowing where body parts are in space. Sensory input, such as through tactile teaching, can aid in guiding the participant through skill development and can reduce confusion and nervousness about doing new skills.

• Keep in mind that decreased spasticity may result from placing the participant in the supine position and performing lateral swaying with a rotational motion at the end of each sway. Two instructors are needed for this or one instructor and a flotation device near swimmer's head (Campion 1985).

Safety Issues

• Be aware of sudden spastic movements, which may be dangerous during transfers in and out of the pool.

• Although warm water is essential for relaxation, whirlpools and saunas may be too hot for persons with temperature regulation problems or with decreased sensation due to paralysis.

• Position yourself at the head of the swimmer with spasticity as movements may cause the head to submerge.

Goals to Target

Strive to decrease spasticity, increase voluntary motor control, and improve quality of voluntary motor skills.

Common Related Conditions

Commonly seen in individuals with cerebral palsy, spinal cord injury, traumatic brain injury, multiple sclerosis, and other neurological impairments.

HYPERACTIVITY

Hyperactivity is overresponsivity to stimuli that causes the individual to move excessively. Typical characteristics include difficulty standing or sitting still, fidgeting, running, or climbing excessively, which occurs for at least six months. The individual with hyperactivity may have such problems as listening and doing written work because these require staying still for a period of time. The individual never seems to tire and may often act impulsively.

Teaching Tips

• Decrease stimuli in environment by limiting number of participants in the group.

• Reduce the amount of space used for lessons by sectioning off an area in the pool with buoys (see figure 9.6).

• Establish a routine and keep the instructional time structured.

• Be consistent with praise, cues, and consequences.

• Don't put out equipment until it is time to use it.

• Use bright colors to focus attention on an object or a learning center, but avoid wearing bright bathing suits or having too many colors total.

• Provide relaxation activities emphasizing slow movements and self-control.

• Follow logical skill progressions during each lesson.

• Build success into every lesson.

• Task-analyze each motor skill, because presenting one small part of the skill will increase success as opposed to the frustration of trying to do the entire skill at once.

• Provide specific feedback regarding performance of motor skills.

• Provide positive reinforcement for each accomplishment.

• Be consistent with rules, procedures, presentation of tasks, and reinforcement and punishment, thereby setting the tone for sessions that are free of misunderstandings and frustrations.

• Incorporate five-minute free swims into your sessions to provide less structured time.

• Keep structured lessons 5 to 30 minutes, depending on the swimmer's attention span.

• Consult with the swimmer's psychologist for a behavior modification program.

• Speak with the participant in response to poor behavior, explaining how the behavior is not appropriate.

• Keep in mind that frequently changing activities and offering limited choices helps to decrease restlessness and increase motivation.

Figure 9.6 Sectioning off an area of the pool can help swimmers with hyperactivity maintain their personal space.

Safety Issues

• Consult with caregivers, physicians, and table 8.1 for medication side effects related to physical activity.

• Position yourself between the individual with hyperactivity and the pool when walking on the slippery deck or near the deep end.

Goals to Target

Encourage individuals with hyperactivity to increase movement time on-task, increase quality of movement, increase self-control, and improve self-concept.

Common Related Conditions

Commonly seen in individuals with ADHD, severe learning disabilities, autism, pervasive developmental disabilities, and individuals prenatally exposed to alcohol or other drugs.

INTERACTION DIFFICULTIES

Participants with cognitive, social, or behavioral conditions may have difficulty learning in a group. Individuals with a multitude of behavioral conditions and emotional disturbances require adaptations to communication, environment, and teaching strategies. Some interaction problems are withdrawal, anxiety, noncompliance, social maladjustment, disruptiveness, self-injurious and self-stimulatory behavior, phobias, obsessions, compulsions, and schizophrenia. Emotional and learning support personnel may accompany students who are in school-based physical education aquatic programs.

Teaching Tips

• Provide clear limits and rules that participants can understand and achieve.

• Provide structure and routine within the aquatic lesson.

• Be consistent with cues, rules, and consequences.

• Tell participants what you are going to do before touching them.

• Reinforce appropriate behavior with specific, positive praise.

• Check with caregivers as to appropriate consequences and applied behavior analysis plans.

• Since eye contact may be a problem, repeat demonstrations, and guide participant's face toward the demonstrations with your hand or move the participant physically if he tolerates that.

• Start with a very small group of two or three and move to a larger group if participant feels comfortable and is learning.

• Collaborate frequently with caregivers and school vocational or rehabilitation personnel to determine proper approach to behavior management.

• Teach participants to demonstrate respect for themselves, others, and property.

Safety Issues

• Since biting, scratching, or hitting may be behaviors exhibited by those with extreme interaction problems, make sure your tetanus and hepatitis series shots are up-to-date.

• Know the medications the participant takes so that you may note, report, or prevent side effects.

• Some participants with interaction problems do not possess danger awareness skills. This can be a safety issue in the pool area due to deep water, slippery decks, and diving boards.

• Emotional lability (mood swings) in some individuals with interaction problems may cause the participant to be happy one moment and have a crying tantrum the next. Be alert for spontaneous, impulsive behavior.

Goals to Target

Individuals with interaction problems need to increase ability to solve problems, make positive choices more often, increase awareness of others' feelings and rights, increase self-direction, improve safe swimming behavior, increase number of people socialized with, improve self-esteem through success in swimming, improve independence in the aquatic environment, decrease inappropriate behaviors, increase awareness of dangers in the aquatic environment, increase self-control, and improve quality of swim skills.

Common Related Conditions

Interaction difficulties are commonly seen in individuals with autism, pervasive developmental disabilities, mental retardation, schizophrenia, severe emotional disturbance, bipolar disorders, prenatal exposure to alcohol or other drugs, and Fragile X Syndrome.

JOINT DYSFUNCTION

A joint is an articulation of two bones with a smooth inner lining or fluid sac called the "synovium" and an enclosure of fibrous outer tissue called the "capsule" (Blauvelt and Nelson 1994). Disease, trauma, or degenerative disabilities can cause joint dysfunction and changes in joint structure. Infection, inflammation, and trauma may lead to loss of joint function or severe limitations to range of motion, such as joint contracture (see also the section in this chapter on "Contractures and Limitations to Range of Motion").

Joint complications such as arthrogryposis produce stiffness and joint deformity, whereas arthritis is manifested by stiffness, swelling, pain, and soreness. Weak muscles surrounding the joints result from and are complicated by not moving joints through a normal range of motion during activities of daily living and leisure activities. Experts strongly recommend swimming and other aquatic activities.

In this section, we'll focus on joint dysfunction due to arthritis and joint replacement. Teaching tips, safety information, and goals to target for individuals with arthrogryposis are located in the "Contractures and Limitations to Range of Motion" section, since this joint dysfunction is also known as "multiple congenital contracture."

Teaching Tips

• For range of motion limitations and contractures, see the contracture section in this chapter.

• Pain tolerance, swelling, and range of motion may change daily so communicate with the participant frequently, adapting activities to changing symptoms daily.

• Avoid activities that compress the bones and joints, such as jumping and contact activities.

• Offer aquatic activity that lends itself to increasing the range of motion of as many joints as possible.

• Perform exercises and activities slowly underwater.

• Provide weight-bearing activities.

• Offer less strenuous activities during "pain days."

• Monitor postactivity condition to determine next session's work plan.

• Use isometric exercises to improve strength of muscles around a joint.

• Stretch after entire body is warmed up.

• Use aquatic activities consistently and regularly.

• Consult physical therapist to devise appropriate swim plans.

• Have swimmers avoid tight swimsuits and wearing oversized shirts in the pool as they limit movements.

• Plan for gradual increase in activity frequency, intensity, and time.

• Avoid excessive fatigue, fast movements, and competitive atmosphere.

• Avoid excessive back extension, such as prone strokes with face out of the water.

• Be aware that warm water is most often recommended (83 to 88°F), but some participants may feel better in cooler water.

• Provide a water table, tot dock, or chair in the water for resting.

Safety

• Protect against falls, bumping, and colliding with equipment or others.

• Pain and limited range of motion may be manifested by movement difficulties.

• Provide hydraulic lift and easy-access stairs with wide and gradual descending stairs. Many participants with arthritis may fall trying to get their feet on the small recessed ladders in most pools.

• Install handrails and hand grips in and around pool for balance during activities and transfers.

• Rinse off chlorine as people with arthritis may experience a chemical reaction to chlorine caused by their medication.

• Do not force participants to "work through the pain."

Goals to Target

Individuals with joint problems should strive to increase frequency, intensity, and time in aquatic activities without pain, improve strength in muscles around affected joints, improve or maintain range of motion, improve cardiorespiratory endurance, balance, and functional gait, increase tolerance of weight bearing and independence, prevent further contractures, and reduce pain and inflammation.

Common Related Conditions

Common disabilities associated with joint dysfunction include osteoarthritis, rheumatoid arthritis, juvenile rheumatoid arthritis, fibromyalgia, and lupus.

KINESTHETIC SYSTEM DISORDERS

Sensory stimuli enters the kinesthetic system via muscles, tendons, and joints, letting us know where the body and extremities are in space and how they are moving. Disorders in input and interpretation cause deficits in movement (dyskinesia) because the body and its extremities cannot interpret where it is in space or at what speed it is moving. Individuals who cannot identify where the body is while swimming will demonstrate inconsistent movements and skills as corrections in stroke mechanics are based on being able to feel subtle changes in arm, leg, and trunk angles, and speed at which each movement is accomplished.

Teaching Tips

- Create turbulence around an extremity to increase awareness of its position in space.
- Use manual guidance to manipulate the participant's body.
- Apply mild joint pressure to increase awareness of extremities.
- Provide activities through which you challenge the person to vary swimming speed.
- Attach a five-foot-long piece of surgical tubing to a weight lifter's belt. Have swimmer wear belt and tie tubing to the gutter. Have the swimmer try to swim away on this tethered line; this creates increased awareness of the body and its movements.

- Ask participants to bring in old clothes and swim or walk in neck-deep water. The weight of the clothes provides increased awareness that can help them feel stroke corrections until the correction is more automatic.
- Bearing weight on the hands (as in handstands) provides kinesthetic input.
- Lightweight water weights that you can Velcro to a body part can increase kinesthetic awareness.

Safety Issues

Lack of awareness of body parts causes the individual to be clumsy, and therefore he or she may hit others or the wall when swimming.

Goals to Target

Individuals with kinesthetic awareness problems need to increase body awareness and understanding of how body parts function for swimming and water safety, increase awareness of both sides of the body and how they work together (laterality) and directionality (awareness of the body in relation to objects), and increase ability to cross midline by making 90-degree turns while swimming on front.

Common Related Conditions

Kinesthetic system disorders are manifested in individuals with traumatic brain injury, stroke, severe learning disabilities, mental retardation, cerebral palsy, neuromuscular disabilities, autism, prenatal exposure to alcohol and other drugs, and pervasive developmental disabilities.

MEMORY AND UNDERSTANDING PROBLEMS

Memory and understanding problems may be a primary disability or secondary to other disabilities. The diagnosis of cognitive impairment does not give adequate information regarding understanding and ability to recall previously learned tasks. A participant's primary disability may be a physical disability, such as cerebral palsy, but accompanying secondary problems may also exist, such as disorientation, memory deficits, and cognitive impairment. Thus, you must be able to assess the individual's ability to follow multistep directions, understand what you are requesting, and remember the task for use at a later time.

Difficulties with understanding directions and problems with memory interfere with the development of health-related physical fitness and acquisition of motor skills. If a participant cannot recall how to perform a skill from session to session, you may have to plan for adequate repetition. If a participant has a problem understanding, she may learn the skill immaturely and store it incorrectly in the memory. Thus, you must work to help the participant maintain and generalize the skills she has learned. This takes careful planning and continuous spot-checking for skill retention (Jansma and French 1994). Have the participant try the skill in different situations, such as in a game, in the deep end, in another setting (e.g., home pool), and with another instructor to facilitate generalization.

Teaching Tips

To help you better serve such individuals, we have divided the teaching tips into three parts: "Memory Difficulties," "Generalization," and "Poor Understanding of Information."

Memory Difficulties

• Use verbal cues often, such as "Move arms now."

• As visual cues can prove invaluable, you should model desired position and have the participant copy.

• Be aware that tactile cues are often the best means of cueing a person who does not remember what to do next; for example, tap person on shoulder to cue breathing at the right time.

• Have participant carry notebooks into locker room and pool area to help remind them of rules, duties, or sequence for dressing.

• Use Plexiglas and grease pencils. List the tasks the participant must accomplish and stand list by pool edge. As each task is completed, encourage participant to check it off (see figure 9.7). This keeps the person oriented to what is going on.

• Use lap counters to help participant keep track of laps.

• Use a kitchen timer to help a person know when to leave or how much time he has spent on a task.

• Consistency, repetition, and review are good strategies to increase memory.

• Post written handouts and lesson or skill checklists in pool area to show completed tasks and successes.

• Use basic orientation questions at each session; for example, "Where is the best place to enter the lap pool?"

• Use visual imagery to facilitate recall.

• Employ as many sensory modalities as possible, but not all at once.

• Simplify, demonstrate, and repeat.

• Use a hierarchy of cues; for example, start with a nonverbal cue, and if that doesn't work, move on to more intrusive cues, such as verbal cues, visual modeling, and finally physical assistance.

• Use few and simple words.

Generalization

• Remember that the swimmer will need much cueing to generalize skills.

• Have the participant practice the skills in as many situations as possible.

• Use verbal cueing to discuss ways in which the participant may use aquatic-related skills.

• Try having participant role-play and discuss how a skill might apply in various situations.

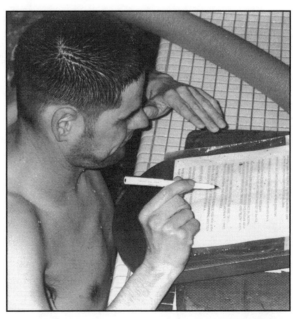

Figure 9.7 Using appropriate memory devices can help an individual become an independent swimmer.

Note: Many professionals feel that generalization of skills is impossible for individuals with severe memory and understanding problems. Strive for an interdisciplinary approach, using words, cues, and reinforcements that are used in other areas of the person's life. Specifically relate what participant is doing in the pool to the participant's life.

Poor Understanding of Information

• Start with one-step directions and gradually move on to two- and three-step directions.

• Repeat directions or ask swimmer to repeat directions.

• Keep in mind that a sterile environment devoid of as many visual and auditory stimuli as possible is best.

• After giving a command or asking a question, keep in mind that you may have to wait for a reply for more than 30 seconds.

• Visual and verbal prompts are helpful instead of long explanations.

• When working with an adult, speak in an adult-like manner; in other words, use simple phrases but not baby talk.

• If you are a fast talker, slow down but don't exaggerate the slowness.

• Inform participants of class expectations daily.

Safety Issues

• Emphasize and repeat safety directions.

• Never assume any safety issue is minor.

• Accident prevention is an issue that is abstract to this group.

• Cause and effect relationships are hard to understand. Be specific about simple rules.

• To make safety issues come alive, demonstrate and use verbal and physical cues for safety information (see figure 9.8).

Goals to Target

Individuals with poor understanding of directions need to improve following of multistep directions, recollection of safety rules, generalization of aquatic skills to home pools, beaches, and other community facilities, and understanding of directions while in a large group and increase awareness of safety issues and independent swim skills.

Common Related Conditions

Common disabilities include mental retardation, traumatic brain injury, severe learning disabilities, stroke, autism, individuals prenatally exposed to drugs, and those with pervasive developmental disability.

Figure 9.8 Giving a physical prompt is a concrete means of teaching someone with difficulty understanding verbal language.

MULTISENSORY DEPRIVATION

Individuals with visual and hearing difficulties in combination may be referred to as deaf-blind (D/B) or multisensory deprived (MSD). Individuals with MSD may have residual hearing and/or vision or may be totally deaf and blind. Communication may be difficult as many use hand-over-hand signing. Allow these participants to manipulate the aquatic environment because they view the world from a tactile, kinesthetic, and vestibular perspective. Often medical problems are secondary characteristics of individuals with MSD. Some may be mislabeled as mentally retarded and some are, in fact, mentally retarded (McInness and Treffry 1982). Those with MSD with other disabilities may not be successful in ordinary (on land) physical activities and may need an aquatic program in order to establish some amount of mobility and independence (Curren 1971). You may have to spend a great amount of time establishing meaningful relationships.

Teaching Tips

- Establish trust through touch.

- Provide tactile orientation to the pool area, encouraging touching of pool gutters, ladders, and water returns.

- Establish signs for emergencies, commands, and positions. Figure 9.9 is from Grosse (1985) and describes commands used with a deaf-blind youth in the pool.

- Structure lessons to establish a typical routine. This will make the participant feel safe, helping her begin to achieve a sense of independence through knowing what will happen next. Add skills to already established ones as participant experiences success, but maintain a routine sequence.

- Use skill commands followed by moving the person through the motion of the skill (see figure 9.10). Then have her feel you performing the movement. Follow with the command again and the sign for "go."

- Until the participant is an independent swimmer, use the same activities and drills in the same pool location from lesson to lesson.

- Provide concrete methods of praise, such as a hand shake or pat on the back for good progress, since typical reinforcements such as smiles and verbal praise probably won't be useful.

- Incidental learning is nonexistent. You must consciously teach each behavior and skill that you want the individual to do.

- Take advantage of any residual vision by using bright-colored objects.

- Do not surprise participant by pulling him into position.

- To give participant a sense of security, give command or explanation and gradually move into the skill.

- Use co-active movement, in which your body are in as much contact as possible with the swimmer, gradually increasing space between the bodies (Sherrill 1993). Link and use signs and cues once body contact is no longer needed.

Safety Issues

- One-on-one supervision is required for nonswimmers and low student-to-teacher ratio for swimmers (one instructor per three swimmers).

- Be aware that disorientation may cause nonswimmers to venture into deep water. Lifeguards and instructors should know their swimmers. Guide disoriented participants back to appropriate depth water. Try roping off an area in the pool for beginners to improve orientation and decrease wandering into deep water.

- Don't leave equipment scattered around deck.

Goals to Target

Individuals with MSD should work on skills to increase self-directed movement, improve awareness of water safety, increase swim skills without flotation devices, and develop fitness through increased mobility.

Common Related Conditions

Commonly associated with MSD are people who are both deaf and blind and people with Usher's syndrome, and other conditions acquired through maternal infections, such as rubella, drug and alcohol abuse, and sexually transmitted diseases, or acquired after birth as a result of meningitis or scarlet fever.

Signs and Positions

Skill	Sign	Position
Enter pool	Hand gesture for come and slight tug on arm.	From seated position on side he comes to the edge, sits, rolls to stomach, and slides in feet first over the edge, finishing standing facing the side.
Walk	Gentle pull on both hands, sign for come.	Instructor faces student, holding both hands. Instructor walks backward as student walks forward.
Dunk head*	Gentle press on back of head.	In the walking position, the instructor reaches along side of student's neck and around to the back of the head, placing hand on the back of the head. This hand gives the sign and then also helps the student make the initial short dunk. Once the student has learned the sign, it can be given from any position.
Blow bubbles*	Blow on hand.	In the walking position, the instructor takes one of the student's hands and blows against that hand. He then holds the student's hand in front of the student's mouth. This needs *much repetition*. Action is repeated with mouths close to and on the water so that bubbles result when the instructor blows.
Prone kick*	Tap on thigh.	Student is positioned at the side with arms extended, hands holding gutter. Instructor then taps thigh and motors through the kicking as the student holds the wall. Once the student can kick a little, he can also be asked to dunk in this position.
Back float*	Tap on back of shoulder.	Instructor stands behind student and taps back of one shoulder. The instructor then reaches under both armpits until he can reach in front of the student's shoulders. From this position, the instructor gently tips the student onto his back, supported by the instructor's body. The instructor can gradually lessen support by dropping his hips and lowering the hand position. Tipping the student's chin can be done with one hand if he does not do it himself (though he probably will to keep his face out of the water).
Use arms	Tap or press on back or underside of upper arms.	Can be given in any position. This is used to cue the use of crawl arms as well as to cue "keep going."
Climb out	Grasp wrist and tug gently and tap pool deck.	From a position at the pool side the instructor climbs onto the deck and gently tugs. Student climbs out.
Jump in	Gently push in center of back.	Standing next to the student at the deep end, the instructor gives the sign, grasps the upper arms of the student, and both jump in. Once student is familiar with the sign, he will jump without the instructor. Note: The student should not try the jump until he can swim the width with complete independence.
Roll over	Grasp upper arm. Lift on the arm and push it across the front of the swimmer's body.	This sign is used for both types of rolls: prone to supine and supine to prone. The arm is held until 90 degrees of the roll is completed.

*Indicates a skill that the swimmer should "feel" the instructor demonstrate.

Figure 9.9 Commands for a deaf-blind youth (Grosse, 1985).

Figure 9.10 Tactile teaching is helpful for blind or deaf-blind swimmers.

ORAL MOTOR DYSFUNCTION

Lip closure and breath control may be difficult for participants with neuromuscular disabilities affecting the cranial facial muscles or who have suffered facial trauma. Many individuals with oral motor dysfunction drink the water instead of keeping their lips closed or exhaling.

Teaching Tips

• Use activities that stress blowing against resistance, such as blowing Ping-Pong balls, making bubbles with mouth in the water (see figure 9.11), and blowing up floats, swimmies, and beach balls.

• Try having toddlers and preschoolers with problems drinking pool water hold a pacifier in their mouths to encourage lip strength and decrease the amount of pool water they drink.

• Manually close lips while giving verbal cue "Close your lips."

• Have participant say certain sounds as cues to encourage lip closure, such as "MMM" and humming.

• Be aware that individuals with moderate to high cognitive awareness might be able to keep their mouths open while underwater while keeping their throats closed to prevent swallowing or inhaling water.

• Encourage participant to flex the head slightly, because this may help with lip closure.

When the head is in extension and participant is lying on her back, the mouth tends to open.

• Keep participant stable, as unstable positions in the water or a feeling of falling causes the body to stiffen, the arms and legs to involuntarily extend and flex, and the mouth to open.

Safety Issues

• Excessive drinking of pool water due to poor oral motor control (or low cognitive ability) may lead to vomiting, diarrhea, and even hypernutremia (sodium imbalance) in those who are small in stature and low in weight (infants, toddlers, young children, and small adults).

Goals to Target

Individuals with poor oral motor coordination should perform activities to improve lip closure, facial muscle tone, and breath control, to increase awareness of lips, mouth, and facial movements, and to decrease drinking of pool water.

Figure 9.11 Blowing bubbles helps improve oral-motor control.

Common Related Conditions

Commonly seen in individuals with low muscle tone, cerebral palsy, severe multiple disabilities, stroke, hemiplegia, mental retardation, traumatic brain injury, and Down syndrome.

PARALYSIS, PARESIS, AND ATROPHY

Paralysis is the result of interrupted nerve innervation between the brain and muscles as a result of birth defects, disease, tumors, trauma, or infection. Paralysis usually refers to loss or impairment of voluntary muscle function while paresis refers to incomplete loss of voluntary muscle function. Atrophy refers to wasting away or reduction in size of muscle tissue due to disuse, disease, trauma, bed rest, infection, or tumor. These conditions lead to changes in muscle tone, range of motion, ambulation, organ function, sensation, health-related physical fitness, and motor skills. Other complications may result in postural problems, hypotension, pressure sores, bone ossification, and blood clots (Garvey 1991). Depending on the source of the paralysis or paresis, a variety of symptoms may be present that are not the same from one disability to the next.

Teaching Tips

• Paralysis causes alterations to floating positions. Look for ways to streamline the body, such as changing head position, attaching flotation devices or weights to lower or raise body position. Achieve a balanced body position by experimenting within proper safety limits.

• Modify strokes, entries, and water safety skills on an individual basis after determining extent of involvement.

• Encourage independence as much as possible, especially in self-care and locomotion.

• Plan extra time and, if necessary, assistance for self-care and locker room activities.

• Individuals whose legs are atrophied and therefore have little muscle weight in them often have lower bodies that float excessively, so, if necessary, place a light weight-belt around the hips, lowering the body somewhat, making it easier to get the head out of the water for breathing.

• Check skin for abrasions before and after swimming due to decreased sensation.

• Do not allow swimmers to bump or drag buttocks along pool deck.

• Be aware that obesity might be a factor due to passive lifestyle.

• Keep in mind that fatigue is common among individuals with muscle degeneration disabilities (muscular dystrophy, Lou Gehrig's disease) and in deconditioned individuals with spinal cord injuries. If necessary, allow frequent rest periods.

• Encourage use of aquasocks to decrease abrasions from transferring and scraping feet when swimming.

• If atrophy has caused posture problems, check with physician for specific movements that improve posture (see also section on "Posture Disorders").

• Be aware that muscle spasms and strange sensations sometimes interrupt the aquatic session.

• Encourage participant to communicate with physician about medications and proper positioning.

• Become knowledgeable of proper assistance in taking off and on braces and other **orthotic** devices.

• Work within trunk limitations as individuals with para- or quadriplegia will have had spinal fusions or other operations to stabilize the spine.

• See section in this chapter on "Contractures and Limitations to Range of Motion," as contractures are common among individuals with muscle tone problems.

• See sections in this chapter entitled "Cardiovascular Disorders" and "Respiratory Disorders," as muscle-weakening disabilities, such as muscular dystrophy or traumatic spinal cord injuries (SCI), will result in impaired respiration function; therefore, you may need to adjust fitness heart rate zones (see chapter 12). In addition, keep in mind that these participants are shallow breathers and coughing is difficult.

• Place special emphasis on upper body development. Include stretching and strengthening, focusing on deltoid and pectoral stretching.

• Be aware that stabilization of other body parts or trunk—such as belting lower extremities together—may be necessary for the swimmer to focus on one part of the body.

• Alter stroke mechanics as necessary due to uneven muscle strength and abnormal centers of gravity and buoyancy. Change stroke as little as possible from "normal" efficiency. Use trial and error to compensate for structural inefficiencies, limited range of motion, uneven strength, and a variety of other problems. Try having participant use smaller range of motion or sculling arm movements.

• To overcome difficulties in turning at the wall for swimming laps, have participant approach wall from an angle and use arm push-offs.

• If upper body impairment causes difficulty lifting or turning the head to breathe, encourage using mask and snorkel or rolling over onto the back to breathe. Initially, teach the back crawl or elementary backstroke.

• Try having participant use hand paddles as these may help with weak hand function by increasing surface area.

• Try having participant use fins if upper body is weak and lower body has some movement, but keep in mind that fins can be heavy and burdensome (see figure 9.12).

• Be aware that sidestroke may be difficult for individuals with lower body paralysis and atrophy because of balance problems and the importance of the kick in this stroke.

Safety Issues

• Discourage individuals with **decubitis ulcers**, or pressure sores, from participating in aquatics due to risk of infection.

• Ensure that individuals with halo braces are medically stable and that the linings of braces are replaced following swimming Avoid getting the head wet.

• Participants should avoid swimming if low blood pressure or autonomic dysreflexia (as could be seen in many with paraplegia and quadriplegia) impedes their on-land therapy treatments (Garvey 1991).

• Ensure that all collection bags are emptied before swimming.

• Check skin frequentlys as decreased sensation leads to unnoticed bruising.

• Avoid prolonged heat and cold and sudden temperature changes.

Goals to Target

Individuals with paralysis or atrophy should perform activities that increase balance and trunk stability, endurance, stability of posture, weight bearing (if feasible), number of pain-free positions, and independence, that increase or maintain range of motion and strength, and that improve ambulation, circulation, and transfers.

Figure 9.12 Swimming with fins can increase surface area for better propulsion.

Common Related Conditions

Common disabilities associated with paralysis, paresis, and atrophy include traumatic brain injury, stroke, spinal cord injury, orthopedic disabilities, prolonged bed rest with immobility, multiple sclerosis, spina bifida, muscular dystrophy, and myasthenia gravis.

POSTURE DISORDERS

Problems with posture may be a primary result of an orthopedic disability or a secondary result of a neuromuscular disorder. Posture disorders such as kyphosis, lordosis, or scoliosis may be of a functional nature (caused by day-to-day improper body mechanics) due to lifestyle, but proper exercise and conscious changes in walking, sitting, and standing alignment may correct it. They may, however, be of a structural nature; structural problems can only be corrected through surgery or other medical intervention, such as electrical stimulation.

Kyphosis is extreme flexion of the thoracic vertebrae causing the upper back to be humped, or rounded. The muscles that extend the upper back are weak and the pectorals may be tight as a result.

Lordosis is extreme hyperextension of the lumbar spine causing a "hollow" lower back, or "swayback." The muscles of the abdomen are usually weak and lax, the gluteals are weak, the hip flexors are tight, and the lower back muscles are short and tight. This combination causes the pelvis to tip forward, and the body compensates by leaning back, causing swayback.

Scoliosis is a rotolateral curvature of the spine in which the vertebrae are rotated and tilted to the side. Muscles on the tilted side of the back are short and tight while the muscles on the other side are weak and elongated, or lax.

Posture problems that affect the trunk cause poor body alignment during aquatics and other physical activity, poor functioning of internal organs, and sometimes pain. A severe problem affects breathing and flexibility.

Teaching Tips

• Seek information regarding home exercise programs to integrate into the aquatic program.

• Stick to recommended strokes that stress even muscle development, including the following:

1. Wide-sweep–arm breaststroke—helps improve symmetry in those with scoliosis and stretches chest muscles in those with kyphosis.

2. Double-arm backstroke—helps improve symmetry in those with scoliosis and stretches chest muscles and strengthens upper back muscles in those with kyphosis (see figure 9.13).

• Emphasize proper posture, stretching, and strengthening of both sides of the body.

• Capitalize on swimming time, the only time individuals who use back braces may take braces off.

• Discuss any range of motion limitations an individual who has had spinal surgery may have with the participant, caregiver, and physician.

• Adapt strokes and aquatic activities as necessary, based on range of motion limitations.

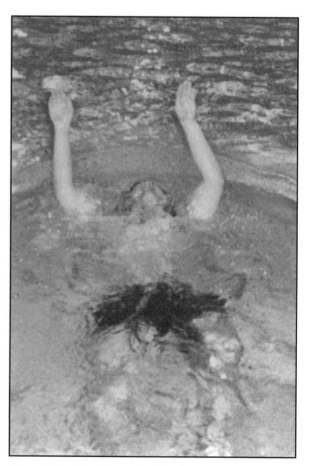

Figure 9.13 Double-arm backstroke can strengthen upper back muscles.

Safety Issues

• In juvenile kyphosis (Scheuermann's disease) vigorous flexion of the trunk is contraindicated in the acute stage of the condition

Goals to Target

Individuals with posture problems should perform activities that improve flexibility in limited body parts, enhance swim strokes to the best of limits, strengthen in targeted muscle groups, and that decrease pain and increase body awareness.

Common Related Conditions

Scoliosis is commonly seen in individuals with leg-length differences, quadriplegia, osteogenesis imperfecta, and dwarfism, such as spondyloepophyseal dysplasia.

Lordosis is commonly found in individuals with myelomeningocele spina bifida, muscular dystrophy, polio, paraplegia, cerebral palsy, spondylolisthesis, and osteogenesis imperfecta.

Kyphosis is commonly associated with older women (due to osteoporosis), individuals who are blind (due to walking with shoulders and head forward when using a cane or having a dog pulling them), individuals in wheelchairs (due to leaning and pushing forward), and individuals with cerebral palsy, Scheuermann's disease, quadriplegia, juvenile rheumatoid arthritis, and dwarfism conditions (such as spondyloepiphyseal dysplasia and diastrophic dysplasia), osteogenesis imperfecta, Friedreich's ataxia, and spina bifida.

PRIMITIVE REFLEX RETENTION

Primitive reflexes are normal, involuntary spinal cord and brain stem motor responses to stimuli. During infancy, primitive reflexes such as the grasp reflex, Moro reflex, asymmetrical tonic neck reflex, and symmetrical tonic neck reflex are inhibited by the maturing of the central nervous system and replaced by righting and equilibrium reactions and coordinated, voluntary motor output. When the CNS fails to mature due to brain damage, the individual may retain these primitive reflexes, interfering with normal, orderly motor development, posture, and voluntary motor control. Involuntary reflexes can affect muscle tone and compromise balance.

Teaching Tips

• During activities, use positions that inhibit reflexes such as a neutral head position or a slightly tucked chin position, with the head in midline of the shoulders, and hips and knees flexed.

• Use symmetrical activities (both sides of the body doing the same thing at same time) such as the breaststroke, elementary backstroke, inverted breaststroke, finning, and sculling.

• Use caution with scissor kick and flutter kick as these tend to promote the crossed extension reflex, causing scissoring of legs.

• Use caution in supine positions as neck extension stimulates the symmetrical tonic neck reflex, causing arms to extend and legs to flex.

• Consult with physical therapist as to proper positioning of body for increased extremity control (figure 9.14).

• See Harris 1978, for further information about head and jaw control positions.

Figure 9.14 Positioning someone with primitive reflexes to "break up" poor postural patterns will improve voluntary motor control.

• Be aware that rhythmic breathing to the side in front crawl may be impossible for those with severe asymmetrical tonic neck reflex (ATNR) retention. Turning the head to the side causes limbs to extend on face side and limbs to flex on skull side, thereby eliminating propulsion. Yet, those with mild ATNR retention may be able to rhythmic breathe to the side without interfering with the stroke.

Safety Issues

• Be aware that when swimming prone, individuals with tonic labyrinthine reflex retention will have difficulty raising their heads to breathe.

• Remain at the head, as position of the head and neck controls most movements in those with primitive reflex retention.

• Keep in mind that sudden noises, movements, or splashing may cause sudden reflex activity, possibly causing participant to lose safe position.

• While participant is in the supine position, guard against sudden submersion of face.

Goals to Target

Individuals with reflex retention problems should perform activities to increase extremity coordination by controlling positioning and to improve functional and independent swimming and voluntary motor control.

Common Related Conditions

Commonly affected are individuals with cerebral palsy, traumatic brain injury, stroke, neurological impairment, severe learning disabilities, and severe mental retardation.

PROPRIOCEPTIVE DISORDERS

See "Kinesthetic System Disorders."

RANGE OF MOTION DYSFUNCTION

See "Contractures and Limitations to Range of Motion."

RECEPTIVE-EXPRESSIVE LANGUAGE DISORDERS

See chapter 7 section entitled "Strategies for Overcoming Communication Barriers."

RESPIRATORY DISORDERS

Disorders of the respiratory system have a profound affect on aquatic activity because they limit the amount of air the participant may inhale or exhale. Respiratory disorders may cause narrowing of the bronchial tubes, increased mucous secretions, or destruction of lung elasticity. These may result in decreased vital lung capacity, decreased chest expansion, uncoordinated breathing patterns, labored breathing, difficulty with exhalation, nonfunctional coughing, and poor respiratory control for speech (Charness 1983). Medication may control symptoms but will not cure the disorder. "Swimming traditionally has been the sport of choice because it seems to interrupt **homeostasis** less than activities that cause perspiration and require breathing dry, cold or pollen laden air" (Sherrill 1993, p. 483).

Teaching Tips

• Use the double-arm backstroke, elementary backstroke, and inverted breaststroke to stretch chest muscles and expand chest area.

• Hydrostatic pressure of water on chest wall stimulates chest expansion, but have participant move slowly into chest- and neck-deep water.

• Focus on activities that encourage trunk mobility to facilitate increased vital lung capacity.

• Encourage individuals with respiratory problems to drink plenty of water outside of swim class.

• Warm water (greater than 93°F) helps spastic intercostal muscles relax, which improves the individual's capacity to expand the chest.

• Use breath control activities, such as bobbing and rhythmic breathing, which are good for increasing exhalation. Remind participant to breathe deeply and slowly.

• Keep in mind that intense activity combined with high emotional states and fatigue may provoke an asthma episode in some individuals with asthma. Therefore, limit competition within the instructional program.

• Provide rest periods commensurate with an individual's needs during activity.

• Keep in mind that low-intensity activity over a longer duration is usually more successful with fewer breathing problems.

• Use a long slow warm-up of 15 to 30 minutes.

• Keep activity changing area as clean as possible (dust- and mold-free).

• Avoid extreme changes in temperature. Maintain approximately a four-degree difference between air temperature in the locker room and natatorium and water temperature in the pool.

• Provide a place to expel coughed-up mucous.

Safety Issues

• Ensure that you understand the effect of medication on the individual's physical and mental performance, including heart rate and blood pressure.

• Communicate effectively with participant and physician to gather information concerning medication needs and safe intensity and duration levels.

• Be aware that for children with cystic fibrosis, excessive loss of sodium chloride in perspiration is dangerous. Insist that participant avoid strenuous activity out of pool and use caution in high-intensity workouts in very warm water (greater than 86°F) in which participants will sweat.

• Receive instruction from parents or physician on how to dislodge mucous plugs during activity in individuals with cystic fibrosis.

• Be aware that chronically ventilator-dependent individuals can use the pool as a means of therapy and enjoyment, but the participant's condition may require full emergency equipment and, possibly, the combined services of a doctor, nurse, anesthetist, physical therapist, or swim instructor and parent or caregiver (Carter 1988). The participant may need to be hand-ventilated or use a heavy grounded electrical cord and prepare for power outages (Carter, Dolan, and LeConey 1994). The participant will need calm water with no others splashing and the area where the ventilator is inserted should remain above water (neck for tracheostomy and nose for nasal endotracheal tube).

Goals to Target

Individuals with respiratory problems should perform activities to improve rhythmic breathing patterns by incorporating slow, deep breaths, increase time in activity, improve self-monitoring of warm-up and exercise time within limitations, improve or maintain chest and trunk flexibility, improve strength in diaphragm, chest, back, and neck to help muscles involved in breathing, and improve relaxation during activities.

Common Related Conditions

Common disabilities with respiratory disorders include chronic obstructive pulmonary diseases (COPD), cystic fibrosis, ankylosing spondylitis, kyphoscoliosis, severe scoliosis, severe kyphosis, emphysema, allergies, and bronchitis.

SEIZURES

Seizures are manifestations of a central nervous system disorder that upset electrical activity in the cerebrum. This upsets causes abnormal, involuntary, and unpredictable brain behavior, ranging from focal seizures, which are localized in one part of the brain causing short-term behavior changes or jerking of limbs, to generalized seizures, which range from unconsciousness and total body convulsions to limited impairment of consciousness (semiconsciousness). You may observe a participant who appears to be daydreaming, disoriented, or not paying attention during swim instruction; or, you may see a participant who suddenly drops underwater or has convulsions—all these behaviors may signify that the participant is having a seizure.

Signals of a seizure vary according to the type of seizure. Minor seizures may be characterized by staring off into space for several seconds followed by a quick return to full alertness. More intense seizures may include a combination of signals. The individual may experience an aura characterized as a strange sensation that lasts a few seconds prior to the seizure. The individual may perceive an aura as a visual or auditory hallucination, a painful sensation, a peculiar taste or smell, or a sensation warning him to move to safety. The person may also suddenly become rigid. Loss of consciousness is possible. Uncontrollable muscular movement and accompanying loss of bladder and bowel control may result. Breath-holding, salivation, and rapid pulse are also common during a seizure.

Teaching Tips

• Keep in mind that medication may reduce coordination and concentration, slow reaction time, blur vision, and increase sleepiness and irritability.

• Contact a physician and refer to the Physicians' Desk Reference (1996) for information regarding side effects of medication.

Safety Issues

• Obtain medical clearance that lists contraindicated activities.

• Be aware that certain factors may provoke the onset of a seizure, such as hyperventilation, emotional stress, a menstrual period, excessive caffeine, strobe lights, and illness.

• Devise plan of action for clearing pool and seizure management (not restraining convulsions, not putting anything in the mouth, and knowing when to call EMS; see also "Seizure Management" section in chapter 7). Fill out appropriate incident report following seizure.

• Maintain close supervision during aquatic activities.

• Exercise caution for diving board activities, including having an aide walk with participant, if necessary.

• Discourage holding breath for "as long as you can" as well as hyperventilation before underwater swimming.

• Discuss scuba diving with participant and physician before attempting deep dives.

• Monitor drinking of pool water as hyperhydration or hyponutremia are known to induce seizures.

• Monitor heat tolerance as **hyperthermia** is known to induce seizures.

• Report sudden changes in behavior to caregivers.

• Use caution in highly competitive, extended, or emotional activities.

• In outdoor pool, encourage participant to wear sunglasses or tinted goggles if looking into the sun induces seizures.

• Use the buddy system.

• Be aware that some seizure medications increase photosensitivity. Outdoors, swim in early evening or have participant use sunscreen or wear a tight T-shirt.

Goals to Target

Individuals with seizures should improve independent swimming, increase self-esteem, and learn to avoid conditions and activities that may precipitate a seizure in the aquatic environment.

TACTILE SYSTEM DISORDERS

Individuals who experience disturbances in tactile input or integration may have several problems in an aquatic program. Those who are hyperresponsive to tactile information may experience problems with the following: elastic parts of bathing suits touching the skin, the feeling of a towel on the body, the sensation of water all over the body or the instructor's hands as he or she guides the person. Individuals who are hyporesponsive to tactile information generally crave tactile stimulation and need to feel and touch everything.

Teaching Tips

• Find out how intensely you should touch an individual, because some individuals respond better to light touch and pressure while others need heavy touch.

• Consult an occupational therapist if an individual who is hyperresponsive to touch becomes irritable or uncomfortable with touch (tactile defensive). Sometimes the occupational therapist or other practitioner prescribes aquatics for such an individual because the overall pressure of water on the body helps the individual adjust to normal levels of touching.

• Use activities such as washing with sponges and washcloths, swimming underwater, playing games that require body contact with another person, and moving or feeling the water coming out of the jets (see figure 9.15).

Goals to Target

Individuals with tactile problems need to increase tolerance to tactile input and decrease resistance to others touching them.

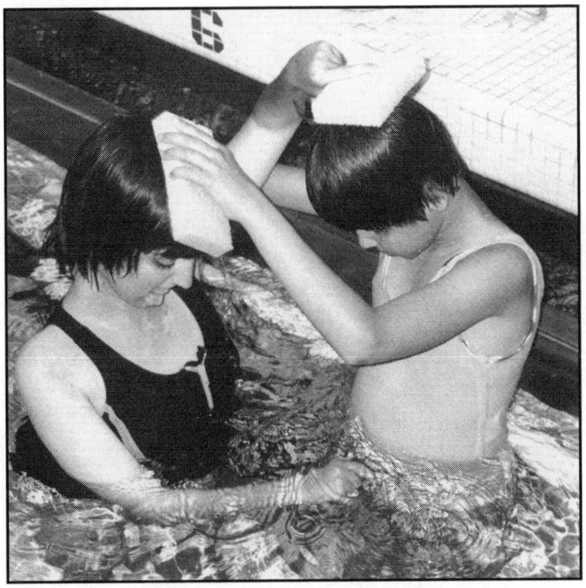

Figure 9.15 Washing with sponges helps to stimulate the tactile system.

Common Related Conditions

Commonly seen in individuals with severe learning disabilities, pervasive developmental disabilities, autism, prenatal exposure to drugs, and mental retardation.

TEMPERATURE REGULATION DISORDERS

Temperature regulation disorders may result from impaired sympathetic nervous system flow, ". . . inadequate secretion by sweat glands, or inappropriate distribution of blood due to impaired cardiovascular system control" (Glaser et al. 1996, p. 7). The impaired autonomic nervous system in spinal cord injury causes problems with **vasoconstriction** and **vasodilation**. This results in the inability to control body core temperature effectively. The body takes on the temperature of the outside environment and therefore hypothermia or hyperthermia may result if the susceptible person becomes cold or overheated (Rogers 1996). High humidity, extreme heat, high-intensity exercise, and improper clothing for the temperature can lead to hyperthermia because the body cannot release enough heat. Conversely, impaired cardiovascular control and inability to shiver due to muscle paralysis can lead to excessive heat loss in the cold and therefore hypothermia.

Teaching Tips

• Allow the individual to wear a neoprene vest or wet suit to keep warm in cooler pools.

• In outdoor pools or where temperature is hot, encourage cool water spray bottles to mist head, neck, and face.

• Encourage bringing plastic water bottles to the pool and drinking water in hot and humid environments during class.

• Put towels in the sauna so they are warm as participant comes out of a chilly pool, always having someone check the towels to make sure they will not burn the participant.

Safety Issues

• Minimize exposure to overheating and overcooling.

• Watch for signs of overexposure and cold in pool or locker areas, such as blue lips.

• Offer warm drinks after swimming in cold water (less than 82°F).

Goals to Target

Individuals with temperature regulation disorders should minimize overexposure and increase awareness of the effects of cold or hot conditions on themselves.

Common Related Conditions

Temperature regulation disorders are commonly seen in individuals with spinal cord injury above T8 and in some individuals with traumatic brain injury and multiple sclerosis.

VESTIBULAR SYSTEM DISORDERS

Where a person's head is in space affects what sensory information enters the vestibular system. The semicircular canals in the inner ear respond to head position and interpret if we are off-balance. Information from the eyes also helps the brain interpret balance information at the same time that the vestibular system coordinates proper alignment of body parts, balance, equilibrium, and body posture. Deficits in input and interpretation of vestibular information result in poor balance (ataxia) while walking in the pool; using the ladder; recovering to vertical from front or back; centering self on floats, kickboards, or tubes; and difficulty controlling the body's adjustments to gravity.

Teaching Tips

• Have the participant use a floating mat for practicing various balance positions. Keep mat away from the sides of the pool while individual is balancing on it. Make sure water is deep enough so that if the individual falls off the mat, she will not hit bottom (see figure 9.16).

• Provide activities that put the person slightly off-balance to practice recovery, such as underwater log rolls, somersaults, swinging, and twirling.

• Have participant jump up and down or side to side over the lines on the bottom of the pool to help with balance and postural orientation.

• Have participant straddle long, foam solid tubes (noodles) to practice balance. Once participant can balance on a tube at rest, create turbulence or pull tube around with the individual astride it.

Safety Issues

• Provide assistance for balance problems while on deck.

Figure 9.16 A floating gym mat can facilitate balance practice while having fun

• Encourage use of aquasocks while on a slippery deck or doing quick movements as in water aerobics class.

• Use spotters for individuals with vestibular system problems when they are using the diving board or jumping in from the side.

• Recognize that recovery from a prone or supine to a vertical position is difficult and may even lead to drowning.

Goals to Target

Individuals with vestibular problems should perform activities to increase ability to recover to vertical from prone and supine floats and to improve balance while using flotation devices and while walking in the pool with turbulence (e.g., several people moving around).

Common Related Conditions

Commonly seen in individuals with cerebral palsy, traumatic brain injury, stroke, severe learning disabilities, and inner ear damage.

VISUAL IMPAIRMENT AND BLINDNESS

Visual impairment is a term encompassing the whole range of disabilities that affect sight, from problems with distance and peripheral vision to color blindness and double vision. Although visual perception problems may be considered a visual impairment, our discussion in this section will focus on visual acuity problems, and in the next section we'll turn to visual perception deficits. Several terms describe degree of sight and visual acuity. Total blindness and legal blindness are two of the more frequently used terms.

Total blindness refers to individuals who cannot see light, forms, or shapes. These individuals learn through kinesthetic experiences, hearing, and braille. Individuals with legal blindness have some usable vision (20/200 or worse in the better eye with correction or a field of vision of less than 20 degrees). These individuals can see bright objects, shapes, and figures that have a distinct outline and are within their sight range.

Teaching Tips

• Adapt visual demonstrations, directions, and environment. Encourage individuals who are not totally blind (those with residual vision) to make full use of the vision they still have. Wear a bright lycra shirt or tights to draw attention to your legs or arms.

• If tunnel vision is a problem, demonstrate at no more than five to seven feet away, directly in front of the person.

• For a participant with a loss of central vision, demonstrate in peripheral vision.

• Either allow individual with total blindness to place his hands on you while you demonstrate or manipulate the participant's body through the motions (see figure 9.17).

• Keep directions concise and accurate and provide specific cues as to where to go and to do. Use directions that make use of a clock face, such as "Swim seven strokes to 12 o'clock." Use the terms left, right, and number of strokes or steps to be taken.

• Avoid using gestures, such as pointing.

• Offer a running commentary to describe what others are doing and use names frequently.

• The environment needs very little adaptations, but use lane lines for swimming laps and practicing strokes.

• Use auditory signals, such as a radio near the deep end, if it can be heard over the noise of a typical pool.

• Place a child's water sprinkler attached to a hose near the end of the pool to signal that the swimmer is nearing the end.

• Have an assistant use a tennis ball impaled on a long folding cane to tap the head or shoulder of a lap swimmer, warning of the coming of the pool end.

• Put raised tape (that used for sealing windows and doors) on the wall of the pool at the corresponding height as the water depth next to it. Also, put raised numbers on the wall next to the corresponding depth so individuals can trail down the wall, feel the appropriate height independently, and get in at the depth they want to.

• Have participant bring magnet to put on locker with letters or specific shapes so she can find her locker more easily. Remove when finished.

• Allow participant to grasp you above the elbow for mobility.

Figure 9.17 Physically moving someone through a skill provides kinesthetic and tactile cues.

• Have individual experience the environment in and around the pool with a sighted buddy. This will help orientation and mobility.

Safety Issues

• Know where the individual is at all times to prevent disorientation.

• Communicate effectively with participant to avoid hazards in the environment.

• Be aware that individuals with partial retinal detachment must avoid bumping the head or eyes. You may need to require a somewhat segregated environment, using a sighted spotter to intercept balls, kickboards, and other people.

• Have sighted spotters provide cues for individuals who want to jump or dive.

Goals to Target

Individuals who are blind or visually impaired should perform activities to improve overall fitness, fluidity of movement (to address the tendency to have rigid posture and mobility), posture (shoulders and head in alignment with trunk), mobility, orientation, independence, body image, spatial awareness, and sound localization.

Common Related Conditions

Disabilities commonly associated with visual impairment include congenital blindness, adventitious blindness, glaucoma, retinitis pigmentosa, optic nerve disease, retinopathy, tumors of the eye, albinism, diabetes, myopia, nystagmus, early stages of multiple sclerosis, and prenatal exposure to drugs.

VISUAL PERCEPTION DEFICITS

Visual perception problems may be due to difficulty with eye coordination or due to inaccurate interpretation of speed, size, distance, and location. Visual perception deficits relate to judging and interpreting what one sees, including such components as figure-ground discrimination (locating an object against a background), tracking across midline and up and down (following an object from one point to another), seeing the whole picture, depth perception, binocular vision, and eye-hand and eye-foot coordination. Naturally, these problems reduce visual efficiency and interpretation will be reduced (Van Witsen 1979). When this happens, motor output is of poor quality.

Teaching Tips

• Put brightly colored tape or paint on edges of steps.

• Place a bright-colored bath mat on bottom of neck-deep water where the participant will be jumping in to help with depth perception.

• Guide foot placement when walking in the pool by using your feet to help guide participant's feet.

• Use brightly colored equipment.

• Decrease extraneous visual stimuli, such as the instructor wearing a tie-dyed bathing suit or lots of people behind the instructor as she does a demonstration.

• Have participant practice swimming under lane lines, through hoops, and between people (figure 9.18).

• Manipulate body parts physically to offer kinesthetic instead of visual input.

• Use key cue words, such as "elbow high," to give a mental picture of the task.

Figure 9.18 Swimming through a hoop is a visual perception activity.

• Hold a pole at various heights under shallow water and encourage participant to step, leap, hop, and jump over it.

• Wear a bright, one-color bathing suit and, if needed, bright, one-color lycra tights and shirt to draw attention to your limb actions during demonstrations.

• Have individual experience the environment in and around the pool with a buddy. This will help orientation and mobility.

Safety Issues

• Be aware that due to depth perception problems, individuals may misjudge depth of water, not recognizing it is too shallow or too deep.

• Provide "No Jumping" and "No Diving" signs and verbal reminders.

• Provide spotters for pool entries and exits as tripping on stairs and ladders may be a problem due to overstepping or understepping.

• Keep in mind that because visual perception is involved in knowing how far a person is away from us, deficits in this area can result in bumping into others, equipment, or walls and throwing balls too hard.

Goals to Target

Individuals with visual perception problems should perform activities to improve lane swimming without bumping into lane lines or others, increase accuracy of imitation of visual demonstrations, improve abilities to use ladder and stairs safely, to distinguish depths, and to differentiate among sizes, shapes, and colors of pool equipment.

Common Related Conditions

Disabilities in which visual perception deficits are common include cardiovascular accident (CVA or stroke), traumatic brain injury, multiple sclerosis, cerebral palsy, learning disabili-

ties, severe mental retardation, and prenatal exposure to drugs.

SUMMARY

Each individual that you encounter will be a unique person with unique characteristics. Refer to this chapter to better understand the multitude of disabilities that individuals may have and the kinds of attributes these disabilities may involve. Use table 9.1, along with teaching tips, safety issues, and goals to target sections for the challenges you face to help you meet the individual needs of swimmers with disabilities in a safe, successful, and satisfying manner.

CHAPTER 9 REVIEW

1. Explain the concept of "labeling" and how it may negatively impact an individual.

2. What aquatic activities should be avoided by a participant with atlantoaxial instability syndrome (AAIS)?

3. What are some conditions in which it is helpful to give a physical prompt? When might a physical prompt be a poor choice?

4. Explain how to help a person with memory and understanding problems maintain and generalize skills.

5. How may a disturbance in the autonomic nervous system impair performance in aquatics?

6. What are contractures? How do they impair swimming performance?

7. List several hints for working with individuals with problems understanding directions.

Part III

PROGRAM ENHANCEMENT

ADAPTED AQUATICS PROGRAM SELECTION

Adapted aquatics programs are increasingly more available, accessible, and affordable, giving individuals with disabilities many options from which they may select a program that best meets their needs and interests. Naturally, such diversity offers a range of services and benefits, varying from meeting basic therapeutic, fitness, or swim instruction needs to providing enrichment activities through recreation, competition, or sports. Moreover, programs are conducted in a variety of settings and sponsored by many types of organizations. The information in this chapter provides an overview of program characteristics and features you should know when starting, selecting, or referring an individual to an adapted aquatics program. Figure 10.1 summarizes various considerations for program selection. Use it and the adaptations and enhancements that other programs have made when tailoring your own decisions.

PROGRAM ENVIRONMENTS

The mission of an organization often guides the decisions administrators and other staff make regarding program development and delivery. Those in charge must determine which groups the program will serve (age, disability, or factors related to target population), what methods the instructors will use (group, individual, segregated, integrated), and what specific content the curriculum will include (social, water safety, therapeutic, recreational). Collectively, these decisions help a program establish its unique approach within its setting. Figure 10.2 lists some criteria for assessing and matching an adapted aquatics program to the specific needs and interests of an individual with disabilities. Consider these criteria when reviewing the differences among adapted aquatics programs in the following sections.

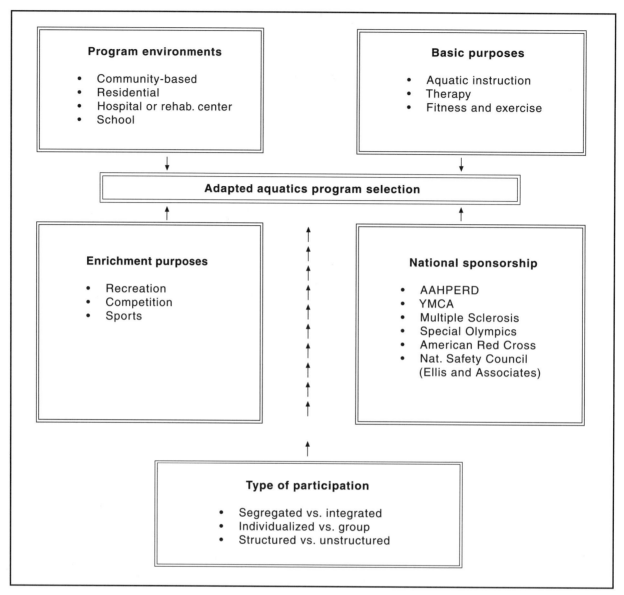

Figure 10.1 Considerations for adapted aquatics program selection.

Community-Based Programs

Organizations providing community-based delivery of adapted aquatics services account for many of the aquatic programs that are available and accessible to individuals with disabilities. We can characterize these organizations according to their type of funding, governance, membership, and advocacy. They vary with respect to private (not-for-profit) or public status, religious affiliation, and level of volunteer involvement.

Private, not-for-profit organizations include YMCAs, YWCAs, Boys and Girls Clubs, Jewish Community Centers, and Boy and Girl Scouts, all of which serve the general public. Participants in these programs are generally members who must pay dues or other fees. These organizations may receive further funding through grants, private contributions from individuals, or funding agencies, such as the United Way. They may allow nonmembers to take classes or attend a particular program at the agency by paying on a per-day or per-course basis.

The adapted aquatics programs provided through these organizations serve many purposes. For example, a Jewish Community Center might offer an instructional program or open recreation swim. A YMCA might offer fitness, instructional,

- Aims or goals of the program
- Program delivery models
- Target groups served
- Contents of the program
- Qualifications and training of staff
- Type and amount of structure
- Services availability
- Accessibility to facility and program

Figure 10.2 Adapted aquatics program selection criteria.

recreational, or therapeutic programs. Moreover, individuals may choose from segregated or inclusive programs, group or individual instruction, and structured or unstructured sessions.

Public organizations, those organizations primarily funded by federal, state, or municipal government, providing adapted aquatics programs include parks and recreation departments, schools, and other publicly funded institutions. As with other not-for-profit organizations, the programs conducted in public agencies vary. Participation may be subsidized or offered through membership or program fees. Community-based organizations or service groups might sponsor programs using public facilities.

Community-based affiliates of disability-specific organizations include the Spina Bifida Association, National Multiple Sclerosis Society, United Cerebral Palsy, and Special Olympics. Although some of these organizations may own aquatic facilities, many secure pool time from public and private facilities, such as high schools, community centers, health clubs, and rehabilitation facilities.

Some camp programs include adapted aquatics as part of the curriculum. However, the day or residential camp environment may impact participants with disabilities in several ways. The duration of the program is generally limited to the summer. Participants may require time and energy to adjust to camp factors, including the weather, other social and recreational activities, daily routines, movement throughout the camp, and camp regimens.

Adapted aquatics programs with a therapeutic focus have increasingly turned to community-based resources. In these programs, allied health professionals, such as physical and occupational

therapists, contract with the organization to use a community pool for individual or group therapy. Such a program may offer patients medically prescribed therapy as well as exercise, fitness, and swim instruction. Medical insurance usually covers part or all of the fees for such services.

Community-based settings may provide an inclusive atmosphere and a convenient geographic location, thereby encouraging participation in adapted aquatic programs. Their appeal, however, may be influenced by such factors as adequate accessibility, ease of transportation to the facility, appropriate pool design and air temperature, the comprehensiveness of programs, and the quality of instruction.

Residential Programs

Although the trend in the United States is toward community-based, integrated living, some individuals with disabilities or their caregivers choose a residential facility for care and educational, recreational, and therapeutic opportunities. These facilities may be public or private, for-profit or not-for-profit; they may offer nursing or medical care or long-term or intermediate care community living arrangements (CLAs); or they may be residential schools. Such programs may offer aquatics to residents if the program has a pool or has the ability to transport residents off-site to an aquatic facility.

Residents may vary in their abilities and disabilities from mildly disabled to profoundly involved. Indeed, residential facilities use many criteria to establish whom they will serve, what programs they will provide, and how they will provide programs and services. A facility might provide services to individuals based on age or establish specific physical or cognitive requirements. Staff tend to follow a transdisciplinary or cross-disciplinary approach. They communicate with each other, pursue similar objectives, and reinforce similar tasks, such as activities of daily living and functional skills.

Residency can facilitate the delivery of adapted aquatics programs. Obviously, the program itself is more readily accessible and accommodating, giving residents more opportunities to participate in aquatic activities. Since the residential facility is designed to meet the needs of its residents, the aquatic facilities are usually accommodating and accessible. Staff most likely adjust the pool conditions to the needs of the residents.

Staff face several challenges in a residential

facility, however. They must maintain their enthusiasm and commitment to the same residents, day after day. They must deal with burdensome paperwork as various organizations, such as Medicare or other funding sources, impose regulations and require documentation regarding the amount and type of services offered the residents. Staff should also strive to implement individual goals and objectives which not only seek to maintain function, but also develop new skills.

A RESIDENTIAL PROGRAM

The Mary Campbell Center is a private facility that serves approximately 50 adults with severe physical impairments (figure 10.3). Residents have access to a range of social, recreational, physical therapy, and daily care services. The aquatic facility includes a 15' x 32' pool with a hydraulic floor, an 8' x 10' spa pool with a hydraulic lift, fully accessible showers and locker rooms, a laundry facility adjacent to the deck, and a fitness area with weights and aerobic exercise equipment. Program personnel include aquatic staff with training in physical education and aquatic certifications, about 30 volunteers, and ancillary PTs, OTs, and nurses.

The aquatics program provides each individual the support and skills necessary to achieve maximum independence and freedom of movement, directing its efforts at establishing a safe environment for all participants; promoting independence, growth, and opportunities for new experiences; and teaching swimming skills. All these endeavors increase self-esteem.

Staff individualize all programs by focusing on specific instructional, recreational, therapeutic, and social needs. They make comprehensive individual assessments, combining physical therapy, occupational therapy, and physical development recommendations. Staff assess participants one-on-one to determine aquatic skill level, then make recommendations at annual Individualized Aquatics Program Plan meetings.

To implement the aquatics program, staff or volunteers work on-on-one with most individuals and collect data from each session to provide feedback. Each session consists of a review of the parts of the skill, practice, and application.

The following high praise from three residents and one parent demonstrate how the pool program has become an integral part of their lives:

Figure 10.3 Mary Campbell Center pool program.

"The pool makes my legs feel very good."

"The only place I can walk is in the pool."

"I hate when the pool needs to be cleaned."

"It was great to see my daughter compete at the Aquatic Expo."

Information provided by Andrea Youndt, The Mary Campbell Center, 4641 Weldin Road, Wilmington, DE 19803, 302-762-6025

Hospital and Rehabilitation Center Programs

Treatment, care, and therapy are primary concerns for individuals participating in aquatics programs sponsored by hospitals and rehabilitation centers. Such organizations may also provide supplemental programs that emphasize swim instruction, recreation, fitness, or competition, creating diversity in programs. An organization's aquatic facilities may range from a small therapy pool to a full-scale swimming pool. Program staff may include physical therapists, occupational therapists, certified therapeutic recreation specialists, certified swimming instructors, aides, and volunteers. If needed, such programs offer special equipment to accommodate participant mobility and therapy. They may have to deal with accrediting agencies and governmental or private insurance carriers who may impose regulations that affect program delivery. Moreover, therapeutic pools often have different requirements regarding lifeguarding, sanitation, and pool operation.

Aquatic programs conducted by rehabilitation hospitals may combine aquatic instruction with physical therapy. The programs may be augmented with other recreational or fitness activities. Such programs may limit delivery to the specific times the therapist or instructor is available to work with patients one-on-one. They are usually limited to people who are inpatients or outpatients of that hospital and are likely to be covered by insurance submitted through the physical therapy department. The pool is usually small, very warm (88-90°F), and usually not conducive to lap swimming or competition.

A hospital or rehabilitation center that has no pool may choose to cosponsor an adapted aquatics program with a community organization. Participants referred by the hospital or affiliated doctors may pay reduced fees. In such an arrangement, the hospital and community organization must determine how to distinguish or share personnel, program expenses, and program responsibilities. A benefit of this arrangement is that individuals with disabilities gain more exposure to and involvement with the community. They can practice social and community living skills with receptionists, volunteers, and other members of the facility and meet other individuals, with or without disabilities, in informal settings outside the hospital. The community-based pool may also be more suited to swimming instruction, recreational lap swimming, or competition. The disadvantages of this arrangement are that the program is still not fully integrated, pool temperature may be too low to be appropriate for specific physical limitations, some architectural barriers may exist, and staff or volunteers may need training to assist with a particular special population.

School Programs

Schools, elementary through college level, may conduct adapted aquatics programs for the students during school hours and may sponsor programs for the community throughout the week. As a part of the school curriculum, the adapted aquatics program is generally conducted by a regular or adapted physical educator with aquatic expertise. The adapted aquatics instructor may support the regular aquatic instructor when including an individual with a disability or provide service in a supplemental or partially segregated program. The adapted aquatics program may serve the students of that particular school or the district.

As an adjunct to the physical education program, the primary purpose of these school-based programs is to provide swimming instruction. Participants acquire aquatic skills that permit them to attain buoyancy, comfort, safety, fitness, and mobility in the water. Participants may also enjoy recreational and competitive swim activities.

A SCHOOL-BASED PROGRAM

The Osborn Aquatic Center is an indoor, community pool used by the Corvallis School District to provide adapted aquatics programs as part of their special education services (figure 10.4). The program strives to provide an environment in which individuals with physical or mental disabilities are able to participate, regardless of their limitations. Staff encourage an atmosphere of acceptance and personal challenge, emphasizing activities that increase strength, endurance, and water skills. Participants encourage and help one another through peer tutoring.

The adapted aquatics program director designs a specific program for each student based on his or her physical abilities and limitations, taking into account input offered by the school district's physical therapist, classroom teachers,

Figure 10.4 Osborn Aquatic Center program.

and parents. Programs might include assisted stretching, assisted walking, swimming with and without flotation devices, group activities, and free time to explore and play.

Students are bused to the program throughout the day, five days per week. Students' physical and mental disabilities include cerebral palsy, autism, mental retardation, Down syndrome, Prader-Willi syndrome, and developmental and emotional delays.

Information provided by Christine King, Osborn Aquatic Center, 1940 NW Highland Drive, Corvallis, OR 97330, 503-757-5854.

PROGRAM PURPOSES

A fundamental criterion for selecting an adapted aquatics program is matching the purpose of the program with the needs and interests of an individual. Informal discussions, self-assessments, or formal evaluations may determine what type of program best meets the needs and interests of individuals with disabilities. Programs categorized as meeting basic purposes might include aquatic instruction, fitness, exercise, and therapy. We discuss such programs and their purposes in many places throughout this book, especially in chapter 2, in which we examine the four models of service delivery. Aquatic enrichment programs include recreation, sports, and competition. See chapter 11 for more information about enrichment programs.

Basic Needs and Interests Programs

The ability to move safely and comfortably in the water is achieved through programs whose basic purpose is aquatic instruction. These programs include safety and swimming skills. Competency with the following skills help to ensure swimmer safety and survival in the water.

1. Submerging and breath holding
2. Prone floating, back floating, and survival floating
3. Treading water
4. Turning over and changing directions
5. Elementary propulsive movements of arms and legs
6. Recovery from horizontal and vertical positions

Another purpose of aquatic instruction is to develop good swimming strokes—strokes that maximize efficiency and minimize effort. Individuals should acquire effective locomotion in the water by improving head and body position, arm and leg propulsive movements, and rhythmic breathing and coordination. The instructor's role is to customize the swimming stroke to best accommodate an individual's abilities.

Therapy is a basic purpose of adapted aquatics programs in several environments. Many hospitals, rehabilitation centers, and residential facilities provide aquatics programs to supplement, complement, or replace land-based physical therapy. The aquatic regimen may be prescribed to improve range of motion, muscle tone, balance, ambulation, and circulation. An adapted aquatics instructor may be asked to provide aquatics and swimming activities which involve specific movements to achieve desired results.

Individuals with disabilities may also seek adapted aquatics programs to fulfill fitness and exercise needs. Although these aquatic activities may result in improvements similar to therapy regimens, the activities may not be monitored nor prescribed by medical professionals. Such programs may supplement physical education or the programs available through residential facilities. Individuals may simply be interested in their personal wellness through the pursuit of lifetime fitness activities.

Enrichment Programs

Our society has progressed past the philosophy that our duty is to simply meet the basic needs of individuals with disabilities. Fortunately, the growing support for inclusion encourages opportunities and empowers individuals with disabilities to seek other opportunities that will enrich their lives. Due to organizational efforts to maintain customer satisfaction, the development of expanded programs and facilities that meet the desires, not just the needs, of individuals with disabilities has been pursued. The field of aquatics has been impacted by these developments and has responded with challenging and fulfilling opportunities in sports, competition, and recreation. Swimming may be used as a focus on a sport interest or combined with other aquatic skill pursuits. Inner tube water polo or water basketball provides opportunities for sports and recreation and general fitness. Recreational swimming, pool volleyball, and lap swimming are recreational activities that revolve around aquatics as an enriching activity.

Competitive swimming is another obvious example of an enriching aquatic activity. Disability sports groups provide competitive swimming outlets to all populations of swimmers with disabilities. These groups may provide local, regional, and national meets but have very few full-time training programs. An individual with a disability who wants to swim competitively usually self-trains, finds an interested coach to help individually, goes to a community-based organization or rehabilitation hospital that sponsors a particular disability group swim team, or participates in a community-based, nonsegregated competitive swim program.

A COMPETITIVE FOCUS

The Virginia Wadsworth Wirtz Sports Program is conducted by the Rehabilitation Institute of Chicago (RIC). The RIC Wirtz Sports Program's swim program is organized as a recreational and competitive swim program and is not meant to be a therapeutic aquatic program. A basic mission of the program is to include individuals with any physical disability in a competitive swimming and training program. Participants are encouraged to strive to compete. As stated by one participant: "Swimming has improved my ability to perform ADL (activities of daily living) activities. It has increased my fitness level and enabled me to compete again when I thought I never would be able to."

During the required, initial pool evaluation, new participants must demonstrate the potential to achieve independence with recreational or competitive swimming, including recovery skills from each stroke position and the ability to negotiate the pool environment (locker rooms, pool deck, and pool access points). Training during the swim season includes drills, dry land training, and cardiovascular fitness. Swimmers and coach develop training goals together. Swimmers are evaluated each meet to monitor their progress from the previous year.

Individuals are provided opportunities to achieve goals at various competitive levels. Three swimmers competed in the 1994 World Swimming Championships in Malta.

Information provided by Pamela J. Redding, Coach, The Virginia Wadsworth Wirtz Sports Program, Rehabilitation Institute of Chicago, 345 E. Superior, Chicago, IL 60611, 312-908-4292.

TYPES OF PARTICIPATION

Equally as important as the previous features for selecting an adapted aquatics program is determining the type of participation offered through a program. Programs may be segregated (focus on individuals with disabilities) or inclusive (individuals with and without disabilities in the program together) with respect to the individuals being served. A community facility may provide programs for the general public in which individuals with disabilities are integrated with regularly scheduled programs. The same facility may opt to conduct a program just for individuals with physical disabilities who have limited ambulation or a program targeted just for individuals with mental retardation. The organization may serve only a segregated population such as a school for students who are blind.

The type of program may dictate the ratio of instructors and aides to participants. A residential facility with individuals who have profound disabilities may provide one-on-one instruction and attention. Even if the individuals are brought together for a group activity, the program maintains individualized assistance. Other programs may routinely instruct groups of 5 to 10 participants. The individual's abilities, instructional needs, and personal desires should determine which setting is most beneficial.

The amount of structure provided during an aquatics program impacts the needs and desires of the participants. Highly structured instructional classes or fitness activities may produce the best results for some. This environment permits achievement through logical learning progressions, corrective and positive feedback, and sufficient practice. Others may prefer an unstructured environment that allows them to progress at their own rates, self-direct and explore their aquatic abilities at will, and select desired aquatic activities. Perhaps more common and helpful, however, are those programs that provide a balance of both approaches.

NATIONALLY SPONSORED AQUATICS PROGRAMS

Several national organizations have recognized, nationally developed, sponsored, and supported aquatics programs (see chapter 1 for the histories of several). They either provide or can support programs in adapted aquatics. In this chapter, we'll highlight organizations that provide swimming programs, meeting a variety of purposes for delivering adapted aquatics programs. Our selections represent comprehensive program development and delivery. See chapter 11 for organizations that support nonswimming, adapted aquatics enrichment activities.

American Alliance for Health, Physical Education, Recreation and Dance (AAHPERD)

AAHPERD's adapted aquatics program has received increasing attention because of the phasing out of the American Red Cross adapted aquatics program and instructor course, moving to the forefront in adapted aquatics with the reintroduction of their Teacher of Adapted Aquatics credential in 1993.

An AAHPERD Teacher of Adapted Aquatics functions independently to develop and implement adapted aquatics programs. AAHPERD instructors conduct programs in schools, community-based organizations, or residential facilities. The objectives of these program fulfill aquatic instruction, fitness, and recreation needs of participants.

American Red Cross

Since the 1940s, the American Red Cross has provided various types of adapted aquatics programs and special training for instructors who wished to conduct such programs. The primary focus of these programs has been to provide instruction in aquatic and safety skills.

Since 1992, the American Red Cross has embraced the philosophy of inclusion of individuals with disabilities into regular programs, integrating professional development materials with the regular Water Safety Instructor (WSI) program. This redesign resulted in the elimination of a segregated American Red Cross adapted aquatics program.

The American Red Cross Learn-to-Swim program includes seven levels of aquatic and safety skill achievement presented in a logical learning progression. Each level provides a different developmental focus including water exploration, primary skills, stroke readiness, stroke development, stroke refinement, skill proficiency, and advanced skills (American Red Cross 1992b). Program participants learn to adapt a swimming stroke to their individual abilities and body characteristics, no matter the disability.

National Multiple Sclerosis Society

In 1991, in response to clients with Multiple Sclerosis (MS), the National Multiple Sclerosis Society—Georgia Chapter developed a comprehensive aquatic program for use at community facilities (National Multiple Sclerosis Society Client and Community Service Division 1993). This program provides people with MS an opportunity to engage in structured exercise after they are discharged from a formal physical therapy program. In addition, the aquatic setting allows participants to become reinvolved in social activities within the community following diagnosis or exacerbation (flare-up).

The program includes warm-up, stretching, and strengthening exercises, an endurance component, a cool-down or relaxation activity, and free time. Program exercises

1. reduce spasticity,
2. maximize strength potential,
3. maintain or increase endurance potential,
4. maintain or improve the range of motion and flexibility of joints,
5. prevent symptoms secondary to MS (e.g., muscle atrophy and joint contracture),
6. aid in weight control,
7. improve socialization and decrease isolation, and
8. promote an inner sense of achievement and improved self-esteem (National Multiple Sclerosis Society Client and Community Services Division 1993, p. 17).

National Safety Council and Ellis and Associates, Inc.

A recent entry to the national swimming instruction scene is the National Safety Council Learn-To-Swim Program. Developed with Ellis and Associates, Inc. and endorsed by the National Recreation and Park Association, this program teaches basic swimming skills. Its objective is to provide young children with a positive, fun-filled opportunity to learn skills that will reduce the number of drownings and provide lifelong aquatic enjoyment.

Three different program components are available, depending on the swimmer's age. The Exploration Series is designed for children ages 6 months through 3 years. It introduces children and their caregivers to developmentally appropriate water activities that permit a safe and shared experience. Children ages 4 through 7 can participate in the Journey Series. This series emphasizes interaction between child and caregiver, integrating the parent with the child's learning process. Objective-driven, this series leads participants through progressive levels aimed at developing a broad range of swimming skills and strokes. The Challenge Series is a performance-based swimming program designed for all ages through adult. Structured in a flexible lesson format for novice, advanced, and expert levels, this series presents three "challenges" including "Stroke and Safety," "Fitness," and "Sprint."

Although this community-based program is not specifically designed as an adapted aquatics program, it features developmentally appropriate, progressive skills that facilitate the inclusion of children and adults with disabilities in a standard aquatics program. Instructors decide what, when, and how to teach, making it possible for them to meet the needs of individuals with disabilities. The program is administered by licensed coordinators who must meet training and auditing criteria to retain their licenses. In 1996, Ellis and Associates released a manual, Adapted Aquatics (Priest 1996), making this program an even better option for individuals with disabilities.

Special Olympics International

Special Olympics International is an organization that provides aquatics programs for several purposes, only one of which is competition. These purposes are clearly expressed in the mission of Special Olympics, which describes the additional benefits that children and adults with mental retardation receive through its competition program: developing physical fitness, demonstrating courage, experiencing joy, and participating in a sharing of gifts and friendship with their families, other Special Olympics athletes, and the community (Special Olympics International 1994). The aquatics programs sponsored by Special Olympics provide opportunities for participation in aquatic instruction, fitness, and recreation activities, competition and sports, and psychological and social development activities.

Special Olympics exists through volunteer resources. Individuals volunteer their time to manage, coordinate, and conduct all parts of the program. Organizations voluntarily give pool time and space for aquatic activities. Special Olympic programs are often conducted in schools, residential facilities, and community-based centers.

Participation in Special Olympics aquatics programs has traditionally been segregated with both individual and group instruction. Coaches structure activities, based on long-term goals and short-term objectives for each participant.

Unified Sports, a registered program of Special Olympics International, combines approximately equal numbers of Special Olympics athletes with peer athletes without mental retardation to train and compete together on sports teams. The program expands opportunities for athletes to seek new challenges and promotes inclusion in the community (Special Olympics International 1993). Special Olympics Partners Club achieves a similar purpose through which high school students and Special Olympics athletes practice sports skills together on a regular basis (Special Olympics International n.d.). (See also chapter 11.)

Young Men's Christian Association (YMCA)

Unlike the American Red Cross and AAHPERD, YMCAs do not need to depend on other organizations to sponsor their adapted aquatics programs. They have their own community-based facilities and camps in which they provide programs in adapted aquatics, including opportunities for aquatic instruction, recreation, fitness, and competition. YMCAs may offer either segregated or inclusive programs for individuals with disabilities or both.

The YMCA has also collaborated with the Arthritis Foundation to provide a nationwide program called the Arthritis Foundation YMCA Aquatic Program (AFYAP). In this program, groups of individuals with arthritis are lead through a regimen of exercises that includes an aerobic endurance component and strength and flexibility exercises (Arthritis Foundation and National Council of YMCAs of the USA 1990).

SwimAmerica

Relatively new among nationally sponsored learn-to-swim programs is the American Swimming Coaches Association's (ASCA) program, SwimAmerica. Designed by professional swim coaches, this program emphasizes the **"station method"** to teach infants through adults to swim. The program identifies general goals and corresponding levels of advancement, including the following 10 stations, or levels (SwimAmerica n.d.):

1. Bubbles
2. Floats and glides
3. Kicking
4. Crawl stroke
5. Freestyle
6. Backstroke
7. Breaststroke
8. Turns
9. Lifetime strokes
10. Individual medley

Swimmers must meet a total of 25 objectives to advance through the 10 stations. Each objective includes specific skills and criteria for advancing to the next station. Thus, through the station method, instructors use logical teaching progressions to introduce and build new skills while constantly reviewing previous skills.

Although SwimAmerica does not specifically provide guidelines for the inclusion of children and adults with disabilities in its programs, with the proper training and licensing, you could use it as an alternative or supplemental program for teaching adapted aquatics (see chapter 1).

Coaches are eligible to operate SwimAmerica programs after appropriate training and licensure as a program director. Program directors may train their own staff. Licenses never expire and continuing education is provided in monthly newsletters. Individuals who operate SwimAmerica programs must adhere to the following requirements (SwimAmerica n.d.):

- Be a Certified Coach Member of ASCA
- Train coaching staff with materials and methods described in the operations manual
- Use the SwimAmerica awards system
- Program director (or site supervisor) must be present on deck, actively directing each lesson
- Submit appropriate records to SwimAmerica on schedule

SUMMARY

Many adapted aquatics program options are currently available. Make it your aim to meet the developmental needs and interests of each individual seeking a program. To this end, use the overview in this chapter of various program characteristics, features, and factors when selecting an adapted aquatics program. Consider the basic purposes of each program, including aquatic instruction, therapy, fitness, and enrichment (see also chapter 11). Choosing the most suitable environment—whether community-based, residential, hospital, rehabilitation center, or school—is also basic to meeting individual needs and interests. Selecting the type of participation permitted from segregated to integrated, individualized to group, and structured to unstructured is another important issue. Finally, examining the structure and standards practiced by nationally sponsored programs will help you compare programs as you strive to select the best option for each individual with disabilities.

CHAPTER 10 REVIEW

1. Describe four types of settings in which an adapted aquatics program might be provided and how program goals might vary among these settings.

2. List several types of community-based organizations that could sponsor or implement adapted aquatics programs.

3. Identify two purposes for providing adapted aquatics programs and the types of programs which represent such purposes.

4. Describe how adapted aquatics programs might vary among organizations with respect to types of participation.

5. Identify five national organizations which provide swimming programs that can support the implementation of an adapted aquatics program.

COMPETITIVE AND RECREATIONAL ACTIVITIES

Aquatic participation for individuals with disabilities now extends far beyond traditional water safety and swim stroke instructional programs. The world of competitive swimming, recreational, and water adventure activities, including scuba diving, boating, open water swimming, and water skiing, is now open to individuals with disabilities, and the opportunities are continually expanding. In this chapter, we will focus primarily on competitive swimming for individuals with disabilities, equitable competition and classification, coaching swimmers, and recreational aquatic activities for individuals with disabilities (see figure 11.1). Make it your goal to either provide these opportunities as appropriate or serve as a well-informed liaison between your participants and the appropriate enrichment programs, making the transition from basic to enrichment activities go more smoothly.

COMPETITIVE SWIMMING FOR INDIVIDUALS WITH DISABILITIES

Although passive recreational opportunities have been available for decades, competitive sporting opportunities are a more recent phenomenon for individuals with disabilities. While not all desire to participate in competitive events, an ever-increasing number of individuals are continuing to define competition in numerous ways from competing with their own personal bests to competing against others (Priest 1990). Competitive opportunities exist in a variety of settings including short- and long-course swimming, in which events are conducted in typical Olympic style; triathlons for the physically challenged, in which swimming events are divided into quadriplegic and either paraplegic or "others" divisions; and diving, which is only offered by Special Olympics International (SOI) and the American Athletic Association of the Deaf (AAAD).

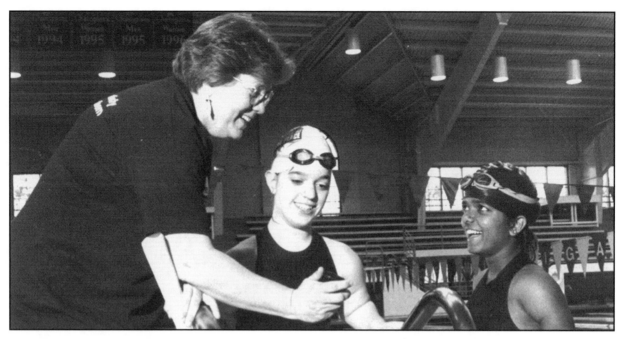

Figure 11.1 True competition recognizes ability.

As you probably well know, United States Swimming (USS) is the national governing body for all competitive swimming in the United States. Competitive swim events are conducted according to United States Swimming rules, which also address swimmers with disabilities. USS rules provide guidelines for officiating swimmers with disabilities, such as alternate starting positions and signals. Article 105 states "The USS rules and regulations grant the Referee the authority to modify the rules for the swimmer with a disability. Disability is defined as a physical or mental impairment that substantially limits one or more major life activities" (United States Swimming 1997, p. 47).

Philosophy of Competitive Swimming

Since World War II, and particularly in the last 25 years, an increasing number of sporting associations have provided competitive opportunities in aquatics for individuals with disabilities. Although water is a great equalizer, swimming ranks only third as the sport with the greatest number of disabled competitors (Paciorek and Jones 1994). Lack of participation in aquatics for people with disabilities may be due to transportation difficulties, poor accessibility of facilities, or the time and effort it takes to access a pool, perform the necessary activities of daily living, and perform all the necessary transactions for pool use. Additional reasons for nonparticipation include lack of enjoyment of the activity, poor quality of coaching, and lack of exposure to youth sport programs.

Despite the difficulties, competitive swimming has many benefits. Competition within USS and Disabled Sports Organization (DSO) focuses on ability, rather than disability, and on enjoyable activity, rather than therapeutic manipulation. Individuals with disabilities choose to participate, as opposed to being forced, and are active participants in goal setting. These factors motivate those who are interested to participate and improve.

Competitive swimming can be a useful psychological outlet for individuals involved in the workforce, caring for a home or children, and educational or rehabilitative programs. Competition can enhance self-confidence, encourage normalization, and release stress. Moreover, competitive opportunities promote a feeling of belonging and self-reliance. Athletes who are considered elite, those who compete at a level at which they must meet rigorous national standards, train hard year-round (Montelione and Davis 1986). They want the same recognition as nondisabled athletes who train and compete at the national level.

Competitive swimming can turn a sedentary adult, teen, or child into a physically active one. Health benefits are the same for disabled as nondisabled participants, including increased caloric expenditure, maintaining or decreasing weight, improved cardiorespiratory endurance, increased muscular strength and endurance, and improved range of motion (ROM). It can also decrease injury and illnesses due to increases in flexibility and respiratory health (Cocchi 1997).

Disabled Sports Organizations

Individuals with disabilities may compete in either segregated, integrated, or inclusive programs, including school-based intramural activities, interscholastic and intercollegiate opportunities, and community-based amateur sport programs for individuals with disabilities (Jansma and French 1994). Most competitive swim programs for individuals with disabilities are run in conjunction with rehabilitation centers, community sport clubs, or segregated residential or day schools, although many teens can compete on their own high school teams. Most serious, elite swimmers train with USS clubs (Dummer 1997).

DSOs in the United States belong to the Committee on Sports for the Disabled (COSD), a subcommittee of the United States Olympic Committee (USOC). The COSD is largely comprised of representatives of seven DSOs. These organizations, serving the interests of individuals with disabilities in sport and athletic endeavors, are the American Athletic Association of the Deaf, Disabled Sports USA, Dwarf Athletic Association of America, Special Olympics International, United States Cerebral Palsy Athletic Association, United States Association for Blind Athletes, and Wheelchair Sports USA. We'll look more closely at each of these organizations in the following sections.

American Athletic Association of the Deaf

The American Athletic Association of the Deaf (AAAD) began in 1945 and is the oldest DSO in America. Approximately 25,000 individuals who are deaf or hard of hearing participate in a multitude of sports through some 2,000 clubs in the United States. The criterion for participating is a hearing loss of 55 decibels or greater in the better ear (DePauw and Gavron 1995). Although many multisport clubs exist, relatively few "deaf only" swim clubs in the United

States have been established, and those are all at schools for students who are deaf (Dummer 1997). The AAAD is the United States affiliate of the Comite International des Sports des Sourds (CISS), which sponsors the World Games for the Deaf. This Olympic-style sports competition is the showcase of sports for people who are deaf and is held every four years in the years immediately following the Olympic Games.

Swimming and diving events are conducted following United States Swimming rules. USS rules allow for arm signals for starting swimmers who are deaf. There is no separate junior and senior division and no classification system except for separate male and female divisions. The United States Aquatic Association of the Deaf is the National Sports Organization Affiliate of the AAAD and handles queries about swimming for people who are deaf (see appendix E).

Disabled Sports USA

Disabled Sports USA is a national organization providing opportunities to participate in year-round sports and recreation to children and adults with disabilities. It was founded in 1967 as the National Handicapped Sports and Recreation Association by disabled Vietnam veterans and serves individuals with physical disabilities that restrict mobility, such as amputations, paraplegia, quadriplegia, cerebral palsy, head injury, multiple sclerosis, muscular dystrophy, spina bifida, stroke, and visual impairments (DSUSA 1996). (Prior to becoming DSUSA, the organization was known as National Handicapped Sports.) DSUSA offers noncompetitive sport clinics and recreational activities, such as instructional boating. Swim competition is not a large part of the organization's efforts, but DSUSA does jointly sanction and cosponsor various cross-disability training camps and swim competitions, primarily supporting amputees and other orthopedically impaired (les autres) people, such as those with multiple sclerosis, muscular dystrophy, and arthrogryposis (Bauer 1997).

Dwarf Athletic Association of America

Individuals with dwarfism and congenital short stature participate in the DAAA, founded in 1985. The purpose of the organization ". . . is to develop, promote and provide quality amateur athletic opportunities for dwarf athletes in the United States" (DePauw and Gavron 1995, p. 56). Participants must be 4'10" or less and classified as dwarfs due to chondrodystrophy or other related causes of short stature. Swimming is one of the major sports offered at local, regional, and national competitions. In national events, which are segregated from those with other disabilities, participants are divided into three classifications for open events, based on body size proportions. In competitions in which people with dwarfism are integrated with people with other disabilities, such as the Paralympics and other international competitions, organizers use an integrated swimming classification system (International Paralympic Committee 1995). DAAA also offers noncompetitive developmental clinics for Futures (children under 6), Juniors (ages 7-9, 10-12, and 13-15), Open (any age), and Masters (age 40 and older). DAAA further separates athletes by gender.

Special Olympics International

The first SOI competitive swimming event was held in Chicago in 1968 (see also chapter 1). Today, SOI competitions include 34 official events, including 1-meter diving events and 25 Olympic-type events, qualifying athletes for national and international competition. The swimming events include 50 meters of each of the four competitive strokes, a variety of individual medley events, and freestyle and medley relays. Athletes with severe limitations may participate in 1 of 9 events, including 25 meters of one of the four competitive strokes, a 15-meter walk or flotation race, a 25-meter flotation race, a 10-meter assisted swim, or a 15-meter unassisted swim.

SOI separates each event into heats, according to age, gender, and ability level. Although not a rule, to make competition more equal, in a heat the most crucial criterion for dividing athletes is the 10 percent guideline: variance between the highest and lowest swim times (or scores in diving) should not differ by more than 10 percent (Special Olympics International 1994). Some events are coed, although SOI encourages organizers to plan gender-segregated heats as long as there are enough competitors. The official age groupings are 8-11, 12-15, 16-21, 22-29, and 30 and over.

To help you brainstorm ways to adapt aquatics for competition in your program, we have taken the following examples of some rule modifications from the Official Special Olympics Summer Sports Rules, 1992-1995 edition.

1. Flotation devices during the flotation races must be secured on (wrapped around) the athlete and may not be something to hold, such as a kickboard or foam noodle.

2. Walking events should take place in water no more than three and a half feet (one meter) deep, and the athlete must keep one foot in contact with the pool bottom at all times.

3. During the assisted swim events, the athlete must provide her own assistant. The assistant may not support or assist in forward movement; only touching, guiding, or directing the athlete is allowed.

Special Olympics divides diving into four levels, assigning different levels of competency to each category. For example, athletes participating in level 1 diving competition must be capable of performing two dives, level 2 must do three dives, level 3, four dives, and level 4, five dives. Federation International de Natacion Amateur (FINA) rules for senior competition apply.

In addition to Special Olympics segregated competitive swim programs, Unified Sports team participation is available, in which athletes with mental retardation and partners without mental retardation train for competitive swimming on the same team. Considerations for starting the team include having participants of approximately the same age and similar ability; ages should be within a 3- to 5-year age span for athletes under 21 and within a 10- to 15-year age span for swimmers 22 and older. In addition, opportunities exist for noncompetitive instructional teams for which these age ranges may not apply.

Unified Sports, a registered program of Special Olympics International, combines approximately equal numbers of athletes with mental retardation and athletes without mental retardation (called partners) to train and compete together on sports teams, including swim teams. During training, the partners should train together but the nondisabled partner should not be given the role of coach as this is a team with equal status given to all members. Experienced coaches have found that siblings and other relatives of Special Olympics athletes make good Unified Sports swim team members. As with segregated Special Olympics swim teams, eight weeks of swim training is mandated before competing in a meet and Special Olympics official swim rules apply. The official events consist of freestyle and medley relays and team (one athlete and one partner) one-meter diving events. The diving teams, which must compete at the same diving level, have their scores added together as the final score. Each relay team must have two SOI athletes and two partners. A similar program called Partners Club involves high school students and Special Olympics athletes practicing sport skills together on a regular basis (Special Olympics International n.d.).

United States Association of Blind Athletes

The USABA was established in 1976 as an organization whose mission is to ensure that legally blind athletes have the same opportunity in sport that sighted people have. USABA publishes a swimming rules book, available through their national office, which modifies United States Swimming rules. For national competition, USABA prefers 50-meter pools, which reduce the need for turns; it also recommends a modified swim turn. Other modifications USABA sanctions include the following:

1. Coach tapping a swimmer to indicate a turn or the finish line.*

2. Speaking to a swimmer if he drifts into the wrong lane.

3. Hanging continuous ribbon low enough to touch, lowering the backstroke flags, using bubbling devices, or showering water from the backstroke flags. (Although these are suggested, they must be approved by the USABA swimming technical committee.)

4. Giving swimmers the option of starting on the diving blocks, the pool edge, or in the water.*

5. Coach giving a deaf-blind athlete a starting signal.*

6. For relays, the coach or another swimmer can start any relay participant with a nonverbal signal such as touching.*

7. Giving totally blind swimmers some leeway in touching the wall with hands on the same level for breaststroke and butterfly.

These items are already sanctioned under United States Swimming rules.

USABA divides competitors into three classes, according to degree of vision, and four age groups: open (any age), youth 8-13, and masters 30-49 and 50+.

United States Cerebral Palsy Athletic Association

The first national program in competitive sports for individuals with cerebral palsy started as the National Association of Sports for Cerebral Palsy in 1978 (Jones 1988). In 1986, the administrative component of the organization was restructured, and the organization broke away from their parent group, United States Cerebral Palsy Associations and became the United States Cerebral Palsy Athletic Association (USCPAA), an independent association. The organization supports athletes with cerebral palsy and those who have had head injuries or a stroke. They have provided swimming competition and other athletic events through local, regional, national, and, in conjunction with other international organizations, international competitions. Even its main office in Newport, Rhode Island, includes a swimming pool! The future of USCPAA includes recreational sports advocacy as well as competitive events.

The USCPAA uses a complex classification system according to functional ability in order to ensure equitable competition due to the wide variation in degree of physical involvement in USCPAA swimmers. Physical therapists and adapted physical educators who are trained in the classification system evaluate an athlete's functional ability and the quality of her performance in swimming. More on classification is included later on in this chapter. The USCPAA Classification and Rules Book (USCPAA 1997) is an important reference to have when training athletes with cerebral palsy; you can obtain it through their national office (see appendix E).

Wheelchair Sports USA

Formally the National Wheelchair Athletic Association (NWAA), this organization has roots in the mid-1940s, officially becoming the NWAA in 1956. Wheelchair Sports USA (WSUSA) generally serves individuals with spinal lesions, although it does serve some other individuals with mobility impairments who use wheelchairs, such as amputees. United States Wheelchair Swimming is the subsidiary of WSUSA that conducts and advocates swimming competition and training programs. United States Wheelchair Swimming classifies participants according to gender, age (junior and senior), and for international meets, the integrated, functional classification system.

Wheelchair Sports USA uses United States Swimming rules, which allow for various starting positions for starts, turns, and strokes (see figure 11.2).

Integrated Versus Segregated Activities

Most individuals with disabilities who have an ambitious spirit thrive in competitive aquatics. As with instructional aquatics, participation in competition should be in the most inclusive setting possible; this is an inherent right (Kozub and Poretta 1996). Indeed, school and community competitive swim coaches should consider recruiting and accommodating individuals with disabilities. Winnick's (1987) continuum of sports participation (figure 11.3) asserts that you should allow individuals with disabilities to start out participating in the regular swim team program, exploring other options (segregation, partial participation) only after concluding that an individual is not having safe, successful, and satisfying experiences in the regular program. There is a need for a continuum of opportunities from segregated to integrated—the swimmer should be afforded a choice (Dummer 1997).

Our research reveals successful inclusion of swimmers who are visually impaired, deaf, learning disabled, and mentally retarded. These are exceptional athletes who excelled in spite of their

disabilities and who usually initiated adaptations themselves. However, some individuals with disabilities may have some physical disadvantage, possibly creating a barrier to inclusion of individuals with disabilities in typical athletic programs because of the highly competitive nature of interscholastic programs. Such a philosophy of elimination and elitism in which only the most gifted are on school teams limits participation and skill development of individuals with disabilities. Some states, however, such as Minnesota, have integrated a large variety of students with disabilities into the state high school athletic association structure (Kozub and Poretta 1996).

We encourage you to educate nondisabled swimmers and their coaches about the integrated team approach practiced by Minnesota Athletic Association and Special Olympics Unified Sports, which benefits all participants. Work to develop a positive attitude toward diversity and point out how proud both disabled and nondisabled participants will be when they unselfishly work together to accomplish their goals. Moreover, explain that this approach meets the spirit of the Americans With Disabilities Act, providing equal opportunity (Block 1995), and expands the base of school pride by involving individuals traditionally excluded.

But don't think of participation in segregated sports programs as a last resort. Although many people feel that segregated competition only serves to protect individuals from the mainstream world, the competitive adapted aquatics

Figure 11.2 A person with amputations can compete.

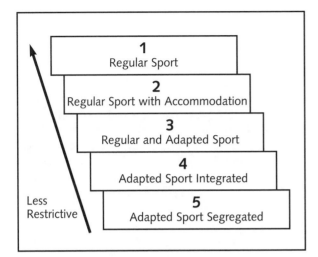

1 Regular Sport	
2 Regular Sport with Accommodation	
3 Regular and Adapted Sport	
4 Adapted Sport Integrated	
Less Restrictive	**5** Adapted Sport Segregated

Figure 11.3 Sports integration continuum.

Reprinted from Winnick 1987.

environment, with a productive atmosphere and supportive coach, can improve activities of daily living, independence, self-esteem, health-related fitness, and feelings of well-being.

Critics of segregated programs note that individuals who participate in these programs don't get to meet and talk to friends who are nondisabled. They also believe that participation in sports for the disabled perpetuates the stereotype of segregation. Proponents of segregated activities feel that sport is just one avenue of socialization and opportunities for persons with disabilities in sport would not exist to the extent that it does if not for segregated DSOs.

EQUITABLE COMPETITION AND CLASSIFICATION

Classification in sport competition for individuals with disabilities is the practice of organizing athletes into groups by some set of criteria to take into account the varying degrees of disability (Vanlandewijck and Chappel 1996). This practice is intended to create fair and equal competition by accounting for differences in body functioning, muscle mass, body proportion and size, and bodyweight. It is not intended to provide a means of making every individual a winner, but means by which every swimmer in an event has equal possibilities to become a winner (Lindstrom 1986). Indeed, for some individuals with disabilities, such as the most disabled, competition would lead to constant "failure" unless

a grading or classification system existed. Furthermore, without classification, the competition might be very unequal due to the wide range of abilities associated with each disability group.

Grouping by Function Versus Disability

Organizations train classifiers who either classify participants separately for each sport or in a general assessment of generic functional skills. Unfortunately, when an athlete is classified by disability without regard to the sport in which the person will participate, they give little consideration to the demands of the sport (DePauw and Gavron 1995). We believe, for example, that different categories should exist for sports in which a person can propel his wheelchair versus aquatic events in which a person cannot use mobility devices. Grouping by functional ability usually produces more equitable competitive events, thereby providing more incentive to try harder (Groves 1979).

Until recently, United States DSOs and some international DSOs used segregated classification systems based on specific medical diagnosis and levels and sites of injury or disability. In the mid 1980s and early 1990s, however, a movement within the International Paralympic Committee fostered the development of a system placing greater emphasis on sport performance. Following the 1988 Seoul Paralympics, DSOs are exhibiting less autonomy and moving toward eliminating their disability-specific classifications in favor of the Integrated Functional Classification System. This system integrates people with a variety of disabilities into a single event or heat, basing criteria on the function of the individual (Vanlandewijck and Chappel 1996), including factors such as strength, quality and quantity of active muscle mass, and performance within a specific sport (Ferrara and Davis 1997).

Swimming and the Functional Classification System

Swimmers competed under this cross-disability classification system during international competition at the 1992 Barcelona Paralympics. In this system, swimmers with various physical disabilities are combined and compete against each other in 10 functional classes at the international level. Blind athletes are not involved and compete only against each other in 3 classes.

Functional Swim Classification Components

The Integrated Functional Classification for swimming was extensively studied by Blomgwist of Germany and Williamson of England in the early 1980s and modified by the International Paralympic Committee (Sherrill, Adams-Mushett, and Jones 1986). Currently, a group of individuals, trained as swimming classifiers, examines each athlete who has locomotor impairments prior to each meet. This is done in two phases, a medical evaluation and an evaluation of actual sport performance (Davis 1997).

Changes in classification are still evolving (Ferrara and Davis 1997). Evaluators at the 1996 Atlanta Paralympics tested the medical components, which included evaluation of range of motion, strength, coordination, and trunk and limb length through bench testing, choosing test items depending on type of disability. In bench testing, each evaluator assigns zero to five points to each component. For example, an evaluator assigned zero points for zero range of movement, one point for minimal ROM, two for a quarter of typical movement, three points for half of typical range of movement, four points for three-quarters of typical range of movement, and five points for full range of movement (International Paralympic Committee 1996). Evaluators conducted the testing based on actual sport performance. Evaluators assigned up to 300 points for swim stroke mechanics, including functioning of the hands, arms, trunk, and legs and body position displayed for the particular stroke. In addition, they scored diving starts and turns and push-offs (International Paralympic Committee 1996). For a clearer picture of the classification system, a nondisabled swimmer with efficient swim strokes earned 300 points; a quadriplegic with complete injury below C4/5 and with very limited movement of all limbs for propulsion earned about 50 total points; a person with a double–above-elbow amputation earned about 200 points. Finally, evaluators combined the subtotals of the two phases of evaluation and used the grand total to determine classification for that event (Davis 1997).

Administrative Benefits and Burdens

Many people have debated over and criticized the Integrated Functional Classification System. But proponents of such a classification system believe that administrative benefits outweigh any problems. This classification system simplifies the administration of a competition by reducing the number of events (Dummer 1997). Moreover, with the functional classification system in place, usually enough competitors participate in almost every event, resulting in true competition. Prior to the functional system, the immense number of classifications resulted in too few competitors in each event heat, resulting in confusion to the general public and sports media regarding who the true champions within each event were. For example, the 100-meter freestyle may have had 50 or more "winners" at a swim meet in which each DSO used their own classification system.

Those opposed to functional classification, however, argue that, at times, swimmers have been classified and then reclassified during a competition, adding to administrative burdens. Specifically, reclassification can waste time, wreak havoc on seedings and organization, and disrupt schedules at the last minute (Richter et al 1992). We believe, however, that such administrative difficulties and classification ambiguities will ease once all parties become more familiar with the system.

Difficulty in Accurately Classifying Function

Of course, the swimmers themselves have had much to say about the classification debate. In some swimmers' opinions, administrative convenience and opinions of the sports media and general public do not justify the decision to move to the Functional Classification System. They argue, for example, that some swimmers with cerebral palsy and those with more severe physical disabilities may have underlying neurological issues that sometimes appear and sometimes do not. Primitive reflex retention is one example in which early infant reflexes may still be present in an athlete with cerebral palsy. Although such an athlete may outwardly be physically functioning similar to an amputee, once the starting signal goes off, the startle reflex may impair his movements, but not that of the amputee athlete who is in the same classification.

Worries About Elitism

Another issue that some swimmers—and athletes with physical disabilities in all venues of sport—present is the notion of elitism. Disability-specific aquatic competitions and classifications fostered a large number of groupings and heat events, so that all levels of athletes could participate. Eliminating events generally reduces the number of events for more severely disabled athletes. Some think the Functional Classification

System, which integrates all disability groups, is, in effect, an attempt to provide more elite athletes with the opportunity to display their talents in order for the disabled sports movement to move toward an "authentic" sports movement. Shepherd indicates that this is ". . . moving away from the rehab model into an era of true elite athleticism" (Kaminker 1996).

Some maintain that the Functional Classification System favors the least disabled, who are the most skilled. Therefore, athletes with traumatic brain injury, for example, experience rejection due to neurological manifestations preventing the same type of physical performance as amputees or those with spinal injuries or dwarfism. Some say integrated classifications will have a greater impact on the audience and mainstream America by portraying only the most "able" disabled, who present an image of ability that is more analogous with typical Olympic competition. Athletes with more severe disabilities feel that more elite disabled athletes are embarrassed to compete at the same games as them (Kaminker 1996). The International Paralympic Committee has convened a Most Severely Disabled in Sport task force in response to these opinions, and in the 1996 Paralympic Games, the classification system was revised to make the system more equitable to swimmers with cerebral palsy.

Whether at the local, national, or international level, the classification debate goes on, however, fostering strong emotions. It is healthy and typical of any organization that continues to grow through a dynamic process. Despite its detractors, however, integrated classification is now an important component of competition for individuals with physical disabilities.

Special Olympics and Classification

Classification and participation in world class events for athletes with mental retardation or mental impairments is quite different from the Integrated Functional Classification System used by the Paralympic Committee. First, Special Olympics International requires that athletes involved in Special Olympics International competitions verify mental impairment and meet qualifying standards. The qualifying standards are listed in Article II, Section AA of the Official Special Olympics Summer Sports Rules (Special Olympics International 1992). The rules further divide competitors according to age, gender, and ability. Athletes submit their best

times for an event, then organizers seed them into heats or divisions according to the 10 percent rule (i.e., within a division, an athlete can have no more than a 10 percent difference between the top and bottom times for the event [DePauw and Gavron 1995]).

Paralympics for Persons With Mental Handicaps

A challenger to Special Olympics International (SOI) competition at the international level has been the Paralympics for Persons With Mental Handicaps, organized in 1986 by the International Sports Federation for Persons With Mental Handicaps (INAS-FMH). The INAS-FMH is the official governing body of sport for individuals with mental handicaps (INAS-FMH 1996). Although not an administrative goal of SOI, INAS-FMH gained momentum to include athletes with mental disabilities at the Paralympics, which has traditionally been for persons with physical disabilities. The INAS-FMH does not use a classification system, but prerequisites for competition include international qualifying standards, a verified status of mental handicap, and an age of at least 15 years. In comparison, to participate in Special Olympics International Games, prerequisite requirements include swimming training lasting at least eight weeks, placing first, second, or third at national competition in their division, and being at least 8 years old.

COACHING SWIMMERS WITH DISABILITIES

Youth and adults with disabilities are often deprived of competitive swim opportunities because of the lack of empathetic, knowledgeable coaches. Although training techniques are similar, coaching knowledge about specific disabilities is important to the success of the athlete. Many times, individuals with disabilities take longer to progress, and far too often, parents and coaches who are not experienced with coaching sports for the disabled become discouraged by the minimal progress that takes place in one swim season (Mushett, Wyeth, and Richter 1995). Thus, swimming professionals should take advantage of coaching clinics to learn the nuances associated with disabled sports. For starters, an athlete should not be allowed to attempt competition unless she has mastered basic swim skills, attained some endurance, and developed a positive attitude toward competition. Initial training should focus on slow, quality movements, rather than on swimming as fast as one can. Initially, it is OK to allow an athlete to use flotation devices, however, phasing these out will enhance progress toward independent swimming. As a coach, you should focus on the stroke or the position in which the individual is most comfortable, whether prone or supine. Then you should develop this strength before introducing another stroke, concentrating on sound individual functional mechanics, rather than on traditional stoke techniques.

Responsibilities

As a coach, you have responsibilities to your athletes with disabilities and should maintain high standards for yourself and your swimmers. As a coach of swimmers with disabilities, you should have the same goals as coaches of typical swimmers. Specifically, your primary goal should be to improve swimming performance through instruction and proper training and feedback as well as through building strength, flexibility, and endurance for the events that the swimmer wants to participate in (Miller 1985).

One difference a coach needs to learn is what modifications are possible and helpful for swimmers with disabilities, preferably through formal coach's training. You should become a member of your athlete's organization in order to keep up with modifications and event announcements. Then, you should read and become familiar with the rules and classification systems the swimmer will need to comply with through the DSO swim rule book and United States Swimming rules. Several DSOs conduct training clinics for coaches and some distribute management guides for conducting swim training, events, or both. As a coach, you must be willing to get in the water with an athlete to demonstrate and physically manipulate to facilitate better communication with the athlete.

Training Tips

Competitors who are not elite athletes often do not receive ample training from experts in competitive swimming (Persyn et al 1975). Many times, coaches are rehabilitation specialists, family, or friends. In contrast, athletes are primarily interested in coaches who are experts in swimming and care about them as people (Dummer 1997). Training in coaching swimming is the most important background for a coach of individuals with disabilities, but it is extremely wise for the coach to attend clinics, view videos, and read articles pertaining to specific disability implications.

Individuals with disabilities do not have the opportunities that individuals without disabilities have to participate in interscholastic or intramural sports and therefore have sporadic training regimes, which may consist of only one two-hour training session a week, culminating eight weeks later in a state or local meet. This is hardly the ideal. Year-round training to maintain some level of fitness is paramount in developing an active lifestyle, improving quality of life. In a study by Davis and Ferrara (1991), it was reported that elite athletes in wheelchairs trained an average of about 3.5 days per week versus 5 or 6 days for other elite athletes.

Since there are a variety of types of disabilities and athletes, we cannot offer one formula for training. Refer often to this chapter and the teaching and safety tips we reviewed in chapter 9 as an important first step to training swimmers with disabilities.

Before Training

Before beginning training first find out what type of functional abilities the person has through talking to them and their caregivers and through more formal assessment of function such as problems with memory or lower body spasticity. Then look up the disability and learn about the possible problems with function (see table 9.1) and read the corresponding material regarding those issues. Secondly, put together a swim plan incorporating the information you have gathered and the goals the swimmer has set.

Setting Goals. Teaching swimmers with disabilities how to set goals empowers them to exercise control over their futures. In fact, goal setting is the most critical component of competition, and without it, the coach and swimmers can lose focus (Davis and Ferrara 1995). When setting goals, swimmer and coach need to examine current swim skills and fitness of the athlete, the time commitment that will be necessary, pool and other training space in an available facility, and how long term the goals are. As a swimmer reaches goals, the coach should work with him to set new goals. If a swimmer does not reach his goals within an ample period of time, help him reconceptualize and task-analyze his goals into simpler, more discrete components.

Developing a Progressive Training Program. Apply principles of general swim training to develop a progressive training program that considers the goals of the swimmer, medical indications or contraindications, present level of swimming performance and fitness, and anatomical limitations. In addition, analyze the event in which the swimmer will compete, taking into account specificity of training principles. For sprints, for example, the swimmer needs to develop the strength, power, and anaerobic performance for short distances. Moreover, incorporate the principles of FITT (frequency, intensity, time, and type; see chapter 12) to apply the overload principle. Have the swimmer keep a training log, recording workouts and anecdotal notes regarding soreness, spasticity, and fatigue experienced during and the day after a workout.

Trouble Spots: Legal Strokes, Starts, and Turns

Some specific aspects will require more of your and your swimmers' time. A significant issue is adjusting the swim stroke to the capabilities of the individual while keeping the stroke legal from a stroke judge's point of view. But turns and starts can be the most difficult part of training. As a coach, you must decide how to deal with strokes, starts, and turns, based on what the rules say and what functional ability an athlete has.

Starts. Should the person start on the starting blocks? If the person has good standing balance and can perform a shallow dive, the answer is yes. If the person has good sitting balance, but no legs or leg strength, a sitting dive from the pool deck is more appropriate. If a sitting dive is not appropriate due to poor trunk or head control, spasticity, or missing lower body parts, starting in the water is best. A swimmer who cannot grasp the wall and needs to start in the water can have someone on deck hold them at the wall, then let them go at the start without giving them a push-off advantage.

Turns. Swimmers with mobility impairments may not have the ability to push off with their feet, legs, or hands. Swimmers with one leg or

hemiplegia may have difficulty coming straight off the wall and may need to adjust the foot on the wall or hand and body position before the push-off. Elite athletes with one functioning leg learn to compensate. Keep in mind, however, that swimmers who are classified as not able to use their legs for push-offs cannot use them at all—even if they have some leg strength. Become aware of any legal useful movement for a push-off, whether it is a single joint (ankle only) or hand and arm action.

Often when paraplegics or quadriplegics approach the wall to turn, they begin their turn prior to the wall and push off at an oblique angle to provide propulsion to complete the turn, similar to rounding first base in baseball. Specifically, they push off with the pad portion of the palm of one hand and lean one shoulder on the wall, quickly moving their head toward the lane they are swimming in.

Stroke Mechanics. Concerns about stroke mechanics and propulsion exist in swimmers with impairments to trunk, hip, and leg function. These swimmers, such as those with spina bifida, spinal cord injuries, or polio, may have intense arm power with no power in their legs, which may cause stroke imbalance or excessive swaying of the hips and legs or both. This affects hydrodynamics, causing drag and poor streamlining. Lack of leg power can also be a problem for swimmers who are doing the breaststroke and butterfly. Initially, you can walk backward in front of a swimmer to cut a path in the water, allowing the athlete to propel herself more easily by reducing water turbulence (Scull and Athreya 1995).

Many factors can impair balance, making breathing difficult: excessive body roll, swaying of hips and legs, uneven muscle control, and problems with buoyancy due to muscle atrophy or limb loss. To compensate, those with one functional leg might kick that leg inward and downward, crossing over midline, helping balance the body and making breathing easier (Persyn et al 1975). It may also be helpful to perfect a two-beat kick in this situation (for front-crawl). To help her build the strength she needs to perform stokes correctly, you can allow a swimmer to wear a flotation device or weight belt during the initial stages of training but not in major competitions. Tethered swimming is another option because it keeps the swimmer close to the edge of the pool, making feedback easy due to the proximity of the instructor. Tethering makes swimming in place possible by attaching surgical tubing or other elastic cord to a belt worn by the swimmer and tying the other end to the end of the pool or a pole. In addition, emphasize to your athletes the benefits of experimenting with various training adaptations to fully use any remaining functions they have.

RECREATIONAL AQUATIC ACTIVITIES

Beyond traditional passive aquatics programming, federal legislation has empowered individuals with disabilities to participate in recreational adventure activities in greater numbers as well. While as you know legislative mandates require recreational facilities to eliminate architectural and programmatic barriers, it is individuals with disabilities themselves who have proven to the nondisabled in society that they have an inalienable right to take controlled risks and that they can be safe and successful consumers of recreational aquatic opportunities.

Individuals of all ages with disabilities enjoy water sports as much as their nondisabled counterparts, providing outlets for persons with disabilities to participate in aquatic recreational opportunities with their peers, families, and community members. In the following sections, we will expand on how these activities can serve as avenues for increasing independence and normalizing existence.

Water Skiing

Although water skiing is a relatively new sport, it continues to gain in popularity and is the most rapidly growing aquatic sport (Kelly and Frieden 1989). Sport associations and facilities, including the American Water Ski Association, Adapted Aquatics, and the Mission Bay Aquatic Center (see appendix E), promote the sport, improve skiing technique, and advance equipment design. With adequate instruction and equipment, this activity gives an individual with disabilities the opportunity to participate in a popular recreational activity alongside family and friends.

Safety

Prerequisites to skiing include participants consulting with their physicians, becoming aware of the risks of hypothermia, and recognizing limitations each individual's level of sensation and muscle function may dictate. Of course, participants with disabilities need to observe the same basic safety precautions as nondisabled participants. Possessing basic swim skills and knowing how to use a personal flotation device (PFD) are essential. All skiers should practice using a PFD that meets their needs for support and buoyancy in a controlled environment before using a PFD in open water. In addition, skiers should be knowledgeable of state and local regulations regarding water skiing. The driver of the boat, the observer, and the skier should be thoroughly familiar with verbal commands, whether hand or head movement signals, to make this a safe activity for all.

Equipment and Technique

To make skiing easier for the beginner and those with disabilities equipment modifications must be made, especially for those with lower extremity involvement. A ski bra is one piece of equipment that keeps the skis together for those with leg weakness or paralysis. A knee board, ski biscuit (inflatable inner tube with a floor cover), or specially designed sit-ski can accommodate the skier who cannot stand up (figure 11.4). Two popular sit-skis are the KAN SKI and Wake Jammer. These feature high seat-backs, an aluminum seat tube or "cage," and quick-release tow rope attachments and foot bindings on a wide- or regular-width ski. Outriggers are also available for the novice or skier with severe balance impairment. After a significant amount of practice, skiers who use the sit-ski learn to lean to one side or the other in order to change direction. (For additional information, contact Mission Bay Aquatics Center, listed in appendix E, and refer to Bowness and Wilson n.d.)

Scuba Diving and Snorkeling

Traditionally, scuba diving was not a sport open to individuals with disabilities, but during the last decade, scuba and snorkeling have become part of a nucleus of adventure-based activities offered to individuals with numerous disabilities. These are activities that the disabled can share with nondisabled participants with only minor modifications.

Before beginning training, the instructor and diver need to discuss specific water access and entry techniques from the pool, beach, or boat

Figure 11.4 Water skiing is apprropriate for all ages.

(Petrofsky 1995; Robinson and Fox 1987). Once in the water, however, no architectural barriers prevent interaction with nature and there is little gravity to restrict mobility. Individuals with disabilities, accustomed to being creative in everyday life to work their way around physical and attitudinal obstacles, simply carry this ingenuity into their dive plans and equipment problems. "Success is pragmatic and limited only by human ingenuity" (Jankowski 1995). As an aquatic instructor, collaborate with individuals with disabilities to help them access the underwater world through the technology available within the scuba world.

A wide variety of scuba training programs are available that share the goal of diver certification, such as the National Association of Underwater Instructors (NAUI), the Professional Association of Diving Instructors (PADI), and the YMCA. Also available to meet the more specific needs of individuals with disabilities is the Handicapped Scuba Association (HSA), founded in 1981 by Jim Gatacre. Unlike the more traditional scuba certification programs, HSA uses a multilevel credential that classifies divers according to physical performance standards regardless of type of disability. Level A consists of diving students who can care for themselves and others, level B are students who need partial support, and level C are students who need

full support. (See also HSA, listed in appendix E, and refer to Jankowski 1995, Paciorek and Jones 1994, and Robinson and Fox 1987.)

Safety

While all agree that certified divers should possess requisite knowledge and skills for a safe and successful experience, controversy surrounds the diving community in regard to medical clearance and certification. Scuba diving has been generally accepted for most individuals with orthopedic, sight, and hearing disabilities, but secondary disabilities, such as limited breathing capacity, osteoporosis, poor circulation, temperature regulation disorders, medication, psychological conditions, and medical conditions, such as seizure disorders, insulin-dependent diabetes, and asthma, present a real concern for physicians and dive instructors (Lin 1987; Paciorek and Jones 1994; Petrofsky 1994a, 1994b). Presently, the only sound advice is for the prospective diver with a disability to consult with a physician experienced in hyperbaric medicine, use caution when diving, and be conservative.

Equipment and Technique

Since snorkeling and scuba require a significant financial investment, and individuals with disabilities often need specialized equipment that is not available by renting, they should approach the purchasing of equipment cautiously. You may consider working collaboratively with the diver, the scuba instructor, and the dive shop to ensure equipment is appropriate. The dive instructor can recommend the proper equipment, and you can assist by knowing the strengths and weaknesses of the disabled diver. Some modifications to equipment might include pressure gauges that have braille numbers or that emit auditory signals, divers tethered together, hand paddles or swim mitts, diving boots, low-volume masks, octopus regulators, jacket-type buoyancy compensators, flexible vented fins, wet suits, and diver propulsion vehicles for those who cannot propel themselves (Paciorek and Jones 1994).

Boating

Boating is a generic term used to represent a variety of water activities using a small craft. Boating activities are especially good for the individual with lower body involvement since paddling, rowing, and sailing emphasize upper body strength, allowing him to participate with his nondisabled peers and family members. As the national governing body for canoeing and kayaking, the American Canoe Association (ACA) is the nation's largest and most active nonprofit paddle sports organization. Likewise, the Disabled Paddler's Committee of the ACA dedicates itself to promoting canoeing and kayaking as lifetime recreational activities for individuals with physical disabilities.

Sailing opportunities have expanded rapidly during the last decade through new programs and adapted boats for individuals with disabilities. The United States Sailing Association (United States Sailing), formerly known as the North American Yacht Racing Union, became the national governing body for the sport of sailing under the Amateur Sports Act of 1978 and continues to promote sailing at all levels in the United States. One of the first adapted sailing programs in the United States, the Lake Merritt Adapted Boating Programs of the Office of Parks and Recreation in Oakland, California, began in 1981. Glo Webel, Boating Programs Coordinator, pioneered the development of sailing facilities for individuals with disabilities and has coauthored a text entitled, Open Boating: A Handbook (Webel and Goldberg 1982).

Another pioneer and innovator in sailing is Harry Horgan, founder of Shake-A-Leg of New-

port, Rhode Island. In the early 1980s, Horgan approached Everett Pearson, president of Tillotson Pearson, regarding the construction of a boat that could be sailed by individuals with spinal cord injuries. Their efforts led to the construction of Tillotson-Pearson's Freedom Independence 20 in 1986 (McCurdy 1991). The design, with its "Freedom Seat," proved to be successful, and participants consider it to be the benchmark of modified sailing vessels. In addition, the National Ocean Access Project, now associated with Disabled Sports USA, has continued to improve accessibility of sailing vessels by modifying traditional designs, such as with the Kaufman "Drop-in Seat" and by otherwise customizing boats for sailors with disabilities. Competitive sailing opportunities continue to grow nationally and were most recently showcased at the 1995 International Special Olympics Games and at the 1996 Atlanta Paralympic Games.

The United States Rowing Association is the national governing body for rowing. Its Adaptive Rowing Committee has developed educational materials and is dedicated to promoting rowing among individuals with disabilities and providing the same spectrum of opportunities as is enjoyed by nondisabled rowers (Tobin 1990).

Safety

Safety and risk management are concerns for everyone in boating, but some individuals with disabilities need to take extra precautions. If you plan to teach boating as part of your adapted aquatics programs, you should become a certified instructor through the American Canoe Association or the Level I Coaching Program, available through USRowing. Webre and Zeller (1990) suggest that safety planning of any boating class should include considerations for accessibility to the boating site, reviewing medical information and considerations involved with any medical condition, assessing what the participant can do on land, and determining what medical information needs to be shared with others in the group in relation to an emergency action plan. While boating offers a tremendous opportunity to participate in outdoor activities and enhance fitness and motor skill performance, it is still a water-based adventure sport; thus, students should not venture out into moving water until they have demonstrated competence in still water.

The amount of responsibility a paddler or rower should have should depend on functional ability. Ensure that you test balance, stability, and buoyancy of the boat with paddlers or rowers and equipment before undertaking a river or lake trip. Other elements of safety are problems with embarkation and disembarkation, instructor-to-student ratio, and—as with all water sports—an emergency action plan. In order to determine which boat, method, and paddle are most appropriate, consider the participant's balance, grip strength and endurance, coordination, and upper extremity range of motion. Consider, too, how much sight and hearing the person possesses, her ability to make decisions, and her knowledge of cause and effect.

Equipment and Techniques

The instructional process parallels that for nondisabled individuals, however, choosing the content, techniques, and equipment may involve extra thought, time, and money. Water orientation should be the first step; it should include instruction in safety, personal rescue, and using a PFD. After the water orientation, boat orientation may begin on land, moving into a pool, then to still open water, and finally to moving open water. Boat orientation should include terminology in a form that is understandable to the participant, exploration of the boat by blind participants, entry and exit procedures, and propulsion and steering techniques. It is at this time that participant and instructor must work together to modify equipment through trial and error, based on knowledge of available commercial equipment.

You can modify entry and exit procedures several ways. For example, a modification may be as simple as your standing in the water stabilizing the boat. Or you and an aide or two may opt to use a transfer mat to move the participant from the dock into the boat. If the river or lake bed is firm enough, consider pushing a water wheelchair into shallow water for water entries, having assistants help lift and transfer.

You can help a participant further modify equipment to enhance propulsion techniques by printing the words "right" and "left" on the opposite paddle blades on a double-blade paddle or on the inside of the boat to help a cognitively impaired paddler, painting the inside of the boat with nonslip paint, using suction cup bath mats on the bottom or seats of the boat, having various paddle lengths available, and having the participant use rubber or leather palm gloves for a better grip.

Commercial equipment for seating and gripping is available, such as a custom-made seat, ensolite on the seat to protect those with skin problems, Row Cat mitts for grasping, and sling-back seats to help with sitting balance (Andrews 1981). There are several models of canoes and kayaks to choose from, and you should analyze the participant's ability and intended use prior to suggesting a boat. A sea kayak is the most stable of kayaks and a rowboat is the most stable small craft; therefore, they are both good for beginners. Specially designed boats, such as the Row Cat II, which is an "untippable" catamaran that is easy to board and propel, and the Modified Alden Ocean Shell provide extra stability for the paddler or rower with a disability. The Modified Alden Shell is made by Special Sports Corporation of Knoxille, Tennessee and Row Cat II is made by Martin Marine Company of Kittery Point, Maine (see appendix E).

SUMMARY

Use this chapter as an overview of competitive and recreational opportunities in aquatics for individuals with disabilities. Remember, recreational and competitive opportunities are part of the typical lifestyle of most United States citizens. The importance of athletics and physical recreation is evident by the popularity of local sports teams, professional athletics, and excitement about the Olympics (Kennedy et al. 1987). Organized sport has influenced our culture and extends into all aspects of our lives. We must afford individuals with disabilities the same opportunities to participate in aquatic recreation and competition to develop skills not only in swimming and diving but also in the ancillary skills that come with such participation: independence, a healthy competitive spirit, justification for an active lifestyle, use of community facilities, release from everyday tensions, and networking with people of similar interests. Competitive swimming also provides public awareness of individuals with disabilities as active people with a great deal of ability.

Not all individuals want to participate in the competitive aspects of aquatics, however; therefore, recreational opportunities must provide the person with activities to challenge and compete with themselves, and the ability to develop the basic and ancillary skills we have mentioned. Individuals with disabilities could benefit greatly from the transition from instructional aquatics, in which participation and goals are instructor-directed, to competition and recreation activities in which independence and goal setting prepares individuals with disabilities for community living. Aquatics as a lifelong endeavor is a worthwhile activity because it develops valuable skills needed throughout life.

CHAPTER 11 REVIEW

1. List the seven DSOs that represent adapted aquatic competition in the United States.

2. List three modifications to competitive swimming sanctioned by United States Swimming.

3. Discuss the controversies over the issues regarding segregated (based on disability) versus integrated (cross-disability) aquatic competition.

4. What are some benefits of inclusion of athletes with disabilities in regular aquatic teams to the individuals without disabilities?

5. Define the term "classification" as it applies in adapted swim events.

6. Describe the cross-disability Integrated Functional Classification System for swimming.

7. What are the two components of the Integrated Functional Classification System test?

8. What are some responsibilities of swim coaches of athletes with disabilities?

9. List ways that you could adapt three recreational, nonswimming aquatic activities for individuals with disabilities.

AQUATIC FITNESS AND REHABILITATION

Individuals with disabilities are often perceived as unhealthy, although this is not true in most cases. Indeed, being healthy does not mean freedom from disability or disease. "Health is optimal well being that contributes to quality of life" (Corbin and Lindsey 1990, p. 10). Wellness is a state of physical, emotional, spiritual, and mental health that is achieved through preventing **hypokinetic disease**, avoiding unhealthy behaviors, practicing healthy behaviors, and decreasing the effects of heredity factors. As you well know, aquatics can provide rehabilitation and fitness training for all individuals—with or without disabilities and whether or not the disabilities are temporary or permanent. But you must work to change your own attitude as well as those of staff, participants, and the other aquatic patrons of a facility; furthermore, as we have discussed throughout this book, you must adapt exercise techniques and equipment to encourage people with disabilities to make necessary lifestyle changes, thereby ensuring long-term success. Ultimately, physical fitness is more than simply one aspect of wellness: it can also act as a catalyst to improve the other aspects of a person's health, including mental, social, emotional, and spiritual well-being.

In this chapter, we will introduce the concepts of health-related physical fitness and relate them to aquatics. We'll offer tips for dealing with various disabilities and circumstances as you strive to increase the fitness of your clients with disabilities. Then we will offer tips and address contraindications related to aquatic rehabilitation. You should not, however, substitute reading this chapter for formal training in rehabilitation. Instead, use this chapter both as a basic guide to appropriate practices and a springboard for further study. Contact the aquatic fitness organizations listed in appendix E for course and certification information that will enhance your professional knowledge of health-related physical fitness.

HEALTH-RELATED PHYSICAL FITNESS CONCEPTS AND AQUATIC EXERCISE

Of course, regular exercise is the key to physical fitness. Specifically, health-related physical fitness refers to a person's ability to work effectively, enjoy leisure time, resist hypokinetic diseases, and meet emergency situations (Corbin and Lindsey 1990). It includes cardiorespiratory endurance, flexibility, muscular strength and endurance, and body composition.

Aquatic exercise has become a popular activity that meets the needs of a culturally diverse society. Water-walking, shallow- and deep-water–jogging, water aerobics performed to music, sport-specific workouts, aqua-step aerobics, and circuit training are only a few examples of ways to use aquatics to enhance physical fitness. You should help participants choose a program or combination of programs based on interest, physical ability, and program availability. Then to integrate individuals with disabilities into an aquatic exercise program, find an instructor with a good attitude toward inclusion, make sure participants can regain their footing as needed, or provide a physical support person in the water with them at all times.

To put together a safe and sound water exercise program, you should have a professional fitness or physical education background or be certified by the Aquatic Exercise Association, AAHPERD, or other national agency. All of the information regarding training we discussed in chapter 11 applies as well. Then continue your education by reading articles, attending courses and conferences, and watching other instructors to stay abreast of current safety, technology, and educational advances.

Who uses aquatic exercise programs? Nondisabled teens and adults, individuals with disabilities, athletes with and without sport injuries, and older people, among others. Individuals with medical disorders, such as coronary heart disease, use aquatic exercise as a rehabilitation tool to return to their former activity levels. Kinesiotherapists and physical therapists often use aquatic exercise as a "work-hardening" tool to build strength and endurance to help injured individuals reenter the working world. Others who commonly use aquatic exercise are those who are obese or pregnant or who have recently had surgery. When prescribed by a physician or a therapist, aquatic exercise is called aquatic therapy (see also chapter 2).

Participation Factors and Challenges

Obstacles may confront a person with disabilities who is trying to achieve physical fitness. Examine the issues we raise in the following sections before helping a participant set goals and embark on a regimen to improve physical fitness.

Present, Preaccident, or Presurgery Fitness Status

If the person was active and involved in fitness activities before injury or surgery, there is a good chance that she will want to use activity as a means of rehabilitation. If a person with long-term disabilities is presently active, she, too, will be more likely to seek aquatic fitness. Individuals with a higher fitness level will be more motivated to perform the fitness routines.

Present, Preaccident, or Presurgery Swimming Abilities

Participants with no previous ability may feel anxiety, fear, and apprehension about beginning a fitness program in water. Jogging, walking, and other water exercises, rather than swimming, may be the way to initially expose participants to the aquatic environment. You should encourage the new or experienced swimmer with positive reinforcement, constantly pointing out small achievements. Participants who have been in an accident and who were swimmers previously may not experience fear but may have unrealistic expectations as to what they can do at present. Often, participants who were competitive swimmers or divers may become frustrated as they recognize that they may never return to their prior skill levels. Approaches you may use to encourage such an individual include:

1. Assist the participant in defining achievable personal goals.
2. Reinforce his goals by emphasizing progress is made by taking small steps.
3. Initiate support for the individual through one-on-one or peer tutoring.
4. Incorporate socialization into the sessions.
5. Encourage the development of new interpersonal relations.
6. Help the participant to realize that no one is staring at him and thinking of his former skills.
7. Convince the individual that if other people have a problem with his skills, it is the other person's problem, not his.

Duration of Sedentary Life

Endurance is a problem for anyone who has been on prolonged bed rest. When working with someone who is severely deconditioned due to prolonged inactivity, start very slowly and monitor progress carefully.

Indeed, you cannot be too cautious. Each person should complete a medical form in which a physician identifies any contraindications to physical activities. Monitor pulse and blood pressure, at least initially. Participants who are usually in a horizontal or sitting-reclining position may develop **orthostatic hypotension** when you ask them to stand or hold themselves in a vertical position in the pool. This extreme drop in blood pressure caused by moving into a vertical position may cause such participants to lose consciousness. Question participants as to whether they have been confined to a horizontal position for an extended duration recently, as in hospitalization.

You should also take precautions with people on certain medications. Seizure medications, for example, may cause side effects that interfere with target heart rates. Furthermore, fatigue is a potential cause of seizures in seizure-prone persons (Eichstaedt and Kalakian 1993). Although physical conditioning should bring a person close to the point of fatigue, you should avoid prolonged exercise and swimming sessions that bring the seizure-prone participant to the point of exhaustion and should keep a careful eye on the fatigued individual. Monitor locker room activities as well. Insist that a person who is fatigued rest before attempting to go home. (See chapters 7 and 9 for more information about managing seizures.)

Tips for developing exercise sessions that take into account the tendency for fatigue include (1) having the swimmer walk or swim widths of the pool at first, rather than lengths, (2) marking the length of the pool into thirds using buoys and lane lines, having each third represent a rest stop until the swimmer has more endurance, (3) setting realistic goals, avoiding pushing the swimmer before he is ready, (4) monitoring pulse (figure 12.1), (5) staying alert for signs of fatigue, such as falling, sloppy swim strokes, irritability, and exaggeration of motor and cognitive deficits, and (6) calling the swimmer the next day to determine if he was too tired following the session.

Physical Abilities

As we discussed in more depth in chapters 3 and 4, once you learn a participant's abilities through assessment, interviews, and reading medical charts or forms, as an aquatic exercise instructor, you can develop a swim program for the participant. Excessive muscle tone, paralysis, and bal-

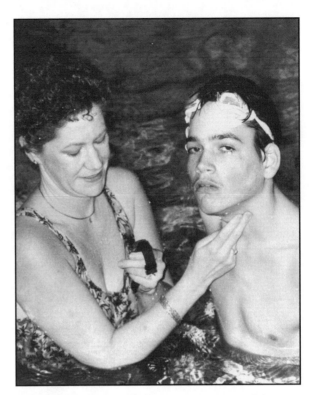

Figure 12.1 Fitness activities are more appropriate when pulse is monitored.

ance problems can limit the types of aquatic activities that a participant can do to improve fitness. Some typical fitness activities, such as unassisted lap swimming, treading water, and walking laps may not be viable options for those with some types of physical disabilities. Flotation devices and stationary objects, such as tot docks and chairs, however, can assist people with balance problems in developing other components of skill-related fitness, such as agility. Still, the less assistance, the more intensely the participant will be able to perform rhythmic, aerobic exercises in water and therefore the more she will be able to improve her level of fitness. Offer, then, the least amount of assistance that is safe and enjoyable for the individual.

Watch closely those with hemiplegia, paraplegia, quadriplegia, or weak or partially paralyzed muscles and follow these hints for exercising:

1. Be alert to how the body parts that lack feeling and movement respond to exercise, especially limbs. Protect these vulnerable areas with cotton gloves, socks, shoes, and shirts as participants can injure themselves on the pool bottom, side, or lane lines without knowing it (figure 12.2).

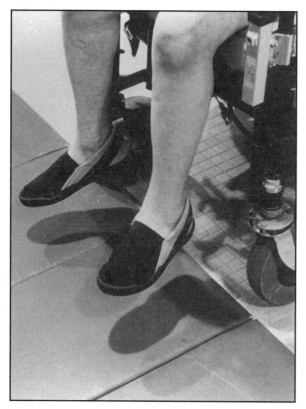

Figure 12.2 Water shoes provide protection and traction.

2. Consult each individual's physical therapist, kinesiotherapist, or athletic trainer regarding how you might assist with range of motion exercises.

3. Don't assume that the affected body parts have no movement; sometimes the part may have residual movement potential.

4. When people with weak or partially paralyzed muscles are involved in physical therapy, they begin with passive range of motion, then move on to active assistive, active, and then resistive. You should follow the same protocol when designing a fitness program.

Participant's Understanding of Fitness Concepts

Fitness is not an easy concept to understand, especially for individuals who have cognitive impairments. During warm-ups is a good time to explain the basics of fitness to get the person fully involved. If the information you need to present is too difficult for the person to understand, pair analogies such as feeling good and looking good with pictures of people getting into shape through aquatic exercise.

As you explain the basics of fitness, strive to teach the participant to view swimming and other water exercise as lifelong activities. If a participant recognizes that more benefits to swimming laps besides recreation and fun exist, they may continue to swim independently. How else can you motivate an individual? Try using the American Red Cross "Swim and Stay Fit" charts and homemade water-walking charts to promote fitness.

Another motivating point to include in fitness discussions is the value of fitness in life outside the pool. Some participants may want to swim when they learn that it helps them gain and maintain the strength and endurance needed to transfer into and out of their wheelchairs or beds. Some may see swimming as a social outlet.

Equipment and Expertise Available

No or little equipment should not mean no fitness class. As long as participants can enter, maneuver around, and exit the pool safely, you can begin your program. You can purchase or make various pieces of equipment to make sessions more interesting, but such items aren't necessary. The Wet Vest, (figure 12.3) a jacket-type flotation device that keeps a person vertical, and fitness paddles, plastic hand paddles to increase resistance during upper body exercise, are just two pieces of equipment that can enhance physical fitness workouts in water. See chapter 6 for more information about equipment.

Cautions: Wet vests are not personal flotation devices, so you must supervise closely non-swimmers who are using them. In addition, it can be dangerous to allow impulsive participants to use water weights.

Although an aquatic fitness program can begin without equipment, it cannot function without knowledgeable and personable personnel. To staff your aquatic exercise program, you can have an aquatic fitness expert develop and conduct classes, have swimming instructors conduct classes and an expert consultant come in several times to give advice, or have swimming instructors attend classes and conferences and read literature, becoming knowledgeable enough to be certified as aquatic exercise instructors. Discuss your program plans with other professionals, such as physical educators, physical therapists, athletic trainers, and exercise physiologists to help you plan a physical fitness program that will meet the needs of your

Figure 12.3 Use of the Wet Vest provides aerobic activity to those who do not like to swim laps.

participants. (Several resources for general information on aquatic fitness appear in the reference section. Also, see appendix E.)

Enhancing Cardiorespiratory Endurance: Adaptations and Issues

Success in activities that require sustained rhythmic movement depends on a good level of cardiorespiratory endurance. Individuals with disabilities need cardiorespiratory endurance to push their wheelchairs long distances, ambulate with crutches or walkers, perform work and home activities of daily living, and perform manual labor. Cardiorespiratory fitness is the ability of the heart, vascular system, and respiratory system to move oxygenated blood to the muscles efficiently and the ability of the muscles to use the oxygen efficiently. In order for cardiorespiratory training to take place in water exercise, exercise or swim strokes must involve large body muscles of the legs and buttocks and last about 20 minutes while the participant works at the proper target heart rate.

Frequency, Intensity, Time, and Type (FITT)

You should apply general principles of fitness training to swimmers with and without disabilities. To set goals, first discern what the participant wants to achieve. Endurance? Strength? Any other aspect of health-related fitness? Next, help the participant set realistic goals, then plan and follow an appropriately progressive training program. While you may plan for cross-training for strength and flexibility out of the pool, the main component of a swimmer's cardiorespiratory training should occur in the pool. To create a complete and safe plan, follow these FITT guidelines:

- Frequency: Depending on current level of fitness and goals, sessions may be held three times a week or on alternating days
- Intensity: 60 to 80 percent of maximum heart rate, depending on current level of fitness and goals
- Time: At least 20 minutes in the target heart rate zone per workout
- Type: Many aquatic activities facilitate health-related fitness

Frequency. In addition to limiting initial workouts to three times per week, ensure that participants have a 24-hour rest period following maximal swim workouts in order to avoid overtraining. This is especially true for those who both swim and use manual wheelchairs; never giving their arms, wrists, and shoulders a rest can result in injury.

Intensity. The intensity for competitive training should stress the **cardiorespiratory system** at about 80 percent of maximum heart rate (MHR) while maintenance and development of fitness can be 60 to 75 percent (American Red Cross 1996). The most popular way to calculate maximum heart rate is to subtract your age from 220 (200 minus age for those who exercise with arms only). Multiply this number by .60 to find 60 percent of maximum heart rate; multiply by .70 to find 70 percent of maximum heart rate, equalling your target heart rate zone (THRZ). As an example, Jim is a 40-year-old man with cerebral palsy who does not have use of his legs. His MHR would be calculated as:

MHR = 200 - 40 = 160

His THRZ (60 to 80% of MHR) would be:

THRZ = 160 x .60 = 96.00   160 x .80 = 128.00

With these two calculations, you can determine that his heart rate should be between 96 and 128 beats per minute. Have the participant begin by keeping his heart rate around 60 percent of maximum, slowly working up to 80 percent over time.

Due to hydrostatic pressure, thermal response, lack of gravity (easing stress on the heart), and the dive reflex, heart rate is usually lower for aquatic exercise. In fact, heart rates during water exercise are about 13 percent lower than on land (Lindle 1989). Deducting 17 beats per minute from the upper and lower limits of the projected target heart rate zone seems to take into account these phenomena (Windhorst and Chossek 1988). Medication and heart disease may be another confounding component in the calculation of aquatic exercise heart rate zones. (See table 8.1 for a chart of medications.)

Individuals who use their upper bodies for fitness swimming and water exercise movements without using their legs cannot elevate their heart rates to the typical target heart rate zone due to the smaller amount of muscle mass involved; they should subtract age from 200. Those with spinal cord injuries should subtract 40 beats per minute off the 220, then subtract their age from 180 (Lockette and Keyes 1994), due to nervous system dysfunction that prevents normal maximal heart rates and cardiovascular responses. Quadriplegics have even lower exercise heart rate zones, and usually peak heart rates do not exceed 100 to 125 beats per minute (Glaser et al. 1996).

In addition to those water exercisers with spinal cord injury (SCI), individuals with progressive disabilities and neuromuscular disorders that induce early fatigue may find the above formula too aggressive (Lockette and Keyes 1994). The **rating of perceived exertion (RPE)** may be a more reasonable method of describing level of intensity during exercise (Borg 1982).

Finding and monitoring heart rate for those with sensory problems of the hands (quadriplegia, arthritis, peripheral vascular disease, diabetes, multiple sclerosis, and the like) may be difficult (Grosse 1993). You can purchase heart rate monitors for participants to wear on the finger, wrist, arm, or chest from Biosig Instruments and Country Technology (see appendix E). Some individuals may need their blood pressure monitored during and after swimming or water exercise. This group includes those with

SCI who experience exercise hypotension and orthostatic hypotension and those with cardiovascular disease.

Time. Time refers to the duration of the exercise session, not including the warm-up or cooldown. You should encourage exercise participants to spend at least 20 minutes in their target heart rate zones per workout. Of course, those who are in extremely poor condition will have to work up to this duration. Some individuals may not be able to keep the aerobic pace going due to cardiovascular problems or fatigue related to their disability. Specifically, those with quadriplegia, postpolio syndrome, multiple sclerosis, muscular dystrophy, and progressive neuromuscular disabilities might need to take an interval approach to aerobic exercise, doing short bouts of exercise two to five minutes long, taking rest periods of one to two minutes in between (Lockette and Keyes 1994). Individuals with thermoregulation disorders (SCI) or who become excessively fatigued due to heat (multiple sclerosis) should cool themselves off with frequent water breaks and take rest periods when needed. The maximum length of a workout should depend on current condition of the participant and reports of excessive fatigue and soreness following workouts. Naturally, overdoing it does more harm than good as injury or soreness sidelines a participant.

Type. Some specific aerobic activities that will achieve cardiorespiratory training effects are swimming laps, swimming while tethered (figure 12.4), shallow water-walking or -jogging, running while using a water treadmill, aqua-aerobics to music, deep-water jogging with or without flotation, treading water, and water polo. Base type on individual interest, capabilities, and program availability.

Warming Up

As you well know, it is essential to warm up before cardiorespiratory pool workouts. Performing full-body exercise at a low intensity for approximately five minutes should be sufficient in most cases. Swimming elementary backstroke, swimming with a flotation device, treading water, or walking and jogging in shallow water (or in deep water with a flotation device), followed by stretching specific muscle groups that the workout will stress are excellent ways to warm up.

During group aerobic classes, if a participant cannot keep up or cannot perform a specific move, you can modify the steps in several ways: (1) have the participant do a specific arm action, such as pumping her arms as if she were running, (2) have her imitate the leg action with her arms (figure 12.5), (3) have her move her legs with her hands, (4) have her lean her body in the direction the class is moving, (5) allow her to use a tire tube or another flotation device, or (6) have an assistant help the participant move.

Enhancing Flexibility: Adaptations and Issues

Aquatic exercise improves range of motion (ROM) in joints. When swimming, poor ROM of the shoulder, neck, elbow, wrist, hip, and ankle can make it harder for a participant to improve fitness, because the ability to add resistance during the power phase of a swim stroke and to recover the arms above the water will be affected by flexibility.

Aquatic exercise is valuable for improving ROM in specific populations for which ROM is limited by disuse, disease, or disability. Buoyancy, warmth, and resistance are appealing attributes of this rehabilitation mode. Individuals who cannot perform exercises on land against gravity, as well as injured athletes, can make great gains using aquatic exercise. Aquatic exercise can aid in recovery from surgery, increasing

functional ability as well as decreasing pain during exercise (Levin 1991). To prevent injuries caused by poor flexibility, start the participant slowly in chest- to neck-deep water, controlling movements carefully and keeping them underwater. The participant can move to progressively shallower water as his ROM increases and therefore needs more weight and gravity to keep improving.

Specific conditions that inhibit ROM include (1) the abnormal stretch reflex in individuals with cerebral palsy, (2) contractures in individuals with muscular dystrophy, cerebral palsy, spinal cord injury, traumatic brain injury, or stroke, (3) surgery, (4) scar tissue, (5) heterotopic ossification (bone deposited into soft tissue around joints) as in individuals with spina bifida, polio, or multiple sclerosis or who have experienced trauma, a stroke, or traumatic brain injury, or (6) injury or joint capsule damage or both as in sports injuries or arthritis. When these conditions are present, you are more likely to have to alter proper stroke mechanics and exercise techniques to accommodate the individual's abilities.

Figure 12.5 A water chair allows an exerciser (in the right back) to do alternate moves while the class does leg exercises.

Figure 12.4 Use of a tether can keep a participant in close range for feedback or to alleviate fear.

To improve ROM, encourage the participant to stretch every joint twice a day almost to the point of the discomfort threshold (not pain), which is called "overload." Explain that you should never go beyond the initial sensation of discomfort nor should you "bounce" through a stretch, or injury will occur: "To enhance flexibility, move joints through their full ROM so muscles are stretched at least 10 per cent over their resting length and held at the point of tension (not pain) at least 20 to 30 seconds" (Burgess and Davis 1993, p. 120).

A complex subject to broach is the issue of **passive ROM** exercises. If a swimmer cannot move through a normal ROM, does not have a physical therapist or athletic trainer that works with or consults with her, and aquatics is her only form of exercise, should you as the adapted aquatic or water exercise specialist provide this exercise? Where does passive ROM end and tactile teaching begin? How does a nontherapist provide the exercise needed while not crossing over the professional boundary into clinical service?

In the absence of specific requirements, we recommend the following guidelines for passive ROM exercises:

1. Work in tandem for one session with a physical therapist or athletic trainer and learn the specifics for helping the water exercise participant do flexibility activities.

2. Encourage the participant to initiate the movement. To empower the individual in this capacity, use gravity and keep the movements underwater. If hip extension is the goal, for example, it would be appropriate to have the aquatic exercise participant in a supine position so gravity can help pull the leg down.

3. Warm water temperature is important for flexibility, with 88 to 92°F ideal.

4. Individuals with the following conditions need medical clearance and licensed therapists or certified trainers to provide or outline for you range of motion activities or specific movements that you may safely facilitate: severe spasticity, joint contractures, osteoporosis, heterotopic ossification, hypermobility, subluxations, dislocations, tissue adhesions, joint fusions, surgically implanted bars or pins, and pain that has not been evaluated by a physician (Lockette and Keyes 1994).

5. Be aware that wrist extension in quadriplegics may be contraindicated due to preserving **tenodesis** in the hand. Refer to physician or therapist before doing finger extensions, as tenodesis helps with a somewhat functional grip.

Enhancing Muscular Strength and Endurance: Adaptations and Issues

"Muscular strength is the ability to produce force at high intensity over short intervals of time, and endurance is the ability to sustain repeated productions of force at low to moderate intensity over extended periods of time" (Winnick 1995, p. 27). Muscular strength and endurance are essential components for individuals with disabilities to perform activities of daily living (ADLs) including wheelchair propulsion on uneven surfaces, walking with crutches or walker, transferring, performing vocational skills, and using community facilities. Strength and endurance are also important for proper posture and preventing injuries caused by muscle weakness and skeletal instability.

Unfortunately, however, some individuals have disabilities that affect muscle tissue directly or have progressive disabilities that result in muscle atrophy and strength loss; they may not be able to strength-train the muscle groups. If the progression rate is slow and 70 percent of residual muscle mass is available and you are monitoring the rate of intensity and taking into consideration the intensity of the individual's ADLs, then strength training at a low intensity is beneficial (Lockette and Keyes 1994). Individuals who need to have physician-approved strength-training programs include those with muscular dystrophy or other muscular degeneration disabilities, multiple sclerosis, myasthenia gravis, or postpolio syndrome. In these cases, strength training may be contraindicated due to the risk of extreme fatigue or the potential for actually causing permanent damage to muscle fibers. They (and all beginners) may benefit most from muscular endurance training at low intensity and low repetitions (Lockette and Keyes 1994).

You can easily modify muscular strength and endurance training in the pool. For resistance training, participants can use buoyant objects, such as kickboards, pull buoys, floating barbells, "noodles"(figure 12.6), beach balls, and water wings for pushing down into the water with their hands and arms. In addition, participants can wear hand paddles or fins or both, adding larger resistive surfaces for them to move through the water, thereby improving strength and endurance. Strap-on and handheld weights are popular, but you should use them with caution with those with joint problems or acute injuries; instead, have such participants increase the speed of their movements, which will increase the resistance underwater, or increase the resistance by presenting a larger surface area to the water (American Red Cross 1996). For example, a webbed glove (figure 12.7) increases the surface area of the hand without the risk of injury that paddles may present. Doing elbow flexion (biceps curls) underwater with an open hand, rather than with a fist, provides more resistance, making the move harder without resistive equipment.

Typically, the muscles you should help participants strengthen are those that are antagonistic to spastic muscle groups, usually the extensor muscles of the hip and wrist and the muscles on the front part of the lower leg. In addition, work on the strength and endurance of respiratory muscles for those with spasticity, scoliosis, muscular dystrophy, and asthma, which you can help participants develop by doing trunk exercises (e.g., sitting trunk rotation and trunk flexion/extension) and by encouraging exhaling fully through rhythmic breathing and blowing bubbles underwater.

PHYSICAL CONDITIONS AND TIPS FOR AQUATIC REHABILITATION

If as an aquatic instructor you do not have credentials in rehabilitation, you should never administer active therapeutic intervention for individuals with temporary disabilities or who have recently had surgery. If you are a therapist with no aquatic experience who would like to use the water for rehabilitation, however, you should consult an aquatic instructor for information about using aquatics as an adjunct to rehabilitation. We have written this section with the professional therapist in mind. We will discuss the following injuries and conditions: low back pain, frail elderly, obesity, pregnancy, knee surgery, shin splints, stress fractures, **tendinitis**, bursitis, plantar fasciitis, and **chondromalacia**. Remember that when working in aquatic rehabilitation with an individual with a chronic or acute injury, you should first review the participant's medical file to learn about the side effects of medication that may affect performance.

We have taken many of the following tips from Aquatics: The Complete Reference Guide for Aquatic Fitness Professionals by Ruth Sova (1992).

Figure 12.6 Pushing down on a buoyant object is good for resistance training.

Figure 12.7 Webbed gloves.

Low Back Pain

Twisting, jarring, and compressing the lower back are the main contraindications for low back pain. Slow controlled movements, in addition to strengthening the abdominal muscles and stretching the hip flexors, will help prevent or heal low back pain.

Frail Elderly

You should consider someone to be frail elderly if he cannot perform weight-bearing exercises, has some age-related disabilities, or needs assistance to perform activities of daily living and exercise. The aquatic program should offer a physical and emotionally safe environment, limit spinning and turning to lessen the chance of dizziness, use slower movements, and possibly use the gutter or chairs in the pool to help with balance. Many frail elderly need a longer, slower warm-up and need to work at their own paces to feel comfortable. They may need directions repeated due to poor hearing. Some frail elderly may be incontinent and need to wear tight-legged plastic panties. To develop a program for the frail elderly, you must incorporate all aspects of health-related physical fitness as well as fine motor movement. Avoid having participants grip equipment for prolonged peri-

ods as this may aggravate joint problems such as arthritis. Aquamitts or neoprene webbed gloves can be helpful because they increase resistance, thereby reducing the need to grip resistance equipment tightly.

Obesity

Experts consider individuals who are 20 percent over their recommended bodyweights to be obese (Dunn 1996). Workouts that feature low-impact, low-intensity, and high-duration activity are best for this group. If the bodyweight has caused the participant to be clumsy, it may be appropriate to offer a chair or bar in the water to hold on to. Excessive buoyancy may make it difficult for an individual to recover from both front and back horizontal positions. If necessary, teach the recovery to standing using the side of the pool. This population is at a high risk for developing heat-related illnesses due to lack of proper heat dissipation; water above 86°F may be too hot for working out (Sova 1992).

Pregnancy

Aquatic workouts should maintain prepregnancy fitness levels. Be sure, however, that the participant does not become overheated and that her heart rate does not exceed 140 beats per minute.

Workouts should be low-impact, and 80 to 83°F water is ideal. Musculoskeletal injuries are common due to a hormone released during pregnancy that softens joint structures and increases flexibility; therefore, tell the pregnant participant to avoid overstretching. During standing exercises, the swimmer should maintain a pelvic tilt (tighten buttocks and tilt pelvis toward head). Have her avoid equipment that intensifies abdominal work, due to possible separation of abdominal muscles, and stop if any pain or contractions occur. A pregnant swimmer should reduce intensity, frequency, and time as her body tells her to. Finally, never contradict the participant's doctor's advice, even if it seems conservative.

Knee Surgery

During swim strokes and exercise, a swimmer recovering from knee surgery should limit knee flexion to less than 75 degrees, unless instructed otherwise by a physician or therapist. The participant should avoid bouncing and weighted equipment as well as twisting movements with feet planted on the bottom of the pool. Moreover, breaststroke and elementary backstroke kicks are usually contraindicated. During all activities, the participant should keep his knees directly above his feet with the toes on both feet always pointed in the same direction as each other. Using a flotation device enhances exercising in deep water, eliminating weight bearing while encouraging increased ROM.

Shin Splints

Swimmers and water exercisers with shin splints should ice their shins before and after exercise while substituting nonweight-bearing activities such as jogging in neck-deep water. However, proceed with caution as deep-water jogging may be contraindicated due to increased plantar flexion and increased likelihood of pain. During weight-bearing activities, encourage participants to avoid jarring and stress landing on the heel. Participants with shin splints can wear the AquaRunners zero impact footwear, by Excel Sports Science of Eugene, Oregon, during water exercise to decrease the risk of impact-related injuries (see appendix E). Although made to add resistance and buoyancy, participants can wear them during shallow-water exercise as well.

Stress Fracture

An aquatic exercise participant with a stress fracture in the lower extremity should avoid weight bearing and do deep-water exercise while wearing a Wet Vest or an AquaJogger flotation belt.

Tendinitis

Swimmers and water exercisers with tendinitis should ice the affected area 20 minutes before and after exercise, strengthen the weak muscles, and stretch the opposing muscles of the affected joint.

Bursitis

Swimmers and water exercisers with **bursitis** should ice the affected area 20 minutes before and after exercise, and avoid using weighted, buoyant, or resistive equipment.

Plantar Fasciitis

Water exercisers with **plantar fasciitis** should use aquashoes with an arch support during weight-bearing exercises, avoid bouncing and jumping, and do as much deep-water exercise as possible. Incorporate stretching of the calf and Achilles tendon as much as possible during the workout.

Chondromalacia

Water exercisers should avoid high-impact activity and excessive knee flexion and extension. They should also avoid wearing weighted, buoyant, or resistive equipment on their ankles and doing the breaststroke, elementary backstroke, and scissor kicks. Aquashoes with an arch support help during weight-bearing water exercise.

SUMMARY

Individuals with disabilities are often unsuccessful exercising on land and have often been viewed as unhealthy by nondisabled people. But through water exercise, individuals with disabilities can exhibit some control over their lives and contribute to their own health and wellness, thereby enhancing their quality of life. Despite the physical and psychological barriers that still remain in our society, individuals with disabilities can develop and maintain a level of physical fitness that can decrease or prevent the risk of hypokinetic and other diseases. Whether you are an aquatic instructor or a therapist, you should help individuals with disabilities set goals, then help them adapt equipment, environment, and skills to be successful. Moreover, your encouragement is a valuable asset for helping individuals with disabilities overcome the negative factors they must deal with.

Apply the health-related fitness concepts and adaptations to fitness training in the water for individuals with disabilities that we have discussed in this chapter to create programs that will meet your clients fitness needs. Finally, refer to the common conditions for which experts recommend aquatic therapy we have described, using the tips to facilitate rehabilitation.

CHAPTER 12 REVIEW

1. What are some ways you might modify water exercise routines for individuals who cannot stand and do the routine with the class?

2. What questions should you ask of individuals with disabilities before you and they set their aquatics fitness goals?

3. Describe general precautions you should address for individuals taking medication.

4. List tips you can use to develop aquatic exercise sessions for those with low levels of fitness.

5. What are the basic principles for conducting a fitness aquatics program?

6. How do you calculate target heart rate zone for a 20-year-old female who uses her arms and legs during swimming?

7. Discuss programmatic concerns for providing aquatic rehabilitation programs.

8. Provide examples of how you can have participants use equipment to enhance muscular strength and endurance training.

Glossary of Common Disabilities

AIDS—Acquired immune deficiency syndrome is the outcome of HIV infection, causing high susceptibility to all kinds of bacterial and viral infections due to an inadequate immune system.

Alzheimer's disease—A disability of unknown origin primarily affecting an older population. May involve a variety of symptoms from mild memory loss to profound disorientation, passivity to aggression, and physical disabilities.

Amputee—An individual born without a limb (partial or full) or who has lost a limb.

Arthritis—Inflammation of the joints and concurrent damage to the various articulating surfaces within the joints.

Arthrogryposis—A nonprogressive disorder that affects many of the joints, making them weak, stiff, and swollen. Joint angles may be atypical; intelligence is usually normal. Also known as multiple congenital contractures.

Asthma—A respiratory condition in which either exercise or allergens induce bronchial inflammation and increased mucus production, leading to wheezing, coughing, difficulty exhaling, shallow breathing, feelings of chest constriction, and difficulty regulating breathing.

Ataxia (ataxic)—A descriptive term meaning poor balance and general lack of coordination. Also a type of cerebral palsy.

Attention deficit disorder (ADD)—Difficulty focusing on tasks, distractible, difficulty attending to directions.

Attention deficit hyperactivity disorder (ADHD)—The same as ADD but with hyperactivity, which leads to fidgeting, impulsivity, excessive movement, impatience, and low tolerance for frustration.

Autism—A pervasive developmental disability typically revealed before the age of 30 months, in which interaction with people is impaired, activity level is significantly above or below average, and person makes little eye contact. May engage in echolalia, exhibit no fear of real dangers, engage in odd play, and (or) display inappropriate attachments to objects.

Behavior disorders—Behaviors that are exhibited over a long period of time to a marked degree, adversely affecting learning. Severe behavior disorders include noncompliance, self-stimulatory, self-abusive, and aggressive behavior. May also be described as emotionally disturbed, emotionally handicapped, or socially maladjusted.

Blindness—Lack of sight that is severe enough that a person cannot see shapes, shadows, or light. Various terms, such as total, low-partial, and high-partial, describe individuals with visual impairment of one degree or another.

Cancer—An abnormal reproduction of atypical cells that leads to tumors. Chemotherapy and radiation therapy treatments are common.

Cerebral palsy—A general term applied to nonprogressive, neuromuscular disorders affecting normal, orderly motor development and voluntary muscle control caused by brain lesion before, during, or shortly after birth. Common types are ataxia, athetosis, spastic, flaccid, and tremor.

Deafness—Classification of hearing loss in which a person cannot understand speech even with a hearing aid. Also a cultural minority who use sign language as a communication medium.

Diabetes—A metabolic disorder in which the body does not produce or underproduces insulin, preventing body cells from using sugars for energy.

Down syndrome—A congenital disorder in which there is an extra chromosome on the 21st pair. Common characteristics are short stature, cognitive impairment, speech and language disorders, congenital heart defects, visual and hearing impairments, flat feet, lax ligaments, low muscle tone, joint instability, and, sometimes, atlantoaxial instability.

Fetal alcohol syndrome—A condition in which the fetus has been prenatally exposed to alcohol through the mother's abuse. Typical symptoms include small size for age, abnormal muscle tone, developmental delays, and abnormalities in alertness, attention, and learning. It is a leading cause of mental retardation.

Hard of hearing—Classification of hearing loss in which a person can understand linguistic information through the use of amplifiers and hearing aids.

Heart defects—Malformations of the heart, which can be congenital or acquired and may hamper an individual's ability to become or remain fit.

Hemophilia—A blood disorder in which the protein needed to clot blood after injuries or bleeding is lacking, leading to internal or external bleeding or both. Internal bleeding into joints (hemarthrosis) can cause joint dysfunction.

Hydrocephalus—An accumulation of cerebrospinal fluid on the brain, causing enlargement of the head and pressure on the brain. Excessive brain pressure causes cognitive impairments. Often seen in individuals with myelomeningocele spina bifida.

Juvenile rheumatoid arthritis (JRA, or Still's disease)—Inflammation of many joints throughout the body, manifesting itself in childhood. Often symptoms decrease 10 years after onset, but some children may have chronic joint damage and severe disability into adulthood.

Kyphosis—A posture problem in which the upper back muscles are weak, causing poor extension of the upper back, leading to a humpbacked appearance.

Learning disabilities—A dysfunction in one or more of the psychological processes involving written or spoken language that is not caused by deafness, blindness, mental retardation, or environmental disadvantages.

Legal blindness—Loss of vision that equals a visual acuity of 20/200 or worse (with correction) in the better eye, or a field of vision of 20 degrees or less.

Les autres—A term meaning "the others" that includes disabilities *other than* spinal cord injury, cerebral palsy, closed head injury, stroke, amputation, visual impairment, mental impairments, or hearing disabilities.

Lordosis—A postural problem in which the lumbar area is hyperextended (swayback) due to weak abdominal muscles and (or) tight hip flexors and lower back muscles.

Mental retardation—Substantial limitations in functioning due to significantly lower than average general intellectual functioning with limitations in two or more of the following: communication, self-care, home living, social skills, self-direction, health and safety, functional academics, and abilities to pursue leisure, use the community, and perform work (AAMR 1992). Manifested during childhood.

Multiple disabilities—A person with more than one impairment, causing profound problems in learning, such as cerebral palsy with blindness and spina bifida with mental retardation (Individuals With Disabilities Education Act 1990).

Multiple sclerosis—A progressive disorder of the nervous system, characterized by degeneration of the myelin sheath surrounding the nerves. Onset is usually in young adults or middle age and its cause is unknown. Affects more women than men.

Muscular dystrophy—The name for a group of degenerative disorders affecting muscle tissue causing atrophy, weakness, and severe physical disability.

Myelomeningocele—Severe type of spina bifida in which the spinal cord and its covering are herniated through the posterior part of the vertebrae, causing paralysis in the body parts below the site of disorder; most commonly located in the lumbosacral (lower back) region with accompanying paraplegia.

Obesity—For a female, 30 to 35 percent, for males, 20 to 25 percent, above expected weight for height and body frame size; 50 percent over the expected weight and frame size is classified as superobese (Jansma and French 1994).

Osteogenesis imperfecta—A condition of brittle bones with several classifications, in which individuals may or may not have skeletal deformities, may or may not be ambulatory, and may or may not have normal life expectancy (Blauvelt and Nelson 1994).

Paraplegia—Loss of voluntary muscle control in the lower extremities.

Poliomyelitis—Acute phase of inflammation of the gray matter of the spinal cord, causing loss of voluntary muscle control and therefore long-term disability.

Postpolio syndrome—A variety of symptoms and characteristics seen commonly in individuals over 50 who have had polio since childhood, including joint dysfunction, paralysis or paresis, and brittle bones.

Prader-Willi syndrome—A genetic condition marked by mental retardation, low muscle tone, short stature, and obesity (Wiedemann, Kunze, Grosse, and Dibbern 1992).

Quadriplegia—Loss of voluntary muscle control in all extremities.

Scoliosis—A rotolateral posture disorder resulting in a C- or S-lateral (side-to-side) curve.

Seizure disorder—A number of convulsive and nonconvulsive disorders frequently associated with epilepsy. Generalized (grand mal) seizures involve involuntary tensing (tonic phase) and then jerking (clonic phase) of the muscles of the whole body. Other types of seizures are partial, unilateral, and unclassified.

Spina bifida—Congenital neural tube defect, which can be mild (SB occulta) with no disability, severe (SB myelomeningocele), or not as severe (SB meningocele). See myelomeningocele definition for more information.

Stroke (cerebrovascular accident)—Lack of oxygen to a part of the brain due to blood vessel occlusion, hardening of the arteries, embolism, tumor, or aneurysm rupture. Can cause hemiplegia, speech and language disorders, and permanent disabilities.

Traumatic brain injury—Injury to the brain due to a closed head injury or penetrating (open) head injury causing multiple disabilities.

Traumatic spinal cord injury—Trauma to vertebrae or spinal cord or both resulting in loss of sensation and voluntary motor control. Can be mild (simple broken vertebrae), which may result in temporary paralysis, or severe (severed spinal cord), which results in permanent paralysis from about the site of the injury downward.

Glossary of Terms

Academic learning time (ALT)—The amount of time a student spends in learning and engaged in appropriately challenging, on-task behavior.

Active-assistive ROM—Active range of motion where assistance is provided by an outside force.

Active ROM—Movement within the range of motion, initiated and performed by contraction of the muscles and not aided by another person.

Adapted aquatics—A comprehensive label for programs serving individuals with disabilities that use swimming, water safety, and aquatic recreational activities to promote health and rehabilitation. Such programs encompass more than swim strokes, but do not include therapeutic water exercise, hydrotherapy, or aquatic therapy.

Adapted physical education—Any adaptation to the physical education curriculum that allows for safe, successful, and satisfying participation of a student with a disability, including specially designed instruction.

Adapted swimming—A program that modifies swim strokes for individuals who do not have the strength, flexibility, or endurance to perform the standard version. Adapted swimming is part of adapted aquatics.

Adapted water exercise—A program that uses active (not passive) exercises, typically done on land, within the medium of a pool. Such exercises are adapted to the needs of individuals with acute or chronic disabilities.

Adduction—Movement of the extremities toward the body midline.

Ambulation—Capable of walking with or without assistance.

Americans With Disabilities Act (PL 101-336)—Federal law which expanded federally mandated accessibility and participation requirements of the Vocational Rehabilitation Act of 1973, Section 504, to the private sector.

Anemia—A common blood disorder characterized by reduction of oxygen to the tissues.

Annual goals—Broad global statements that provide direction for instruction.

Aphasia—Loss of or impaired expression or comprehension of spoken or written language.

Aquatic therapy—Water exercise that has been prescribed by a physician or therapist.

Assessment—Interpretation of data to develop a student profile influencing placement, goals, and objectives.

Atlantoaxial instability—Unstable joint at cervical vertebrae 1 and 2. When the head is bent forward, the spinal cord can be pinched (Bleck and Nagel 1982).

Atrophy—Reduction of tissue due to disease or injury.

Behavior modification—Changing behavior via systematic application of methods of behavioral science.

Bromine—A group of chemical agents often used in cleaning pool water.

Bursitis—An inflammation of the bursae sacs due to repeated irritation from overuse, or from direct trauma. Bursae help cushion a joint.

Cardiorespiratory system—System that transports oxygen from the lungs, through the heart and to the body by the blood vessels; pertaining to the heart, blood vessels, and lungs.

Center of buoyancy—The area of the body around which buoyancy is evenly distributed; generally located in the chest region.

Chondromalacia—A condition in which the underside of the kneecap degenerates causing bone erosion and pain (Torg, Welsh, and Shephard 1990).

Conjunctivitis—Inflammation of the membrane lining of the eyelid and the eyeball.

Contraindications—An activity or treatment considered undesirable, unwarranted, or improper because of possible deleterious effects.

Coping behavior—Techniques utilized by individuals to avoid learning or practicing what is being taught.

Data-Based Gymnasium Program (DBG)—Noncategorical teaching approach using task analysis, recording of data, and behavioral principles.

Decubitis ulcer—A lesion of the skin and tissue which results in death to the tissue and breakdown of the skin.

Dry ramp—Access constructed into the pool deck outside of the pool.

Education for All Handicapped Children Act of 1975 (PL 94-142)—This law ensures a free, appropriate, public education in the least restrictive environment, including special education and related services, for all handicapped children age 3 to 21 years.

Education for All Handicapped Children (reathorization of 1980) (PL 99-457)—Amendment to 94-142 which mandates and partially funds services down to age three.

Expressive language—Expressing oneself with words in a meaningful, organized way.

Flexibility—The ability of a muscle to relax and stretch.

Germicide—An agent that kills disease-producing microorganisms.

Hemiplegia—Paralysis on one side of the body.

Homeostasis—Regulation of balance of internal bodily functions; a state of internal equilibrium (Sherrill 1993).

Hydrotherapy—The treatment of disease, disability, and ill health using water as the therapeutic medium.

Hyperthermia—Dangerously increased core body temperature.

Hypertonicity—Muscle tone that is too high (tight).

Hypokinetic diseases—Diseases that result from lack of physical activity.

Hypothermia—Dangerously reduced core body temperature.

Individualized Educational Program (IEP)—A written plan of instruction, including present levels of performance, annual goals and objectives, and extent of inclusion, for students qualifying for special education services.

Individualized Family Service Program (IFSP)—A written plan describing the education, therapeutic and social services projected for infants, toddlers, and the child with a diagnosed disability or who are at high risk of having a permanent disability.

Individualized Transition Plan (ITP)—A statement in the IEP of each child no older than 14 years, describing the process that will be used to make transition into community-based living.

Individuals With Disabilities Education Act (IDEA; PL 101-476)—Amendment to 94-142 that changed the name of the law, added requirement of transition plans by age 16, and added autism and traumatic brain injury as disability categories.

Kinesiotherapy—Profession practiced by certified individuals who seek to improve work, leisure, and fitness performance through therapeutic exercises.

Lateral movement—Movement oriented to the right or left or away from the midline of the body.

Least restrictive environment (LRE)—The philosophy that children with disabilities will be provided educational services individually determined to be the best place for the child to learn and to the maximum extent appropriate alongside children without disabilities.

Neurology—Branch of medicine that deals with the nervous system and its diseases.

Objectives—Measurable intermittent steps by which to plan and evaluate progress of instruction.

Occupational therapy—Use of purposeful activity by licensed occupational therapists to assist individuals in acquiring the skills necessary to perform activities of daily living (ADL).

Orthostatic hypotension—A fall in blood pressure while person is vertical that is associated with dizziness and blurred vision.

Orthotic—An orthopedic appliance, such as a brace or other support.

Paralysis—Loss or impairment of motor function due to a lesion of the neural or muscular system.

Passive ROM—Movement within the unrestricted ROM, produced by an external force, rather than the participant voluntarily contracting the muscle.

Peer tutors—Personal assistants for individuals with disabilities of the same age.

Personal flotation device (PFD)—Life jackets and similar devices graded according to buoyancy ability.

Physical therapy—Profession practiced by licensed physical therapists that uses heat, cold, electric stimulation, exercise, water, and massage to improve physical functioning of the individual.

Plantar fasciitis—Inflammation of the connective tissue on the underside of the foot that attaches at the toes to the heel bone. This results in pain and tenderness while walking and running, often due to tight calf muscles (Robbins, Powers, and Burgess 1991).

Prone—Lying on the front.

Proprioceptive—Components of the nervous system that transmit information between the brain and the muscles, joints, and ligaments to let an individual know where the body is in space.

Prosthetics—Artificial substitutes for a missing body part.

Range of motion (ROM)—The amount of motion that occurs between any two bones in a joint.

Rating of perceived exertion (RPE)—A technique in which a person designates how hard he is working by assigning a number (from 1 to 20) to the intensity he believes he is working at.

Readily accessible—Used in conjunction with the Americans With Disabilities Act (ADA) to describe the relative ease of entrance and usability of a facility.

Readily achievable—Used in conjunction with the ADA to describe the relative ease or difficulty of removing barriers in a facility.

Receptive language—A person's ability to organize and derive meaning from what she hears.

Rheumatology—Branch of medicine that deals with rheumatic disorders, such as rheumatoid arthritis.

Risk management—Interventions and activities used by an organization to identify, evaluate, eliminate, reduce, and (or) transfer risks, regarding accidents, unsafe facilities and equipment, legal recourse, inadequate staff, and other related problems.

Seizure—A characteristic of epilepsy manifested by a disturbance in the electrochemical activity of the brain, possibly resulting in unconsciousness and uncontrolled muscular contractions.

Sensory integration—The process whereby an individual develops awareness, discrimination, and recognition of sensory stimuli and subsequently uses the sensory information to direct motor behavior.

Shin splints—A condition characterized by pain in the front lower leg as a result of a sudden return to weight-bearing, high-impact exercise after a layoff (Robbins, Powers, and Burgess 1991).

Spasticity—Abnormally high tension in a muscle.

Station method—A method of teaching whereby participants are directed to specific stations for instruction in specific swimming skills, permitting focused practice and review.

Stimulants—Agents that arouse or produce systemic excitation.

Stoma—A surgical opening in an individual's neck through which the individual breathes.

Stress fracture—The reaction of a bone due to the accumulated stress of repeated actions. Frequent sites of these microscopic breaks in a bone are lower leg and foot (Robbins, Powers, and Burgess 1991).

Subluxation—Incomplete or partial dislocation of a joint.

Supine—Lying on the back.

Tactile—Refers to touch or the method of instruction in which the aquatic instructor uses hand-over-hand touch to move a person's body through an action.

Target heart rate zone—A range in which your heart rate (beats per minute) should remain to achieve cardiorespiratory training effects.

Task analysis—A method of breaking down a task to determine its sequential components.

Tendinitis—Inflammation of tendons (soft tissue that connects muscle and bone) due to repeated stress; can occur at any joint. Tendinitis often occurs in the Achilles tendon and in the shoulder.

Tenodesis—The use of wrist extension, by quadriplegics, to passively put the fingers into flexion. Can be used for functional hand grasp (Lockette and Keyes 1994).

Terminal behavior—Behavior targeted for an individual to achieve.

Therapeutic recreation—Health-related profession that seeks to bring about a change in behavior or function through recreational experiences.

Therapeutic water exercise—These are aquatic movements specially prescribed for a particular individual. Therapeutic water exercise protocols should be authorized by a physician and conducted by a physical therapist, athletic trainer, or kinesiotherapist who has aquatic training.

Therapy hands—A term denoting the efficacious use of touching, supporting, positioning, and handling of people to facilitate greater movement potential (Cratty 1989).

Transdisciplinary—In the context of service delivery, the transdisciplinary approach focuses on sharing and cooperation. The team of professionals, with the caregivers and participant, prioritize goals and provide input in a collaborative manner.

Vasoconstriction—Narrowing or constriction of the blood vessels.

Vasodilation—Enlargement of the blood vessels.

Ventilator—Mechanical device designed to assist or perform ventilation of the lungs.

Vocational Rehabilitation Act of 1973 (PL 93-112, Section 504)—A federal civil rights law prohibiting discrimination based on "handicap" within any facility or program that is federally funded. It mandates accessibility and equal opportunity.

Wet ramp—Access connecting the deck directly into the pool.

≋ Appendix A ≋

AAHPERD-AAALF-AQUATIC COUNCIL ADAPTED AQUATIC POSITION PAPER

ADAPTED AQUATICS

A Position Paper of the Aquatic Council

American Association for Active Lifestyles and Fitness

American Alliance for Health, Physical Education, Recreation and Dance

Adapted aquatics constitutes aquatic instruction and recreation for individuals with disabilities. Individuals of all ages with various physical, sensory, or mental disabilities want, need, and possess the legal right to have opportunities in the same aquatic activities, in the same environments, in the same ways as nondisabled persons. Individuals with disabilities participate in aquatic instruction and recreation for the same reasons as nondisabled persons—learning specific aquatic skills, taking part in leisure recreational activities, developing and maintaining appropriate levels of personal fitness and wellness, responding to individual challenges, having opportunities to socialize with families and friends, taking part in competitive aquatic activities, and having *fun* by enjoying life through the aquatic medium. This position paper delineates the scope of aquatics for individuals with disabilities within the broader frame of aquatic organization, administration, and participation.

Adapted aquatics is a broadly encompassing concept including belief that

- aquatic activities of all types—instructional to competitive swimming, water aerobics, fitness and wellness, water games, crew, diving, small craft, skin and scuba diving, water parks, sailing, motorized water ventures, and surfing—provide opportunities for individuals with disabilities to improve the quality of their lives through active participation, particularly with families and friends;
- individuals with disabilities have a right to participate regardless of where they live—inner city, suburbia, or rural communities; and
- aquatics for individuals with disabilities is a total lifespan activity and should be approached as such.

Aquatic instruction and recreation involving individuals with disabilities should not be confused with aquatic or hydrotherapy, an extremely important part of rehabilitation processes.

- The two are not synonymous: Each has its own distinct goals and specific objectives.
- This distinction does not negate therapeutic contributions from educational and recreational aquatic programs nor educational and recreational values of therapeutic programs.

- Focus must be kept on primary goals and objectives, either instructional or therapeutic, when involved in each of these programs.

Most aquatic instructional sequences and progressions are appropriate and applicable for use with individuals with disabilities, regardless of type or severity of disability. Creativity, innovation, and resourcefulness are keys to successful uses of these progressions and sequences. This might include, but is not limited to

- being sure activities and approaches are age appropriate;
- entering into a sequence at appropriate points for the individual, rather than at predetermined group objectives;
- introducing more basic steps in progressions (starting at lower levels);
- breaking skills down into smaller and more manageable steps;
- basing approaches on functional aquatic skills, not on medical diagnoses, recognizing how an individual's disability affects ability to learn and perform aquatic skills and activities;
- personalizing and individualizing instruction, addressing each individual's ability to perform applicable skills, with or without flotation or assistive devices; and
- introducing accommodations to meet needs of each individual student.

Safety is a critical component. Safety instruction must be a part of all aquatic activities.

- Flotation devices should only be used under direct supervision of an instructor, should not be a substitute for lifeguard surveillance or instruction in skills, and should only be used until independence and appropriate skills can be developed.
- Swimming—competitive, instructional, or recreational—should take place under supervision of a lifeguard whose sole responsibility is surveillance of participants.
- All aquatic instruction should be provided by an individual who has credentials from a national aquatic agency.
- All safety rules and participation safeguards applicable in regular programs apply to adapted aquatics.

- Water safety education and skills must be integrated with all aquatic activities, regardless of the type of aquatic activity or functional level of the participants.

Individuals with temporary or permanent disabilities should participate in regular aquatic activities whenever possible, only being placed in special programs when absolutely necessary. These special programs should be reserved for students who cannot, for whatever reasons (physical, mental, social, emotional), safely, successfully, and with personal satisfaction take part in regular aquatic programs. Participants in special programs should work toward the same basic goals as peers in regular programs. Instructors should always focus on individualized goals and personalized objectives. Emphasis in special classes and activities should be on preparing an individual for active participation in appropriate regular programs. Regardless of setting the total aquatic facility must be accessible—parking entrances, locker rooms, showers, rest rooms, and the pool itself.

There is a need for aquatic specialists with specific training and competence relating to individuals with disabilities. Their roles include

- teaching and leading individuals with disabilities within special programs;
- serving as resources for aquatic generalists—demonstrating and (or) team teaching and conducting various aquatic activities in integrated settings;
- assessing participants with disabilities;
- recommending and providing appropriate flotation and other assistive devices;
- suggesting instructional progression and sequence accommodation for individual aquatic needs;
- furnishing professional resources on adapted aquatics and aquatic recreation for individuals with disabilities; and
- conducting inservice training activities for generalist instructors or program leaders, volunteers, and others involved in any way in the program.

Whether generalist or specialist, instructors must be highly committed and dedicated to fulfilling their moral and ethical responsibilities of meeting the challenges of including participants with disabilities in aquatic activities. They must also be strong advocates for equality of opportunities through aquatics. Instructors must possess empathy for individuals with disabilities. Teamwork through communication, cooperation, and coordination with other individuals and agencies is a *must* for success. General ratio of students to teachers must be less where individuals with disabilities are served. This ratio must be reduced even further when students have more severe conditions.

Adapted aquatics is a service delivery system providing appropriate aquatic instruction and recreation for participants with disabilities. This system includes identifying, assessing, planning, instructing, leading, and coaching individuals with disabilities who desire to participate in aquatic instruction and recreational activities. It also includes education, consultation, and assistance to general aquatic professionals, family members, health professionals, and the community in providing equal opportunities to participants with disabilities and on successfully including them in aquatic programs to fulfill and reaffirm the potential of aquatics to contribute to the quality of their lives.

Aquatic Council, AAALF/AAHPERD, 1900 Association Drive, Reston, VA 22091

The American Association for Active Lifestyles and Fitness is one of six associations of AAHPERD.

⁓ Appendix B ⁓

ASSESSMENT FORMS

Sports Skills Assessment—Level I Swimming

Instructions

The Sports Skills Assessment is designed to determine the athlete's present level of functioning within a specific skill or sport and to determine the athlete's progress through training.

In administering the test, observe each athlete as he or she performs each test item. Score the athlete accordingly by checking the box located to the left of the task performed. If there are any questions as to the athlete's competence in a particular skill, require the athlete to perform the task 3 out of 5 times.

After scoring each athlete, add up the total number of boxes and indicate the athlete's present level of ability (i.e., Beginner, Rookie, Winner). If the athlete is performing at a higher skill level than measured in the Skills Assessment—Level I, reevaluate the athlete using Skills Assessment—Level II.

Skills Assessment—Level I

Prescore Postscore

Test item #1 **Water adjustments**

☐ ☐ Sits on the edge of the pool and kicks.
☐ ☐ Walks across the pool holding onto the side with one hand.
☐ ☐ Walks across the pool alone.
☐ ☐ Puts face in water.
☐ ☐ Exhales through nose and mouth in a relaxed and rhythmical manner (bobs).

Test item #2 **Water entry**

☐ ☐ Enters pool using stairs with assistance.
☐ ☐ Enters pool using stairs without assistance.
☐ ☐ Slides into pool from pool edge.
☐ ☐ Jumps into shallow end.
☐ ☐ Jumps into deep end.

Test item #3 **Prone float**

☐ ☐ Attempts to float on stomach.
☐ ☐ Floats on stomach with assistance (buoyancy belt).
☐ ☐ Performs a prone float for 5 seconds.
☐ ☐ Performs a prone float and recovers to standing position.
☐ ☐ Performs a prone glide with a flutter kick.

(continued)

Prescore Postscore

Test item #4 **Back float**

Attempts to float on back.
Floats on back with assistance (buoyancy belt).
Performs a back float for 5 seconds.
Performs a back float and recovers to a standing position.
Performs a back glide.
Performs a back glide with a flutter kick.

Test item #5 **Kicking**

Kicks legs with instructor's assistance.
Kicks legs using a bilateral movement while holding onto pool side.
Propels kickboard using the flutter kick with instructor's assistance.
Propels kickboard independently.

Test item #6 **Water safety**

Identifies swimming boundaries.
Understands and identifies pool safety rules.
Bobs in neck-deep water.
Demonstrates a vertical float in deep water for 2 minutes.
Demonstrates sculling arm action 5 strokes in neck-deep water.

| _____ Prescore | **Check the skill level achieved:** ❑ 0-10 Beginner ❑ 11-20 Rookie ❑ 21-30 Champ | _____ Postscore | **Check the skill level achieved:** ❑ 0-10 Beginner ❑ 11-20 Rookie ❑ 21-30 Champ | _____ hrs. **Approximate training time** |

Reprinted from Special Olympics International n.d.

Water Adjustment—Level I

1.0 **Given demonstration and practice the student will successfully execute the necessary skills to participate in swimming.**

Water adjustment

1. **Sit on the edge of the pool without resistance 4 out of 5 times.**

   Task analysis
   a. Walk around and familiarize oneself with pool area.
   b. Stand near pool.
   c. Sit near pool with instructor.
   d. Sit on the edge of the pool.

2. **Sit on the edge of the pool and kick for 15 seconds.**

   Task analysis
   a. Sit on the edge of the pool.
   b. Wash hands, arms, feet, face, shoulders, and neck.
   c. Move one foot up and down.
   d. Move other foot up and down.

3. **Enter the water via the ladder.**

   Task analysis
   a. Face toward the wall of the pool.
   b. Grip the appropriate ladder rungs with both hands.
   c. Place feet on the first step.
   d. Continue down one step at a time until both feet are on the bottom.

Teaching suggestions

- Do not spend too much time on these strategies for they are preliminary in nature as a means to adjust the students to the water and overcome their fears associated with the water.

- "Splash"—Student splashes or kicks water while sitting on the side of the pool. The object of this game is to overcome the fear of the water by trying to get the instructor wet. In doing so, the students get themselves wet.

- Physically assist the student as he or she steps down the ladder. Stand in the pool facing the ladder and guide the student's feet one step at a time.

Sports Skills Assessment—Level II Swimming

Instructions

The Sports Skills Assessment—Level II is designed for high skill level athletes. The test determines the athlete's present level of functioning within a specific skill or sport and shows his or her progress through training.

In administering the test, observe each athlete as he or she performs each test item. Score the athlete accordingly by checking the box located to the left of the task performed. If there is any question as to the athlete's competence in a particular skill, require the athlete to perform the task 3 out of 5 times.

After scoring each athlete, add up the total number of boxes, add 30, and indicate the athlete's present level of ability (i.e., Star, Super Champ, Superstar). If the athlete is performing at a lower skill level than measured in the Skills Assessment—Level II, reevaluate the athlete using Skills Assessment—Level I.

Skills Assessment—Level II

Prescore Postscore

Test item #1 **Front crawl**

Makes an attempt to swim on front.
Performs front crawl stroke in waist-deep water.
Performs front crawl stroke using flutter kick a distance of 10 meters.
Performs front crawl stroke with periodic breathing for a distance of 10 meters.
Performs coordinated front crawl stroke with rhythmic breathing a distance of 25 meters.

Test item #2 **Back crawl**

Makes an attempt to swim on back.
Performs back crawl stroke in waist-deep water.
Performs back crawl using a flutter kick a distance of 10 meters.
Performs coordinated back crawl stroke a distance of 25 meters.

Test item #3 **Sidestroke**

Demonstrates a scissors kick while holding onto a kickboard.
Performs sidestroke kick in waist-deep water.
Performs sidestroke using a scissors kick a distance of 10 meters.
Performs sidestroke with rhythmic breathing for a distance of 25 meters.

Test item #4 **Breaststroke**

Demonstrates wedge kick while holding onto a kickboard.
Performs breaststroke in waist-deep water.
Performs breaststroke using a wedge kick a distance of 10 meters.
Performs breaststroke with periodic breathing for a distance of 10 meters.
Performs coordinated breaststroke with rhythmic breathing a distance of 25 meters.

Test item #5 **Water safety**

Follows safety rules and standards while swimming.
Performs sculling action with one arm and other arm holding onto pool edge.
Performs sculling action with arms.
Treads water for 1 minute.
Performs survival float in deep water for 1-1/2 minutes.

Prescore	Check the skill level achieved:	Postscore	Check the skill level achieved:	_____ hrs. Approximate training time
	❏ 31-40 Star		❏ 31-40 Star	
	❏ 41-50 Super Champ		❏ 41-50 Super Champ	
	❏ 51-60 Superstar		❏ 51-60 Superstar	

Reprinted from Special Olympics International n.d.

Sports Skills Assessment—Level II Diving

Instructions

The Sports Skills Assessment is designed to determine the athlete's present level of functioning within a specific skill or sport and to determine the athlete's progress through training.

In administering the test, observe each athlete as he or she performs each test item. Score the athlete accordingly by checking the box located to the left of the task performed. If there are any questions as to the athlete's competence in a particular skill, require the athlete to perform the task 3 out of 5 times.

After scoring each athlete, add up the total number of boxes, add 30, and indicate the athlete's present level of ability.

Skills Assessment—Level II

Prescore Postscore

Test item #1 **Front dive**

❏ ❏ Demonstrates a sitting front dive.
❏ ❏ Performs a kneeling front dive with assistance.
❏ ❏ Performs a kneeling front dive without assistance.
❏ ❏ Demonstrates a standing one-leg front dive.
❏ ❏ Demonstrates a standing front dive.

Test item #2 **Approach**

❏ ❏ Jumps into pool off pool edge.
❏ ❏ Stands and steps into pool off diving board.
❏ ❏ Jumps in pool using a one-step approach.
❏ ❏ Performs a forward dive using a one-step approach.
❏ ❏ Jumps in pool using a three-step approach.
❏ ❏ Performs a forward dive using a three-step approach.

Test item #3 **Backward dive**

❏ ❏ Makes no attempt to perform a backward dive.
❏ ❏ Jumps backward into pool.
❏ ❏ Performs a standing backward dive from pool edge.
❏ ❏ Performs a back dive off a diving board.
❏ ❏ Performs a back somersault.

Test item #4 **Advanced front diving**

❏ ❏ Performs a forward dive in a layout position using a one-step approach.
❏ ❏ Performs a forward dive in a layout position using a three-step approach.
❏ ❏ Jumps to pike position, touching and entering water feet first.
❏ ❏ Performs a forward dive in a pike position using a three-step approach.
❏ ❏ Performs a forward somersault.

Test item #5 **Diving participation**

❏ ❏ Shows an understanding of the sport of diving.
❏ ❏ Identifies diving boundaries.
❏ ❏ Demonstrates diving etiquette.
❏ ❏ Executes a diving routine.
❏ ❏ Originates and performs own diving routine.
❏ ❏ Dives cooperatively and competitively.
❏ ❏ Follows safety rules for diving.

	Check the skill level achieved:		Check the skill level achieved:	
	❏ 31-40 Star		❏ 31-40 Star	_____ hrs.
	❏ 41-50 Super Champ		❏ 41-50 Super Champ	**Approximate**
_____ **Prescore**	❏ 51-60 Superstar	_____ **Postscore**	❏ 51-60 Superstar	**training time**

Water Safety Skill Sheet

Name	Identifies swimming boundaries.	Understands and identifies pool safety rules.	Identifies safety equipment.	Demonstrates a vertical float in deep water for 2 minutes.	Bobs in neck-deep water.	Performs sculling action with one arm while other arm holds onto pool edge.	Performs sculling action with arms.	Treads water.	Performs survival float in deep water.
	%	%	%	sec.	sec.	sec.	sec.	sec.	sec.
	%	%	%	sec.	sec.	sec.	sec.	sec.	sec.
	%	%	%	sec.	sec.	sec.	sec.	sec.	sec.
	%	%	%	sec.	sec.	sec.	sec.	sec.	sec.
	%	%	%	sec.	sec.	sec.	sec.	sec.	sec.
	%	%	%	sec.	sec.	sec.	sec.	sec.	sec.
	%	%	%	sec.	sec.	sec.	sec.	sec.	sec.
	%	%	%	sec.	sec.	sec.	sec.	sec.	sec.
	%	%	%	sec.	sec.	sec.	sec.	sec.	sec.
	%	%	%	sec.	sec.	sec.	sec.	sec.	sec.

Kicking Skill Sheet

Name	Kicks legs with instructor's assistance.	Kicks legs using a bilateral movement while holding onto pool side.	Propels kickboard using the flutter kick with instructor's assistance.	Propels kickboard independently.	Performs wedge kick with instructor's assistance.	Propels kickboard using wedge kick.	Performs scissors kick with instructor's assistance.	Propels kickboard using scissors kick.	
	sec.	sec.	meters	meters	meters	meters	meters	meters	
	sec.	sec.	meters	meters	meters	meters	meters	meters	
	sec.	sec.	meters	meters	meters	meters	meters	meters	
	sec.	sec.	meters	meters	meters	meters	meters	meters	
	sec.	sec.	meters	meters	meters	meters	meters	meters	
	sec.	sec.	meters	meters	meters	meters	meters	meters	
	sec.	sec.	meters	meters	meters	meters	meters	meters	
	sec.	sec.	meters	meters	meters	meters	meters	meters	
	sec.	sec.	meters	meters	meters	meters	meters	meters	
	sec.	sec.	meters	meters	meters	meters	meters	meters	

Diving Participation Skill Sheet

Name	Shows an understanding of the sport of diving.	Identifies diving boundaries.	Demonstrates diving etiquette.	Executes a diving routine.	Originates and performs own diving routine.	Dives cooperatively and competitively.	Follows safety rules for diving.		
	reps.	reps.	reps.	reps.	reps.	reps.	reps.		
	reps.	reps.	reps.	reps.	reps.	reps.	reps.		
	reps.	reps.	reps.	reps.	reps.	reps.	reps.		
	reps.	reps.	reps.	reps.	reps.	reps.	reps.		
	reps.	reps.	reps.	reps.	reps.	reps.	reps.		
	reps.	reps.	reps.	reps.	reps.	reps.	reps.		
	reps.	reps.	reps.	reps.	reps.	reps.	reps.		
	reps.	reps.	reps.	reps.	reps.	reps.	reps.		
	reps.	reps.	reps.	reps.	reps.	reps.	reps.		
	reps.	reps.	reps.	reps.	reps.	reps.	reps.		

Reprinted from Special Olympics International n.d.

DePaepe Positioning & Buoyancy Checklist

Name	Some front buoyancy while assisted	Some back buoyancy while assisted	Retrieves objects in waist-deep water	Bracket for prone float	Prone float, chest-deep with assistance	Chest-deep bend & tuck knees	Jellyfish float with assistance	Jellyfish float without assistance	Jellyfish extending arms and legs	Assistance to standing position	Standing recovery unassisted	Back float with instructor support	Assistance to standing position	Standing recovery unassisted	Kicking on front using a support	Kicking on back using a support	Comments

Reprinted from DePaepe 1980.

DePaepe Propulsion in the Water Checklist

Name	Prone glide push-off from side	Prone glide with recovery	Prone glide for 10 feet	Prone glide with kick, using kickboard	Prone glide with kick	Prone glide with flutter kick 20 feet	Prone glide with flutter kick & breathing	Back glide with push-off from side	Back glide with recovery assistance	Back glide with relaxed flutter kick	Back glide with sculling action	Doggy paddle, arms alone	Doggy paddle with arms & legs	Standing crawl stroke, shallow end	Crawl stroke, fingers dragging in water	Crawl stroke and roll	Crawl stroke and kick	Rhythmic breathing using only arms	Rhythmic breathing using legs only	Rhythmic breathing using combination	Beginning elementary back, arms only	Back glide with sculling & finning	Treading water	Survival floating	Drown proofing

The Water Orientation Checklists

Directions for the Water Orientation Checklist-Basic (WOC-B)

The following 13 items are assessed using a five-choice rating scale. The observer records only successful performances by circling an "s" on the appropriate level of the rating scale. Rating scale choices use the following abbreviations and operational definitions:

- Spontaneous (SP): the subject performs one of the 13 tasks prior to an instructor's verbal directions.
- Verbal (VB): the subject performs the specified task after the instructor's verbal directions.
- Verbal with demonstration (DMO): the subject performs the specified task after the instructor's verbal directions and visual cues.
- Physical guidance (PG): the instructor manipulates the subject's body through the specified task; verbal directions and visual cues accompany manipulation.
- Objection (OBJ): the subject is unwilling to attempt the task either passively or actively.

Directions for the Water Orientation Checklist-Advanced (WOC-Adv)

The following 13 items are assessed by recording both successful and unsuccessful performances on each level of the five-choice rating scale. For each item it is possible to record several unsuccessful performances prior to recording a successful performance. The observer records performance by circling one or more abbreviations. The following abbreviations and operational definitions are used:

- Successful (s): the subject performs the task as defined.
- Unsuccessful (u): the subject demonstrates an overt motor response in which he or she attempts but fails to perform the specified task.
- Passive objection (p): the subject fails to attend to the task, says "no," or shows no overt motor response.
- Active objection (a): the subject pulls away, runs away, throws a tantrum, abuses self, yells, or screams.

Item	WOC-B		WOC-Adv	
1. The instructor holds the subject by the hand as they walk to a predetermined location 8 ft. from the pool. Instructor then releases subject's hand and subject proceeds toward the pool:	SP	s	s	u
	VB	s	s	u
	DMO	s	s	u
	PG	s	s	u
	OBJ	obj	p	a
2. The subject touches the water with either hand or foot:	SP	s	s	u
	VB	s	s	u
	DMO	s	s	u
	PG	s	s	u
	OBJ	obj	p	a
3. The subject enters the pool by placing both feet in shallow water:	SP	s	s	u
	VB	s	s	u
	DMO	s	s	u
	PG	s	s	u
	OBJ	obj	p	a

4. The subject remains in pool throughout the observation:
   a. spontaneously
   b. exits, returns after verbal direction
   c. exits, returns after verbal direction with demonstration
   d. exits, returns with physical guidance
   e. exits, and objects to returning to the pool

(continued)

	WOC-B		WOC-Adv	
5. The subject attains a sitting, squatting, or horizontal position (wet up to waist) in the water:	SP	s	s	u
	VB	s	s	u
	DMO	s	s	u
	PG	s	s	u
	OBJ	obj	p	a
6. The subject blows bubbles (mouth contacts water and exhalation produces bubbles):	SP	s	s	u
	VB	s	s	u
	DMO	s	s	u
	PG	s	s	u
	OBJ	obj	p	a
7. The subject submerges entire face (forehead, eyes, nose, mouth, chin) in water:	SP	s	s	u
	VB	s	s	u
	DMO	s	s	u
	PG	s	s	u
	OBJ	obj	p	a
8. The subject performs a back float (ears in water, arms and legs extended, mouth and nose out of water, feet not touching the bottom):	SP	s	s	u
	VB	s	s	u
	DMO	s	s	u
	PG	s	s	u
	OBJ	obj	p	a
9. The subject performs a back float recovery (attaining a standing position without face submersion):	SP	s	s	u
	VB	s	s	u
	DMO	s	s	u
	PG	s	s	u
	OBJ	obj	p	a
10. The subject performs a prone float (face submersion, arms and legs extended, feet not touching the bottom):	SP	s	s	u
	VB	s	s	u
	DMO	s	s	u
	PG	s	s	u
	OBJ	obj	p	a
11. The subject performs a prone float recovery (attaining a standing position without turning over):	SP	s	s	u
	VB	s	s	u
	DMO	s	s	u
	PG	s	s	u
	OBJ	obj	p	a
12. The subject performs a turnover from back to prone float (without touching bottom):	SP	s	s	u
	VB	s	s	u
	DMO	s	s	u
	PG	s	s	u
	OBJ	obj	p	a
13. The subject swims 5 ft. (any propulsive movement without touching bottom):	SP	s	s	u
	VB	s	s	u
	DMO	s	s	u
	PG	s	s	u
	OBJ	obj	p	a

Note unusual behavior: _____

Reprinted from Killian 1987.

Aquatic Orientation Checklist

Observer checks one behavior for each numbered item:

1. Instructor and subject begin to walk toward pool:
   a. Subject spontaneously leads by pulling instructor's arm. _____
   b. Subject walks voluntarily. _____
   c. Instructor manipulates subject toward pool. _____
   d. Subject objects to task. _____
   Note unusual behavior: _____

2. At edge of pool, subject touches water with hand or foot:
   a. Spontaneously. _____
   b. Voluntarily with demonstration. _____
   c. Subject requires manipulation to touch water. _____
   d. Subject objects to task. _____
   Note unusual behavior: _____

3. Subject enters the pool (both feet in shallow water):
   a. Spontaneously. _____
   b. Voluntarily with demonstration. _____
   c. Instructor manipulates subject into pool. _____
   d. Subject objects to task. _____
   Note unusual behavior: _____

4. Subject attains a sitting, squatting, or horizontal position in the water:
   a. Spontaneously. _____
   b. Voluntarily. _____
   c. After manipulation by instructor. _____
   d. Subject objects to task. _____
   Note unusual behavior: _____

5. Subject blows bubbles (mouth contacts water and exhalation produces bubbles):
   a. Voluntarily. _____
   b. Voluntarily after demonstration. _____
   c. After manipulation. _____
   d. Subject objects to task. _____
   Note unusual behavior: _____

6. Subject submerges entire face (forehead, eyes, nose, mouth, chin) in water:
   a. Spontaneously. _____
   b. Voluntarily after demonstration. _____
   c. After manipulation. _____
   d. Subject objects to task. _____
   Note unusual behavior: _____

Reprinted from Killian 1984.

Beginning Competency Levels of Swimming
Sherrill Model

Level I: Explorer
Movement exploration in water
1. Enters and leaves water alone
2. Walks across pool, holding rail
3. Walks across pool, holding teacher's hand
4. Stands alone
5. Walks across pool, pushing kickboard
6. Jumps or hops several steps alone
7. Walks and does breaststroke arm movements
8. Does various locomotor movements across the pool
9. Blows bubbles through plastic tube
10. Blows Ping-Pong ball across pool

Level II: Advanced Explorer
Movement exploration in water
1. Puts face in water
2. Blows bubbles (5 sec.)
3. Touches pool bottom or toes with hands
4. Retrieves objects from bottom of pool
5. Assumes horizontal position with teacher's help
6. Holds onto kickboard pulled by teacher
7. Jumps into water without help
8. Takes rides in supine position
9. Changes level: squat to stand; stand to squat
10. Plays follow-the-leader–type water games
11. Demonstrates bracketing on back with kick

Level III: Floater
Prebeginning swimming
1. Blows bubbles (10 sec.)
2. Performs bracketing on front with kick
3. Changes position: stands; prone with support; stands
4. Floats prone
5. Changes position: stands; supine with support; stands
6. Floats supine
7. Flutter kicks using board
8. Jellyfish floats
9. Performs breaststroke arm movements
10. Swims one-half width any style
11. Performs at least one stunt, such as standing or walking on hands, front somersault, back somersault, tub, surface dive

Conatser Adapted Aquatics Screening Test Sheet

Name of student _____

Key: (P) Pass = 1, (0) Fail = 0, (–) Emerging, inconsistent = 0 points

A: Psychological and physical adjustment skills　　　　P, 0, –　1 point each
1. Enters pool area displaying adequate behavior　　　　_____　_____
2. Puts feet in water, pool side　　　　_____　_____
3. Puts hands in water, pool side　　　　_____　_____
4. Rubs water or accepts water on shoulders, pool side　　　　_____　_____
5. Sits in chest-deep water, 1 min.　　　　_____　_____
6. Puts chin in water while sitting　　　　_____　_____
7. Puts ears in water while sitting　　　　_____　_____
8. Puts nose in water while sitting　　　　_____　_____
9. Puts forehead in water while sitting　　　　_____　_____
10. Accepts needed level of assistance into deeper water　　　　_____　_____
11. Accepts shoulder-deep water, 30 sec.　　　　_____　_____
12. Approves being supported by evaluator (No Time Requirement)　　　　_____　_____
13. Approves of swaying movement by evaluator (N.T.R.)　　　　_____　_____
14. Approves of vertical position changes by evaluator (N.T.R.)　　　　_____　_____
15. Approves of supine position by evaluator (N.T.R.)　　　　_____　_____
16. Demonstrates relaxation in supine position by evaluator, 15 sec.　　　　_____　_____

B: Entering and exiting the pool　　　　P, 0, –　1 point each
17. Enters and exits via ramp, stairs, ladder, or lift, assisted or unassisted safely　　　　_____　_____
18. Sits pool side and falls forward into evaluator's arms, 3 out of 4 times　　　　_____　_____

C: Range of motion (ROM) in water　　　　P, 0, –　1 point each
19. Accepts passive trunk rotation　　　　_____　_____
20. Accepts passive ROM of upper extremities　　　　_____　_____
21. Accepts passive ROM of lower extremities　　　　_____　_____

D: Breath control and respiratory skills　　　　P, 0, –　1 point each
22. Blows bubbles in instructor's hands, 3 out of 4 times　　　　_____　_____
23. Blows bubbles face submerged in the pool, 3 out of 4 times　　　　_____　_____
24. Closes lips while face is submerged, 3 out of 4 times　　　　_____　_____
25. Puts head under water, 10 sec.　　　　_____　_____
26. Sits pool side, rolls forward into water, remaining prone safely, 8 sec. 3 times*　　　　_____　_____
27. Sits pool side, rolls forward into water, floats to surface prone then to supine, unassisted 3 times　　　　_____　_____

(continued)

E: Balance and flotation   P, 0, –   1 point each

28. Maintains standing or kneeling position in shoulder-deep water,
    2 min.*   _____   _____
29. Walks or moves in shoulder-deep water, 3 yards, 3 out of 4 times*   _____   _____
30. Maintains supine float unassisted, 10 sec., 3 times*   _____   _____
31. Maintains prone float unassisted, 7 sec., 3 times*   _____   _____
32. Maintains supine position with PFD, 2 min.*   _____   _____
33. Rolls from prone to supine floating unassisted, 3 out of 4 times*   _____   _____

F: Active movement in water   P, 0, –   1 point each

34. Kicks on surface of water   _____   _____
35. Moves arms underwater   _____   _____
36. Moves legs underwater   _____   _____
37. Sculls with hands   _____   _____
38. Demonstrates power arm strokes   _____   _____
39. Demonstrates rotary leg kick   _____   _____
40. Holds onto pool side, 1 min.   _____   _____
41. Pushes off from pool side into evaluator's arms, 3 out of 4 times   _____   _____
42. Moves through water with PFD, 3 yards, 3 out of 4 times*   _____   _____
43. Moves through water independently, 3 yards, 3 out of 4 times   _____   _____
44. Moves independently from evaluator to a safe place, 3 yards, 3
    out of 4 times*   _____   _____

                                                              Total   _____

                                                              Percentile   _____

Total points for selected sections: A. _____ B. _____ C. _____ D. _____ E. _____ F. _____

Percentiles for selected sections: A. _____ B. _____ C. _____ D. _____ E. _____ F. _____

*These skills are especially important to attain.

Reprinted from Conatser 1995.

Carter, Dolan, and LeConey Aquatic Assessment

Directions

Prior to instruction, observe and interview the participant and significant others to identify functioning abilities and factors having an effect on performance in the aquatic environment. Report presence (with date accomplished) or absence (left blank) of behaviors and, in some instances, record time and number of behaviors.

Sensory behaviors

Auditory

_____ Deaf
_____ Hard-of-hearing
_____ Hearing loss in ___ right ear in ___ left ear
_____ Wears hearing aid
_____ Listens to speech
_____ Covers ears when hears loud noises
_____ Self-stimulates when hears loud noises
_____ Creates noise or echo in response to noises

Visual

_____ Blind
_____ Visually impaired
_____ Discriminates light and dark
_____ Discriminates shadows
_____ Looks at light reflection on water
_____ Wears glasses in water
_____ Will wear _____ won't wear goggles
_____ Will wear _____ won't wear mask
_____ Opens and closes eyelids
_____ Looks at speaker
_____ Looks at objects in visual field
_____ Looks down _____ does not look down into the water
_____ Watches objects move _____ horizontally _____ vertically
_____ Steps over _____ does not step over lines or objects
_____ Reaches for support when looking down or stepping over
_____ Covers eyes to prevent water entry

Tactile

_____ Touches safety equipment _____ touches flotation equipment
_____ Touches others _____ resists touch of others
_____ Touches others only if controls the touch of others
_____ Holds objects
_____ Wears equipment

(continued)

Speech and breathing

_____ Creates audible speech _____ number of words
_____ Cries _____ laughs
_____ Makes noise _____ number of seconds
_____ Uses manual communication device _____ computer to respond
_____ Drinks _____ licks water
_____ Allows water to move in and out of mouth for stimulation
_____ Breathes through mouth
_____ Breathes through nose
_____ Breathes through mouth and nose
_____ Breathes through mouth with nose pinched
_____ Closes mouth with nose pinched
_____ Opens mouth with nose pinched
_____ With nose pinched, holds breath, blows out for _____ seconds
_____ With nose pinched, breathes in, blows out for _____ seconds
_____ With nose pinched, blows out for _____ seconds, breathes in
_____ Foam appears around mouth from swallowing air
_____ Enlarged tongue
_____ Able _____ unable to open and close mouth
_____ NG tube _____ tracheostomy _____ ventilator-dependent
_____ False teeth _____ braces _____ plate _____ cleft palate

Self-care

_____ Identifies personal belongings
_____ Dresses _____ undresses
_____ Toilets without _____ with assistance
_____ Wears diaper
_____ Wears collection device
_____ Uses catheter
_____ Hair appears washed _____ unwashed
_____ Places hands over face when hair is washed

Emotions displayed

_____ Apprehension _____ Fear _____ Anger _____ Aggression
_____ Happiness _____ Confidence _____ Trust _____ Success

Social interactions

_____ Holds hands of others
_____ Talks with others
_____ Stays in _____ withdraws from group
_____ Seeks to control group dynamics _____ Withdraws when not in controlling position

Cognitive

_____ Identifies directions: ___ up ___ down ___ under ___ over ___ right ___ left
_____ Identifies body parts
_____ Identifies safety and flotation devices
_____ Recognizes and responds to name
_____ Attend to task _____ seconds
_____ Follows 1-2–step _____ 3-5–step directions
_____ Responds to verbal _____ visual _____ written directions
_____ Counts to: ___ 3 ___ 5 ___ 10
_____ Comprehends a count to: ___ 3 ___ 5 ___ 10

(continued)

(continued)

Motor

Stature
____ Trunk long   ____ short

Muscle mass location
____ Upper torso ___ Lower torso ___ Upper limbs (__ R __ L) ___ Lower limbs (__ R __ L)

Adipose tissue location
____ Upper torso ___ Lower torso ___ Upper limbs (__ R __ L) ___ Lower limbs (__ R __ L)

Head control
____ Rotates head ____ R ____ L
____ Lifts head from prone position ____ from supine position

Balance
____ Sits without ____ with assistance
____ Stands without ____ with assistance
____ Stands on ____ R foot ____ L foot
____ Walks without ____ with assistance
____ Walks forward ____ backward
____ Runs forward ____ backward ____ zigzagging
____ Hops foward on ____ R foot ____ L foot
____ Jumps fowards ____ backward with 2 feet off ground

Ambulation
____ Independently

Ambulates with:
____ Prothesis (__ R __ L __ both) ___ Orthopedic device (__ R __ L __ both) ___ Walker
____ Crutches ____ Wheelchair

Walks with:
____ Even cadence ____ On toes ____ Heel-to-toe ____ Feet inverted
____ Feet everted ____ Parallel arm swing ____ Opposition arm swing

Hands, arms, shoulders
____ Arms extended ____ flexed
____ Grasps ____ Releases ____ Claps
____ Transfers objects from one hand to the other
____ Crosses midline with R hand and arm ____ L hand and arm
____ Clamps down on top of instructor's or other's hand(s), arm(s)
____ Shoulders broad ____ narrow

Feet, legs, hips
____ Legs extended ____ flexed ____ in scissors position
____ Legs long ____ short
____ Lifts R foot ____ L foot off ground
____ Squats at knees ____ does not squat at knees
____ Bends at waist ____ does not bend at waist

Muscle tone
____ Flaccid ____ Spastic ____ Contractures ____ Uninhibited reflexes

Martin-Nichols Evaluation of Beginning Swimming Skills of the Severely and Profoundly Retarded

Name _____ Case # _____ P/S _____

Cottage _____ Date of birth _____

Skill Levels:
1. Attempts task
2. Performs task with physical and (or) verbal assistance
3. Performs task independently on verbal command

I			II			Code	TEST ITEMS
1	2	3	1	2	3	1.0	Enters the pool.
1	2	3	1	2	3	2.0	Splashes self with water.
1	2	3	1	2	3	3.0	Jumps and splashes in waist-deep water.
1	2	3	1	2	3	4.0	Walks across width of pool.
1	2	3	1	2	3	5.0	Puts whole face in water.
1	2	3	1	2	3	6.0	Blows bubbles in water.
1	2	3	1	2	3	7.0	Blows bubbles with whole face in water.
1	2	3	1	2	3	8.0	Ducks head underwater holding breath.
1	2	3	1	2	3	9.0	Opens eyes underwater.
1	2	3	1	2	3	10.0	Ducks head underwater and retrieves object
1	2	3	1	2	3	11.0	Ducks head underwater and blows bubbles.
1	2	3	1	2	3	12.0	Jumps into water from side of pool.
1	2	3	1	2	3	13.0	Bobs in and out of water several times breathing rhythmically.
1	2	3	1	2	3	14.0	Performs jellyfish float and recovers.
1	2	3	1	2	3	15.0	Performs prone float and recovers.
1	2	3	1	2	3	16.0	Performs prone glide.
1	2	3	1	2	3	17.0	Jumps into water from side, pushes off bottom, and glides.
1	2	3	1	2	3	18.0	Performs stationary flutter kick.
1	2	3	1	2	3	19.0	Performs flutter kick several body lengths.
1	2	3	1	2	3	20.0	Performs prone glide with flutter kick.
1	2	3	1	2	3	21.0	Performs stationary arm stroke.
1	2	3	1	2	3	22.0	Performs arm stroke with prone glide.
1	2	3	1	2	3	23.0	Performs prone glide with arm stroke and flutter kick.
1	2	3	1	2	3	24.0	Performs front stroke 15 ft. (unrestricted breathing).
1	2	3	1	2	3	25.0	Performs stationary rhythmic breathing.
1	2	3	1	2	3	26.0	Performs rhythmic breathing with forward stroke.
1	2	3	1	2	3	27.0	Performs a dive from a sitting position.
1	2	3	1	2	3	28.0	Performs a dive from a kneeling position.
1	2	3	1	2	3	29.0	Performs a dive from a standing position.
1	2	3	1	2	3	30.0	Dives into water, levels off, and swims.
1	2	3	1	2	3	31.0	Swims underwater several body lengths.
1	2	3	1	2	3	32.0	Swims 20 feet on the front using rhythmic breathing.

_____ Subtotals

_____ Total

Test dates _____

Instructor's signature _____

Comments: _____

Data-Based Gymnasium Swimming Test

A. Adjustment to water

Terminal objective: Student enters waist-deep water, moves through the water for 30 feet, and exits from the pool.

Prerequisites skills:

Phase I	Sits on side of pool and splashes feet
Phase II	Sits on first step in pool
Phase III	Sits on second step in pool
Phase IV	Moves down the steps and stands on bottom of pool
Phase V	Walks across the pool (shallow end) for a distance of 30 feet while holding onto the edge or a rope
Phase VI	Walks across the pool for a distance of 30 feet without holding onto the edge or a rope
Phase VII	Exits from pool using ladder or steps
Phase VIII	Enters waist-deep water, moves through the water for 30 feet, and exits from the pool

The following steps apply to phases I-VIII:

Steps:

1. With physical assistance
2. Without physical assistance

B. Breath-holding

Terminal objective: Student, standing in waist-deep water, places face in the water (water touching ears), and hold his or her breath for 10 seconds.

Prerequisite skills: Swimming, Task A.

Phase I	Holds breath while sitting on deck of pool
Phase II	Stands in pool and puts water on face while holding onto the edge
Phase III	Stands in waist-deep water, puts face into the water (water touching ears), and holds breath for 10 seconds

The following steps apply to phase III:

Steps:

1. Two seconds
2. Four seconds
3. Six seconds

Teaching notes: Student should be discouraged from drinking water.

C. Bobbing rhythmically

Terminal objective: Student bobs independently in chest-deep water in a rhythmical manner 10 times.

Prerequisite skills: Swimming, Task B

Phase I	Bobs while holding onto the side of the pool with both hands
Phase II	Bobs, exhaling underwater with head completely submerged while holding onto side of pool with both hands
Phase III	Bobs while holding onto side of pool with one hand

(continued)

Phase IV	Bobs while holding onto one of teacher's hands
Phase V	Bobs while holding onto a flutter board
Phase VI	Bobs independently in chest-deep water in a rhythmical manner 10 times

The following steps apply to phases I-VI:

Steps:
1. Two times
2. Four times
3. Six times
4. Eight times

Teaching notes: The depth of the water may vary from the waist to the chest, depending on the tolerance level of the student.

D. Back crawl

Terminal objective: Student, in chest-deep water, swims back crawl 20 yards, using a smoothly coordinated flutter kick and back crawl arm stroke.

Prerequisite skills:

Phase I	While standing, moves arms in opposition with arms recovering straight above shoulder and terminating in water directly forward of shoulder for five cycles with physical assistance
Phase II	Wearing a personal flotation device, performs five cycles of arm movement smoothly with a prompt
Phase III	Wearing a PFD, swims back crawl 20 feet in waist-deep water, using a smoothly coordinated flutter kick and back crawl arm stroke
Phase IV	Performs a functional back crawl in chest-deep water without a PFD and with prompt only
Phase V	Swims back crawl 20 yards in chest-deep water, using a smoothly coordinated flutter kick and back crawl arm stroke

The following steps apply to phase V:

Steps:
1. 10 yards
2. 15 yards

Teaching notes: PFD is a personal flotation device.

Reprinted from Dunn and Moorehouse n.d.

≋ Appendix C ≋

GAMES AND ACTIVITIES FOR VARIOUS AGE GROUPS

6-36 MONTHS OLD

GOING TO THE MARKET

Materials	Three dozen pieces of plastic fruit (one dozen of three different kinds), three inner tubes or hoops, laminated pictures of the fruits you have.
Goals	1. To increase familiarity with water by taking their minds off where they are
	2. To improve ability to get child's hands off caregiver and reach out for something
	3. To improve sense of group
	4. To increase comfort on stomach
	5. To develop ability to sort color, shape, and size
How to Play	Have parent-child pairs scatter around shallow, buoyed-off area. Anchor or hold three tubes or hoops by a wall and place a laminated picture above each tube of one of the plastic fruits that are available in the game. Spread fruit around water and ask caregivers to hold participants at their side facing forward and have children make progress toward fruit with caregiver gliding them along with face above the water, on their stomach, encouraging them to kick or use arm stroke. Once child has grabbed a fruit, have caregiver name it. Have child drop fruit into tire with the corresponding picture above it and repeat the process with other two kinds of fruit.
Tip	Hold child's bottom slightly lower (three to four inches) than shoulders so child's head stays more naturally above water.
Adaptations	For students who cannot grasp an object that large, put fruit in a knee-high stocking and tie top so child can grasp stocking top. For students who are visually impaired, use opportunity to describe fruits, have child reach into tire tube first to feel if it matches, or instead of using fruit, use toys with various sounds.

WATER THE GARDEN

Materials	1 small plastic watering can per pair, 12 various fake flowers stuck into the pool gutter or lane lines
Goal	To improve water orientation

278

How to Play	Start with child/adult pairs in a circle, having them bob up and down to shoulders singing a song about rain, flowers, or the like. Use a watering can to wet children's feet, caregiver's shoulders, and so on. Now give each pair a watering can and have everyone water a flower. At each flower, have caregiver gradually pour water on child's various body parts.
Tip	Don't have caregiver pour water on face until child feels very comfortable about having water on neck, chin, and back of head.
Adaptation	For those who cannot perform without independence, caregiver or instructor should provide physical assistance for using the watering can.

MAGIC CARPET RIDE

Equipment	One kickboard per child
Goals	1. To improve head control
	2. To develop confidence in prone position
	3. To introduce kicking
	4. To explore pool
How to Play	Have each caregiver position child's arms and upper body on kickboard, holding the child onto the board. Encourage caregivers to use various speeds of gliding, push off the wall by placing child's feet on wall, and even introduce the flutter kick. Have caregivers go to various places in the pool where there is a laminated picture of children's favorite characters (e.g., Mickey Mouse, Big Bird, or Lambchop). After they visit, have them continue the magic carpet ride, kicking and gliding to another location.
Tip	Show each caregiver how to hold child and kickboard, depending on child's body control and comfort in the water.
Adaptations	Place action figures near pictures for those with poor eyesight to feel. Those with more severe physical disabilities may need to wear a tube or life jacket.

RUBBER DUCKIE

Materials	Tape player with Sesame Street song "Rubber Duckie" playing (record it about five times in a row), 1 floating duckie with a short (4") ribbon (not string) around its neck per child
Goal	To increase comfort lying on back
How to Play	Place ducks in gutter. Have caregiver hold child so that they are facing the gutter with child's back to caregiver's chest, head near shoulder. Have pair walk backward to other side of pool once the child has grabbed the duck's ribbon, happily giving the duck a ride while singing "Rubber Duckie." Have caregiver gradually begin to squat down in water until after a few laps of duck-walking, the child is reclining on adult's shoulder. Child can also place duck on the chest or adult can hold it above child to encourage the child to lie on his back.
Tip	Watch out for ribbons near children's necks and mouths; remove ribbons from ducks' necks for free play.
Adaptation	Use ducks that squeak to motivate all students and to help visually-impaired students.

3-5 YEARS OLD

THE TEAM IS IN THE HUDDLE

Materials	None
Goal	To imitate water orientation skills
How to Play	Form a circle, in water where children can stand, or have aides hold the children facing the middle of the circle. Pick one child to be the captain for each time the game starts, until all the children have had a turn. The game starts by each person putting one hand in the middle of the circle so there is a pile of hands (like a team does before they play). The group chants the cheer "The team is in the huddle; the captain's at the head; they all got together; and this is what he said. . . ." The captain then says a skill or demonstrates a skill (or both) that everyone has to try to do to the best of their abilities. After about 10 seconds of trying, have the group come back in together, each person putting one hand in the middle again, and you pick another captain. Begin the chant again and continue the game until all have had a chance to be the captain.
Tip	Encourage children to do whatever they can to approximate the skill that the captain is demonstrating.
Adaptations	Give children who have problems processing information quickly a warning when they are going to be it, so they have time to think of a skill. Help children with severe cognitive problems demonstrate a skill (like splashing their hand or foot, or jumping up and down). Children with poor range of motion or no hands can put their elbow or foot in the middle of the circle of hands, or put their hand on their assistant's arm and the assistant puts own hand in the circle.

LONDON BRIDGE

Materials	Foam noodles
Goals	To practice creative and individual swimming
How to Play	Hold one end of a foam noodle and put the other end on the deck. Encourage swimmers to swim under the noodle in any manner they wish or in a way you call out. Sing "London Bridge" as all are going under the noodle and then swimming around your back to go under again.
Tips	Putting two noodles together with a foam attachment is easiest. Keep a lookout for those swimming around your back. Bridge can go up and down closer to the water as needed.
Adaptations	Allow physical assistance or flotation device for those who need it. Eliminate singing for those who can't hear. Allow touching of your back (for orientation) and the noodle for those who can't see.

6-8 YEARS OLD

BIRTHDAY PARTY

Materials	Thin corks, several Styrofoam rings, reaching pole, one kickboard per child
Goals	1. To improve breath control
	2. To improve flutter kick
	3. To improve underwater swimming skills

How to Play **Part One:** "Make a Cake." Split group in half on either side of the pool in the water, each participant holding a kickboard. On signal, have participants kick toward the middle and then stop and pile kickboards on each other until the group makes a "layer cake."

Part Two: "Blow Out the Candles." Replace layer cake of kickboards with one Styrofoam ring for every three children. Balance the corks on the ring. After students sing "Happy Birthday," have them blow the corks off the ring, like candles, and then place their mouths in the water to try to blow corks out of the ring.

Part Three: "Limbo." Use reaching pole to do limbo dance. Place pole as far into or out of the water as participant ability allows. Ask students to do whatever movement they want, a different one for each pass under the pole. Challenge with questions such as "Who can let their feet go first?"

Tip	Use limbo music for extra motivation and fun.
Adaptation	Allow individuals with visual impairment to feel bar.

ESCAPE HATCH

Materials	One hoop for every two children
Goals	1. To improve underwater swimming
	2. To increase spatial awareness
	3. To increase independent water movement

How to Play Start with half the group in a circle holding a hoop between each person, at all different levels; some hoops touching bottom, mid-depth of water, and others half out of the water. In the middle of the circle, have the other half of the group perform some swim skills commensurate with each individual's ability (such as bobbing) in the middle of the circle. When you say "Escape hatch!" have all in the middle head for a hoop of their choice and swim through it. Then have them swim around the outside of the circle until you give the signal again. Repeat the process from the outside of the circle to get back inside the circle. Periodically, switch two hoop holders at a time with swimmers, for maximum participation. Encourage participants to swim through as many different hoops as they will challenge themselves with.

Tip	Hoop holders can move in a circle during the game.
Adaptations	Individuals who cannot swim can walk, jog, or be pulled through the hoop while in a PFD. Have those who are nonverbal and cannot swim point to the hoop they want to try and then assist them.

MUSICAL HOOPS

Materials	One hoop per person, music that can be stopped and started
Goals	1. To develop cooperation
	2. To develop confidence submerging
	3. To develop independence and confidence moving in pool without holding the edge
How to Play	Spreads hoops around shallow (or for advanced class, deep) end. Have participants walk or swim around until music stops. Then have them find a hoop and swim into it from underwater. To make this an even more cooperative game, remove several hoops and have participants share hoops when the music stops.
Adaptations	For students with visual impairment, allow them to touch hoops or direct them toward an empty hoop. For students who are hard of hearing or deaf, wave flag or cloth or clap while music is on. For students with mobility difficulties, offer support (aide or PFD) to swim or walk.

9-11 YEARS OLD

BACKSTROKE FLAG TOUCH

Materials	Backstroke flags
Goals	1. To encourage shoulder extension while on back
	2. To improve arm recovery in back crawl
How to Play	String several rows of backstroke flags to within two feet of water surface. Have everyone swim on back, trying to touch the backstroke flags with each recovery of arms.
Tips	Group faster students together so they don't crash backward into slower swimmers. Have faster swimmers complete more widths.
Adaptations	Suspend bells for visually-impaired swimmers. Suspend one row of flags lower for those with short arm or limited range of motion. Offer flotation devices or physical support or both to those who need it.

CHARIOT RACE (AMERICAN RED CROSS 1977©)

Materials	One tube or ring buoy per pair
Goal	To develop bottom arm strength and propulsive skills for sidestroke
How to Play	Conduct this activity in neck-deep or deeper water. Have one person in each pair tow (with the hand that would be the top arm in the sidestroke) the other who is sitting in a tube. Stress using free arm to do the movements of the lower arm in the sidestroke. Have pairs switch at a designated point.
Tip	Attach a short rope to tube for those who have trouble towing.
Adaptations	Place individuals with visual impairment near the lane line to keep oriented. For individual with physical disabilities who cannot tow and swim at same time or who uses a PFD, use bungee cord to connect tube to PFD, shorten distance or allow more time, have instructor help pull, or allow another more appropriate movement instead of sidestroke.

ARE WE THERE YET?

Materials	A large floating foam mat or several foam tubes
Goals	1. To develop leg muscle endurance
	2. To develop flutter kick
How to Play	Place evenly strong participants on each side of a mat or tube with their upper bodies draped on it. On signal, have them kick as hard as they can for 30 seconds. Rest and repeat. It is fun to try to move the mat toward the group on the other side of the mat.
Tips	If the game is getting competitive, stand on one side of the mat to hold on, evening the odds. Or have all the students try to move the mat from one side of the pool to the other.
Adaptations	Keep tire tube around person with poor head control to act as a head prop. Also stay near this person.

POISON

Materials	Floating objects, such as kickboards, balls, hoops, and tubes (about 5 per participant in a cordoned-off area)
Goals	1. To improve direction changing
	2. To increase alertness when swimming
How to Play	Designate all floating items as poison. Have students perform various skills the width of the pool and avoid the poison.
Adaptations	Use some floating objects that have bells in them. Have an aide tap person with visual impairment when poison is near. Place some anchored poisons near wall and have visually impaired swim close to wall.

12-14 YEARS OLD

ROLLING LOG (FROM SPECIAL OLYMPICS N.D.).

Materials	None
Goals	1. To improve turning over from back to front
	2. To improve motionless front float
	3. To improve front crawl or breaststroke speed
How to Play	Mark off spaces at opposite ends of the deep end for two goals. Have one player, the "log," float on back in the center of the pool midway between the two goals. Have the other players swim in a circle around the log, who without warning suddenly rolls over and chases them. Encourage players to try to reach one of the goals without being tagged. Those caught must join the first log in the center, and when the first log rolls over, help tag others.
Tips	In general, slower swimmers need an equalizer in order to catch someone. Having those in the circle of swimmers swim underwater can help slow the faster swimmers down a bit.

Adaptations For students with visual impairment in the group, have "log" yell "log over," and you yell "goal" from the goal area several times for orientation. For students with poor swim skills, a PFD could be helpful as well as a shorter distance to the goal. For those students with no propulsive skills, they can grab onto a string in their lap and hold onto it while you pull them to goal.

SURFIN' USA

Materials One blow-up raft per student (slightly underinflated), tape player with song "Surfin' USA" by Beach Boys, diving bricks on the bottom of pool at the half-way point

Goal To improve front crawl and butterfly

How to Play Play "Surfin' USA" on tape player. Have participants start out lying on raft at one end of the pool. In waves of three, have them do front crawl arms to a location marked with a brick on bottom of pool 10 yards away, then surf on raft for 30 seconds, then resume front crawl arm stroke to other end while next wave begins. Repeat with butterfly arms, then flutter and dolphin kicks.

Tips Do not allow students to surf in lanes closest to walls. Do not allow standing surfing in shallow water. Do not allow diving off the raft.

Adaptations Allow individuals to be creative in surfing (e.g., sit-surfing, knee-surfing, supine-surfing). For individuals with poor range of motion that limits then from reaching over the sides of the raft, use thinner raft or fold sides of raft under and clip with a rope and potato chip clips.

STRIKE A POSE

Materials Music that can be started and stopped

Goals 1. To improve stationary sculling

2. To improve treading water

3. To improve motionless float

How to Play Have participants swim in a circle in deep end while music is on; when music is off, have them strike a pose either treading water, stationary sculling, or floating motionless. When music is on again, have them swim.

Adaptations Individual with poor vision can swim perimeter of area and stay close to wall and lane line or have a buddy next to them. You can tap the shoulder of hard-of-hearing or deaf swimmer with a reaching pole that has a tennis ball impaled on one end. For those with poor swim skills, allow PFDs and allow them to work on the stroke they need most work on.

≋ Appendix D ≋

INFORMATION GATHERING FORMS

West Chester University Community Adapted Aquatics Program

Swimmer's name: _____

Residence: _____

Date of birth: _____

Caregiver at the pool:_____

What are the medical issues we need to know about such as seizures, diabetes, medications, swallowing water, atlantoaxial instability syndrome, toileting issues?

What are five things the swimmer wants to learn?

What are five things the caregiver wants the swimmer to learn?

What are five skills other than swimming that we should encourage?

What are any behavioral issues that we need to address, and how should we address them?

West Chester University
Adapted Aquatics Program

Participant information—To be filled out by parents.

Participant's name: _____ Birthdate: _____

Address: _____

Phone number: _____ Parent's or guardian's name: _____

School or program they attend: _____

Teacher's or leader's name: _____

Address if different from above: _____

Phone number if different from above: _____

Person to call if emergency: Name _____ Phone _____

Participant's disability:

Is child subject to seizures? _____ Yes _____ No   If yes, please describe seizure. Time it usually lasts? Unconscious? What symptoms before it occurs? Is there anything in particular to avoid?

_____

_____

Is child on medication? _____ Yes _____ No   If yes, what type? _____

What (if any) equipment does your child use (e.g., glasses, wheelchair)? _____

What are your child's likes (food, toys, cartoons, anything)?

_____

Please share with us the behavior intervention strategies that best work with your child.

_____

_____

What are your child's dislikes?_____

Is your child on a specific behavior, food, or toileting program that we need to be aware of?

Please explain: _____

_____

Any other health problems that we should be aware of (e.g., allergies, asthma, and so on)?

_____

_____

Statement of release: I understand that West Chester University and the Special Physical Activities Program personnel cannot be held directly responsible for any injuries, thefts, and damage to persons or personal property.

_____
Signature of parent or legal guardian

_____
Date

Photo release: On occasion pictures may be taken to promote the program. It is understood that these pictures will be taken under the supervision of the director and great care will be taken to ensure that the individual will not be embarrassed by their use.

Permission is granted _____   Permission is not granted _____

For pictures to be taken of_____
                                                     Student's name

_____
Signature of parent or legal guardian

_____
Date

West Chester University
Adapted Aquatics Program

Director: Monica Lepore
School Confidential Form

1. Participant's name: _____ 2. Date of birth: _____
3. Teacher name: _____ 4. School phone:_____
5. School name: _____
6. School address _____

Information concerning the individual (Use pen please)

7. Enrolled in a special class? Yes _____ No _____ 8. Type of class: _____
9. Number of years in school: _____
10. Does he or she participate in an aquatics program at school? Yes _____ No _____
11. If yes, how many hours per week? _____
12. Comments about individual's performance in aquatic activities:
    _____
    _____

13. Has the child had any motor assessment done? Yes _____ No _____
14. If yes, identify test used:
    _____
    _____

15. Brief description of individual's relationship and interaction with peers:
    _____
    _____

16. Does the student need a one-on-one working situation in order to function at an acceptable
    level? Yes _____ No _____ Explain _____
    _____
    _____

17. Comments about student's personality:
    _____
    _____

18. Is this client on a formal _____ or informal _____ behavior modification program? Explain.
    _____
    _____

Classroom activities

19. Activities the student excels in: _____
20. Activity the student enjoys the most. Individual activity:_____
21. Group activity: _____
22. Motor development or perceptual activities you would suggest that the student work on:
    _____

23. Additional comments: _____
    _____

Filled out by: _____ Date: _____
Return to: Dr. Monica Lepore
               West Chester University
               West Chester, PA 19383

This part to be filled out by physical education teacher:

Name: _____ Phone:_____

Goals for this student for this school year: _____

_____

_____

_____

_____

Specific objectives: _____

_____

_____

_____

Does the student participate in adapted physical education? _____

How much time per week? _____

Is adapted physical education in the IEP? _____

What *specific* objectives does this student need to learn in order to be more fully able to participate in the school's regular physical education program for this year? _____

_____

_____

_____

_____

What role do you play in the IEP process? _____

_____

What assessment is used to determine appropriate placement in physical education?

_____

Can you share the results of that assessment? _____

_____

West Chester University
Parent or Caregiver Assumption of Risk Form

Informed Consent and Liability Release

Please fill out and return to: Monica Lepore
                                    West Chester University
                                    Health and Physical Education Center
                                    West Chester, PA 19383

I understand that participation in the West Chester University Children's Adapted Multiactivities Program has risks due to the physical demands that are placed on a child during physical activity and recreation participation, and that during physical activity there is a potential risk of physical injury. I agree that I am solely responsible for my child's participation and for his or her physical and emotional well-being. I understand that the program activities are voluntary and after receiving a copy of the activities, I am choosing for my child to participate in each activity to whatever degree possible—with the child's physical, emotional, and medical considerations considered.

I affirm that my child's health is good, and that he or she is not under a physician's care for any *undisclosed* condition that bears upon his or her fitness to participate in physical education, recreation, and aquatic activities. I willingly and knowingly assume risk for my child, myself, my heirs, family members, executors, administrators, and assume all risk of physical injury and emotional upset that may occur during any aspect of the program; and hereby agree to hold West Chester University, its employees, instructors, facilitators, and volunteer counselors blameless for any liability arising out of the child's participation in the program.

This release does not, however, apply to any physical injury or emotional harm caused by negligence or willful misconduct of West Chester University, and the facilitators, employees, instructors, and volunteers of the Children's Adapted Multiactivities Program.

Date: _____

Parent or caregiver's signature: _____

Address: _____

Please attach proof of insurance to this form for our files.

West Chester University
Volunteer and Work Application for Special Physical Activities Program

Please check the program and time you are registering for:

Preschool Movement Program	Mon.	10-11 A.M.	9/23-11/25
Adapted Aquatic Life Skills Program	Tues.	11-12 noon	10/1-11/12
Childrens' Adapted Aquatic Community Program	Tues.	5:30-6:30 P.M.	9/3-10/15
Teen Social Skills & Recreation Program	Tues.	6-7:30 P.M.	10/22-12/3
Children's Adapted Physical Education (3-9 yrs)	Wed.	6-7 P.M.	9/11-11/6
Children's Adapted Physical Education (9-16 yrs)	Wed.	7-8 P.M.	9/11-11/6

Name: _____

Address: _____

Phone number, local: _____

      permanent: _____

Have you had a tetanus shot in the last 10 years? _____

What experience have you had with children with disabilities? _____

_____

Do you have an FBI child abuse check? _____

What is your major? _____

Are you doing this for volunteer work? _____

Are you doing this for work study? _____

Are you doing this for the KIN 251 class? _____

Are you doing this for extracurricular credit? _____

Do you know anyone who has a special talent who would volunteer to come to the program for a few hours and share that with us? _____

_____

Do you know someone who would donate T-shirts, food, drink, or anything else for the kids?

_____

_____

What talents do you bring to the program that you can teach one day? (Music? A sport? Arts and crafts?) _____

_____

_____

≋ Appendix E ≋

ADAPTED AQUATICS PROGRAM RESOURCES

EQUIPMENT AND SUPPLIES

Aquatic/shower chairs

Activeaid, Inc.
1 Activeaid Road
P.O. Box 359
Redwood Falls, MN 56283-0359
507-644-2951   800-533-5330

Water fitness and recreational therapy flotation products

AFA, Inc.
Aquarobics™
Box 5752
Greenville, SC 29606

Large pool equipment: ramps, tot docks, etc.

AFW of North America
1 Aquatic Center
Cohoes, NY 12047
716-372-2935
E-mail: aqdevgrp@wg.net

Aquatic exercise equipment

Aqua-Gym
P.O. Box 270209
Tampa, FL 33688
813-960-9040

Aquanaids lifts

The Whitmer Company
3311 Brookpark Road
P.O. Box 347210
Cleveland OH 44134-7210
216-749-4350   800-362-1162 (USA)
216-749-2078 (Fax)
E-mail: whitmer@whitmer.com
http://www.whitmer.com/

Pool lifts and handicap access equipment

Aquatic Access, Inc.
417 Dorsey Way
Louisville, KY 40223
800-325-5438

Water Walker and other flotation devices

Aquatic Therapy
1903 East B Avenue
Painwell, MI 49080
616-349-9049

Water workout station

Aquatrends
649 U.S. Highway 1, Suite 14
North Palm Beach, FL 33408
407-844-3003
E-mail: aqua649@aol.com

Poolsider lift and other lifts; large equipment

Arjo
8130 Lehigh Avenue
Morton Grove, IL 60053
800-323-1245

Heart rate monitors

Biosig Instruments
P.O. Box 860
Champlain, NY 12919

Flotation Suit for the Disabled (FSD)

Christie Fister
1580 Bud Arthur Bridge Road
Spartanburg, SC 29307

Heart rate monitors

Country Technology, Inc.
P.O. Box 87
Gay Mills, MA 01106

Video: Aquatics for children with disabilities

1997. 25 minutes.
Courage Center of Minnesota
3915 Golden Valley Road
Golden Valley, MN 55422

Diving and snorkeling equipment

Dacor
161 Northfield Road
Northfield, IL 60093
847-446-9555

Swim aids, flotation devices, headgear, positioning aids, etc.

Danmar Products, Inc.
221 Jackson Industrial Drive
Ann Arbor, MI 48103
313-761-1990
800-783-1998
313-761-8977 (Fax)
E-mail: danmarpro@aol.com

Wet Wrap and Wet Pants

D.K. Douglas Co., Inc.
299 Bliss Rd.
Longmeadow, MA 01106
800-334-9070

AquaJogger, AquaRunner foot resistance boots for low-impact, high-intensity workouts

Excel Sports Science, Inc.
450 West 5th Avenue
P.O. Box 1453
Eugene, OR 97440
541-484-2454   800-922-9544
541-484-0501 (Fax)
E-mail: info@aquajogger.com
http://www.aquajogger.com/

Center mount snorkel

Finis, Inc.
700 Beaver Court
Discovery Bay, CA 94514
510-516-1359
Email: Finis@cctrap.com
http://www.cctrap.com/~Finis/

Aquatic exercise equipment

Flaghouse, Inc.
601 Route 46 West
Hasbrouck Heights, NJ 07074
800-793-7900

Body-Gard seat shower

Hospital Therapy Products, Inc.
757 North Central Avenue
Wood Dale, Illinois 60191
630-766-7101

Water aerobics equipment

Hydro-Fit, Inc.
1328 West 2nd Avenue
Eugene, OR 97402
541-484-4361   800-346-7295
541-484-1443 (Fax)
E-mail: hydrofit@insyght.com
http://www.hydrofit.com/

Exercise, therapy, and instructional equipment

Hydro-Tone Fitness Systems, Inc.
16691 Gothard Street, Suite M
Huntington Beach, CA 92647
714-848-8284
800-622-8663
714-848-9035 (Fax)
E-mail: hydrotone@academy.la.ca.us
http://www.youth.net/hydrotone/hydrotone.html

International Swimming Hall of Fame

Mail order company for International Swimming Hall of Fame
5755 Powerline Road
Ft. Lauderdale, FL 33309
954-462-6536   954-522-4521(Fax)
http://www.ishof.org/

Instructional flotation equipment

J & B Foam Fabricators, Inc.
P.O. Box 144
Ludington, MI 49431
800-621-3626   616-843-8723 (Fax)
E-mail: jbfoam@gte.net
http://home1.gte.net/jbfoam/

Pool equipment

Kiefer, Inc.
1700 Kiefer Drive
Zion, IL 60099
847-872-8866
800-654-SWIM (Fax in USA and Canada)
E-mail: catalog@kiefer.com
http://www.kiefer.com/

Rowing equipment

Martin Marine Company
Kittery Point, ME 03905
207-439-1507

AquaCiser (underwater treadmill)

McTaggart Company
201 Gore Creek Drive
Vail, CO 81657
970-476-9164 800-825-8798
970-476-1097 (Fax)
E-mail: AquaCiser@McTaggart
http://www.mctaggartco.com/aquaciser/

Lifts

Morris Independent Lift
3236 Patterson Road
Bay City, MI 48706
517-684-5333

Manuals:

Scuba diving for everyone
Open waters: Scuba instruction by chance or choice
The Americans with Disabilities Act and the scuba industry

Open Waters Project
Alpha One
127 Main Street
South Portland, ME 04106
800-640-7200
http://www.alpha-one.org

Heart rate monitors

Polar Electro, Inc.
99 Seaview Boulevard
Port Washington, NY 11050
800-227-1314

Adaptive water skis and wheelchairs

Quickie Designs, Inc.
2842 Business Park Avenue
Fresno, CA 93727
209-292-2171
800-456-8168
E-mail: quickie1@quickiedesigns.com
http://www.quickiedesigns.com/

Facility and pool equipment, lifts

Recreonics, Inc.
4200 Schmitt Avenue
Louisville, KY 40213
800-428-3254
800-428-0133 (Fax)
E-mail: aquatics@recreonics.com
http://www.recreonics.com/

Swim-Step Pool Access System, ramps, ladders, steps

Rehab Systems, Inc.
1720 3rd Avenue N
Fargo, ND 58102
800-726-8620

Economical flooring materials:

Slip/Safe, Inc.
9160 South 300 West, Suite 11
Sandy, UT 84070
801-569-8821

Rowing equipment

Special Sports Corporation
11020 Solway School Road, Suite 103
Knoxville, TN 37931
615-481-3557

Swim-Lift and Handicap Access Equipment

Spectrum Pool Products
7110 Spectrum Lane
Missoula, MT 59802
800-776-5309

Speedo Exercise Step

Speedo Authentic Fitness Corporation
6040 Bandini Boulevard
Los Angeles, CA 90040
800-5-Speedo (800-547-8770)

Sprint Step and Aquaflex exercise paddles

Sprint-Rothhammer International, Inc.
P.O. Box 3840
San Luis Obispo, CA 93403
800-437-2156
805-541-5339 (Fax)
http://www.sprintaquatics.com/

Hoyer lift

Ted Hoyer & Company
2815 Oregon St.
P.O. Box 2744
Oshkosh, WI 54903
414-236-3460

Pool storage equipment, transfer tiers, and Casey ladder

Triad Technologies, Inc.
219 Lamson Street
Syracuse, NY 13206
315-437-4089
E-mail: triadtech@dreamscape.com

Portable stairs
WMS Aquatic Specialists
P.O. Box 398
Ellensburg, WA 98926
800-426-9460   800-443-7946

ORGANIZATIONS

Access to Sailing
1974 Beach Boulevard, Suite 404
Huntington Beach, CA 92648
714-722-5371

American Alliance for Health, Physical Education, Recreation and Dance (AAHPERD)
Aquatic Council and Adapted Physical Activity Council
1900 Association Drive
Reston, VA 22091
703-476-3400
E-mail: info@aahperd.org
http://www.aahperd.org/

American Athletic Association of the Deaf (AAAD)
3607 Washington Boulevard, #4
Ogden, UT 84403
E-mail: aaadeaf@aol.com
(See also U.S. Aquatic Association of the Deaf, a subsection of AAAD.)

American Canoe Association
7432 Alban Station Blvd., Suite B-226
Springfield, VA 22150
703-451-0141
E-mail: acdirect@aol.com
http://www.aca-paddles.org/

American National Red Cross
8111 Gatehouse Road
Falls Church, VA 22042
703-206-6000

American Swimming Coaches Association
2101 North Andrews, Suite 107
Fort Lauderdale, FL 33311
305-462-6267
800-356-2722
http://www.lornet.com/~asca/

American Therapeutic Recreation Association (ATRA)
P.O. Box 15215
Hattiesburg, MS 39404-5215
800-553-0304
601-264-3413
601-264-3337 (Fax)
http://www.atra-tr.org/index.html

American Water Ski Association
Adaptive Aquatics, Inc.
P.O. Box 337
Bolingbroke, GA 31004
888-825-5530

American Wheelchair Sailing Association
512 30th Street
Newport Beach, CA 92663

Aqua-Percept
Aquatics Department
98 Douglas Shand Avenue
Pointe-Claire, Quebec H9R2A8
Canada

Aqua Sports Association for the Physically Challenged
830 Broadway, Suite 10
El Cajon, CA 92021
619-593-8777

Aquatic Exercise Association (AEA)
820 Albee Road, Suite 9
P.O. Box 1609
Nokomis, FL 34274
941-486-8600

Aquatic Network for Occupational Therapy
Carolyn Johnson
E-mail: johnson2@jeflin.tju.edu

Aquatic Resources Network
4780 Centerville Road, Suite 112
White Bear Lake, MN 55110
612-653-3757 (Voice and fax)
E-mail: ARNetwork@aol.com
http://www.nvi.com/aquaticnet/

Australian Sports Commission
P.O. Box 176
Belconnen, ACT 2616
Australia
06-252-1111   06-251-2680 (Fax)
E-mail: nsic@ausport.gov.au
http://www.ausport.gov.au/ascmenu.html

Disabled Sports USA
451 Hungerford Drive, Suite 100
Rockville, MD 20850
301-217-0960   301-217-0968 (Fax)
301-217-0963 (TDD)
E-mail: information@dsusa.org
http://www.dsusa.org/~dsusa/dsusa.html

Dwarf Athletic Association of America
418 Willow Way
Lewisville, TX 75067
214-317-8299
E-mail: jfbda3@aol.com

Ellis & Associates
3506 Spruce Park Circle
Kingwood, TX 77345
713-360-0606
or
7650 South Tamiami Trail
Sarasota, FL 34231
813-925-8100
813-921-5881 (Fax)

Federation Internationale de Natation Amateur
(FINA)
Avenue de Beaumont 9
1012 Lausanne
Switzerland
+41 21-312-6602   +41 21-312-6610 (Fax)
http://www.fina.org/

Handicapped Scuba Association (HSA)
1104 El Prado
San Clemente, CA 92672
714-498-6128
E-mail: HSDivers@pac-aggressor.com
http://pac-aggressor.com/hsa.html

International Sports Federation for Persons with
Mental Handicap (INAS-FMH)
Roger Biggs, General Secretary
INAS-FMA Secretariat
UK Sports Association
13027 Brunswick Place
London N1 6DX, United Kingdom
+44 171-250-1100   +44 171-250-0110 (Fax)

Mission Bay Aquatic Center
1001 Santa Clara Point
San Diego, CA 92109
619-488-1036

National Association of Underwater Instructors
(NAUI)
4650 Arrow Highway, Suite F-1
Montclair, CA 91763-1150
909-621-5801   800-553-6284
909-621-6405 (Fax)
E-mail: Mike Williams, Communications Director, nauimikew@earthlink.net

National Center on Accessibility
5020 State Road, 67 North
Martinsville, IN 46151
317-349-9240   800-424-1877 (voice/TTY)
317-342-6658
E-mail: nca@indiana.edu
http://www.indiana.edu/~nca/

National Instructors Association for Divers with
Disabilities
P.O. Box 112223
Cambell, CA 95011
408-379-6536

National Ocean Access Project
P.O. Box 10726
Rockville, MD 20849-0726
301-217-9843

National Recreation and Park Association
Aquatics Section
650 West Higgins Road
Hoffman Estates, IL 60195
800-677-2236
E-mail: nrpaaq@aol.com

National Safety Council
1121 Springlake Drive
Itasca, IL 60143
800-NSC-SWIM

National Swim School Association
776 21st Avenue North
St. Petersburg, FL 33704-3348
813-896-7946   813-896-3933 (Fax)

National Therapeutic Recreation Society
c/o NTRS Aquatic Committee Chair
Melissa Stratton, CTRS
Aquatic Specialist
Shepherd Center
2020 Peachtree Road, NW
Atlanta, GA 30309
404-350-7786

Open Waters Project
Alpha One
127 Main Street
South Portland, ME 04106
http://www.alpha-one.org

Professional Association of Diving Instructors
(PADI)
1251 East Dyer Road, #100
Santa Ana, CA 92705
714-540-7234   714-540-2609 (Fax)
http://www.padi.com/

Shake-A-Leg
200 Harrison Avenue
Newport, RI 02840
401-849-8898   401-848-9072 (Fax)
E-mail: shake@mail.bbsnet.com
http://www.shakealeg.org/default.htm

Special Olympics International
1325 G Street, Suite 500
Washington, DC 20005
202-628-3630   202-824-0200 (Fax)
E-mail: specialolympics@msn.com
http://www.specialolympics.org/

SwimAmerica
2101 N. Andrews Avenue, Suite 107
Fort Lauderdale, FL 33311
954-563-4930   800-353-2722

U.S. Aquatic Association of the Deaf (A subsection of the AAAD)
Reed Gerschwind
96 Lomb Memorial Drive
Rochester, NY 14623
716-475-6875 (TTY)
E-mail: ragnbt@rit.edu

U.S. Association of Blind Athletes
33 N. Institute Street
Colorado Springs, CO 80903
719-630-0422
E-mail: usaba@us.net

U.S. Cerebral Palsy Athletic Association
200 Harrison Avenue
Newport, RI 02840
401-848-2460   401-848-5280 (Fax)
E-mail: uscpaa@mail.bbsnet.com
http://www.uscpaa.org/

U.S. Les Autres Sports Association (USLASA)
1101 Post Oak Blvd., Suite 9-486
Houston, TX 77056

U.S. Masters Swimming, Inc.
261 High Range Road
Londonderry, NH 03053-2616
603-537-0203

U.S. Olympic Committee on Sports for the Disabled
1 Olympic Plaza
Colorado Springs, CO 80909
719-390-8900

USRowing Association
201 S. Capital Avenue, Suite 400
Indianapolis, IN 46225-1068
317-237-5656   317-237-5646 (Fax)
E-mail: usrowing@aol.com
http://www.coxing.com/usrowing/

U.S. Sailing Association
P.O. Box 1260
15 Maritime Drive
Portsmouth, RI 02871
401-683-0800
E-mail: 104700.3624@compuserve.com
http://www.olyc.com/ussailing/index.htm

U.S. Swimming
1 Olympic Plaza
Colorado Springs, CO 80909
719-578-4578

U.S. Synchronized Swimming, Inc.
Pan Am Plaza, Suite 901
201 South Capitol Street
Indianapolis, IN 46225
317-237-5700

U.S. Water Fitness Association (USWFA)
P.O. Box 3279
Boynton Beach, FL 33424
407-732-9908

U.S. Wheelchair Swimming
229 Miller Street
Middleboro, MA 02346
508-946-1964

Wheelchair Sports USA (For people with spinal cord injuries)
3595 E. Fountain Boulevard, Suite L-1
Colorado Springs, CO 80910
719-574-1150
E-mail: wsusa@aol.com

YMCA of the USA
101 North Wacker Drive
Chicago, IL 60606
312-977-0031   800-USA-YMCA
http://www.ymca.net/

TECHNICAL AND PROGRAM INFORMATION

Magazines and Journals

Aquatics International Magazine
National Trade Publications
13 Century Hill Drive
Latham, NY 12110
518-783-1281

Journal of Aquatic Physical Therapy
Email:JAQUAPT@aol.com

Pool and Spa News
Leisure Publications
3923 West 6th Street
Los Angeles, CA 90020
213-385-3926

Swim Magazine
Swimming World Magazine
Swim Technique Magazine
Sports Publications, Inc.
228 Nevada Street
El Segundo, CA 90245
310-607-9956

Manuals

Fantastic Water Workouts
MaryBeth Pappas Gaines

Fitness Aquatics
LeAnne Case

Both available from Human Kinetics (800-747-4457)

Texts

Aquatics Therapy Programming: Guidelines for Orthopedic Rehabilitation
Joanne M. Koury, M.Ed.

Water Exercise
Martha D. White, OTR

Water Fitness After 40
Ruth Sova

All available from Human Kinetics (800-747-4457)

Videos

Adapted Aquatics Teacher Training
Peter Gregory Angelo, Ph.D.
Department of Physical Education and Athletics
SUNY—Stonybrook
515-632-9225 516-632-7122 (Fax)

Just Add Water
U.S. Swimming
1 Olympic Plaza
Colorado Springs, CO 80909
719-578-4578

Programming of Adapted Aquatics Activities for Children with Serious Motor Handicaps
Lourdes Macias, P.T., and Joaquim Fagoaga, P.T.
TherEd Resource
800-610-4278 305-378-4107 (Fax)

≋ References ≋

AAMR. 1992. *Mental retardation: Definition, classification, and systems of support.* 9th ed. Washington, DC: American Association on Mental Retardation.

ACSM. 1991. *Guidelines for exercise testing and prescription.* 4th ed. Philadelphia: Lea & Febiger.

Albright, C. 1995. Swimming techniques for individuals with physical disabilities. *Palaestra* 11(2):16-21.

American Alliance for Health, Physical Education and Recreation (AAHPER). 1969. *A practical guide for teaching the mentally retarded to swim.* Washington, DC: AAHPER.

American Red Cross. 1977a. *Adapted aquatics.* Garden City, NY: Doubleday.

———. 1977b. *Focus on ability.* Washington, DC: Author. Videocassette.

———. 1977c. *Methods in adapted aquatics: A manual for instructors.* Washington, DC: Author.

———. 1988. *Infant and preschool aquatic program.* Washington, DC: Author.

———. 1992a. *Swimming and diving.* St. Louis: Mosby Year Book.

———. 1992b. *Water safety instructor's manual.* St. Louis: Mosby Year Book.

———. 1996. *Swimming and diving.* St. Louis: Mosby Year Book.

Andersen, L. 1988. Swimming to win. In *Training guide to cerebral palsy sports,* ed. J.A. Jones, 68-88. Champaign, IL: Human Kinetics.

———, ed. 1992. *United States Swimming handbook for adapted competitive swimming.* Colorado Springs: U.S. Swimming.

Andrews, M. 1981. Row Cat mitts. *Sports 'n Spokes* 7(1):6.

Aquatics International. 1995. Program options: National agencies find many ways to structure learn-to-swim classes. *Aquatics International* March/April:16-22.

Arreola, R.A. 1966. Evaluating the dimensions of teaching. *Instructional Evaluation* 8(2):4-12.

Arthritis Foundation and the National Council of YMCAs of the USA. 1990. *Arthritis foundation YMCA aquatic program (AFYAP) and AFYAP PLUS: Instructors' manual.* Atlanta: Arthritis Foundation.

Austin, D.R., and M.E. Crawford. 1991. *Therapeutic recreation: An introduction.* Englewood Cliffs, NJ: Prentice-Hall.

Auxter, D., J. Pyfer, and C. Huettig. 1993. *Adapted physical education and recreation.* 7th ed. St. Louis: Mosby.

Ayres, A.J. 1989. *Sensory integration and praxis test.* Los Angeles: Western Psychological Services.

Back Letter, The. 1991. Aquatic therapy. *The Back Letter* 6(2):6.

Bauer, K. 1997. Personal communication, 7 February.

Bedini, L.A., and C.A. McCann. 1992. Tearing down the shameful wall of exclusion. *Parks and Recreation* April:40-44.

Bigge, J.L. 1991. *Teaching individuals with physical and multiple disabilities.* New York: Macmillan.

Bigler, E.D., ed. 1990. *Traumatic brain injury.* Austin, TX: PRO-ED.

Blauvelt, C.T., and F.R.T. Nelson. 1994. *A manual of orthopedic terminology.* 5th ed. St. Louis: Mosby Year Book.

Bleck, E.E., and D.A. Nagel, eds. 1982. *Physically handicapped children: A medical atlas for teachers.* 2nd ed. New York: Grune and Stratton.

Block, M.E. 1994. *A teacher's guide to including students with disabilities in regular physical education.* Baltimore: Paul H. Brookes.

———. 1995. Americans With Disabilities Act: Its impact on youth sports. *Journal of Physical Education, Recreation and Dance* 66(1):28-32.

Block, M.E., and P.L. Krebs. 1992. An alternative to least restrictive environments: A continuum of support to regular physical education. *Adapted Physical Activity Quarterly* 9:97-113.

Bloomquist, L.E.C. 1997. *Adapted aquatics program manual.* 5th ed. Charleston, RI: Colson Publishers Foundation.

Borg, G. 1982. Psychophysical bases of perceived exertion. *Medicine and Science in Sports and Exercise* 14:377-381.

Boulter, P. 1992. Using hydrotherapy: Maximizing benefits. *Nursing Standard* 7(4):25-27.

Bowness, B., and J. Wilson. n.d. Disabled water skiing coaching manual. Australian Sports Commission, 1-25. (Available from Western Australian Water Ski Association, P.O. Box 52, Victoria Park, 100, Western Australia.)

Bradtke, J.S. 1979. Adapted devices for aquatic activities. *Practical Pointers* 3(1):1-5.

Brandt, R. 1990. On learning styles: A conversation with Pat Guild. *Educational Leadership*, October:10-13.

Bruininks, R.H. 1978. *Bruininks-Oseretsky test of motor proficiency manual.* Circle Pines, MN: American Guidance Service.

Bryant, C.L. 1951. Aquatics for the disabled and handicapped. In *NSWA Aquatics, winter sports and outing guide,* AAHPER, (July), 1951-1953. Washington, DC: AAHPER.

Burgess, S., and T. Davis. 1993. Water exercise. In *Play and recreation for individuals with disabilities: Practical pointers,* eds. S. Grosse and D. Thompson, 117-131. Reston, VA: AAHPERD.

Calarusso, R.P., and D.D. Hammill. 1972. *Motor-free visual perception test.* Novato, CA: Academic Therapy Publications.

Campion, M.R. 1985. *Hydrotherapy in pediatrics.* Rockville, MD: Aspen Systems Corporation.

Canadian Red Cross. 1969. *Manual for teaching swimming to the disabled.* Toronto: Author.

Canadian Red Cross Society. 1980. *Adapted aquatics recertification.* Ottawa, Ontario: Canadian Red Cross.

———. 1989. *Adapted aquatics: Promoting aquatic opportunities for all.* Ottawa, Ontario: Author.

Carter, B. 1988. Simple pleasures. *Nursing Times* 84 13(March):38-39.

Carter, M.J., M.A. Dolan, and S.P. LeConey. 1994. *Designing instructional swim programs for individuals with disabilities.* Reston, VA: AAHPERD.

Carter, M.J., G.E. Van Andel, and G.M. Robb. 1985. *Therapeutic recreation: A practical approach.* St. Louis: Times Mirror Mosby.

Charness, A. 1983. *Aquatics for the physically disabled.* Unpublished paper.

Cocchi, R.C. 1997. Swimming: The sport for all abilities. *Advance for Physical Therapists* 8(19):23.

Conatser, P. 1995. *Adapted aquatics swimming screening test.* Charlottesville, VA: Author.

Corbin, C.B., and R. Lindsey. 1990. *Concepts of physical fitness.* 7th ed. Dubuque, IA: Brown.

Council for Exceptional Children. 1993. Council for Exceptional Children policy on inclusive schools and community settings. *Teaching Exceptional Children* 25(May, Supp.):4.

Cratty, B.J. 1989. *Adapted physical education in the mainstream.* 2nd ed. Denver: Love Publishing.

Cratty, B.J., and M.M. Martin, Sr. 1969. *Perceptual-motor efficiency in children.* Philadelphia: Lea & Febiger.

Crawford, M. 1988. Adapted aquatics programming for persons with severe disabilities: An overview of current best practice standards. In *Adapted physical education: A comprehensive resource manual of definition, assessment, programming, and future predictions,* 3rd ed., ed. P. Bishop, 193-213. Kearney, NE: Educational Systems Associates.

Crawford, M.E. 1991. Formation and organization of the profession. In *Therapeutic recreation: An introduction,* eds. D.R. Austin and M.E. Crawford. Englewood Cliffs, NJ: Prentice-Hall.

Curren, E.A. 1971. Teaching water safety skills to blind multi-handicapped children. *Education of the Visually Handicapped* 3(March):29-32.

Daniels, A.S., and E.A. Davies. 1975. *Adapted physical education.* 3rd ed. New York: Harper and Row.

Dardig, J.C., and W.L. Heward. 1981. A systematic procedure for prioritizing IEP goals. *The Directive Teacher* 3:6-7.

Dauer, V., and R. Pangrazi. 1986. *Dynamic physical education for elementary school children.* 2nd ed. Minneapolis: Burgess.

Davis, R. 1997. Classification: A form of athlete evaluation. *Athletic Therapy Today* 2(1):11-15.

Davis, R.W., and M.S. Ferrara. 1991. Training profiles of elite wheelchair athletes. Paper presented at the 8th International Symposium of Adapted Physical Activity, Miami.

———. 1995. Sports medicine and athletes with disabilities. In *Disability and sport,* K.P. DePauw and S. J. Gavron, 133-149. Champaign, IL: Human Kinetics.

Davis, W.E. 1989. Utilizing goals in adapted physical education. *Adapted Physical Education Quarterly* 6:205-216.

Deno, E. 1970. Special education as developmental capital. *Exceptional Children* 37:229-237.

DePaepe, J.L. 1980. A present level of performance assessment for children with developmental lag or low motor ability. Unpublished master's thesis, State University of New York, Brockport, NY.

———. 1985. The influence of three least restrictive environments on the content motor-ALT and performance of moderately mentally retarded students. *Journal of Teaching in Physical Education* 5:298-303.

Department of Justice, Office of the Attorney General. 1991. Nondiscrimination on the basis of disability by public accommodations and in commercial facilities: Final rule. Part III of the Americans With Disabilities Act. *Federal Register* 56(144): 35544-35691.

DePauw, K.P., and S.J. Gavron. 1995. *Disability and sport*. Champaign, IL: Human Kinetics.

Dieffenbach, L. 1991. Aquatic therapy services. *Clinical Management* 11(1):74-78.

Disabled Sports USA. 1996. *DSUSA introductory packet*. Rockville, MD: DSUSA.

Division of Vocational Rehabilitation, Department of Labor. 1991. *Americans With Disabilities Act*. Wilmington, DE: State of Delaware.

Dulcy, F.H. 1983a. Aquatic programs for disabled children: An overview and an analysis of the problems. *Physical and Occupational Therapy in Pediatrics* 3:1-20.

———. 1983b. A theoretical aquatic service intervention model for disabled children. *Physical and Occupational Therapy in Pediatrics* 3:21-38.

Dummer, G. 1997. Personal communication, May 19.

Dunn, J. 1978. Handicapped legislation and the public agency. In *New horizons in aquatics: Proceedings of the Twentieth National Aquatic Conference*, ed. B.E. Empleton, 63-66. Toledo: Council for National Cooperation in Aquatics.

Dunn, J., J. Morehouse, and B. Fredericks. 1986. *Physical education for the severely handicapped: A systematic approach to a data-based gymnasium*. 2nd ed. Austin, TX: Pro-Ed.

Dunn, J., and H. Fait. 1989. *Special physical education: Adapted, individualized, developmental*. 6th ed. Dubuque, IA: Brown.

Dunn, J.M. 1996. *Special physical education: Adapted, individualized, developmental*, 7th ed. Dubuque, IA: Brown & Benchmark.

Dunn, K. 1981. PFD's for the handicapped: A question of responsibility. *The Physician and Sportsmedicine* 9(8):147-152.

Edlich, R.F., D.G. Becker, D. Phung, W.A. McClelland, and S.G. Day. 1988. Water treatment of hydrotherapy exercise pools. *Journal of Burn Care Therapy* 9(5):510-515.

Eichstaedt, C.B., and L.H. Kalakian. 1993. *Developmental and adapted physical education: Making ability count*. 3rd ed. New York: Macmillan.

Eichstaedt, C.B., and Lavay, B.W. 1992. *Physical activity for individuals with mental retardation—Infancy through adulthood*. Champaign, IL: Human Kinetics.

Exceptional Parent. 1993. Aquatic sports. *Exceptional Parent* July-August:30-31.

Federal Register. 1977a. Final regulations of education of handicapped children, implementation of Part B of the *Education of the Handicapped Act*. Department of Health, Education, and Welfare, Office of Education, 42(163), part II, section 121a307 Physical education, p. 42489 and section 121a14, special education, p. 42480, April 23.

Federal Register. 1977b. *PL 93-112, The Rehabilitation Act of 1973, section 504*, May 4.

Federal Register. 1980. *PL 99-457, The Education of the Handicapped Act*, June 22.

Federal Register. 1991. *PL 101-336, Title III of the Americans With Disabilities Act*, July 26.

Ferrara, M.S., and R.W. Davis. 1997. Disability sports and medical professions. *Athletic Therapy Today* 2(1):7-9.

Finnie, N.R. 1975. *Handling the young cerebral palsied child at home*. 2nd ed. New York: Dutton-Sunrise.

Fisher, C.W., D.C. Berliner, N.N. Filby, R. Marliave, L.S. Cahen, and M.M. Dishaw. 1980. Teaching behaviors, academic learning time, and student achievement: An overview. In *Time to learn: A review of the Beginning Teaching Evaluation Study*, eds. C. Denham and A. Lieverman, 7-32. Sacramento: California State Commission for Teacher Preparation and Licensing (ERIC Document Reproduction Service No. ED 192 454).

Fitts, P.M., and M.I. Posner. 1967. *Human Performance*. Belmont, CA: Brooks/Cole.

Fitzner, K. 1986. Aqua-Percept program. *The National Aquatics Journal* 2(2):8.

Foxx, R.M., and N.H. Azrin. 1973. *Toilet training the retarded: A rapid program for day and night time independent toileting.* Champaign, IL: Research Press.

Framroze, A. 1991. Water's healing powers. *Rehab Management* 4(5):56-66.

French, C., R.T. Gonzalez, and J. Tronson-Simpson. 1991. *Caring for people with multiple disabilities: An interdisciplinary guide for caregivers.* Tucson, AZ: Therapy Skill Builders.

Garvey, L.A. 1991. Spinal cord injury and aquatics. *Clinical Management* 11(1):21-24.

Genuario, S.E., and J.J. Vegso. 1989. The use of a swimming pool in the rehabilitation and reconditioning of athletic injuries. *Postgraduate advances in sports medicine: An independent study course designed for individual continuing education.* Philadelphia: University of Pennsylvania School of Medicine.

Glaser, R.M., W.J. Janssen, A.G. Suryaprasad, S.C. Gupta, and T. Matthews. 1996. The physiology of exercise. In *Physical fitness: A guide for individuals with spinal cord injury*, ed. D. F. Apple, Jr., 1-24: Washington, DC: Department of Veterans Affairs.

Golland, A. 1981. Basic hydrotherapy. *Physiotherapy* 67(9):258-262.

Green, S. 1996. Specific exercise programs. In *Physical fitness: A guide for individuals with spinal cord injury*, ed. D.F. Apple, Jr., 45-96. Washington, DC: Department of Veterans Affairs, Veterans Health Administration.

Grineski, S. 1994. Dilemma of educational placement for students with severe disabilities. *Palaestra* 10(4):21-22.

Grosse, S.J. 1985. Introduction of a deaf-blind swimmer. *National Aquatics Journal* 1(3):14-16.

———. 1993. Aerobic dance. In *Play and recreation for individuals with disabilities: Practical pointers*, eds. S.J. Grosse and D. Thompson, 107-116. Reston, VA: Adapted Physical Activity Council of the ARAPCS of AAHPERD.

———. 1996. What's in a name? Adapted aquatics—back to the future. *Palaestra* 12(3):20.

Grosse, S.J., and D. Thompson, eds. 1993. *Leisure opportunities for individuals with disabilities: Legal issues.* Reston, VA: AAHPERD.

Groves, L., ed. 1979. *Physical education for special needs.* Cambridge, Great Britain: Cambridge University Press.

Hale, G. 1979. *The source book for the disabled.* New York: Paddington Press.

Harris, S.R. 1978. Neurodevelopmental treatment approach for teaching swimming to cerebral palsied children. *Physical Therapy* 58:979-983.

Heckathorn, J. 1980. *Strokes and strokes.* Reston, VA: AAHPERD.

Hicks, L. 1988. Systematic desensitization of aquaphobic persons. *The National Aquatics Journal* 4(1):15-18.

Hirst, C.S., and E. Michaelis. 1972. *Developmental activities for children in special education.* Springfield, IL: Charles C Thomas.

Hopkins, H., and H. Smith. 1988. *Willard and Spackman's occupational therapy.* 7th ed. Philadelphia: Lippencott.

Horine, L. 1995. *Administration of physical education and sport programs.* 3rd ed. Madison, WI: Brown and Benchmark.

Horvat, M.A., W.R. Forbus, and L. Van Kirk. 1987. *Teacher and parent guide for the physical development of mentally handicapped in the aquatic environment.* Athens, GA: The University of Georgia, Department of Physical Education.

Houston-Wilson, K. 1993. The effect of untrained and trained peer tutors on the motor performance of students with developmental disabilities in integrated physical education classes. PhD diss., Oregon State University.

Hunter, M. 1982. *Mastery teaching: Increasing instructional effectiveness in elementary schools, colleges, and universities.* El Secunda, CA: TIP Publications.

Individuals With Disabilities Education Act of 1990 (IDEA). U.S. Public Law 101-476. 20 Congress 30 October 1990. Chapter 33.

International Paralympic Committee. 1995. *IPC SAEC-SW swimming rules.* Rev. ed. Sweden: Author.

———. 1996. General and functional classification guide. International Sports Federation for Persons With Mental Handicap (INAS-FMH). *Information about our work* (pamphlet). Sweden: Author. (Available from INAS-FMH, Solecast House, 13-27 Brunswick Place, London N16DX, United Kingdom.)

Jankowski, L.W. 1995. *Teaching persons with disabilities to scuba diving.* Montreal: Quebec Underwater Association.

Jansma, J., and R. French. 1994. *Special physical education: Physical activity, sports and recreation.* Englewood Cliffs, NJ: Prentice Hall.

Johannsen, S. 1987. A process toward the integration of mentally handicapped students into community learn to swim programs. In *International perspectives on adapted physical activities,* eds. M.E. Berridge and G.R. Ward, 109-117. Champaign, IL: Human Kinetics.

Jones, J.A., ed. 1988. *To float or not to float: Training guide to cerebral palsy sports.* Champaign, IL: Human Kinetics.

Kaminker, L. 1996. Change, growth and exclusion: A Paralympic identity crisis. *New Mobility* April:33, 63.

Kelly, J.D., and L. Frieden. 1989. *Go for it.* Orlando, FL: Harcourt Brace Jovanovich.

Kennedy, D.W., D.R. Austin, and R.W. Smith. 1987. *Special recreation: Opportunities for persons with disabilities.* Philadelphia: Saunders.

Killian, K.J., S. Arena-Ronde, and L. Bruno. 1987. Refinement of two instruments that assess water orientation in atypical swimmers. *Adapted Physical Activity Quarterly* 4(1):25-37

Killian, K.J., R.A. Joyce-Petrovich, L. Menna, and S.A. Arena. 1984. Measuring water orientation and beginner swim skills of autistic individuals. *Adapted Physical Activity Quarterly* 1(4):287-295.

Kozub, F.M., and D. Poretta. 1996. Including athletes with disabilities: Interscholastic athletic benefits for all. *Journal of Physical Education, Recreation and Dance* 67:3, 19-24.

Kraus, R. 1971. *Recreation and leisure in modern society.* New York: Appleton-Century-Crofts.

Langendorfer, S., E. German, and D. Kral. 1988. Aquatic games and gimmicks for young children. *The National Aquatics Journal* 4(Fall):11-13.

Langendorfer, S., D.K. Harrod, and L.D. Bruya. 1991. Prescriptive aquatic instruction: A developmental approach. *The National Aquatics Journal* 7(1):14-15.

Lepore, M. 1991. Teaching aquatic activities to people with traumatic brain injury: A self-instructional manual for aquatic instructors. PhD diss. New York University, New York.

Levin, S. 1991. Aquatic therapy: A splashing success for arthritis and injury rehabilitation. *The Physician and Sportsmedicine* 19(10):119-120, 123-124, 126.

Lin, L.Y. 1987. SCUBA divers with disabilities challenge medical protocols and ethics. *The Physician and Sports Medicine* 15(6): 224-228, 233, 235.

Lindle, J. 1989. Water exercise research. *The AKWA Letter* 3(4):11-13.

Lindstrom, H. 1986. Sports classifications for locomotor disabilities: Integrated versus diagnostic systems. In *The 1984 Olympic Scientific Congress proceedings* 9:131-136.

Lister-Piercy, S. 1985. A process of the integration of mentally handicapped students into community learn-to-swim programs. Unpublished master's thesis, University of Alberta, Canada.

Lockette, K.F., and A.M. Keyes. 1994. *Conditioning with physical disabilities.* Champaign, IL: Human Kinetics.

Long, E., L. Irmer, L. Burkett, G. Glasenapp, and B. Odenkirk. 1980. PEOPEL. *Journal of Physical Education* 51:28-29.

Mace, R.L. 1993. Making pools accessible. *Athletic Business* 17(8):34-36.

Marano, C. and E. DeMarco. 1984. A new design and construction for a swimming prosthesis. *Orthotics and Prosthetics* 38(1):45-49.

Martin, K. 1983. Therapeutic pool activities for young children in a community facility. *Physical and Occupational Therapy in Pediatrics* 3:59-74.

Masters, L.F., A.A. Mori, and E.K. Lange. 1983. *Adapted physical education: A practitioner's guide.* Rockville, MD: Aspen.

Mastrangelo, R. 1992. Aquatic therapy: Whose turf is it, anyway? *Advance for Occupational Therapists* October 26:14-15.

McCurdy, S. 1991. The great equalizer. *Sailing World* April:48-51.

McDowell, C.F. 1974. Toward a healthy leisure mode: Leisure counseling. *Therapeutic Recreation Journal* 8(3):96-104.

McInnes, J.M., and J.A. Treffry. 1982. *Deaf-blind infants and children: A developmental guide.* Toronto: University of Toronto Press.

Mehta, M., ed. 1996. *Physicians' Desk Reference.* 50th ed. Oradell, NJ: Medical Economics.

Meyer, R.I. 1994. *Kinesiotherapy of New Hampshire.* Pamphlet available from R.I. Meyer, 6 Chenell Dr., Concord, New Hampshire 03301.

———. 1990. Practice settings for kinesiotherapy-aquatics. *Clinical Kinesiology* 44(1):12-13.

Milani-Comparetti, A. 1967. Routine developmental examination in normal and retarded children. *Developmental Medicine and Child Neurology* 9:631, 766.

Miller, B.B. 1985. Coaching the wheelchair athlete to swim competitively. *National Aquatic Journal* 1(2):10-12.

Miller, A.G., and J.V. Sullivan. 1982. *Teaching physical activities to impaired youth: An approach to mainstreaming*. New York: Wiley & Sons.

Miller, P.D., ed. 1995. *Fitness programming and physical disability*. Champaign, IL: Human Kinetics.

Minor, M.A., and S.D. Minor. 1984. *Patient care skills*. Reston, VA: Reston Publishing.

Mirenda, J.J. 1973. Mirenda leisure interest finder. In *Leisure counseling kit*, eds. A.E. Epperson, R. Mirenda, R. Overs, and G.T. Wilson. Washington, DC: AAHPER.

Montelione, T.L., and R. Davis. 1986. Physically disabled athletes successfully compete. In *Sport and disabled athletes: The 1984 Olympic scientific congress proceedings*, ed. C. Sherrill, 225-230. Champaign, IL: Human Kinetics.

Moran, J. 1961. Fear and aquatic instruction. In *DGWS Aquatics guide July 1961-1963*, 15-17. Washington, DC: AAHPER.

———. 1979. Water activity for the handicapped. In *NAGWS aquatics guide: Tips and techniques for teachers and coaches*, ed. AAHPER, 13-14. Reston, VA: AAHPERD.

———, ed. 1981. *Handicapped swimming: A syllabus for the Aquatic Council's courses Teacher and Master Teacher of Handicapped Swimming*. Reston, VA: AAHPERD.

Mori, A.A., and L.F. Masters. 1980. *Teaching the severely mentally retarded: Adaptive skills training*. Germantown, Maryland: Aspen Systems Corporation.

Morris, G.S.D., and J. Stiehl. 1989. *Changing kids' games*. Champaign, IL: Human Kinetics.

Mosston, M. 1992. Tug-o-war no more: Meeting teaching-learning objectives using the spectrum of teaching styles. *Journal of Physical, Education, Recreation and Dance* 63(1):27-31, 56.

Mosston, M., and S. Ashworth. 1986. *Teaching physical education*. 3rd ed. Columbus, OH: Merrill.

———. 1994. *Teaching physical education*. 4th ed. New York: Macmillan.

Muhl, W.T. 1976. Aquatics for the handicapped. *Journal of Physical Education and Recreation* 47(2):42-43.

Mushett, C.A., D.A. Wyeth, and K.J. Richter. 1995. Cerebral palsy. In *Sports and exercise for children with chronic health conditions*, ed. Barry Goldberg, 123-133. Champaign, IL: Human Kinetics.

National Center on Accessibility. 1996. National Center on Accessibility—Swimming pool accessibility.

National Council on Disability. 1994. Recommendation for the reauthorization of the Individuals With Disabilities Education Act. *TASH: The Association for Persons With Severe Handicaps* 20(9):8-9.

National Multiple Sclerosis Society Client and Community Services Division. 1993. *National Multiple Sclerosis Society: Aquatic exercise program*. New York: Author.

Nearing, R.J., D.A.K Johansen, and C. Vevea. 1995. Gymnastics mats in the pool? *Palaestra* 11(2):22-30, 64.

O'Morrow, G.S. 1980. *Therapeutic recreation: A helping profession*. 2nd ed. Englewood Cliffs, NJ: Prentice Hall.

Orelove, F.P., and D. Sobsey. 1987. *Educating children with multiple disabilities: A transdisciplinary approach*. Baltimore: Brookes.

Osinski, A. 1989. Warm water pool and spa problems. *The National Aquatics Journal* Winter:12-13, 15.

———. 1993. Modifying public swimming pools to comply with provisions of the Americans With Disabilities Act. *Palaestra* 9:13-18.

Paciorek, M. J., and J.A. Jones. 1994. *Sports and recreation for the disabled: A resource manual*. 2nd ed. Indianapolis: Masters Press.

Palmer, M.L., and J.E. Toms. 1986. *Manual for functional training*. 2nd ed. Philadelphia: Davis.

Persyn, U., E. Surmont, L. Wouters, and J. De Maeyer. 1975. Analysis of techniques used by swimmers in the Para-Olympic Games. In *Swimming II international series on sport sciences, Volume 2: Proceedings of the Second International Symposium on Biomechanics in Swimming*, Brussels, Belgium, eds. L. Lewillie and J. Clarys, 277-280. Baltimore: University Park Press.

Petrofsky, J.S. 1994a. Diving with spinal cord injury. Part I. *Palaestra* 10(4):36-41.

———. 1994b. Diving with spinal cord injury. Part II. *Palaestra* 11(1):30-31, 49-51.

———. 1995. Diving with spinal cord injury. Part III. *Palaestra* 11(2):34-38.

Piper, C.L., ed. 1983. *Aquatics.* Englewood, CO: Morton.

Pratt, P.N., and A.S. Allen. 1989. The role of occupational therapy in pediatrics. In *Occupational therapy for children*, 2nd ed., eds. P.N. Pratt and A.S. Allen, 3-9. St. Louis: Mosby.

Priest, E.L. 1979. Integrating the disabled into aquatics programs. *Journal of Physical Education and Recreation* 50(2):57-59.

———. 1986. Warm water for cold spring. *The National Aquatic Journal* 2(2):10.

———. 1990. Aquatics. In *Adapted physical education and sport*, ed. J. Winnick, 391-408. Champaign, IL: Human Kinetics.

———. 1996. *Adapted aquatics.* Kingwood, TX: Jeff Ellis and Associates.

Rakich, J.S., B.B. Longest, Jr., and K. Darr. 1985. *Managing health services organizations.* 2nd ed. Philadelphia: Saunders.

Rainforth, B., J. York, and C. Macdonald. 1992. *Collaborative teams for students with severe disabilities: Integrating therapy and educational services.* Baltimore: Paul H. Brooks.

Randall, L.E. 1992. *Systematic supervision for physical education.* Champaign, IL: Human Kinetics.

Rantz, M.F., and D. Courtial. 1981. *Lifting, moving, and transferring patients.* 2nd ed. St. Louis: Mosby.

Recreation Access Advisory Committee. 1994. Recommendations for accessibility guidelines: Recreational facilities and outdoor developed areas. Washington, DC: U.S. Architectural and Transportation Barriers Compliance Board.

Recreation Resources. 1993. Bringing facilities up to code with ADA guidelines. *Recreation Resources* 13(8):14.

Rehabilitation Institute of Chicago. 1991. Sensory integrative water activities. Unpublished paper.

Reid, G. 1979. Mainstreaming in physical education. *McGill Journal of Education* 14:367-377.

Reid, M.J. 1980. Programmed recreational activity in water. In *Adapted aquatics recertification*, ed. Canadian Red Cross, 20-25. Ottawa, Ontario: Canadian Red Cross. (Reprinted from *Physiotherapy Canada Journal*, 1976, 28[5].)

Reister, V.C., and B. Ellis. 1993. Current trends in aquatic therapy. Paper presented at the meeting of the Tennessee American Occupational Therapy Association, November, Johnson City, TN.

Reynolds, G.D., ed. 1973. *A swimming program for the handicapped.* New York: Association Press.

Richter, K.J., C. Adams-Mushett, M.S. Ferrara, and B.C. McCann. 1992. Integrated swimming classification: A faulted system. *Adapted Physical Activity Quarterly* 9:5-13.

Rider, R.A., and S. Modell. 1996. Aquatics for children with Angelman syndrome: Earning your water wings. *Palaestra* 12(4):28-33.

Robbins, G., D. Powers, and S. Burgess. 1991. *A wellness way of life.* Dubuque, IA: Brown.

Robinson, J., and A.D. Fox. 1987. *Diving with disabilities.* Champaign, IL: Human Kinetics.

Roeser, R.J., and M.P. Downs. 1981. *Auditory disorders in school children.* New York: Thieme-Stratton.

Rogers, S.M. 1996. Factors that influence exercise tolerance. In *Physical fitness: A guide for individuals with spinal cord injury*, ed. J.D. Apple, 25-32. Department of Veterans Affairs—Veterans Health Administration.

Savage, R.C., and R. Carter. 1984. Re-entry: The head injured student returns to school. *Cognitive Rehabilitation* 2(6):28-33.

Scott, K., ed. 1990. *The Americans With Disabilities Act: An analysis.* Silver Springs, MD: Business Publishers.

Scull, S.A., and B.H. Athreya. 1995. Childhood arthritis. In *Sports and exercise for children with chronic health conditions*, ed. B. Goldberg, 136-148. Champaign, IL: Human Kinetics.

Seaman, J.A., and K.P. DePauw. 1989. *The new adapted physical education: A developmental approach.* Mountain View, CA: Mayfield.

Selepak, G. 1994. Aquatic therapy in rehabilitation. In *Rehabilitation techniques in sports medicine*, ed. W.E. Prentice, 195-203. St. Louis: Mosby.

Sherrill, C. 1986. *Adapted physical education and recreation: A multidisciplinary approach.* Dubuque, IA: Brown.

———. 1993. *Adapted physical activity, recreation and sport: Crossdisciplinary and lifespan.* 4th ed. Dubuque, IA: Brown & Benchmark.

———. 1993. Least restrictive environment and total inclusion philosophies: Critical analysis. *Palaestra* 10(3):25-35, 52-53.

———. 1998. *Adapted physical activity, recreation and sport: Crossdisciplinary and lifespan.* 5th ed. Dubuque, IA: WCB McGraw-Hill.

———, and N. Megginson. 1984. A needs assessment instrument for local school district use in adapted physical education needs. *Adapted Physical Activity Quarterly* 1:147-157.

Sherrill, C., C. Adams-Mushett, and J.A. Jones. 1986. Classification and other issues in sports for blind, cerebral palsied, les autres, and amputee athletes. In *Sport and disabled athletes: The 1984 Olympic scientific congress proceedings, Volume 9*, ed. C. Sherrill, 113-130. Champaign, IL: Human Kinetics.

Shurte, B. 1981. Adapted aquatics bulletin #101. Ann Arbor, MI: Danmar Products.

Shriver, E.K. 1972. Special Olympics. *Swimming World* 13(7):40.

Skaros, S. 1993. Bloodborne pathogens and contagion risks for aquatic personnel. *National Aquatic Journal* 9:3.

Skinner, A.T., and A.M. Thompson, eds. 1983. *Duffield's exercises in water.* 3rd ed. London: Bailliere Tindall.

Smith, R. 1992. Kids take the plunge. *Rehab Management* December/January:31-32, 34-36.

Snell, M.E. 1987. *Systematic instruction of persons with severe handicaps.* 3rd ed. Columbus, OH: Merrill.

Snider, V. 1990. What we know about learning styles from research in special education. *Educational Leadership* October:53.

Sova, R. 1992. *Aquatics: The complete reference guide for aquatic fitness professionals.* Boston: Jones & Bartlett.

Special Olympics. n.d. *Special Olympics swimming and diving sports skills instructional program.* Washington, DC: Author.

Special Olympics International. n.d. *Partners Club.* Washington, DC: Joseph P. Kennedy Jr. Foundation.

———. 1992. *Official Special Olympics Summer Sports Rules.* 1992-1995 rev. ed. Washington, DC: Joseph P. Kennedy Jr. Foundation.

———. 1989. *Special Olympics motor activities training guide.* Washington, DC: Author.

———. 1993. *Special Olympics unified sports guidebook.* Washington, DC: Joseph P. Kennedy Foundation.

———. 1994. *Special Olympics aquatics: Sport management team guide.* Washington, DC: Joseph P. Kennedy Foundation.

Stein, J. 1993. The Americans With Disabilities Act. In *Leisure opportunities for individuals with disabilities: Legal issues*, eds. S.J. Grosse and D. Thompson, 1-11. Reston, VA: AAHPERD.

———. 1994. An editor's response. *Palaestra* 10(4):23-24.

Summerford, C.F. 1993. Apparatus used in teaching swimming to quadriplegic amputees. *Palaestra* Spring:54-57.

Surburg, P.R. 1995. Other health impaired students. In *Adapted physical education and sport*, ed. J.P. Winnick, 213-226. Champaign, IL: Human Kinetics.

SwimAmerica. n.d. Organizational documents provided by SwimAmerica, 2101 N. Andrews Ave., Suite 107, Fort Lauderdale, FL 33311.

Telzrow, C.F. 1987. Management of academic and educational problems in head injury. *Journal of Learning Disabilities* 20:536-545.

Thiers, N. 1994. Taking rehab to the pool. *OT Week* January 6:22-24

Thomas, G.J. 1989. Swimming: An alternate form of therapy. *Clinical Management in Physical Therapy* 9(3):24-26.

Tobin, R. 1990. The second decade: The progress of U.S. disabled rowing. *Row* 1(1):38.

Torg, J.S., R.P. Welsh, and R.J. Shephard. 1990. *Current therapy in sports medicine—2.* Philadelphia: B.C. Decker.

Turner, A. 1987. *The practice of occupational therapy.* 2nd ed. New York: Churchill Livingstone.

United Cerebral Palsy. 1976. *Staff development handbook: A resource for the transdisciplinary process.* New York: Author.

United States Cerebral Palsy Athletic Association (USCPAA). 1997. *USCPAA Classification and Rules Book.* Harrison, RI: Author.

United States Department of Education, Office of Special Education and Rehabilitative Services. 1993. *Fifteenth annual report to Congress on the implementation of the Individuals With Disabilities Education Act.* Washington, DC: Author.

U.S. Government Printing Office. 1991. *The Americans With Disabilities Act.* Title II, Subtitle A, Section 202; Title III, Section 302: Prohibition of discrimination by public accommodations (b):(1) (A) (1-iii) and (2) (B) (I-v). Washington, DC: U.S. Government Printing Office.

United States Swimming. 1997. *1997 United States Swimming rules and regulations.* Colorado Springs: Author.

Vanlandewijck, Y.C., and R.J. Chappel. 1996. Integration and classification issues in competitive sports for athletes with disabilities. *Sports Science Review* 5(1):65-88.

Van Witsen, B. 1979. *Perceptual training activities handbook.* 2nd ed. New York: Teachers College Press.

Vest, S. 1995. Sound sanitation. *Athletic Business* 19(3):39-44.

———. 1994. Hidden risk. *Athletic Business* 18(12):71-76.

Webel, G., and Goldberg, C. 1982. *Open boating: A handbook.* Oakland, CA: City of Oakland, Office of Parks and Recreation.

Webre, A., and J. Zeller. 1990. *Canoeing and kayaking for persons with physical disabilities.* Newington, VA: American Canoe Association.

Webster, G.E. 1987. Influence of peer tutors upon academic learning time—Physical education of mentally handicapped students. *Journal of Teaching in Physical Education* 7:393-403.

Weiss, R., and W.B. Karper. 1980. Teaching the handicapped child in the regular physical education class. *Journal of Physical Education and Recreation* 51:22-35,77.

Wessel, J. 1976. *I CAN: Aquatic skills.* Northbrook, IL: H. Hubbard. (Now available from Pro-Ed, Austin, TX.)

Wessel, J., and L. Kelly. 1986. *Achievement-based curriculum development in physical education.* Philadelphia: Lea & Febiger.

West, J., ed. 1991. *Americans With Disabilities Act: From policy to practice.* New York: Milbank Memorial Fund.

Westbrook, W. 1992. In the clear. *Athletic Business* 16(7):39, 41-43.

Wiedemann, H.R., J. Kunze, F.R. Grosse, H. Dibbern. 1992. *An atlas of clinical syndromes: A visual aid to diagnosis for clinicians and practising physicians.* Aylesbury, England: Wolfe.

Wilbur, R.H., S.K. Finn, and C.M. Freeland, eds. 1994. *The complete guide to nonprofit management.* New York: John Wiley & Sons.

Williamson, D.C. Principles of classification in competitive sport for participants with disabilities: A proposal. *Palaestra* 13(2):44-48.

Windhorst, M., and V. Chossek. 1988. *Aquatic exercise association manual.* Port Washington, WI: Aquatic Exercise Association.

Winnick, J.P. 1987. An integration continuum for sport participation. *Adapted Physical Activity Quarterly* 4:157-191.

———. 1995. Personalizing measurement and evaluation for individuals with disabilities. In *Physical best and individuals with disabilities*, ed. J.A. Seaman, 21-31. Reston, VA: American Association for Active Lifestyles and Fitness/AAHPERD.

———. ed. 1995. *Adapted physical education and sport.* 2nd ed. Champaign, IL: Human Kinetics.

Winter, K. 1992. *Effects of the Americans With Disabilities Act on sports and recreation programs.* Paper presented at the meeting of the Rehabilitation Institute of Chicago: Sports and Recreation for the Disabled Conference. Chicago.

Witt, P., and G. Ellis. 1985. Development of a short form to assess perceived freedom in leisure. *Journal of Leisure Research* 17:225-233.

Woodruff, G., and M.J. McGonigel. 1988. Early intervention team approaches: The transdisciplinary model. In *Early childhood special education: Birth to three*, eds. J.B. Jordan, J.J. Gallagher, P.L. Hutinger, and M.B. Karnes, 163-182. Reston, VA: Council for Exceptional Children.

Wright, J. 1986. *CREOLE: Leisure and recreation curriculum for severely handicapped secondary students.* Gretna, LA: Jefferson Parish Public Schools.

Yacenda, J. 1988. Injury rehabilitation, aquatics style. *Fitness Management* 27:31, 51.

YMCA of the USA and the Arthritis Foundation. 1985. *Arthritis Foundation YMCA Aquatic Program (AFYAP) and AFYAP PLUS: Guidelines and procedures.* Champaign, IL: Human Kinetics.

≋ Index ≋

A

AAHPERD
    certification 47
    development of adapted
        aquatics 6-7
    position paper 253-255
    programs 214
abilities, accommodating 55
abuse 135
accessibility of facility 98-100
    guidelines 99
accountability 21
activity analysis example 54
ADA. *See* Americans with Dis-
    abilities Act
ADA Accessibility Guidelines
    for Buildings and
    Facilities 97
adapted aquatics definition 14
"Adapted Aquatics Program"
    (Red Cross) 5
adapted physical education 15
adapted water exercise 14
ADL skills in locker room 139
adult classes 58-59
age-appropriate goals 37
age considerations 51-53
age-targeted class structure 57-
    58
alternative lesson plans 159-160
ambulation assessment 63
ambulation assistance 136-137
American Alliance for Health,
    Physical Education, Recre-
    ation and Dance. *See*
    AAHPERD
American Athletic Association
    of the Deaf 219
American Red Cross
    development of adapted
        aquatics 4-5
    programs 214
Americans with Disabilities Act
    (ADA) 9-11
annual budget, organizational
    81
annual goals, IAPP 72
anxiety and learning 151-152
aphasia 118
appeal of water activity 12

aqua-aerobics classes 58-59
Aqu-Achievements strategic
    assessment 80
AquaJogger 109
Aqua-Percept program 24
aquatherapy 18
Aquatic Assessment Checklist
    274
Aquatic Council Position Paper
    253-255
Aquatic Orientation Checklist
    268
aquatic therapy 14-15, 18
Archimedes' Principle 133
architectural barriers 98-100
Architectural Barriers Compli-
    ance Board 97
Are We There Yet Game 283
Arthritis Foundation YMCA
    Aquatic Program 5
assessment
    and placement 36-37
    plan 61-62
assisting ambulation 136-137
associative learning stage 149
ataxia 199-200
atlantoaxial instability 171
atrophy 192-194
attention deficit 171-172
attention span difficulties 147
auditory perception disorders
    172-173
autonomic dysreflexia 173
autonomous learning stage 149

B

Backstroke Flag Touch Game
    282
balance disorders 199-200
    See also vestibular system
        disorders
    and hearing impairment 180
barriers to communication,
    overcoming 117-118
basic needs programs 212
basis of placement choice 38
bathing assistance 140
beginner swim class, adult 58
behavior correction, DBG pro-
    gram 145-146

behavior problems 144-147
benefits
    of aquatic participation 12-
        14
    of inclusion 46-47
Birthday Party Game 281
blindness 200-203
blood pressure, effect of med-
    ications 163-168
board of directors 81
boating 231-232
boats, modified 231-232
body mechanics and safe trans-
    fer 119
body system, effect on learning
    150
bone disorders 174
bowel management 140
brittle bones 174
brochures 83
Bruininks-Oseretsky Motor
    Development Scale 62-63
budget development, organiza-
    tional 81
buoyancy 132-134
bursitis 243

C

camp programs 209
Canadian Red Cross integration
    models 40
cardiorespiratory benefits 12
cardiovascular disorders 175
cardiorespiratory endurance,
    improving 237-239
cardiovascular effects of med-
    ications 163-168
care of equipment 110-111
care of participants 138-140
center of buoyancy 132
certification
    aquatic therapist 19-20
    MS aquatic instructor 6
    therapeutic recreation spe-
        cialist 28
    YMCA instructor 5
Chariot Race Game 282
chondromalacia 243
circulatory disorders 176

civil rights and continuum concept 38
classification for competition 223-228
class size vs. age 53
class structure 56
coaching for competition 225-228
cognitive benefits 13
cognitive learning stage 149
cognitive problems, memory and understanding 186-188
cognitive readiness 152-153
collaborative model 29, 29-33
    assessment 69-71
command teaching style 155
communication
    barriers, overcoming 117-118
    collaborative model 33
    skills 116-118
community-based programs 208-209
community support 83
Competency Levels Checklist 269
competitive swimming 217-225
Conaster Skill Test Sheet 270-271
conferences 47
confidentiality form 287
consent form 289
consistency and safety 141
Consumer Satisfaction Survey 90, 91
continuum concept 37-42
continuum of supports 39
contraindications 18
    fitness training 235
"Convalescent Swimming Program" 4
convergent discovery teaching style 156
cooperative vs. competitive activities 55
Council for Exceptional Children 36
credentials staff 92
criteria for selection of adapted aquatics
    program 209
cross-disability competitive classification 223-225
CTRS (certified therapeutic recreation specialist) 28
curriculum-based assessment 65
curriculum development 22

D

Data-Based Gymnasium Program (DBG) 67-69
    behavior correction 145-146
deaf-blind command list 190
deafness 179-180
deck design 101-102
deck to wheelchair transfers
    with backward movement 131
    independent 130
    standing pivot transfer 123-124
    two-person through-arm lift 123
deconditioning 234-235
dependent transfers 119-126
depth of water and buoyancy 134
depth perception problems 202-203
design of program 87
design requirements of facilities 97-105
development of staff 93
developmental aquatic readiness concept 22
developmental delays, addressing 57-58
dimensions of pool 103-104
directions, clarity 160
direct solicitation for funds 84
disabilities glossary 245-247
disability reference sheet 170
disability-specific
    organizations 209
    treatment 18
Disabled Paddlers' Committee 230
disabled sports organizations 219-222
Disabled Sports USA 219
disease transmission and temperature 104-105
disorientation 147
divergent production teaching style 156
Diving Participation Skill Sheet 263
Dix, Dorothea 26
dressing assistance 139
drills, emergency 141
drugs
    effect on heart rate/blood pressure 163-168
    side effects 150-151
dry ramp 102
Dunn and Moorehouse Swimming Checklist 276-277

duration of exercise 238
Dwarf Athletic Association of America 219-220

E

ecologically-based assessment 65-66
educational model 21-26
    assessment 65-69
educational program checklist 67
Education for All Handicapped Children Act 7-8
Eichstaedt and Lavay, least restrictive
    environment 38
elderly participants 242
elitism 224-225
emergency plans 141
emergency procedures 85
empowering participants 117
endurance 234-235
enrichment programs 212-213
entrances 100
    equipment 105-108
    to pool 102
environmental prerequisites for inclusive
    participation 44-45
equipment
    adult 59
    for facility 105-111
    fitness 236-237
equitable competition 223-228
Escape Hatch Game 281
evaluation of program 87-90
evolution
    of adapted aquatics 3-7
    of recreation for therapy 26
exercise prescription 18
exercise principles 237-238
exits 100
    equipment 105-108
    from pool 102-104
expansion of organization 78
extrinsic motivation 152

F

facilitating inclusion 55-59
facilities
    See also settings
    acquisition 84-86
    design guidelines 97
    evaluation 88
    safety 84-86
familiarity with equipment 116

fear physiological responses 152
feedback to participants 161
fee for participation 84
financial development of organization 83-84
fiscal management of organization 81
fitness
    definition 233-234
    equipment 109
fitness program participation 233-234
501(c)(3) status 81
flexibility
    enhancing 239-240
    programmatic 45-46
flotation equipment 108
formal instructor certification 47
form drag 134
for-profit status 81
frequency of exercise 237-238
functional classification for competition 223-225
funding sources 83-84

G

games 278-279
    adapting for inclusion 55-60
    analysis model, example 56
generalizations, avoiding 42
glossaries
    disabilities 245-247
    terms 248-252
goals
    organization 81
    program vs. participant 87
goals and objectives
    collaborative model 32
    educational model 22-24
    medical-therapeutic model 18-19
    therapeutic recreation model 27
    writing for IAPP 72-74
Going to the Market Game 278
governance of organization 81-82
gravity effect in water 133
grooming assistance 140
grouping for competition by function vs. disability 223
group lesson example 158
group makeup, age dependence 52
guided discovery teaching style 156

H

head control difficulties 180-182
hearing difficulty 179-180
    See also auditory perception disorders
heart rate
    effect of medications 163-168
    in water vs. on land 238
    monitors 238
hierarchy of skills 21
high muscle tone 182
history 3-7
hold harmless forms 86
holding participants 136
Horgan, Harry 230
hospital programs 210-211
Hoyer lift 106
human resource development 93-94
human resource management 90-94
hydraulic lift transfer 125
hydraulic pool floor 103
hydrodynamics 132-135
hydrotherapy 18
hyperactivity 183
hyperreflexia 173
hypertonicity 182

I

IAPP
    group lesson sample 157-159
    implementing 75
    success in group setting 75
IDEA. See Individuals with Disabilities Education Act
ignoring inappropriate behavior 146
impatient participants 147
inappropriate behavior 144-147
inclusion
    facilitating 55-59
    health and safety concerns 43
    National Council on Disability position 36
    prerequisites 42-46
    teaching style 156
inclusion groups, developing and maintaining 46-53
Individualized Aquatics Program Plan (IAPP) 22, 61

development 71-75
Individualized Educational Program (IEP) 8, 22
Individualized Family Service Plan (IFSP) 8, 22
Individualized Transition Plan 8-9
individual program teaching style 156
Individuals with Disabilities Education Act 8-9
information gathering forms 285-290
informed consent form 289
inhibition of range of motion 239-240
initial communication 116
injury prevention 140-144
in-kind support 84
inservice education programs 47
instructional delivery 159
instructional design 154-157
instructional time estimate 74
instructor functions 90
instructor-participant interaction 116-118
instructor preparation 47
insurance, third party 18
insurance protection 85
integrated vs. segregated competition 222-223
integration model
    Canadian Red Cross 40
    Sherrill adapted physical education 42
intensity of exercise 237-238
interaction difficulties 184-185
interactive skills 116-118
interagency communications 82
interdisciplinary service 30
intrinsic motivation 152
issues ogranizational 78

J

jellyfish float 132
job analysis 92
joint dysfunction 185-186

K

Kicking Skill Sheet 262
kinesiotherapy assessment 63
kinesthetic system disorders 186
knee surgery 243
knowledge of performance 161

L

ladders 103, 107
Lake Merritt Adapted Boating
    Programs 230
land exercise in water 63
learner-initiated teaching style
    157
learning
    environment structure 147
    process 149-154
    support 48-50
    theory 21-22
least restrictive environment 7,
    22, 37
    total inclusion vs. 25-26
legal issues 85-86
    collaborative model 33
legislation 7-11
    impact on organizational
        planning 78
leisure and independence 27
leisure counseling 27
Leisure Diagnostic Battery 69
leisure integration network
    (LINK) 40
lesson content 22
lesson plans 21-22
    evaluation checklist 76
    for IAPP 75
Level II Diving assessment form
    260
Level II Swimming assessment
    form 259
Level I Swimming assessment
    form 256-257
level of difficulty adjusting 55
liability release form 289
lifts 105-106
limitations of medical-therapeu-
    tic model 20-21
locker design 100
locker room design guidelines
    100-101
locker room safety 138-139
London Bridge Game 280
low back pain 242
Lowman, Charles 4
LRE. See least restrictive envi-
    ronment

M

Magic Carpet Ride Game 279
Martin-Nichols Skills Checklist
    275
maximizing time on-task 57

maximum heart rate 237-238
media relations 82
medical prescription 18
medical-therapeutic model 18-
    21
    assessment 62-64
medication
    effect on heart rate/blood
        pressure 163-168
    effect on learning 150-151
memory problems 186-188
Milani-Comparetti Motor
    Development Screening
    test 62-63
minimun requirements of pro-
    gram 11-12
Mirenda Leisure Interest Finder
    69
mission statement 78-79
mobility of class and safety
    142-143
modifying instruction 159-160
monitors, heart rate 238
motivational supplies 110
motivation for learning 152
Motor-Free Visual Perception
    Test 62-63
multidisciplinary approach 29-
    33
multiple sclerosis and water
    temperature 134
Multiple Sclerosis Society
    development of adapted
        aquatics 6
    programs 214
multisensory deprivation 189-190
muscular endurance training
    240-241
musculoskeletal benefits 12
Musical Hoops Game 282
Music, in adult classes 59

N

National Council on Disability
    36
nationally sponsored programs
    213-216
National Multiple Sclerosis
    Society programs 214
National Ocean Access Project
    230-231
National Safety Council/Ellis
    and Associates develop-
    ment of adapted aquatics 7
National Safety Council/Ellis
    and Associates program
    214-215

National Wheelchair Athletic
    Association 221-222
needs assessment, for educa-
    tional model 22
neurological maturity level
    150-151
newsletters 83
nonprofit status 81

O

obesity 242
objectives, grouping into goal
    areas 72f4.5
occupational therapy assess-
    ment 62-63, 64f4.1
oral motor dysfunction 191-192
organizational foundations 77-
    82
orthostatic hypotension 235
Osborn Aquatic Center pro-
    gram 211-212
overcoming hesitation 116

P

Paralympics for Persons with
    Mental Handicaps 225
paralysis 192-194
parental consent forms 86
paresis 192-194
participant goals 28
    collaborative model 32
    educational model 24
    medical-therapeutic model
        19
    therapeutic recreation model
        28
participant information form
    286
participant input and program
    evaluation 90
participant objectives 24
    collaborative model 32
    therapeutic recreation model
        28
participant prerequisites to
    inclusion 42-43
Partners Club program 50, 221
passive range of motion exer-
    cise 240
peer groups age appropriate 51
peer tutors 49-50
perceived exertion 238
perceptual stimulation 12
performance assessment land
    vs. water 63

performance objectives examples 74
performance of staff appraisal 94
personal flotation devices 109, 231
pharmacological agents 163-168
philosophy of competitive swimming 218-219
physical ability and fitness training 235-236
physical benefits 12
physical environment prerequisites 44-45
physical support 48-50
physical therapy assessment 63, 66
Physicians' Desk Reference 151
physiological factors and learning 150-151
PL 101–336 9-11
PL 101–476 8-9
PL 93–112 7
PL 94–142 7-8
placement
    concepts 36-37
    questions 35
    school settings 39-42
planning for organization future 79
plantar fasciitis 243
Poison Game 283
policies of organization 85
pool area design 101-105
Position and Buoyancy checklist 264
positioning participants 134-138, 137-138
positive reinforcement of appropriate behavior 146
posting safety rules 141
posture disorders 194-195
practice teaching style 155
Praxis tests 62-63
preferred learning modality 153-154
pregnancy 242-243
prerequisites
    inclusion 42-46
    staff 92
prescription 18
present level of performance 71
primitive reflex retention 195-196
principles of organization 81
prioritizing for IAPP 72
prioritizing goals checklist 73
problem behaviors 144-147

problem-oriented report 18
process of learning 149-154
program
    development and evaluation 86-90
    evaluation form 89
programmatic prerequisites 45-46
Project Aquatic Mainstreaming 5
Project CREOLE 50
Project Mainstreaming Activities for Youth 5
Project PEOPEL 50
promotion of program 82-83
proprioceptive disorders. *See* kinesthetic system disorders
propulsion equipment 109
Propulsion in Water checklist 265
provider role release 31-32
providers
    collaborative model 33
    educational model 25
    medical-therapeutic model 19-20
    therapeutic recreation model 28
psychological factors and learning 151-154
psychosocial benefits 13
public awareness of programs 82
public laws 7-11
publicity 82
purposes of program 212-213

Q

qualified individual, definition 9-10

R

raft ball 54
ramps 107
range of motion
    improving 239-240
    limitations 177-179
rapport with participants 117
rating of perceived exertion (RPE) 238
readily accessible 100
    definition 11
readily achievable 100
    definition 11

reasonable accommodation, definition 10-11
receptive-expressive language disorders 117-118
reciprocal teaching style 155
record keeping
    organizational 85
    problem-oriented reports 18
recreational aquatic activities 228-232
recreational benefits 13-14
recreational model assessment 69
recruitment, staff 93-94
Red Cross progressive swim levels 65
redirecting inappropriate behavior 146
referral, physician 18
reflex, primitive 195-196
rehabilitation 20, 241-243
Rehabilitation Act of 1973 7
rehabilitation center programs 210-211
removing participant from class 146
residential programs 209-210
resistance of water 134
respect for participants 117
respiratory disorders 196-197
responsibilities of competitve coaches 226
restlessness 147
retention of staff 94-95
revenue generation 84
reverse mainstreaming 39
risk management 85-86
risk transfer 86
role of therapeutic recreation 28
Rolling Log Game 283-284
ROM. *See* range of motion
Rubber Duckie Game 279
rules
    competitive swimming 218
    safety 141
    for transfer 118-119

S

safety 138-140, 140-144
    boating 231
    collaborative model 33
    equipment 108
    physical environment 44-45
    scuba diving 230
    snorkeling 230
    water skiing 228-229

safety audits 85
safety measures list 142
sailboats, modified 230-231
schedule
    competitive training 226-228
    of program evaluation 88
school programs 211
scuba diving 229-230
SCUBA skills 65
sedentary lifestyle 234-235
segregated competitive pro-
        grams 58
segregated programs 15
seizure management 143-144
    hold in water 144
seizures 197-198
selection of adapted aquatics
        program 208
self-check teaching style 155
Self Leisure Interest Profile 69
self-monitoring 147
self teaching style 157
seminars 47
sensory stimulation 12
sequence of skills, IAPP 72
settings
    collaborative model 33
    educational model 24-25
    medical-therapeutic model 19
    therapeutic recreation model
        28
Shake-A-Leg sailing program
        230
shape of pool 103-104
Sherrill, Claudine 21
Sherrill Model, beginning
        swimming competency
        levels 269
shin splints 243
short-term objectives IAPP 72
shower area safety 138-139
shower design 100
size of group vs. age 52
size of pool 103-104
sliding board transfer 124-125
sling hoist transfer 126
snorkeling 229-230
social ability and learning 153
social minority model 21
South Carolina flotation device
        109
spasticity 182
    and water temperature 134
special education teacher 25
special events and fund raising
        84
Special Olympics International
        220-221

classification 225
development of adapted
        aquatics 5-6
    peer tutor program 50
    programs 215
specific gravity 132
sports medicine assessment 63
Sports Partnership program 50
Sports Skills Assessment forms
    Level II Diving 260
    Level I Swimming 256-257
    Level II Swimming 259
staff
    development functions 94
    fitness training 236
    hierarchy 93
    requirements 92-93
    training 86
stages of learning motor skills
        149-150
stairs 107
standardized OT assessment
        62-63
standing pivot transfer 123
starts for competition 227
steps, sloping 103
stereotyping, avoiding 36
storage of equipment and sup-
        plies 110-111
strategic organizational plan-
        ning 78
strategic plan sample 80
strategic planning model 79
strength differences, gender-
        related 57-58
strength enhancement 240-241
stress fractures 243
Strike A Pose Game 284
stroke mechanics, competitive
        227-228
structure of learning environ-
        ment 147
style of learning 153-154
successful teaching strategies
        154-157
supervision and safety 140-141
supplies 105-111
    locker room 139
support continuum 39
supporting participants 134-138
Surfin' USA Game 284
SwimAmerica programs 215-
        216
swimming ability fitness train-
        ing 234
"Swimming for the Handi-
        capped" program 4
SWOT organizational analysis 78

T

tactile system disorders 198-199
tactile teaching 135
target heart rate 237-238
target objective 54
task analysis example 54, 69
task presentation framework 53
teaching practices 55
teaching styles 155-157
team approach 29-33
Team is in the Huddle Game
        280
temperature of water 104-105
temperature regulation disor-
        ders 199
temporary staff 94
tendinitis 243
terminal behavior 68
terms, glossary 248-252
test of buoyancy 132
therapeutic goals 18-19
therapeutic recreation model
        26-29
    assessment example 70
    links to educational model
        27
    links to medical-therapeutic
        model 26-27
therapeutic water exercise defi-
        nition 14
"therapy hands" 135
time instructional 74
touching participants 135
training
    instructor 47
    staff 94
training competitively 226-228
training seminars 17
transdiciplinary cooperation
        29-33
transferring techniques 118-131
transfer steps 107
travel in pool area 142-143
trust 117, 135
turns for competition 227
Twentieth century evolution 4
two-person standard lift 120-
        121
two-person through-arm lift
        122
    deck to wheelchair 123
types
    of exercise 238
    of participation 213

U

understanding problems 186-188
undue hardship, definition 10
unidisciplinary model, failure 30
Unified Sports program 50
Unified Sports team participation 220-221
United States Association of Blind Athletes 221
United States Sailing Association 230
United States Swimming rules 218
urinary management 140

V

vestibular system disorders 199-200
vision of organization 79
visual impairment 200-203
visual perception deficits 202-203
volunteer staff 93-94

W

warm up for exercise 238-239
Water Adjustment form 258
Water Orientation Checklists 266-267
water quality 104-105
Water Safety Instructor Program 5
Water Safety Skill Sheet 261
water skiing 228-229
water temperature 104-105
Water the Garden Game 278-279
wave drag 134
weightlessness in water 133
wet ramps 102-103
Wet Vest vs. PFD 236
Wet Wrap 110
Wheelchair Sports USA 221-222
wheelchair storage 100
wheelchair-to-deck transfers
    independent 127-128
    two-person standard lift 120-121
    two-person through-arm lift 122
    using forward pivot 129

Winnick's sports integration continuum 223
word-of-mouth promotion 83
work application form 290

Y

YMCA
    certification 47
    development of adapted aquatics program 5
    programs 215

≋ About the Authors ≋

Monica Lepore, EdD, has been an adapted aquatic instructor since 1978 and a trainer of adapted aquatic instructors since 1980. A professor of kinesiology at West Chester University in West Chester, Pennsylvania, she directs two community adapted aquatic programs during the school year. She also directs aquatics at a camp for youths who are blind or visually impaired and at a camp for children with developmental disabilities.

Lepore coauthored the Adapted Aquatic Position Statement in 1995 for the American Alliance for Health, Physical Education, Recreation and Dance (AAHPERD) Aquatic Council. She is also a recipient of a citation from the Pennsylvania House of Representatives acknowledging her work on behalf of children with disabilities.

Lepore is a member of AAHPERD's Adapted Physical Activity and Aquatic councils and the National Consortium for Physical Education and Recreation for Individuals With Disabilities. She earned a doctor of education degree in leadership in adapted physical education from New York University.

G. William Gayle, PhD, has taught aquatic programs to individuals with disabilities since 1977. He has worked with individuals with spinal cord injuries, cerebral palsy, muscular dystrophy, and other neurological and musculoskeletal disorders. Since 1990, he has worked with preschool and early childhood populations with disabilities. In 1988, he was inducted into the Ohio Wheelchair Sports Hall of Fame for his work with athletic programs. Gayle is chair of the Department of Health, Physical Education, and Recreation at Wright State University in Dayton, Ohio. He holds a doctorate in adapted physical education and psychology of mental retardation and developmental disabilities from The Ohio State University. He is a member of the American Alliance of Health, Physical Education, Recreation and Dance (AAHPERD), the National Consortium of Physical Education and Recreation for Individuals with Disabilities, and the Council for Exceptional Children.

Shawn F. Stevens, EdD, served as an adapted aquatics instructor trainer with the American Red Cross for 15 years. Since 1977 he has been a water safety instructor trainer, planning and implementing aquatic programs in community-based organizations. He is currently the Executive Director of the Edgemoor Community Center in Wilmington, Deleware, and previously directed health and safety programs with the American Red Cross for 16 years. Stevens holds a master's degree in health administration, and a doctorate of education in leadership and innovation from Wilmington College.